T0361204

Electromagnetic Ergonomics

Ergonomics is the branch of engineering science in which biological science is used to study the relationship between workers and their environments. Because of the widespread use of electricity for many purposes, one environmental factor that has become omnipresent today is the electromagnetic field, also referred to as electromagnetic radiation or a fraction of the non-ionising radiation. The complex interactions of electromagnetic energy with material objects contribute to ergonomics issues because they can cause health hazards in workers, trigger accidental situations, limit the ability of workers to work safely and disturb the function of electronic devices, including medical implants, etc. A better understanding of complex electromagnetic issues in the work environment is considered in this book.

This title will be beneficial to workers affected by electromagnetic hazards including wireless transfer of information or power, wireless (induction) heating, joining metal elements with electric-supplied techniques, capacitive heating of dielectric materials, physiotherapeutic or cosmetic electromagnetic treatments, antitheft gates, and other monitoring or control systems using wireless solutions, electric transportation and many more. It will help prevent common misunderstandings about electromagnetic hazards and sufficiently reduce their appearance.

Electromagnetic Ergonomics is designed to have a positive influence on public health and worker safety in the work environment, and brings broad benefits, in particular, with respect to research planning and the interpretation of the results, as well as the implementation of science-based evidence regarding the evaluation and elimination of EMF hazards in the operations of enterprises and environmental, labour and sanitary inspections, as well as government regulators responsible for environmental safety issues in the workplace and the daily life environment.

Occupational Safety, Health, and Ergonomics: Theory and Practice

Series Editor: Central Institute for Labour Protection—National Research Institute (Danuta Koradecka)

This series will contain monographs, references and professional books on a compendium of knowledge in the interdisciplinary area of environmental engineering, which covers ergonomics and safety, and the protection of human health in the working environment. Its aim consists in an interdisciplinary, comprehensive and modern approach to hazards, not only those already present in the working environment, but also those related to the expected changes in new technologies and work organisations. The series aims to acquaint both researchers and practitioners with the latest research in occupational safety and ergonomics. The public who want to improve their own or their family's safety and the protection of health will find it helpful too. Thus, individual books in this series present both a scientific approach to problems and suggest practical solutions; they are offered in response to the actual needs of companies, enterprises and institutions.

Electromagnetic Ergonomics – from Electrification to Wireless Society
Jolanta Karpowicz

Visual and Non-Visual Effects of Light: Working Environment and Well-Being
Agnieszka Wolska, Dariusz Sawicki, and Małgorzata Tafil-Klawe

Occupational Noise and Workplace Acoustics. Advances in Measurement and Assessment Techniques
Dariusz Pleban

Active Noise Control – Systems, Algorithms, Applications
Leszek Morzyński and Grzegorz Makarewicz

Virtual Reality and Virtual Environments as a Tool for Improving Occupational Safety and Health
Andrzej Grabowski

Head, Eye, and Face Personal Protective Equipment: New Trends, Practice and Applications
Katarzyna Majchrzycka

Nanoaerosols, Air Filtering and Respiratory Protection – Science and Practice
Katarzyna Majchrzycka

Microbial Corrosion of Buildings: A Guide to Detection, Health Hazards, and Mitigation
Rafał L. Górny

Respiratory Protection Against Hazardous Biological Agents
Katarzyna Majchrzycka, Małgorzata Okrasa, Justyna Szulc

For more information about this series, please visit: https://www.crcpress.com/Occupational-Safety-Health-and-Ergonomics-Theory-and-Practice/book-series/CRCOSHETP

Electromagnetic Ergonomics

From Electrification to a Wireless Society

Edited by

Jolanta Karpowicz

CRC Press is an imprint of the
Taylor & Francis Group, an informa business

First edition published 2024
by CRC Press
6000 Broken Sound Parkway NW, Suite 300, Boca Raton, FL 33487-2742

and by CRC Press
4 Park Square, Milton Park, Abingdon, Oxon, OX14 4RN

CRC Press is an imprint of Taylor & Francis Group, LLC

ISBN: 9780367896102 (hbk)
ISBN: 9781032529134 (pbk)
ISBN: 9781003020486 (ebk)

DOI: 10.1201/9781003020486

Typeset in Times
by codeMantra

To my parents, who made this book possible, and to all those whose hearts and support gave me the time to complete it

[Moim Rodzicom, którzy poświęcili życie,
aby ta książka mogła powstać,

i Wszystkim, których życzliwość i pomoc
dały mi czas, żeby ją skończyć]

Contents

All authors declared that the research was conducted in the absence of any commercial or financial relationships that could be construed as a potential conflict of interest.

Preface

Ergonomics is the branch of engineering science in which biological science is used to study the relation between workers and their environments.

On one side, ergonomics covers the study of people in relation to the environment in which they work, along with the application of anatomical, physiological, psychological and engineering knowledge to the problems involved.

The other side of ergonomics science coordinates the design of devices, systems and physical working conditions for the workplace environment, with the capacities and requirements of the workers—their productivity and their safety and health along with their families. This is intended to maximise productivity by reducing operator fatigue and discomfort, while also having a positive influence on workers' health. It therefore also helps public health, given that nearly half of the population are workers, and benefits the environment of human life, given that humans generally share at least half of their lives between family and leisure activities and work, and a significant percentage of the workspace is accessible to non-workers (e.g. in commercial or public services buildings and open spaces).

One environmental factor that has become omnipresent today is the electromagnetic field (EMF), also referred to as electromagnetic radiation or a fraction of non-ionising radiation. Most frequently, discussions related to EMF have tended to focus on the medical benefits from therapeutic or diagnostic technologies involving EMF interaction on a patient's body or on public concerns related to health hazards from wireless communication systems (such as mobile phone or wireless internet access base stations and terminals) or on high-voltage electric power lines. However, the use of EMF is much broader, and may cause EMF exposure to workers and the general public (many EMF-emitted technologies are used in factories and offices, as well as in daily life). Among other things, this covers: wireless transfer of information and power, wireless (induction) heating, joining metal elements with electric-supplied techniques, capacitive heating of dielectric materials, microwave heating, medical and cosmetic treatments, antitheft gates and other monitoring systems using wireless solutions, as well as media control smart metering, scientific and military applications, electric power production and distribution, electric transportation, and many more traditional and developing technologies.

However, the use of EMF may also cause various direct and indirect interactions of electromagnetic energy with humans and the material environment, which could cause health hazards in workers, trigger accidental situations, limit the ability of workers to work safely, and disturb the function of electronic devices, including medical implants, etc. A better understanding of these complex issues has a positive influence on public health and worker safety in the work environment. It also helps to prevent common misunderstandings about EMF hazards and discover ways to reduce them.

The requirements for evaluating EMF in the environment and the application of sufficient protection measures are covered by labour law and public law, as well as other standards and guidelines (such as European Union directives, international standards from IEC and CENELEC, guidelines and standards such as ANSI/IEEE/ICES, ICNIRP, legislation/guidelines in various countries, etc.). This means that an Electromagnetic Ergonomics approach (the methods used in the studies, and broad protection measures that may easily be undertaken in an EMF-exposed workplace, as well as in the daily use of EMF) must be applied in the evaluation of the influence of electromagnetic energy on humans and technical infrastructure, as well as the adaptation of the work environment and work practices across various fields of the economy (such as industry, medicine, energy, radiocommunication, military and the sciences), as well as the use of EMF emitters in daily life.

This book focuses on the developments in using EMF in the work and daily life environments, from the early stages of systems supplying electricity and electric-powered tools and devices to today's wireless technologies, which provide unlimited potential for the beneficial use of EMF in manufacturing and at home. It sets out examples of variations in certain aspects of electromagnetic ergonomics between various work environments, various jobs, various workers, various work practices, etc., as well as on how society (workers and the general public) may adapt to the EMF influence from the environment (e.g. by certain changes in the work practice or the way of using tools emitting a strong EMF).

Ergonomics is, by definition, an interdisciplinary science. It has elements of basic science but is closer to applied science dealing with the art or science of applying scientific knowledge to practical problems. Given that and the common exposure to EMF in today's society among workers and the general public, we believe that the knowledge provided in our book may bring broad benefits, in particular, with respect to research planning and the interpretation of the results, to researchers and students involved in studies covering environmental issues (research related to EMF sources, the influence of EMF on humans, environmental exposure monitoring and protection against unwanted exposure) at various faculties, including environmental engineering, biotechnology, human engineering, human factors engineering, biomedical engineering, technology, electrical engineering, physiology, psychology, public health, occupational medicine, economy, labour law and ICT applications, etc. It must also be pointed out that the book covers issues that are important in the planning and interpretation of research focused on EMF, as advised by research agendas published by World Health Organisation (WHO).

The second general audience potentially interested in the content of our book includes consultants and engineers responsible for occupational health and safety or for public health issues in enterprises and environmental, labour and sanitary inspections, as well as governmental regulators responsible for environmental safety issues in the workplace and the daily life environment.

Jolanta Karpowicz

Acknowledgements

The compilation of our interdisciplinary book was supported by many scientific and practical directions.

Special thanks go to the panel of reviewers, who provided detailed evaluations of particular chapters: Vitas Anderson (Two Fields Consulting and University of Wollongong, Australia), Dana Dabala (Railways Medical Clinic, Romania), Efthymios Karabetsos (Greek Atomic Energy Commission (EEAE), Greece), Tarmo Koppel (Tallinn University of Technology, Estonia), Leena Korpinen (Elenhe, Finland), Roman Kubacki (Military University of Technology, Poland), Simona Miclaus (Nicolae Balcescu Land Forces Academy, Romania), Kjell Hansson Mild (University of Umeå, Sweden), Mihaela Morega (University 'Politehnica' of Bucharest, Romania), Rauno Pääkkönen (Tmi Rauno Pääkkönen, Finland), Charles V. Sammut (University of Malta, Malta) and Dina Šimunić (University of Zagreb, Croatia).

Special thanks go to Patryk Zradziński (Central Institute for Labour Protection—National Research Institute, Poland), who provided excellent technical assistance in the final formatting and editing of the book, and to Nicolas Faulkner, who provided excellent assistance with the proofreading and editing of the book.

Acknowledgements

Editor and Contributor

Jolanta Karpowicz earned her Master's and Engineering degrees in Medical and Nuclear Electronics (1990) and D.Sc. (Habilitation) in Biomedical Engineering (2020) from the Warsaw Technical University (Poland); as well as Ph.D. (Doctorate) in Environmental Engineering (2004) from the Central Institute for Labour Protection—National Research Institute (CIOP-PIB) (Warszawa, Poland), where she is a researcher, the Head of the Bioelectromagnetics Department (research unit as well as a laboratory accredited in the evaluation of electromagnetic field and the calibration of measurement devices). Her main area of research is the electromagnetic environment, and its influence on humans and environmental safety, focusing primarily on worker safety through measurements, numerical modelling, safety standardisation, and legislation, as well as education under national research programmes and international collaboration (such as European Framework Programmes and The European Cooperation in Science and Technology, known as COST Actions). She has contributed to over 100 journal research articles and conference short papers, and more than 400 expert opinions in the field of evaluating electromagnetic hazards commissioned mainly by industry and healthcare institutions. She also serves as a reviewer for many international scientific journals (such as *JOSE*, *Bioelectromagnetics*, *IJERPH*, *International Journal of Radiobiology*).

Dr. Karpowicz is a member of the BioEM society (previously the Bioelectromagnetics Society (BEMS) and the European Bioelectomagnetics Association (EBEA)), the International Union of Radio Science (URSI) and the International Commission on Occupational Health (ICOH), as well as the Polish Society of Radiation Research (PTBR) and the Polish Society of Biomedical Engineering [PTIB affiliated to the International Federation for Medical and Biological Engineering (IFMBE)]. Her activities also cover collaboration with international scientific and technical bodies: URSI, Commission K—Electromagnetics in Biology and Medicine, the Institute of Electrical and Electronics Engineers/International Committee on Electromagnetic Safety (IEEE/ICES) and the International Electrotechnical Commission (IEC)/European Committee for Electrotechnical Standardization (CENELEC). She was an expert in electromagnetic hazards at work to the European Council, the European Commission and the Ministry of Labour in Poland (among other things as a member of the Interdepartmental Commission for the Maximum Admissible Concentrations and Intensities for Agents Harmful to Health in the Working Environment in Poland and Vice-Chair of the group on Electromagnetic Fields of Panel of Experts on Physical Factors at this commission).

Contributors

Vitas Anderson, ***Two Fields Consulting and University of Wollongong, Australia***
Dr. Vitas Anderson has dedicated most of his professional career to the research and management of safe human exposure to radiofrequency (RF) electromagnetic fields (EMF). He received his undergraduate training in medical sciences and engineering at the University of Melbourne and was awarded a Doctorate in Biophysics from Swinburne University of Technology (Australia). His research activities in RF-EMF bioeffects have included experimental and numerical radiofrequency dosimetry, the development of EMF survey techniques, neurophysiological human experiments, in-vitro studies, examinations of theoretical bioeffect mechanisms and testing of EMF hypersensitivity. Dr Anderson has actively participated in national and international standards committees for radiofrequency safety and exposure assessment, including Standards Australia, ARPANSA, the IEEE and the IEC. He is currently an honorary principal fellow with the University of Wollongong and an honorary technical assessor for the Australian National Association of Testing Authorities (NATA).

Leyre Azpilicueta, ***Department of Electrical, Electronic and Communication Engineering, Public University of Navarre (UPNA), Spain***
Leyre Azpilicueta earned her Telecommunications Engineering degree (2009), her Master's degree in Communications (2011) and her Ph.D. in Telecommunication Technologies (2015) at the Public University of Navarre (UPNA) in Spain. In 2010, she started working as a radio engineer in the R&D department of RFID Osés. From 2015 to 2022, she was an Associate Professor and Researcher at Tecnologico de Monterrey, Campus Monterrey, Mexico. Currently, she is a Ramon y Cajal Fellow (Researcher & Professor) at UPNA, in Spain. Her research interests are on radio propagation, mobile radio systems, ray tracing and channel modelling. She has over 150 contributions in relevant journals and conference publications.

Mikel Celaya-Echarri, ***Department of Statistics, Computer Science and Mathematics, Public University of Navarre (UPNA), Spain***
Mikel Celaya-Echarri earned a Computer Science Engineering degree and an MSc in Project Management from the Public University of Navarre (UPNA), in 2011 and 2015, respectively, as well as a Ph.D. in Engineering and Sciences from Tecnologico de Monterrey, Mexico, in 2022. From 2011 to 2014, he worked as R&D Engineer at Tafco Metawireless, Spain. From 2015 to 2017, he was a visiting assistant in the Networks and Telecommunications Research Group at Tecnologico de Monterrey, Mexico. He is currently working as a postdoctoral researcher at UPNA, in Spain. His research lines are focused on radio frequency electromagnetic dosimetry, radio propagation, wireless sensor networks, project management and computer science.

Maria Christopoulou, ***Non Ionizing Radiation Unit, Greek Atomic Energy Commission (EEAE), Greece***
Maria Christopoulou is a Dipl. Electrical Engineer, and she holds a Ph.D. in Biomedical Engineering. In 2007–2008, she joined the IT'IS Foundation, the Swiss Federal Institute of Technology Zurich (ETHZ), as an Academic Visitor, contributing to two radiofrequency safety and dosimetry projects. In June 2012, Maria was awarded a personal excellence grant of EUR 150K, entitled: 'microDIAGNOSIS: Microwave-based diagnosis for pneumothorax and detection of air cavities in body' at the University of Patras. Her research interests include electromagnetic field measurements, bioelectromagnetics and biomedical engineering. She has authored/co-authored 62 articles in refereed international/national journals, conference proceedings and scientific books. She has served as a reviewer for 11 international scientific journals and participated in organising and scientific committees of 8 international conferences. She has served as substitute member of the Management Committee (MC), representing Greece for COST BM1309 EMF-MED Action, and she has participated in 2 other COST Actions. Since 2019, she belongs to the scientific personnel at the Non-Ionizing Radiation Unit of the Greek Atomic Energy Commission (EEAE).

Fabriziomaria Gobba, ***Chair of Occupational Medicine, Department of Biomedical, Metabolic and Neural Sciences, University of Modena & Reggio Emilia, Italy***
Fabriziomaria Gobba is a Professor of Occupational Medicine and Director of the Postgraduate Specialisation School of Occupational Medicine at the University of Modena & Reggio Emilia. Since the early 2000s, he has been conducting extensive research on EMF exposure, health risks and prevention in workers, publishing several peer-reviewed scientific papers on this topic. He is a co-author of the guidelines on the prevention of the occupational EMF risk of the Italian Medical Radioprotection Association (AIRM) and the Italian Society of Occupational Medicine (SIML). A former chair of the International Commission on Occupational Health (ICOH) Scientific Committee 'Radiation and Work', and currently President of the Occupational Medicine section of the European Union of Medical Specialists (UEMS), vice-president of the AIRM, a Board Member of the SIML and of the Interuniversity National Research Centre on Interactions between Electromagnetic Fields and Biosystems (ICEmB). He actively collaborates within the WHO 'International EMF project'.

Krzysztof Gryz, ***Department of Bioelectromagnetics, Central Institute for Labour Protection—National Research Institute (CIOP-PIB), Poland***
Krzysztof Gryz obtained his Ph.D. in Environmental Engineering in 2004 from the Central Institute for Labour Protection—National Research Institute (CIOP-PIB). In 2019, he obtained a Postdoctoral degree in Electrical Engineering from the Warsaw University of Technology. He is a researcher in the Laboratory of Electromagnetic Hazards at CIOP-PIB. His research is associated with the assessment and mitigation of electromagnetic hazards, performing various activities including research, standardisation, training and education, as a leader or performer of many research

projects. He has contributed to over 100 journal research articles and conference short papers, as well as over 500 expert opinions in the field of electromagnetic hazards evaluation, commissioned mainly by industrial and healthcare institutions. He is a member of the Polish Society of Radiation Research (PTBR) and an expert on electromagnetic field in the Panel of Experts on Physical Factors at the Interdepartmental Commission for Maximum Admissible Concentrations and Intensities for Agents Harmful to Health in the Working Environment in Poland.

Kjell Hansson Mild, ***Department of Radiation Sciences, Umeå University, Sweden***
Kjell Hansson Mild has a background in Physics and Theoretical Physics, but he has been working on biological systems for a long time. He obtained his Ph.D. in 1974 from the University of Umeå. His thesis was on intracellular water structure and cell membrane water permeability. He worked as a researcher at the Swedish National Institute for Working Life (NIWL) until it closed in 2007. Then he was a researcher at the Department of Radiation Sciences of Umeå University, from which he retired in 2012. He now holds a position as a Senior Consultant. At NIWL, he conducted research into the bioeffects of electromagnetic fields. The work covered all levels from molecular level to epidemiology. Since the mid-90s, the research has been mainly associated with mobile phone use and related health effects. He has published over 300 articles and 200 conference abstracts. He was the first person from Europe to serve on the Board of the Bioelectromagnetics Society and was President of the society from 1995 to 1996. He served as an Associate Editor for the *Journal of Bioelectromagnetics* between 1988 and 1996. He has also served as a member of the board of the European Bioelectromagnetics Association.

Efthymios Karabetsos, ***Directorate of Training, Regulatory Policy, Infrastructure and Research, Greek Atomic Energy Commission (EEAE), Greece***
Efthymios Karabetsos is an Electrical Engineer, M.Sc. and he also holds a M.Sc. title in Quality Management and Technology and a Ph.D. in Biomedical Engineering. From 2/2000 to 9/2022, he was Head of the Non Ionizing Radiation Office of the Greek Atomic Energy Commission (EEAE) and from 9/2022 he is Director of the Directorate of Training, Regulatory Policy, Infrastructure and Research of EEAE. He is a member of the International Advisory Committee of the International EMF Project of the World Health Organization (WHO) and a member of the IEEE International Committee on Electromagnetic Safety (ICES). He is also a member of the core group formed by WHO for the development of the Non-Ionizing Radiation Basic Safety Standards. In 2011, he became a member of the European Commission's DG SANCO expert group of stakeholders on electromagnetic fields. He also acts as national delegate to IEC, CENELEC, IMEKO and European Commission's meetings and activities and participates in several expert groups and committees concerning electromagnetic safety, metrology, radiation policies and electrotechnical standardization. His expertise and his research interests include electromagnetic fields measurements, interlaboratory comparison programmes, bioelectromagnetics and biomedical engineering. He has authored or coauthored more than 80 papers in

scientific journals and conference proceedings. He is a Senior member of IEEE and a member of the Bioelectromagnetics Society.

Jarosław Kieliszek, ***Department of Microwave Safety, Military Institute of Hygiene and Epidemiology, Poland***
Jarosław Kieliszek is the main specialist in the Department of Microwave Protection at the Military Institute of Hygiene and Epidemiology (Warsaw, Poland), where he is the Head of the Electromagnetic Hazard Analysis Team with over 25 years of experience in measuring electromagnetic radiation. His research interests are focused on the metrology of electromagnetic radiation, bioelectromagnetic and health hazards of electromagnetic fields, with respect to radar-pulsed radiation. He is the head of an accredited electromagnetic radiation measurement laboratory specialising in evaluating radar emissions in the environment. He has 20 years of experience as a technical auditor at the Polish Centre for Accreditation. He has drafted several national and departmental regulations and standards regarding electromagnetic radiation measurements and assessment of electromagnetic hazards in the workplace.

Dimitris Koutounidis, ***Non Ionizing Radiation Unit, Greek Atomic Energy Commission (EEAE), Greece***
Dimitris Koutounidis is a physicist with a Master's degree in Electronic Physics (Radio-electrology) in the area of Electronic Telecommunication Technology. He is also a graduate (2013) of the Department of Informatics at the Open University of Patras (Greece). Since 2001, he has been working as a special technical scientist at the Non-Ionising Radiation Unit of the Greek Atomic Energy Commission (EEAE). During this time, he has performed thousands of measurements near to antenna stations (mobile base stations, radio and television antennas, radar, wi-fi, etc.), and hundreds of measurements involving all types of devices and installations of static and low-frequency electric and magnetic fields. He also performed the duties of Chairman of the International Competitions Committee of EEAE for many years (during 2012–2022), being responsible for measurements at antenna stations throughout Greece, coordinating and overseeing the good execution of the overall project. From December 1, 2022, he is Head of the Non-Ionizing Radiation Unit.

Roman Kubacki, ***Faculty of Electronics, Military University of Technology, Poland***
Roman Kubacki is a professor at the Faculty of Electronics at the Military University of Technology (Poland). His research interests include the metrology of electromagnetic radiation, bioelectromagnetic and health hazards of electromagnetic fields. In the area of electromagnetic compatibility, his research interests include permittivity and permeability measurements, electromagnetic interaction with materials and new technologies of electromagnetic radiation absorbers. He was the chairman of Warsaw Section of the Polish Radiation Research Society. Currently, he is a member of the main board of the Polish Society of Applied Electromagnetics.

Theodora Kyritsi, ***Non Ionizing Radiation Unit, Greek Atomic Energy Commission (EEAE), Greece***
Theodora Kyritsi is a physicist who holds a Master's degree in Management and Technology. Since 2001, she has been working in the area of Electronic Telecommunication Technology. She has performed and examined technical studies evaluating the levels of radiofrequency (RF) fields near antenna stations, has performed measurements of radiofrequency fields, and low-frequency electric and magnetic fields according to the requirements of the EN ISO/IEC 17025 standard, and deals with communication matters concerning electromagnetic radiation with the general public. She has worked as a Special Technical Scientist at the Non-Ionising Radiation Unit of the Greek Atomic Energy Commission (EEAE) since 2006.

Alberto Modenese, ***Chair of Occupational Medicine, Department of Biomedical, Metabolic and Neural Sciences, University of Modena & Reggio Emilia, Italy***
Alberto Modenese is an Occupational Physician and a Tenure-track Post-Doc Researcher in Occupational Medicine at the Department of Biomedical, Metabolic and Neural Sciences of the University of Modena & Reggio Emilia (UniMoRe). His main area of research at present is studying preventive measures, exposure evaluation methods and health effects related to Non-Ionising Radiation (NIR) exposure in workers. Since 2012, he has been a member of the International Commission on Occupational Health (ICOH) and within ICOH an active member of the Scientific Committee 'Radiation and Work'. Since 2018, he has been the Secretary of this committee. He is member of the board of the Italian Association of Medical Radioprotection (AIRM). He actively collaborates within the WHO 'International EMF project', and he has been appointed since 2022 as member of the WHO Technical Advisory group for the preparation of the new Environmental Health Criteria publication on Radiofrequency fields.

Victoria Ramos, ***Telemedicine and Digital Health Research Unit, Instituto de Salud Carlos III, Spain***
Victoria Ramos has a Ph.D. in Biomedical Engineering and Telemedicine (2005) from the University of Alcala, Madrid, Spain. A tenured scientist at the Instituto de Salud Carlos III, Ministry of Science and Innovation, in the Research Area of Telemedicine and Digital Health, in Madrid. Her research focuses on wireless communications in new emergent healthcare services, standards related to human exposure to EMF, medical devices immunity and safety evaluation related to non-ionising radiation. She is the author of books, journals papers and contributions for scientific congresses. She sits on several European and Spanish Standardisations Committees, and is deeply involved as a referee of proposals for European and Spanish calls for funding.

Dina Šimunić, ***Faculty of Electrical Engineering and Computing, University of Zagreb, Croatia***
Dina Šimunić is Professor of Wireless Communications at the University of Zagreb in the Faculty of Electrical Engineering and Computing, Department of

Communication and Space Technologies. Her international activity started in 1997 when she accepted the position of Vice-Chair of The European Cooperation in Science and Technology, known as COST Actions—the Pan-European COST Action 244bis: 'Biomedical Effects of Electromagnetic Fields'. From 2001 to 2004, she served as the Deputy President of the Croatian Telecommunications Council. From 2001 to 2013, she served as a Vice-Chair of EU-COST ICT Domain of the European Commission. Prof. Šimunić serves as the President of the Technical Committee for Telecommunications at the Croatian Standardisation Institute

Tomasz Tokarski, ***Department of Ergonomics, Central Institute for Labour Protection—National Research Institute (CIOP-PIB), Poland***
Tomasz Tokarski is a Graduate of Doctoral Studies at the Józef Piłsudski University of Physical Education in Warsaw in the field of Biomechanics, explaining the functioning of the musculoskeletal system. He is a researcher in the Department of Ergonomics, the Laboratory of Biomechanics at the Central Institute for Labour Protection—National Research Institute (CIOP-PIB). He researches strength and fitness capabilities, and assesses the ability to work, including people with musculoskeletal system disabilities. He has contributed to over 40 journal research articles and conference short papers, and over 70 expert opinions in the field of ergonomic evaluations in the workplace. He also provides training in ergonomics and musculoskeletal load assessment. He is a member of the Polish Society of Ergonomics.

Sachiko Yamaguchi-Sekino, ***Work Environment Research Group, National Institute of Occupational Safety and Health Japan (JNIOSH) and Electromagnetic Compatibility Laboratory, National Institute of Information and Communications Technology (NICT)***
Sachiko Yamaguchi-Sekino is a Senior Researcher at the National Institute of Occupational Safety and Health, Japan. She has published a number of articles related to biological effects, measurements and surveys of occupational static magnetic field exposure. She served as a member of the technical committee and publicity committee of the IEEE Magnetics Society.

Karol Zajdler, ***Polskie Sieci Elektroenergetyczne S.A.—Transmission System Operator (PSE S.A.), Poland***
Karol Zajdler is a graduate of the Lublin University of Technology, the Faculty of Electrical Engineering. His Master's thesis, defended in the specialisation of processing and using electricity, concerned ways of eliminating interference in electronic devices (EMC area). After graduation, he started working in a company dealing with the construction and renovation of power installations. Later, he started working at the Radom Branch of Polskie Sieci Elektroenergetyczne S.A. (Transmission System Operator). He has been the Technical Manager in the accredited Measurement and Research Laboratory in Radom for 10 years, run as part of the activities of Polskie Sieci Elektroenergetyczne S.A. This laboratory conducts specialist measurement and diagnostic work on power facilities, with a particular emphasis on harmful factors, i.e. electromagnetic fields.

Patryk Zradziński, ***Department of Bioelectromagnetics, Central Institute for Labour Protection—National Research Institute (CIOP-PIB), Poland***
Patryk Zradziński obtained his Ph.D. in 2011 from the Central Institute for Labour Protection—National Research Institute (CIOP-PIB). His thesis was on an assessment of occupational hazards at the manual operating of industrial electromagnetic field sources using computer modelling. In 2019, he obtained a Postdoctoral degree in Electrical Engineering from Warsaw's University of Technology. He is a researcher at the Laboratory of Electromagnetic Hazards of Department of Bioelectromagnetics at CIOP-PIB. His research is associated with computer modelling of the interaction of the electromagnetic field with the human body. He has contributed to over 80 journal research articles and conference short papers and conducted more than 200 expert opinions in the field of evaluating and managing electromagnetic hazards. He also provides lectures and training on assessing electromagnetic hazards in working and living environments. He is a member of the the BioEM society, the International Union of Radio Science (URSI) and Polish Society of Radiation Research (PTBR) and an expert on electromagnetic fields in the Panel of Experts on Physical Factors at the Interdepartmental Commission for Maximum Admissible Concentrations and Intensities for Agents Harmful to Health in the Working Environment in Poland.

1 Electromagnetic Fields in Human History

Dina Šimunić
University of Zagreb

CONTENTS

1.1 INTRODUCTION: BACKGROUND

Humans and the human environment include electromagnetic fields (EMFs). Natural EMFs are generated by the earth. Artificial, or man-made, sources are everywhere around us; this is the technology basis not only for industry, science, medicine and the military, but also for 'smart' human life, having ICT in a core of power transmission, wireless communications, various biomedical applications in diagnostics and healing, and generally, overall in the 'smart cities'. Nowadays, we understand that human activities are also generators of EMFs. Therefore, ergonomics has to account for this and plan the working environment accordingly. This chapter gives an overview of natural and man-made EMFs, the history of EMFs and the current status of industrial development.

1.2 NATURAL EMFs

1.2.1 Thunderstorms

The atmosphere forms a global atmospheric electrical circuit by the movement of charge between the earth's surface, the atmosphere and the ionosphere, creating

DOI: 10.1201/9781003020486-1

natural EMFs in our environment. This interdisciplinary topic, with its long history, involving concepts from electrostatics, atmospheric physics, meteorology and earth science, is called atmospheric electricity.

A very important part of atmospheric electricity studies both the thunderstorms with lightning bolts and the rapid discharge of huge amounts of atmospheric charge stored in storm clouds (Golubenko et al., 2020). This also means that our atmosphere is never electrically neutral. The atmosphere is positively charged, while the earth's surface is negatively charged. Balance is achieved by an atmospheric potential gradient leading to an ion flow towards the surface. The magnitude of the field created by this phenomenon is, on average, 100 V/m at the surface, up to many kV/m below thunder clouds or in desert regions. The United States (US) National Lightning Safety Institute (NLSI) presents numbers of victims of lightning statistics in various countries (NLSI, 2020). Any death incidence in the world is too high, considering human knowledge and the possibility prediction of the phenomenon. This unfortunate statistics starts with Mexico and 223 deaths annually, through USA with 50 deaths annually to many European countries with 1 dead person annually.

1.2.2 Schumann Resonance

What Nikola Tesla (1856–1943) predicted and tried to use for the wireless transfer of energy (1900–1917, Wardenclyffe) (Tesla, 1905), Winfried Otto Schumann (1888–1974) had predicted theoretically in 1952 (Schumann, 1952a). The phenomenon of global electromagnetic resonance occurs in the cavity between the conducting ground and the lower edge of the ionosphere (The height of the dielectric interface region is less than 100 km.). Thus, very low-frequency radio waves travel in the cavity around the earth and return to the starting point, enabling global resonance. Nowadays, Schumann resonance is a recognised branch of radio science. It is used in the global sensing of thunderstorm activity, as the major field source of the resonance, and of the lower ionosphere on planetary scales.

The Schumann resonance formula (Schumann, 1952b) for a cavity with perfectly conducting boundaries is:

$$f_n = \frac{c}{2\pi a}\sqrt{n(n+1)} \tag{1.1}$$

where the resonant frequency of the nth mode is f_n, a is the earth's radius of 6,400 km, and c is the speed of light in an ideal cavity.

Since a height of 100 km is much less than the earth's radius of 6,400 km, and the cavity height is small in comparison with the wavelength, which is comparable with the circumference of the equator of 40,000 km, the resonance frequencies are: $f_1 = 10.6\,\text{Hz}$, $f_2 = 18.3\,\text{Hz}$, and $f_3 = 26.0\,\text{Hz}$. Theoretical calculations give approximate values, but experimental results show that, due to losses, the expected earth–ionosphere waveguide is not perfect. The waveguide acts as a cavity for extremely low frequency (ELF) electromagnetic waves due to the finite dimensions of the earth. The fundamental mode appears when the wavelength is equal to the earth's circumference. The cavity is excited by the natural phenomenon of electric currents from lightning. The measured resonance frequency is lower than calculated. In addition, various earlier known phenomena are present, such as diurnal–nocturnal differences in the ionosphere height, sudden ionospheric disturbances, variations in the earth's radius, changes in the earth's magnetic field at different latitudes, etc. The typical resonance amplitude of the vertical electric field components is relatively small, at around 0.3–1 mV/m/Hz, whereas peak frequencies appear around 7.83 Hz (fundamental), 14.3, 20.8, 27.3 and 33.8 Hz.

1.2.3 Earth's Magnetic Field

Another very important natural source of EMFs is the magnetic field of the earth. This field is static, with some very slow time variations over different time periods, such as diurnal, 27 days and annual. In fact, this is 'natural magnetic' noise. Amplitudes of geomagnetic fields range from 22 to 67 μT at various locations along the globe, varying from tenths of nT (diurnal variation) to hundreds, or even thousands of nT (in strong magnetic storms) (Merrill et al., 1998; British Geological Survey, 2022). The variations in nT need attention because they affect instruments that measure, e.g., electroencephalogram (EEG). Lower frequency geomagnetic pulsations appear in the ultra low frequency (ULF) band with frequencies of 1 mHz to 1 Hz because of the magnetosphere interacting with the solar wind that is a stream of charged particles. Electrons, protons and alpha particles with kinetic energy between 0.5 and 10 keV can be a part of that stream released from the upper atmosphere of the Sun called the corona. The estimated values of Earth's magnetic field, including magnetic declination (D), can be calculated based on the current World Magnetic Model or the International Geomagnetic Reference Field model. This valuable calculation requires location (latitude and longitude), elevation (recommended for aircraft and satellite use) in feet, meters, or kilometers above mean sea level, date in year, month, day and date step size. It is given as a free service by National Oceanic and Atmospheric Administration (NOAA) National Centers for Environmental Information (NCEI) (NOAA, 2022).

1.2.4 Humans and EMFs

The human body itself is a generator of endogenous electric and magnetic fields. Therefore, a part of standard medical procedures today measures endogenous electric fields, i.e. an electrocardiogram (ECG) for measuring cardiac electric signals (e.g., ECG Schematic diagram of normal sinus rhythm for a human heart as seen on ECG, 2022), an electroencephalogram (EEG) for measuring brain electric signals at various human activities (e.g., The sample of human EEG with prominent resting state activity - alpha-rhythm, 2022), an electromyogram (EMG) for measuring muscular electric signals and electrooculogram (EOG) for measuring the existing resting electrical potential between the cornea and Bruch's membrane. Furthermore, the following magnetic signals can also be measured for medical purposes: a magnetocardiogram (MCG) with the heart signals, a magnetoencephalogram (MEG) with the brain signals; a magnetomyogram (MMG) with the muscles signals, and a magnetooculogram (MOG) and magnetoretinogram (MRG) with the eyes signals.

1.3 BRIEF HISTORY OF ELECTRICITY, MAGNETISM AND ELECTROMAGNETISM

In the 19th century, Isidore Marie Auguste François Xavier Comte (1798–1857), a French philosopher, believed that there is a strong interaction between history and its related EMFs (ACHS, 1911). Our civilisation today relies entirely on EMFs phenomena. Therefore, when discussing EMFs and their effects on humans, it is useful to take a brief overview of the human understanding of electromagnetic phenomena. This is especially important in light of reducing worker discomfort, strain and fatigue as well as preventing work-related injuries, which is the goal of ergonomics.

William Gilbert (Gylberde) (1544–1603), a pioneering researcher into magnetism who became the most distinguished man of science in England during the reign of Queen Elizabeth I, understood that 'positive' and 'negative' charges 'appear' when some substances like amber and glass have a mechanical interaction with other materials like fur and silk. He also observed an electrical attraction of the opposite charges and repel of the same charges, which he explained by the operation of a compass (Gilbert, 1600). Later on, René Descartes (1596–1650) offered a mechanistic explanation of the spinning nature of a magnetic field. He introduced cork-screw-shaped particles moving from the South Pole in one direction and those from the North Pole in the opposite direction. He understood that magnetised needles align with their flow (Descartes, 1644). In the mid-18th century, Benjamin Franklin (1706–1790) was sure of the existence of charge conservation. Franklin's extremely dangerous experiments with a kite during thunderstorms showed that lightning is an electrical discharge (Aldridge, 1950).

Charles-Augustin De Coulomb (1736–1806) understood the electric force law with an inverse squared dependence, as well as the proportionality of electric force with its surface charge density (De Coulomb, 1785).

At the end of the 18th century and the beginning of the 19th century, Alessandro Giuseppe Antonio Anastasio Volta (1745–1827) contradicted Luigi Galvani in relation to his theories on the electrical nature of animal tissue (Galvani, 1791). Thus, in the year 1800, Volta proved the flow of electricity in a wire. He sent a letter to the Royal Society of London, describing Volta's pile or the voltaic pile (Wikipedia Volta, 2022). The voltaic pile, as can be seen from Figure 1.1, was a cylindrical stack

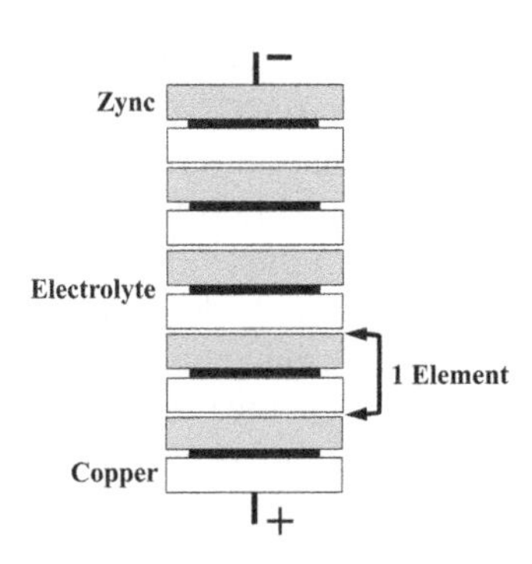

FIGURE 1.1 Voltaic pile [Based on (Wikipedia Volta, 2022)].

of interchanging discs of zinc, felt, paper or leather soaked in a salt solution or dilute acid, and a copper disk, another zinc disk, another pad, etc.

Especially important discoveries of this effect came from the year 1600 from Gilbert with his book on magnetism (Gilbert, 1600) to the year 1800 from Volta with his constant-current electric cell (Wikipedia Volta, 2022). As seen in Figure 1.2, a span of 200 years framed the development of electricity. Gilbert opened the knowledge of a force necessary for explorers of the time, navigating boats and finding the correct routes. Volta discussed the area of electric sources, opening the large doors of the electric world and man-made EMFs emissions in our environment. However, as stated, it was Franklin who understood that lightning is an electric phenomenon.

In the first half of the 19th century, Johann Carl Friedrich Gauss (1777–1855), known as '*Princeps mathematicorum*' formulated electrodynamic laws including Gauss's law; though it remained unpublished until the second half of the century (Huurdeman, 2003), as shown on Figure 1.3. In the same period, Hans Christian Ørsted (1777–1851) understood and proved that a magnetic field is generated by an electric current (Huurdeman, 2003), and André-Marie Ampère (1775–1836) understood and showed the repulsion and attraction of parallel currents, depending on their direction (Malik, 1986). Jean-Baptiste Biot (1774–1862) and Félix Savart (1791–1841) proved that the magnetic force falls off with an inverse proportion of distance, with a perpendicular orientation (Hammond and Purington, 1957). Michael Faraday (1791–1867) showed the induction of currents by changing the currents of a neighbouring circuit. He also presented the analogue of induced electricity in insulators and induced magnetism in magnetic materials. However, by presenting lines of force, he was sure that action at a distance is not feasible (Dalton, 1975).

In the same period, as shown in Figure 1.4, Georg Simon Ohm (1789–1854) understood that voltage drives electric current, and furthermore proved the relation between potential, current, and resistance (Ohm's law) (Ohm, 1827). James Prescott

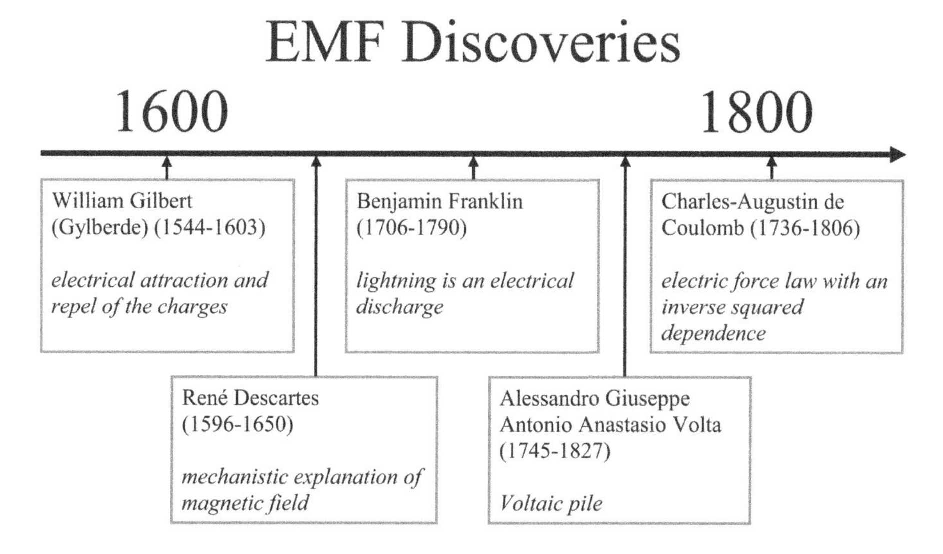

FIGURE 1.2 Two framing centuries for the development of electrical era.

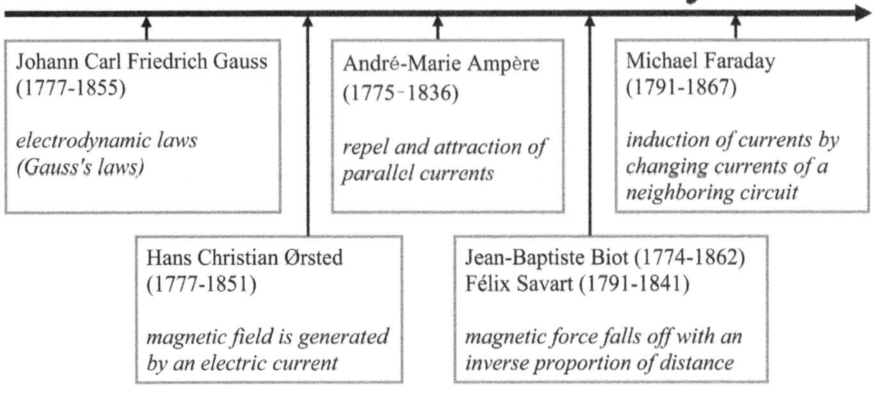

FIGURE 1.3 Discoveries in electromagnetism from Gauss to Faraday.

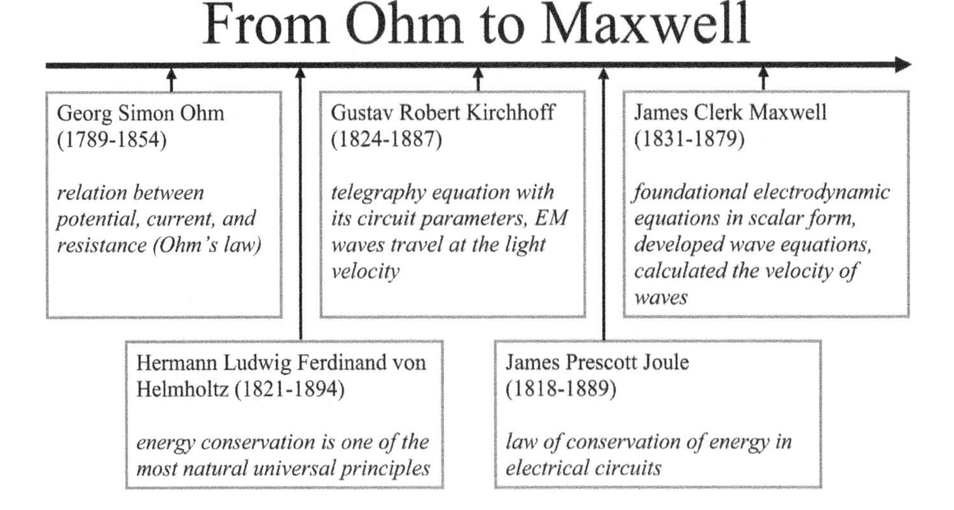

FIGURE 1.4 Discoveries in electromagnetism from Ohm to Maxwell.

Joule (1818–1889) proved the law of the conservation of energy in electrical circuits, chemical and thermal processes (Joule, 1837–1843). Just a few years later, Hermann Ludwig Ferdinand von Helmholtz (1821–1894) discovered that energy conservation is one of the most natural universal principles, whereas energy forms convert into another form (von Helmholtz, 1867).

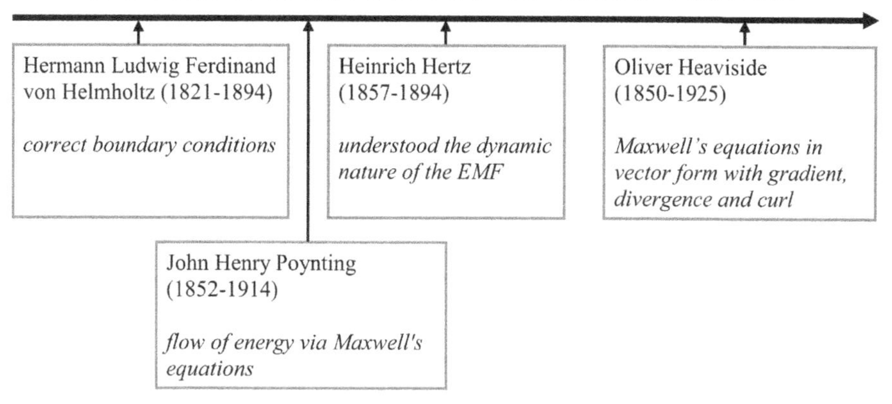

FIGURE 1.5 Discoveries in electromagnetism from Helmholtz to Heaviside.

The second half of the 19th century was crucial for electrodynamics as we understand it today. Gustav Robert Kirchhoff (1824–1887) developed the telegraphy equation with its circuit parameters (Kirchhoff, 1824–1887). He understood that it is not a mere coincidence that the electromagnetic (EM) waves travel at the velocity of light.

James Clerk Maxwell (1831–1879) published his mechanical model of EMFs, in which he formulated foundational electrodynamic equations in scalar form: electric fields as elastic displacements and magnetic fields as rotating vortices, thus presenting the elemental nature of EMFs and EM waves (Maxwell, 2010). Furthermore, this allowed him to develop wave equations as well as to calculate the velocity of waves. Thus, he concluded that the EM waves propagate with a velocity like that of light. In this way, Maxwell presented the coupling between light waves and EM waves.

As shown in Figure 1.5, Hermann Ludwig Ferdinand von Helmholtz used correct boundary conditions that led to the correct expressions of reflection and refraction from Maxwell's equations. Approximately 10 years later (approaching the end of the 19th century), he suggested the coupling of particle and wave theory by the possibility that atoms have charged particles. In the same decade, John Henry Poynting (1852–1914) explained the flow of energy via Maxwell's equations (Poynting, 1894, 1913), and Heinrich Hertz (1857–1894) understood the dynamic nature of EM waves (Hertz, 1893). Hertz started to work on probably the most important experiments in radio, first proving Maxwell's theory with an electric source. Thus, Hertz started the 'wireless' domain by understanding the resonance phenomenon in an open secondary electric circuit when near a primary circuit with an oscillating spark. He showed that the EM waves propagate along wires with the same velocity as in the air and that is: the velocity of light. In those experiments, he generated, transmitted, polarised, diffracted, concentrated to a beam and detected EM waves of 50 MHz (6 m wavelength), 100 MHz (3 m wavelength), and later at 430 MHz (70 cm wavelength)

(Bryant, 1988). Hertz understood EMFs and waves very well; thus, it was possible for him to build elegant and functional solutions by simple means, e.g. various shapes of metal, including wire, wood, sealing wax and glass. Hertz wrote 12 scalar Maxwell equations (instead of the 20 given by Maxwell) and discarded the others.

Oliver Heaviside (1850–1925) presented Maxwell's equations in vector form with gradient, divergence and curl (Heaviside, 2011). At the same time, he also introduced the voltage–current ratio and coined it as 'impedance'.

John William Strutt, also known as 3rd Baron Rayleigh (1842–1919), introduced the radiation model of wave propagation (Rayleigh, 1914).

Wilhelm Eduard Weber (1804–1891), together with Carl Friedrich Gauss and Carl Wolfgang Benjamin Goldschmidt, published 'Atlas of Geomagnetism, Designed according to the elements of the theory' (Gauss and Weber, 1840). It is a series of magnetic maps resulting from the institution of magnetic observatories.

1.4 DEVELOPMENT OF AN ARTIFICIAL EMFs WORLD

The theoretical ideas and experimental verification of EMFs-related phenomena described in the preceding section created many opportunities for their practical applications.

Johann Carl Friedrich Gauss (1777–1855) and Wilhelm Eduard Weber (1804–1891) built a telegraph as an electromagnetic relay for sending signals between Gauss's laboratory and two observatories around 1.7 km away. The authors did not find the invention to be important enough to make it public.

In the first half of the 19th century, Samuel Finley Breese Morse (1791–1872) demonstrated the one-needle telegraph to USA President Martin Van Buren (Yenne, 1993). Approximately a decade later, Morse transmitted, until that time inconceivable, long-distance communications in real time. In this period, Alexander Graham Bell (1847–1922) invented the magneto-telephone and patented it later in the mid-second half of the 19th century. The first versions of the telephone enabled only short-distance communication; but its development was accelerated with higher quality microphones approaching the end of the 19th century (Haykin, 1988).

1.4.1 Alternate Current Systems

Nikola Tesla developed polyphase alternating current systems of generators, motors and transformers, eventually holding 40 basic US patents for those (List of Patents N. Tesla, 2022). The world still uses the same alternating current (AC) system that enabled a new era in the development of human society. The electric transmission of power, Patent number 382, 280 from 1 May 1888 (Tesla, 1888), starts as:

> *Be it known that I, NIKOLA TESLA, from Smiljan, Lika, border country of Austria-Hungary, and residing in New York, in the city, county and State of New York, have invented certain new and useful Improvements in Transmission of Power, of which the following is a specification, reference being had to the drawings accompanying and forming a part of the same.*
>
> *This application is a division of an application, filed by me October 12, 1887, No. 252,132.*

George Westinghouse Jr. (6 October 1846 – 12 March 1914) purchased all of Tesla's patents related to AC motors and system. Westinghouse had a vision to supply USA with AC electricity using the Tesla system. Tesla systems are the standard for power delivery still used in the 20th and the 21st century (Tesla Life and Legacy, 2022). Therefore, Tesla wrote (Westinghouse, 2022):

> *George Westinghouse was, in my opinion, the only man on this globe who could take my alternating-current system under the circumstances then existing and win the battle against prejudice and money power,* and *He was one of the world's true noblemen, of whom America may well be proud and to whom humanity owes an immense debt of gratitude.*

Westinghouse built the first large-scale power plant at Niagara Falls, with three two-phase generators, each of 5,000 hp, a nominal voltage of 2.2 kV and a nominal frequency of 25 Hz, which began operations in 1895 (Delimar et al., 2007).

The outcome of Tesla's inventions is extremely broad, ranging from all kinds of AC motors to fluorescent light bulbs, high-voltage AC devices, high frequency transmitters and devices, transformers, transmission lines, switch gear, radio, TV, radar, X-ray, cell phone, remote control devices, ray gun, etc. His basic patents were the backbone of many of these devices. At the end of the 19th century, Tesla was the first to receive radio waves from the stars by a primitive receiver. In 1943, in the lawsuit Marconi Wireless Tel. Co. v. United States, 320 U.S. 1 (1943) No. 369, argued 9–12 April 1943, decided 21 June 1943 (U.S. Supreme Court, 1943), the US Supreme court gave Tesla credit for the radio over Marconi, giving Tesla the flattering title 'Father of Wireless'. According to IEEE (IEEE Transmitter, 2022), Tesla obtained 278 patents in 26 countries. Tesla was active in the presentation of his research and experiments, e.g. in 1888 and 1891 to members of the American Institute of Electrical Engineers (AIEE which merged with the Institute of Radio Engineers and became IEEE) at Columbia University in New York. In 1892, he was elected as the Vice-President of AIEE for two consecutive years.

In the present day, AC electricity powers many industrial generators and motors for the conversion of mechanical to electrical energy and vice-versa. These generators and motors are the primary power source and driving systems for much of modern industry; examples include cranes, hoists, lifts, conveyor systems, etc. Meanwhile, many other uses of EM components were developed, such as various sensors, converting a physical quantity (e.g. flow, pressure, level, temperature, proximity, …) into an electrical signal and actuating devices, driving the load at specific conditions (e.g. relays, solenoid valves, motors, ...).

As with Hertz, Tesla also understood the nature of EMFs, requiring no metal contact to conduct electricity. This was contrary to the theory at that time; but he too proved it to be correct. By using magnetic induction, Tesla transmitted currents through various non-metal materials over short distances. His wish was to transmit energy to the whole world wirelessly. Thus, he built Tesla Laboratory at Wardenclyffe, featuring a 185-foot tower with metal bars extending below ground. Unfortunately, the concept was not successful. Figure 1.6 shows inventor Nikola Tesla, with his equipment in his laboratory in Colorado Springs in December 1899, supposedly sitting and reading next to his giant 'magnifying transmitter' high-voltage generator while the machine produced huge bolts of electricity.

FIGURE 1.6 Inventor Nikola Tesla with his equipment in his laboratory in Colorado Springs December 1899. (https://commons.wikimedia.org/wiki/File:Nikola_Tesla,_with_his_equipment_EDIT.jpg)

The use of the 50/60 Hz concept comes from the standardisation of AC systems as the most appropriate for energy transfer. The first AC systems, designed by Tesla, operated at 25 Hz (the Niagara Falls Plant from 1895). A very important application of AC was arc-lighting equipment (designed by Tesla) (Tesla, 1886). This equipment was too sensitive for human eyes at frequencies lower than 40 Hz, due to the flickering effect; Westinghouse Electric raised the standard to 60 Hz after learning that the human eye does not sense response to changes of the existing arc-lighting equipment and, thus, can take it as a standard 'continuous' light for human eyes. In Europe, the leader was the German company AEG (Allgemeine Elektrizitäts-Gesellschaft Aktiengesellschaft) (Owen, 1997). The company had been founded as Deutsche Edison-Gesellschaft (DEG), in 1883. AEG also understood the flickering effect and built the first 50 Hz generating station. In Europe, AEG had a virtual monopoly. Thus, the 50 Hz standard was adopted for of the whole Europe.

The selection of a specific operating frequency, such as 50 Hz, 60 Hz or any other frequency, depends on the specific purpose of a device application. For example, vehicles like aircraft use electrical devices and components at 400 Hz because electric power produced at a higher frequency, such as 400 Hz, requires generators that are smaller and lighter.

1.4.2 Contribution to the Wireless Communications

On 10 June 1941, Hedwig Eva Maria Kiesler (known as Hedy Lamar) and George Antheil filed a patent that was published on 11 August 1942, under application number:

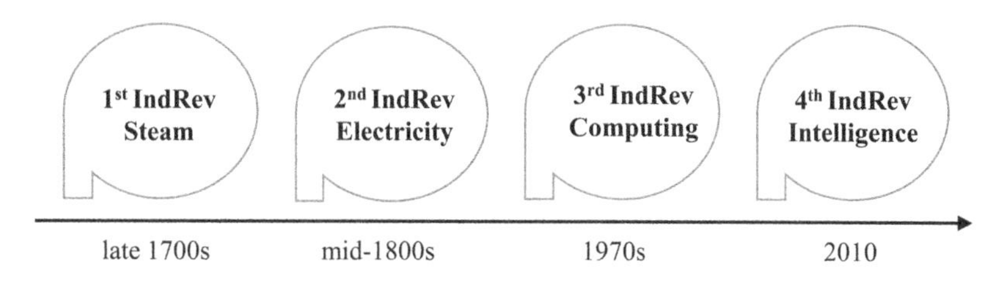

FIGURE 1.7 The four industrial revolutions.

US39741241A (Kiesler and Antheil, 1942). The patent title is 'Secret Communication System'. The patent was donated to the US Navy. Thus, the famous Austrian and American film actress Hedy Lamarr, who lived from 1914 to 2000, patented the basis for today's wireless communications using spread spectrum technology.

1.4.3 Industry in the 21st Century

Until the recent crisis (2008), European industrial policy was based on the selectively targeted strategies of national governments for the development of the national economies by the creation of leading industries. In principle, these were industries to cover the technology gap between Europe and the USA. After the crisis in 2008, the focus was more on forming intra- and extra-European horizontal approaches to enable the creation of competitive companies. This choice was due to the need to increase productivity in the context of the new globalisation, because of the global economy liberalisation.

The fact that the history shows already three industrial revolutions—the first with steam power combined with mechanical production in the late 1700s; the second, which began with the launch of electricity and assembly lines and related mass production from the mid-1800s; the third with the combination of advanced electronics, IT and globalisation from the 1970s—enabled the creation of the fourth industrial revolution, based on the links of intelligent factories (utilising algorithms for various purposes), and all the links of the production chain and next generation automation, starting in 2010 (Figure 1.7).

Although Industry 4.0 is based on autonomously communicating devices and on the involvement of disruptive innovations in industrial processes, thus resulting in significantly higher productivity of 'smart' factories and being excellent characteristics for society, it has to take into account the challenging tasks of the availability of workers, their professional development, new business models, the standardisation of systems, platforms, protocols and the whole technology, safety and security, know-how protection, and the legal framework. Unless all these societal challenges are carefully designed, the complete industrial automation and evolution cannot occur.

1.5 CONCLUSIONS

Tesla's idea of 'instant communication', including the idea of a 'smart phone' in 1901, approximately 100 years before global wireless communications appeared, is given in his wording:

With these developments we have every reason to anticipate that in a time, not very distant, most telegraphic messages across the oceans will be transmitted without cables. For short distances we need a 'wireless' telephone, which requires no expert operators...

This chapter provides a short overview of the increasing significance of EMFs for humans across the history. As described, EMFs are everywhere. It is probably the most complex physical phenomenon that is present everywhere, starting from the space and air around us and ending inside living organisms, while being named by a single term: electromagnetism. Thus, a proficient, and sufficient knowledge and understanding of EMFs should be considered as the main key for achieving EMFs-safe coexistence with human populations and individuals.

Finally, Tesla said:

Let the future tell the truth and evaluate each one according to his work and accomplishments. The present is theirs; the future, for which I have really worked, is mine.

ACKNOWLEDGEMENT

The author appreciates very much the invested time and energy of Mr Timothy Harrington, taken to help and improve this paper.

REFERENCES

Aldridge, A.O. 1950. Franklin, B, J. Edwards on lightning and earthquakes. *Isis* 41(2): 162–164.

American Catholic Historical Society. 1911. The compass of Columbus. The American Catholic Historical Researches. *New Series* 7(1): 1–7.

British Geological Survey, The Earth's Magnetic Field: An Overview, 2022 http://www.geomag.bgs.ac.uk/education/earthmag.html (accessed 11 November 2022).

Bryant, J.H. 1988. The first century of microwaves-1886 to 1986. *IEEE Trans Microw Theory Tech* 36(5):830–858. DOI: 10.1109/22.3602.

Dalton, W.M. 1975. *The Story of Radio*, Vol. I(I). London: Hilger.

De Coulomb, C.A. 1785. Second mémoire sur l'électricité et le magnétisme. *Histoire de l'Académie Royale des Sciences* 578–611.

Delimar, M., A. Szabo, and L. Lugarić. 2007. First integrated electric power system in Croatia. *EUROCON 2007 The International Conference on "Computer as a Tool"*, Warsaw, September 9–12, 2648–2651.

DesCartes, R. 1644. *Principia Philosophiae*. Amsterdam: Elsevier. https://www.loc.gov/resource/rbc0001.2013rosen1431/?sp=1&st=image (accessed 11 November 2022).

ECG Schematic diagram of normal sinus rhythm for a human heart as seen on ECG. 2022. Contributed by Wikimedia Commons, Anthony Atkielski (Public Domain-Self). (accessed 11 November 2022).

Galvani, L. 1791. *Aloysii Galvani De viribus electricitatis in motu musculari commentarius*. Bononiae: Ex Typographia Instituti Scientiarium. DOI: 10.5479/sil.324681.39088000932442.

Gauss, C.F., and W.E. Weber. 1840. *Atlas Des Erdmagnetismus: Nach Den Elementen Der Theorie Entworfen*. Leipzig: Weidmann'sche Buchhandlung.

Gilbert of Colchester, W. Physician of London. 1600. On the Loadstone and Magnetic Bodies, and on the great Magnet the earth. A New Physiology, Demonstrated with many Arguments and Experiments. A Translation by P. Fleury Mottelay, London: Bernard Quaritch, 1893.

Golubenko, K., E. Rozanov, I. Mironova, A. Karagodin, and I. Usoskin. 2020. Natural sources of ionization and their impact on atmospheric electricity. *Geophys Res Lett* 47: e2020GL088619. DOI: 10.1029/2020GL088619.

Hammond, J.H. Jr., and E. S. Purington. 1957. History of some foundations of modern radio -Electronic technology. *Proc IRE*, 45(1): 1191.

Haykin, S. 1988. *Digital Communications*. New York: John Wiley & Sons, Inc.

Heaviside, O. 2011. *Electromagnetic Theory (1893–1912)*, 1st ed. Three volumes published separately in 1893, 1899 and 1912. Cambridge: Cambridge University Press.

Hertz, H. 1893.. *Electric Waves: Being Researches On the Propagation of Electric Action With Finite Velocity Through Space*. London, New York: Macmillan and co. Authorised English translation by Jones, D. E., Professor in the University College of Wales, Aberystwyth, with a preface by Lord Kelvin, LL.D., D.C.L., University of Glasgow

Huurdeman, A.A. 2003. *The Worldwide History of Telecommunications*. Hoboken: John Wiley & Sons.

IEEE Transmitter. 2022. Nikola Tesla 162nd birthday, Internet page, https://transmitter.ieee.org/tesla/ (accessed 11 November 2022).

Joule, J.P. 1837–1843. On the production of heat by voltaic electricity. *Philos Trans R Soc Lond* 4: 280–282.

Kiesler, M. H., and G. Antheil. 1942. Secret communication system. Patent No. US39741241A, U.S. Patent and Trademark Off., Washington, DC.

Kirchhoff, G.R. 1824–1887. *Vorlesungen über mathematische Physik*. Leipzig: B.G. Teubner.

List of patents Nikola Tesla. 2022. https://web.mit.edu/most/Public/Tesla1/alpha_tesla.html (accessed 11 November 2022).

Malik, M.C. 1986. Chronology of developments of wireless communication and electronics. *IETE Tech Rev* 3(9): 479–522. DOI: 10.1080/02564602.1986.11438016.

Maxwell, J. 2010. *A Treatise on Electricity and Magnetism*. Cambridge: Cambridge University Press. DOI: 10.1017/CBO9780511709333.

Merrill, R.T., M. W. McElhinny, and P. L. McFadden. 1998. *The Magnetic Field of the Earth: Paleomagnetism, the Core, and the Deep Mantle*. Cambridge: Academic Press.

National Lightning Safety Institute (NLSI). 2020. http://lightningsafety.com/nlsi_pls/lightningstatistics.html (accessed 11 November 2022).

National Oceanic and Atmospheric Administation (NOAA). 2022.
https://www.ngdc.noaa.gov/geomag/magfield.shtml (accessed 11 November 2022).

Ohm, G.S. 1827. *Die Galvanische Kette, Mathematisch Bearbeitet*. Berlin: J.G.F. Kniestädt for T.H. Riemann.

Owen, E. 1997. The origins of 60-Hz as a power frequency. *Ind Appl Mag IEEE* 3(6): 8, 10, 12–14.

Poynting, J.H. 1894. The mean density of the earth. *Nature* 48, 370. DOI: 10.1038/048370c0.

Poynting, J.H. 1913. *The Earth; Its Shape, Size, Weight and Spin*. Cambridge: Cambridge University Press.

Rayleigh, Lord. 1914. On the theory of long waves and bores. *Proc R Soc Lond, Series A* 90(619): 324–328.

Schumann, W.O. 1952a. Über die Dämpfung der elektromagnetischen Eigenschwingungen des Systems Erde — Luft — Ionosphäre. *Zeitschrift für Naturforschung* 7a: 250–252. DOI: 10.1515/zna-1952-3-404.

Schumann, W.O. 1952b. Über die strahlungslosen Eigenschwingungen einer leitenden Kugel, die von einer Luftschicht und einer Ionosphärenhülle umgeben ist. *Zeitschrift für Naturforschung A* 7(2): 149–154. DOI: 10.1515/zna-1952-0202.

Tesla, N. 1886. Electric-arc lamp, letters. Patent No. 335,787, U.S. Patent and Trademark Off., Washington, DC.

Tesla, N. 1888. The electric transmission of power. Patent No. 382,280, U.S. Patent and Trademark Off., Washington, DC.

Tesla, N. 1905. Art of transmitting electrical energy through the natural mediums. Patent No. 787,412, U.S. Patent and Trademark Off., Washington, DC.

Tesla Life and Legacy. 2022. https://www.pbs.org/tesla/ll/ll_colspr.html (accessed 11 November 2022).

The sample of human EEG with prominent resting state activity - alpha-rhythm. 2022. Left - EEG traces (horizontal - time in seconds; vertical - amplitudes, scale 100uV). Right - power spectra of shown signals (vertical lines -10 and 20Hz, scale is linear). Alpha-rhythm consists of sinusoidal-like waves with frequencies in 8–12Hz range (11Hz in this case) more prominent in posterior sites. Alpha range is red on a power spectrum graph.(accessed 11 November 2022).

US Supreme Court. 1943. Marconi wireless Tel. Co. v. United States, 320 U.S. 1. https://supreme.justia.com/cases/federal/us/320/1/ (accessed 11 November 2022).

von Helmholtz, H.L.F. 1867. *Handbook of Physiological Optics*. Leipzig: Leopold Voss.

Westinghouse. 2022. https://westinghouse.com/ (accessed 11 November 2022).

Wikipedia Volta. 2022. Voltaic pile. https://en.wikipedia.org/wiki/Voltaic_pile (accessed 11 November 2022).

Yenne, B. 1993. *100 Inventions That Shaped World History*. San Mateo: Bluewood Books.

2 Electromagnetic Formalities Regarding Work-Related Environmental Issues

Jolanta Karpowicz
Central Institute for Labour Protection—
National Research Institute (CIOP-PIB)

CONTENTS

2.1 INTRODUCTION

Today, it is hard to find any location not affected by man-made electromagnetic energy [also recognised as the electromagnetic field (EMF) or radiation], whether emitted intentionally or leaked unintentionally. The mass of electric appliances and systems today are constantly functioning in radiocommunication, industrial, medical, office, household and other purposes, forming what we call the electromagnetic environment. Various technologies emitting EMF—known as electromagnetic technologies—have been used over the past decades; others are emerging or changing with respect to the way they are used or their purpose. The more complex the

DOI: 10.1201/9781003020486-2

electromagnetic energy affecting the biosphere and technosphere, the more urgent it is to achieve a relevant characterisation of its significance in the environment and an influence on human safety, health and wellbeing, as well as its electromagnetic coexistence with other elements of the biosphere and technosphere (considering electromagnetic energy to be a dominating single factor in the space, or complex factor or co-factor during the life of a particular organism). Given the use of stronger (consuming higher electric power) EMF sources in the work environment, the priority for such considerations should be on potentially strong, work-related EMF exposure before weak (by definition) public exposures (Hansson Mild et al. 2009, IARC 2002, 2013, ICNIRP 2020, IEEE 2019, Karpowicz and Gryz 2007, 2010, SCENIHR 2015). This includes relations between parameters of sources of electromagnetic energy, the way in which they are used and the effects of exposure to various objects (characterised by analytical considerations, measurements, numerical simulations, and laboratory or epidemiological investigations, etc.) regarding the evaluation of the short-term and long-term, reversible or irreversible, environmental impact of electromagnetic technologies.

Ergonomics is the branch of engineering science in which biological science is used to study the relation between workers and work environment. From one side, ergonomics covers the study of people in relation to the environment in which they work, along with the application of anatomical, physiological, psychological, and engineering knowledge to the problems involved. The opposite side of ergonomics science coordinates the design of devices, systems, and physical working conditions for the workplace environment, with the capacities and requirements of the workers. This is intended to maximize productivity by reducing operator fatigue and discomfort, and also has a positive influence on workers' health, and therefore on public health, given that nearly half of the population are workers, as well as on the environment of human life, given that humans generally share at least half of their lives between family and leisure activities and work, and significant percentage of the workspace is accessible for non-workers (e.g. in the commercial or public services buildings and open space).

The domain of electromagnetic ergonomics (EM-ergonomics) analyses technical and organisational problems related to the impact of the use of electromagnetic technologies on humans (both directly, when the free-standing body comes into contact with EMF, and indirectly, through the electromagnetic impact on the material environment where humans are present). Summarising, EM-ergonomics aims to give a systematic review of the technical and organisational problems related to the impact of EMF on humans in the work environment, considering entire range of possible EMF properties, as well as the work tasks and inter-person variability of workers population (including general issues, such as: anatomical characteristic of the body, age, health conditions, temporary conditions such as pregnancy or simultaneous load by other workplace factors, etc., as well as specific ones caused by electronic devices sensitivity to electromagnetic influence, what make necessary to consider workers' characteristic also including electronic devices assisting their body, such as medical implants used, but also other electronic devices worn on body because of medical purposes, or with any other function, such as rapidly growing use of so called Internet of Thing applications, which may change the sensitivity of worker's body to the electromagnetic energy or triggering various hazards caused by malfunctions of mentioned devices itself).

2.2 ELECTROMAGNETIC ENVIRONMENT AND HAZARDS

Time-varying EMF can be characterised by any frequency of variability over time. The following frequency ranges are typically distinguished: EMF and optical radiation, which are together a non-ionising radiation, along with ionising radiation, subdivided into X-ray, gamma and cosmic radiation with respect to the types of sources (Figure 2.1). In EM-ergonomics, the EMF considered as an environmental factor is a component of the non-ionising part of the spectrum of electromagnetic radiation, with frequencies up to 300 GHz (i.e. with a wavelength greater than 1 mm). Such radiation does not cause the ionisation of the medium they go through.

This frequency range is usually split into several sub-ranges: the static magnetic field (SMF), the static electric field (SEF), and EMF of low and intermediate frequencies [i.e. quasi-static EMF (QSF)]. Next comes the range of frequency exceeding several MHz, also called electromagnetic radiation. Consequently, EMF of high frequency is recognised as being radiofrequency EMF/radiation (RF-EMF/ EMR) or microwaves (MW). The other notations of EMF frequency bands are used, for example, in the technical specifications of radiocommunication devices and systems (Table 2.1).

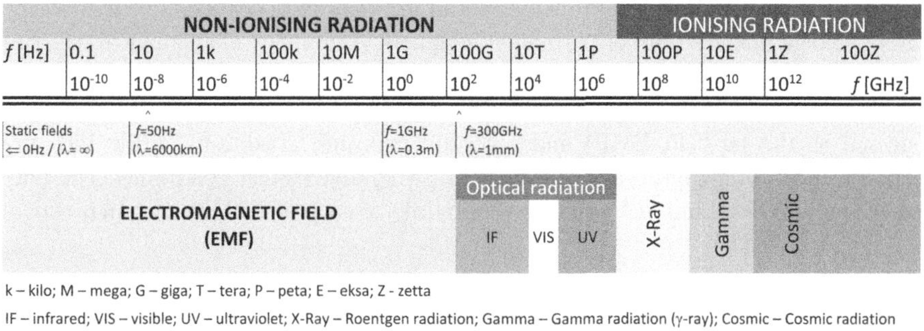

FIGURE 2.1 Frequency spectrum of the electromagnetic field and radiation.

TABLE 2.1
Notation Regarding the Frequency Bands Applicable in Technical Specifications

Band	Frequency	Wavelength (Inversely Proportional to Frequency)
EHF, extremely high frequency	300–30 GHz	1–10 mm
SHF, super high frequency	30–3 GHz	1–10 cm
UHF, ultra high frequency	3–0.3 GHz	10–100 cm
VHF, very high frequency	300–30 MHz	1–10 m
HF, high frequency	30–3 MHz	10–100 m
MF, medium frequency	3–0.3 MHz	100–1000 m
LF, low frequency	300–30 kHz	1–10 km
VLF, very low frequency	30–3 kHz	10–100 km

2.2.1 General Description of Electromagnetic Interaction with Material Objects

The influence of EMF on the material environment induces complex energy processes that are not only used, among other things, in industrial, radiocommunication and medical technologies, but they can also have an unintentional effect on the functioning of organisms and electrical devices. EMF are, therefore, classified as a harmful and annoying factor in the work and life environment. Various biophysical properties related to the electromagnetic issues change along with the frequencies of EMF time-variability in any environment of propagation (including the tissues of the human body). The most significant of these properties in the considered issues are the conductivity and permittivity of medium. These vary, for example, with the type of body tissue and also depend on the frequency of the affecting EMF (Figure 2.2).

In practical environmental studies, the properties of electromagnetic energy are usually analysed with respect to two EMF components: the electric field (EF) and the magnetic field (MF). The MF is present around electric charges in motion (i.e. creating an electric current) or as a result of the magnetisation of certain materials, whereas the EF exists both around moving and motionless charges. The SEF is present around motionless charges, and the SMF is present in the vicinity of conductors energised by direct voltage (and current) or permanent magnets. A complex mathematical description of EMF requires the use of the set of Maxwell's equations (see the appendix).

The EF and MF are inseparable; however, they are correlated to each other (recognised as the far-field EMF) under certain exposure conditions, while they are non-correlated (recognised as the near-field EMF) under other conditions. The only exceptions are SMF and SEF, which have no links to each other. However, in practical

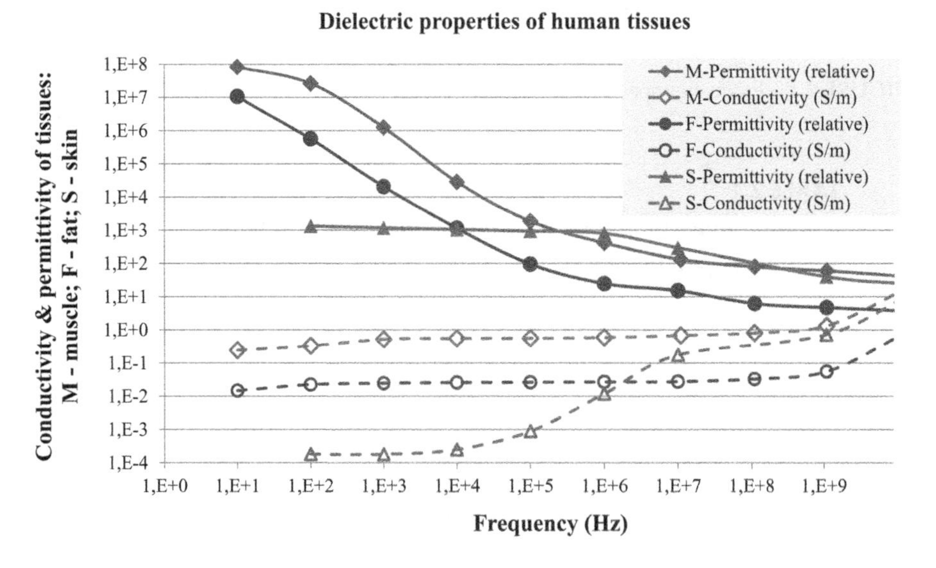

FIGURE 2.2 Permittivity and conductivity of selected human tissues. (Composed from Gabriel et. al., 1996.)

work-related exposure situations, because of the parameters of the electrical structures of EMF sources, one EMF component typically dominates. This makes it possible to significantly simplify the process of analysing EMF hazards in the work environment.

The level of EMF exposure is usually described by relevant parameters: of EF strength (*E*, expressed in volts per metre, V/m), MF strength (*H*, expressed in amperes per metre, A/m), and the frequency (*f*, expressed in hertz, Hz) of the EMF affecting the workplace under question (i.e. affecting a worker's body and any material objects around or inside a body). In the case of electromagnetic radiation, the power density (*S*, expressed in watts per square metre) may also characterise EMF exposure. It is also important to keep in mind that *E* and *H* are vector quantities, which, in practice, means that the scale of influence from EMF is not only related to the magnitudes of affecting field but also its orientation in space (recognised as polarisation).The set of particular parameters of *E* and *H* in a time, space and frequency context, which needs to be evaluated in the EM-ergonomics domain, depends on the considered kinds of interaction mechanisms, the related hazards and the exposure situations under question (usually defined with respect to the EMF frequency, time and spatial distribution of exposure).

The energy of the EF affects both moving and motionless charges, whereas that of MF affects only moving charges. It is also important that the spatial distribution of *E* and *H* near EMF sources differs in the case of both the fields. In practice, the spatial distribution of the MF is defined only by the structure of the EMF source. On the other hand, the EF distribution is highly influenced by the material objects in the vicinity of the EMF source, especially electrically grounded ones with dimensions comparable to the fraction of EMF wavelength (Figure 2.3).

2.2.2 Electromagnetic Interaction with the Human Body Related to the Electric Component of Exposure

The interaction of time-varying EF with the human body results in the electric polarisation of any material object (including the formation of electric dipoles and the reorientation of electric dipoles already present in the tissue) (ICNIRP 1998, 2010, 2020, IEEE 2005, 2019). It may also create an electric current in tissues (i.e. the flow of electric current in tissues from a higher electric potential to a lower one, when possible to the point of electric grounding of the exposed object) and the thermal load there [proportional to the squared value of time-averaged root-mean-square (RMS) value of density of the induced current in the tissues].

The spatial distribution of electromagnetic energy absorbed in the human body depends to a large extent on the frequency. With low-frequency EMF, in practice, only the MF can easily penetrate the body. The internal energy deposition increases in the kHz- and low MHz-frequency EMF. At frequencies in the range 40–100 MHz, the highest energy deposition in the human body occurs because of the phenomenon of the whole-body resonance absorption [whereby, the electric dimensions of the body depend on the posture and grounding conditions, and may fit with the quarters of electromagnetic wavelength (λ): 3.0–7.5 m in that frequency range]. The electromagnetic energy deposition in the body becomes spatially heterogeneous at higher frequencies, and energy absorption occurs primarily near the body's surface above a few GHz (ICNIRP 1998, 2020, IEEE 2005, 2019, Korniewicz 1995).

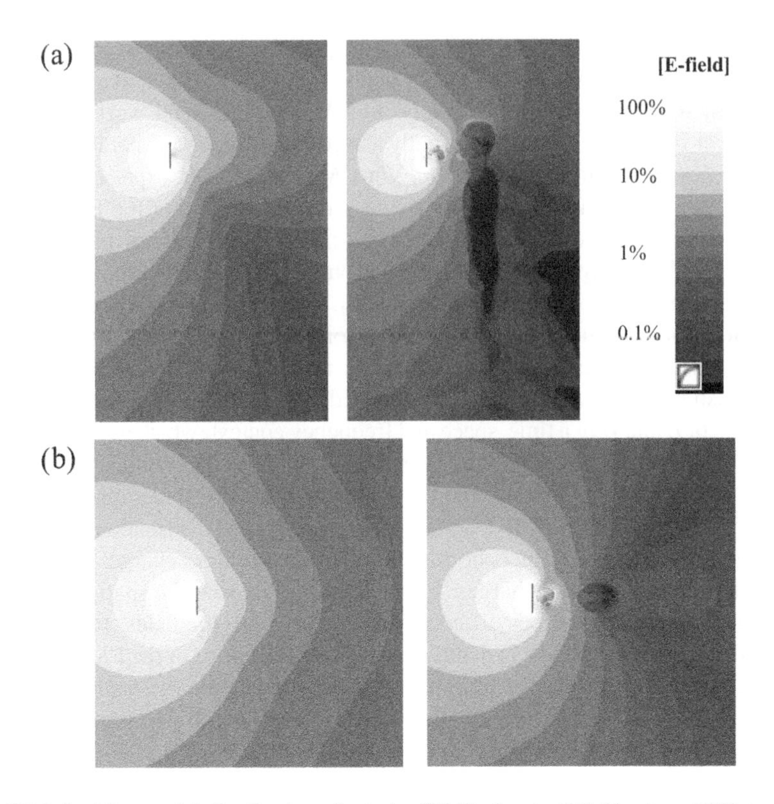

FIGURE 2.3 The spatial distribution of relative EF (the level of RMS value of EF strength) near the model of RFID UHF antenna (operating at 865 MHz): left, distribution of unperturbed EF near antenna located in the free space; right, distribution of EF influenced by the insulated body of human approaching antenna; (a) vertical cross-section, (b) horizontal cross-section.

EMF exposure at frequencies exceeding 100 kHz can lead to significant absorption of electromagnetic energy and temperature increases in the exposed body, with a frequency-dependent spatial distribution (Durney et al. 1985):

- 0.1–20 MHz: Absorption in the trunk rapidly varied proportionally to the frequency, with possible significant absorption in the neck and legs, which have a smaller body cross-section.
- 20–300 MHz: Relatively high absorption in the whole body, with possible resonance increase in body sections (e.g. head) with dimensions coupled to the length of the EMF wave.
- 0.3–10 GHz: Significant local, heterogeneous absorption.
- Exceeding 10 GHz: Absorption primarily near the body surface.

The surface energy absorption is usually characterised by what is known as 'penetration depth' (PE-DE), indicating at what distance from the surface the level of EMF penetrating a particular material object is mitigated at a specific rate because of its absorption, reflection and deflection. PE-DE is a function of the dielectric properties of the exposed object, which means that, in practice, PE-DE is a function of EMF frequency. For example, PE-DE is commonly defined in a way that EF strength is mitigated at approximately three times along the PE-DE in the object (more precisely by $1/e$ times, where $e = 2.72$ is the mathematical constant used as the base of natural logarithm). This definition regarding EF mitigation, when the MF is mitigated to a similar extent, is equivalent to approximately 10 times the mitigation of the power density of penetrating electromagnetic energy along the mentioned PE-DE. In such cases, the EF strength along twice PE-DE would be mitigated approximately 10 times, power density approximately 100 times and so on, for example, the EF strength would be mitigated 100 times along 4 times PE-DE. As an example of the PE-DE values for the skin tissue (dermis), PE-DE at 6 GHz is equal to approximately 8 mm; PE-DE at 10 GHz is equal to approximately 4 mm; PE-DE at 30 GHz is equal to approximately 1 mm; and PE-DE at 60 GHz is equal to approximately 0.5 mm (ICNIRP 2020).

However, it must be stated strongly that the regular mitigation of electromagnetic energy characterises the EMF–material object interaction only in the case of a homogeneous object affected by a homogeneous EMF. Such a simplification of the electrodynamics interaction between EMF and an exposed object (by using the concept of PE-DE) is inadequate in the case that a heterogeneous object (such as human body) is exposed to EMF that is highly heterogeneous (such as localised exposure from a small antenna located near the surface of the object); in such realistic EMF exposure situations, the mitigation of electromagnetic energy penetrating the object is also highly heterogeneous, as shown, for example, in Figure 2.4.

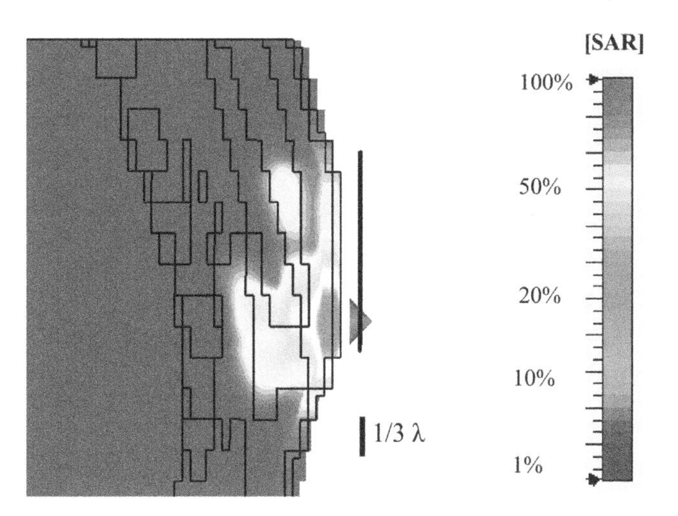

FIGURE 2.4 The example of spatial distribution of electromagnetic energy in the heterogeneous object affected by localised EMF exposure; power density distribution characterised by SAR values numerically calculated in the human body torso model heterogeneous in tissues' dielectric properties.

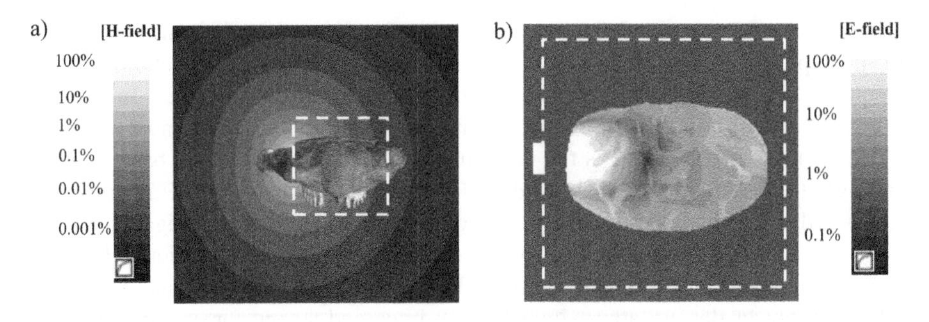

FIGURE 2.5 The distribution of the low-frequency MF (5 kHz frequency) emitted by small-dimensional source located near the hip (a: top view) and EF induced in tissues of the torso (b: horizontal cross-section).

2.2.3 Electromagnetic Interaction with the Human Body Related to the Magnetic Component of Exposure

The physical interaction of the time-varying MF with the human body results in induced EF and circulating electric current, known as eddy current, in the body. The magnitudes of the induced EF and the current density are proportional to the radius of the loop (capturing the body section under question), the electric conductivity of the tissue, and the magnitude and rate of time-variations of the magnetic flux density of MF penetrating the particular body section. The distribution of the current induced in any part of the body also depends on the distribution of the conductivity of the tissues there (Figure 2.5).

It needs to be pointed out that the considered time-variability of exposure to the MF may also be caused by the variability in the level of EMF emitted from the source or the variability of the level and polarisation of EMF affecting a body as a result of the body moving near the SMF source (especially in the highly heterogeneous SMF near its source).

The relative magnitudes of these different effects depend on:

- the conductivity of the exposed object determining the flow of electric current and
- the permittivity of the exposed object determining the magnitude of polarisation effects.

2.3 ELECTRODYNAMIC EFFECTS OF ELECTROMAGNETIC EXPOSURE

Deterministic and linear mechanisms are already the most systematically studied and characterised (parameterised) with respect to various direct biophysical interactions between the tissues of living organisms and time-varying EMF. These are summarised in the following section (ICNIRP 2020, IEEE 2019).

In short, any EF external to the body induce a surface charge on the body, which results in an induced EF and electric current through the body. The MF also induces the EF together with the electric current inside the exposed body but of circulating inside the body nature.

The distribution of induced current depends on exposure conditions—most significantly on the size and shape of the body, on the body's position in the field (with respect to its polarisation and spatial distribution) and on the distribution of electric grounding of objects considered in a particular exposure scenario (considering the frequency-dependent dielectric properties of insulating materials, including the air). The level of electromagnetic hazards also depends on the relationship between the strength of the EF to that of the MF (recognised to be the wave impedance of the EMF energy in a particular location).

Electromagnetic energy affects the body directly (through electrodynamic interaction) or indirectly (due to the electromagnetic impact on the body and material objects located near to this body or in this body itself).

While the exposure is of sufficient parameters (with respect to its level, frequency, modulation, spatial distribution and duration), the direct electrodynamic effects of EMF exposure may cause the electrostimulation of nervous and muscular tissue due to the influence of the EF induced in the body (the dominant mechanism of EMF interaction at frequencies lower than several hundred kHz) and the heating of tissues from the absorbed electromagnetic energy (the dominating mechanism of the influence of EMF at a frequency exceeding 1 MHz) (Reilly 1998). In principle, the scale of the thermal load in an exposed body is correlated with the time-averaged power density or squared RMS value of the EF strength (E^2), where RMS value is defined as the square root from the time-averaged square of the EF strength of incident EMF (ICNIRP 2020, IEEE 2019). The probability of electrostimulation in exposed tissues is correlated with the peak-in-time value of the EF strength of the EF induced in tissues, independently of whether it is induced by the incident EF or MF (ICNIRP 2010, IEEE 2019).

As a rule, the EMF is not felt by the human senses. Exceptions are sensory impressions during the influence of strong EMF at low frequencies (when the body is being affected by the time-varying EMF or by moving through a heterogeneous SMF), such as visual and taste sensations, balance disturbances, visual–motor coordination disruptions or, when pulsed MW affects a head, hearing sensations (known as the Frey phenomenon) (ICNIRP 2009, ICNIRP 2014, IEEE 2019). Other deeply studied mechanisms and effects of direct EMF influence on the body include magnetohydrodynamic interaction with the bodily fluids, such as the blood, dynamics of the oxidative processes and enzymatic reactions, the pro- and anti-inflammatory protein balance, the integrity of lymphocyte DNA material—with potential significance when the EMF exposure occurs (whether EMF is considered as a single environmental stressor or under the conditions of complex exposure to EMF together with other types of radiation, aggressive chemical substances, nanoparticles, etc.) (IARC 2002, IARC 2013, SCENIHR 2015).

The indirect influence can be seen, for example, as contact currents flowing through the body at the point of galvanic contact with a conductive object (usually metal) with an electric potential induced by EMF other than the induced potential at the body. At frequencies lower than 100 kHz, contact currents can trigger the stimulation of electrically excitable (in principle, muscle and nervous) tissues and can cause pain sensations. Contact currents usually occur where a strong EF affects material objects; but in specific exposure situations, a strong MF is also able to induce electric potentials (e.g. in a large elongated metal object located along a high-voltage power line) sufficient to cause the contact current to be strong enough to be felt in the form of the unexpected perception of electric micro shocks while touching this object. In particular exposure situations, the unexpected perception of an electric microshock caused by the mentioned contact current may have dangerous consequences in the work environment (when it disturbs workers' attention or activities) (Gryz et al. 2004, Hill 1985, Jokela et al. 1994, Korpinen et al. 2009, Wilén et al. 2001). In the case of exposure to RF-EMF, contact current perception is also possible, though instead of direct electrostimulation it involves the perception of pain caused by local thermal effects in the skin (ICNIRP 2020, IEEE 2019). At exposure to EMF at higher frequencies, thermal load (up to thermal damage to the body tissues, known as radiofrequency burns in the literature) is expected in the case of minutes-long lasting contact with an object exposed to EMF or remaining in a certain highly exposed area without sufficient insulation from the base (usually floor or ground).

There are various terms used for this sort of exposure effect: limb current, induced limb current, induced contact current, feet current, etc.

Indirect hazards also include certain undesirable effects of EMF impact on the users of medical implants, such as an increased risk of thermal effects and electrostimulation in tissues adjacent to the implant structure, or electromagnetic interference in the functioning of electronic implants (improper operation, lack of action necessary due to the condition of the user's health or the unnecessary activation of the implant), as well as various wearable electronic devices assisting workers or other electronic infrastructure in the work environment (Directive 2013, Mattei et al. 2021, Zradziński et al. 2018).

Special attention is needed to look at relatively new kinds of work-related hazards that may happen because of the magneto-mechanical influence of SMF on ferromagnetic objects. In a strong SMF near a magnet, various ferromagnetic objects (such as paperclips, keys, mechanic or electric tools and devices, oxygen tanks, or even furniture) may be moved or even levitate when attracting towards the magnet due to the force exerted by the SMF, behaving like bullets flying towards the SMF source. The susceptibility of an object to the magneto-mechanical influence from SMF depends on its magnetic parameters determined mainly by the chemical composition, production method and processing during construction or operation (Karpowicz and Gryz 2013). Consequently, the susceptibility of an object to SMF influence may vary as the object is used and potentially adapted or repaired; so this aspect requires a periodical (continuous) evaluation and supervision. In an SMF at the level of teslas (i.e. very strong), even large and heavy objects may be attracted by magnets, creating an acute danger to health (by serious bodily harm) or even life (by hitting anyone who finds themselves between the magnet and the rapidly moving object attracted to the magnet) of workers and damage to the technical objects used there (Chaljub et al. 2001, Chen 2001, Ducknetweb 2010, ICNIRP 2009, MRI safety.com, WHO 2005). Such hazards are recognised as ballistic hazards, projectile hazards or 'flying objects'.

Various aspects of these EMF exposure effects are discussed in detail in particular chapters of this monograph.

2.4 ELECTROMAGNETIC TECHNOLOGIES AND MANAGING THEIR HAZARDOUS IMPACT ON THE SAFETY AND HEALTH OF WORKERS

In material objects, the electrodynamic effects of the EMF induce an EF and induce electric currents used, among other things, in industrial electrothermic technologies for metalworking processes or in the wireless charging of batteries. EMF propagation is accompanied by the transfer of electromagnetic energy (in the air and in a vacuum at the speed of light) and in the case of propagation of a modulated EMF, also information transfer, used, for example, in radiocommunications and electrothermic processes in dielectric materials. All these exposure effects are also applicable for medical purposes (in diagnostic and therapeutic applications) and many others.

Along with the development of technologies using electromagnetic energy (Figure 2.6), knowledge about the mechanisms and effects of EMF, the associated hazards to human safety and health, methods of analysing parameters characterising hazards in the electromagnetic environment and protective measures reducing the level of exposure or its adverse effects are also developing constantly.

Various effects of EMF influence depend significantly on the complex parameters characterising exposure conditions (EMF frequency and polarisation, level and duration of exposure, the ground conditions of exposed objects, the size of the EMF source and its distance from the body, determining whether the exposure is local or applies to the whole body). Therefore, learning about these is a long and gradual process that continues to develop as new types of EMF sources emerge into the environment, and the effects of their complex impact on people appear and are analysed.

Emerging time	**The frequency range of electromagnetic field/radiation**				
	Static magnetic	**Low frequency**	**Radio-frequency**	**Microwave**	**Terahertz**
before 1918	NCU	Electric lightning Electric engines Telegraph	Analogue radio broadcasting (long wave)	NCU	NCU
1918-1945	NCU	Rail electric vehicles	Radar	NCU	NCU
1945-1970	Galvanic coating of metals	Electric supplying network	Analogue radio broadcasting (AM and UKF)	Radar Analogue TV	NCU
1970-1990	Direct current supplying	Nuclear electric power plants	Industrial electrothermia Physiotherapy diathermia Surgical diathermia	MW cooking	NCU
1990-2020	MRI scanners Mag-lev transportation	Electric vehicles	Digital radio broadcasting RFID	Mobile communication networks Digital TV	NCU
Examples of emerging technologies	Magnetic batteries	Wireless charging of batteries Wireless supplying of vehicles	Internet of Things Industry 4.0 Society 5.0 Digital TV	Oncologic hyperthermia Wideband Internet Wireless energy transfer	THz scanners Wideband Internet

FIGURE 2.6 The emergence of electromagnetic technologies in commercial use—timing related to the most frequently used sources of work-related EMF exposure (an example based on the experience in Poland; may differ between countries); NCU, not in commercial use.

Electromagnetic hazards in the work environment need specific considerations linked with various conditions of workers' activities near EMF sources, which have to be covered by the preventative actions ensuring, or improving, occupational safety and health. In principle, workers' activities at every stage in the 'life' of a device have to be considered in the EMF exposure evaluations and planning of preventative actions (e.g. EN 292-1:1991):

- Construction
- Transport and commissioning (assembly; installation; adjustment)
- Use (setting; teaching/programming or process changeover; operation; cleaning; fault finding; maintenance)
- Decommissioning, dismantling and, as far as safety is concerned, disposal.

When considering of potential EMF exposure situations in the work environment, in classifying EMF exposure levels near particular EMF sources, a statistical approach needs to be incorporated because of their variability along various operating conditions, for example, like specified in Table 2.2.

Another aspect of the mitigation of electromagnetic energy inside an exposed body and one that is highly significant when considering the safety of workers exposed to EMF relates to the strength of the potential electromagnetic influence on the body in the work environment. It needs to be taken into account that certain work-related

TABLE 2.2
Examples of Categories of EMF Exposure Levels Near EMF Sources in Common Use at the Workplace

No	Various Activities Near the EMF Sources (As SPECIFIED by EN 292-1:1991)	Exposure Level	
		Low	High
1.	Induction heater, dielectric heating (RF: glue drying, plastic welding, MW heating & vulcanisation applications), spot welding, RADAR & other systems	x	xxx
2.	Arc welding (MIG, MAG, TIG, etc.), military & research RF systems, industrial magnetisers/demagnetisers; surgical & physiotherapeutic use of diathermy, MRI medical diagnostic equipment	xx	xxx
3.	Electrolytic installations, industrial microwave ovens, electric vehicles (trains, trams, metro), broadcasting systems & devices (radio & TV:AM, VHF, UHF), mobile telephony base stations, radiophones (professional), RFID, EAS & other anti-theft equipment, electricity supplying networks & equipment, electric handheld tools	xxx	xx
4.	NMR spectrometers, wireless local area networks (WLANs), mobile and cordless phones, Bluetooth devices	xxx	x

x, an unexpected situation; xx, a possible situation; xxx, the most common situation.

Note: The parameters of workers' exposure, such as the maximum level of exposure and time-averaged one, are related to the work organization. In the use of the majority of devices mentioned in the table, well organised workers' tasks may be performed without their substantial electromagnetic exposure.

EMF exposure situations might have an EF affecting a worker that is at least 100 times stronger than the typical exposure of members of general public to EMF at a similar frequency. In such cases, it means that the worker's skin and deeper tissues under the skin, up to a depth equal to four times the PE-DE from the body surface, experience EF exposure at levels that never happens in the case of exposure received by tissues in the body of the members of general public. When we consider that even stronger exposures in the work environment may occur, it is clear beyond a shadow of a doubt that the conclusions developed regarding EMF-related health hazards, caused by short-term or long-term general public EMF exposure, are highly inadequate when discussing health implications from strong, work-related electromagnetic exposure.

On the other hand, it is also clear that any parameters of work-related EMF exposure that are proven, on the basis of scientific evidence, to be neutral for the safety and health of exposed workers may be taken, based on that evidence, as being neutral also for the safety and health of healthy adult members of the general public exposed to EMF of comparable parameters or weaker (at a lower level of E and H, or for a shorter duration of exposure).

Various aspects of managing EMF exposure in the work environment are discussed in detail in particular chapters later on in this monograph.

2.5 PARAMETERISATION OF WORK-RELATED ELECTROMAGNETIC EXPOSURE AND ELECTROMAGNETIC HAZARDS

Summarising the principles of electromagnetic interaction with material objects, the relative magnitudes of the various exposure effects depend on the ratio between the EF and MF strength, the spatial distribution of conductivity (σ) and permittivity (ε) of the exposed object, which depend on the frequency (f) of the affecting EMF and the material composition of the object (e.g. vary with the type of body tissue). The effects also depend on the changes in exposed object's behaviour (i.e. on the size and shape of the object/body and on its position in the field, where related with the movements of a worker performing their professional duties) and on the distribution of the affecting EMF in space and time (ICNIRP 1998, 2009, 2010, 2020, IEEE 2005, 2019, Hansson Mild et al. 2009, Karpowicz 2015).

This situation makes it necessary to use '4-dimensional' characteristics of worker exposure in practical cases of managing EMF exposure in the work environment, covering the following contexts:

1. Frequency (frequency pattern of EMF emitted from the source): $E(f)$ and $H(f)$
2. Space (spatial distribution of EMF emitted by the source): $E(\mathrm{x, y, z})$ and $H(\mathrm{x, y, z})$
3. Time (time-distribution of exposure caused by timing of EMF emission and workers activities in the exposed work environment): $E(t)$ and $H(t)$
4. Wave impedance (proportion of tween EMF components affecting worker): $Z=E/H$.

Regarding the wave impedance context ($Z=E/H$) of worker exposure, it may change along with the place and duration of the work performance, and because of that depends on the EMF properties in the work environment as well as the worker's behaviour, and should be evaluated as the fourth dimension of EMF exposure for the entire range of worker's activities, and versus time and location of those activities. In electrical engineering, the wave impedance is defined as the ratio of the transverse components of *E* and *H*, which can only be evaluated by numerical simulations. However, when evaluating workers' exposure to EMF, it may be roughly estimated by using a ratio of independently measured values of *Em* and *Hm* ($Zm = Em/Hm$) using isotropic probes to take measurements in the same time and location. The limitation here is caused, in practice, by the need to use two measurement devices, which make only two cases of evaluation possible: (1) at the same time but not in the same location or (2) in the same location but not at the same time.

This experimentally evaluated impedance (*Zm*) is dependent on *E* and *H* distribution in the work environment; but, when considering workers performing various activities (i.e. moving around in the vicinity of the EMF source and affecting in that way the EF distribution there), these parameters become 'less dependent' on parameters (1)–(3) in the vicinity of EMF source. The independent monitoring of their variability may be necessary in order to sufficiently follow the pattern of EMF exposure during workers' activity with respect to various options of work practice (however that may be challenging from a technical point of view in the case of various exposure situations).

Such experimentally evaluated wave impedance in a real environment would depend on the time-variability, spatial distribution and polarisation of the EMF affecting a worker in any position of the worker's body, but it primarily changes as the worker's position changes while physically performing professional duties. In various work activities, this context of EMF exposure may differ significantly and need more attention through further research, as well as when managing EMF exposure in the work environment aimed, for example, at applying the new guidelines provided by ICNIRP for evaluating RF-EMF exposure (ICNIRP 2020), in practice.

Still, the dynamics of the development of chronic diseases when workers are exposed to EMF is also insufficiently documented. A substantial percentage of studies on the health hazards related to EMF exposure belong to the basic science than to the applied science, and because of it they are still focused on the weak exposure of healthy adults from EMF sources used in public environment, and not on more realistic exposure situations in the public and work environment. Mentioned laboratory studies use EMF exposure set-ups that are inadequate for evaluating health hazards for workers, e.g. exposure to EMF of only a single frequency and a fixed wave impedance, such as: (1) EMF produced by Helmholtz coils, where the MF exists without its tween EF existing always in real exposure situations; or (2) EMF produced in TEM/GTEM cells where far-field exposure conditions are produced that are not able to provide the near-field exposure conditions (with EF not correlated with MF) that, in practice, dominate in cases typical for workers' exposure; and (3) at exposure levels of general public cases (with the motivation for example to guarantee that the studies capture only the non-thermal exposure conditions and exposure effects), whereas workplace exposure may be found to be many orders higher (in some case sufficient to create substantial thermal effects of exposure).

In addition, we are only learning about the effects of chronic exposure to EMF many years after its sources are emerging in the environment (in the context of cancer development, for example, it is assumed that health risks appear after at least a decade or so of chronic exposure). Along with recognising the mechanisms and effects of EMF, we have to learn the parameters characterising the exposure conditions that enable a meaningful analysis of hazards and, consequently, the development of electromagnetic hazard assessment methods that are helpful in evaluating the effectiveness of mitigation through appropriate protective measures (ICNIRP 2020, IEEE 2019, Hansson Mild et al. 2009, SCENIHR 2015, WHO 2010, Zradziński 2013, Zradziński 2015).

At present, the outcome of such studies is summarised, for example, by the International Agency of Research on Cancer (IARC) 2B classification for EMF (the possible carcinogenic environmental factor for humans) (IARC 2002, IARC 2013, SCENIHR 2015). Until such delayed EMF effects can be dismissed as irrelevant, progress in research should be monitored and mitigation of EMF exposure should be applied in workplace.

2.6 CONCLUSIONS

Given the limitations in the available scientific evidence, it still needs to be considered that EMF in the work environment may be less friendly than what emerging technologies try to promise. The main principle of any EM-ergonomics activity should be to move towards the application of available measures mitigating EMF exposure and electromagnetic hazards, even when the legislation does not require it categorically.

However, from another point of view, it must be pointed out that international guidelines, as well as international labour legislation, establishing EMF exposure limits to be applicable in evaluation of the EMF exposure in the work environment (recognised using various wording, e.g. work-related exposure, controlled environment, occupational exposure, etc.), are formulated with cautions that the use of such limits must be restricted to specific work-related situations.

The most fundamental restrictions on the possible use of EMF exposure limits, recognised as 'limits of exposure in the work environment' (where, in principle, the considered exposure may be many times higher than when evaluating cases of public exposure) are as follows: (1) such limits are intended to be applied only to exposure situations that occur in spaces where the relevant practice and protection measures have been already maintained in the workplace and work practices, (2) exposed workers are periodically trained on safety practices necessary while performing hazardous tasks and (3) EMF exposure comes under periodic inspections and evaluation (Directive 2013, ICNIRP 1998, 2009, 2010, 2020, IEEE 2005, 2019, Karpowicz et al. 2006).

ACKNOWLEDGEMENTS

Special thanks go to Dr Patryk Zradziński for providing figures based on numerical simulations of electromagnetic issues to illustrate the issues discussed in this chapter.

This chapter has been based on the results of the research that has been carried out in Poland within the scope of the National Programme 'Improvement of safety and working conditions' (CIOP-PIB is the programme's main coordinator.), partly supported by the ministry for labour issues (within the scope of state services; tasks 2.SP.10).

REFERENCES

Chaljub, G., L.A. Kramer, R.F. Johnson 3rd, R.F. Johnson Jr, H. Singh, and W.N. Crow. 2001. Projectile cylinder accidents resulting from the presence of ferromagnetic nitrous oxide or oxygen tanks in the MR suite. *AJR Am J Roentgenol* 177(1):27–30. DOI: 10.2214/ajr.177.1.1770027.

Chen, D.W. 2001. Boy, 6, dies of skull injury during M.R.I. *NY Times* Jul 31: Sec. B: 1, 5.

Directive 2013/35/EU. 2013. Directive of the European Parliament and of the Council of 26 June 2013 on the Minimum Health And Safety Requirements Regarding The Exposure Of Workers To The Risks Arising From Physical Agents (Electromagnetic Fields) (20th Individual Directive within the Meaning of Article 16(1) of Directive 89/391/EEC). *Official Journal of the European Union* O.J. No. L-179 of 29 June 2013, 1–21, Brussels, Belgium.

Ducknetweb. 2010. MRI Accident Earlier This Year Kills Service Engineer Who Was Sucked in And Pinned to the Unit– FDA Investigation. http://ducknetweb.blogspot.com/2010/06/mri-accident-earlier-this-year-kills.html (accessed September 29, 2022).

Durney, C. H., H. Massoudi, and M. F. Iskander. 1985. *Radiofrequency Radiation Dosimetry Handbook*. Salt Lake City: Utah Univ Salt Lake City Dept of Electrical Engineering.

EN 292-1:1991. 1991. Safety of Machinery - Basic Concepts, General Principles for Design Part 1: Basic Terminology, Methodology. Brussels: CENELEC [European Committee for Electrotechnical Standardization].

Gabriel, S., R. W. Lau, and C. Gabriel. 1996. The dielectric properties of biological tissues: II. Measurements in the frequency range 10 Hz to 20 GHz. *Phys Med Biol* 41(11):2251–2269. DOI: 10.1088/0031-9155/41/11/002.

Gryz, K., J. Karpowicz, M. Molenda, and P. Zradziński. 2004. Indirect hazards in the vicinity of HVPL- analysis with the use of FEM. Przegląd Elektrotechniczny 80(12):1240-1243 (in Polish).

Hill, D.A., and J.A. Walsh. 1985. Radio-frequency current through the feet of a grounded human. *IEEE Trans Electromagn Compat* EMC-27(1):18–23. DOI: 10.1109/TEMC.1985.304241.

IARC [International Agency for Research on Cancer]. 2002. IARC monographs on the evaluation of carcinogenic risks to humans. Volume 80. Non-Ionizing Radiation, part 1: Static and Extremely Low-Frequency (ELF) Electric and Magnetic Fields. Lyon: IARC Press. https://publications.iarc.fr/Book-And-Report-Series/Iarc-Monographs-On-The-Identification-Of-Carcinogenic-Hazards-To-Humans/Non-ionizing-Radiation-Part-1-Static-And-Extremely-Low-frequency-ELF-Electric-And-Magnetic-Fields-2002 (accessed September 29, 2022).

IARC [International Agency for Research on Cancer]. 2013. IARC Monographs on the Evaluation of Carcinogenic Risks to Humans. Non-Ionizing Radiation, Part 2: Radiofrequency Electromagnetic Fields. Volume 102. Lyon, France: IARC Press. http://monographs.iarc.fr/ENG/Monographs/vol102/mono102.pdf (accessed September 29, 2022).

ICNIRP [International Commission on Non-Ionizing Radiation Protection]. 1998. Guidelines for limiting exposure to time-varying electric, magnetic, and electromagnetic fields (up to 300 GHz). *Health Phys* 74(4):494–522.

ICNIRP [International Commission on Non-Ionizing Radiation Protection]. 2009. Guidelines on limits of exposure to static magnetic fields. *Health Phys* 96(4):504–514. DOI: 10.1097/01.HP.0000343164.27920.4a.

ICNIRP [International Commission on Non-Ionizing Radiation Protection]. 2010. Guidelines for limiting exposure to time-varying electric and magnetic fields (1 Hz – 100 kHz). *Health Phys* 99(6):818–836. DOI: 10.1097/HP.0b013e3181f06c86.

ICNIRP [International Commission on Non-Ionizing Radiation Protection]. 2014. Guidelines for limiting exposure to electric fields induced by movement of the human body in a static magnetic field and by time-varying magnetic fields below 1 Hz. *Health Physics* 106(3):418–425. DOI: 10.1097/HP.0b013e31829e5580

ICNIRP [International Commission on Non-Ionizing Radiation Protection]. 2020. Guidelines for limiting exposure to electromagnetic fields (100 kHz to 300 GHz). *Health Phys* 118(5):483–524. DOI: 10.1097/HP.0000000000001210.

IEEE C95.1-2005. 2005. *Standard for Safety Levels with Respect to Human Exposure to Radio Frequency Electromagnetic Fields, 3 kHz to 300 GHz*. New York: IEEE [Institute of Electrical and Electronics Engineers].

IEEE C95.1-2019. 2019. *IEEE Standard for Safety Levels with Respect to Human Exposure to Electric, Magnetic, and Electromagnetic Fields, 0 Hz to 300 GHz*. New York: IEEE [Institute of Electrical and Electronics Engineers].

Hansson Mild, K., T. Alanko, G. Decat, et al. 2009. Exposure of workers to electromagnetic fields. A review of open questions on exposure assessment techniques. *Int J Occup Saf Ergon* 15(1):3–33. DOI: 10.1080/10803548.2009.11076785.

Jokela, K., L. Puranen, and O.P. Gandhi. 1994. Radio frequency currents induced in the human body for medium-frequency/high-frequency broadcast antennas. *Health Phys* 66(3):237–244. DOI: 10.1097/00004032-199403000-00001.

Karpowicz, J., M. Hietanen, and K. Gryz. 2006. EU directive, ICNIRP guidelines and polish legislation on electromagnetic fields. *Int J Occup Saf Ergon* 12(2):125–136. DOI: 10.1080/10803548.2006.11076675.

Karpowicz, J., and K. Gryz. 2007. Practical aspects of occupational EMF exposure assessment. *Environmentalist* 27(4):525–531. DOI: 10.1007/s10669-007-9067-y.

Karpowicz, J., and K. Gryz. 2010. Electromagnetic hazards in the workplace. In: *Handbook of Occupational Safety and Health*, ed. D. Koradecka, pp. 199–218. Boca Raton, FL: CRC Press.

Karpowicz, J., and K. Gryz. 2013. Experimental evaluation of ballistic hazards in imaging diagnostic center. *Pol J Radiol* 78(2):31–37. DOI: 10.12659/PJR.883943.

Karpowicz, J. 2015. Chapter 21: Environmental and safety aspects of the use of EMF in medical environment. In: *Electromagnetic Fields in Biology and Medicine*, ed. M. Markov, pp. 341–362. Boca Raton, FL: CRC Press. DOI: 10.1201/b18148-22.

Korniewicz, H. 1995. The first resonance of a grounded human being exposed to electric fields. *IEEE Trans Electromagn Compat* 37(2):296–299. DOI: 10.1109/15.385898.

Korpinen, L.H., J.A. Elovaara, and H.A. Kuisti. 2009. Evaluation of current densities and total contact currents in occupational exposure at 400 kV substations and power lines. *Bioelectromagnetics* 30(3):231–240. DOI: 10.1002/bem.20468.

Mattei, E., F. Censi, G. Calcagnini, and R. Falsaperla. 2021. Workers with cardiac AIMD exposed to EMF: Methods and case studies for risk analysis in the framework of the european regulations. *Int J Environ Res Public Health* 18(18):9709. DOI: 10.3390/ijerph18189709.

MRIsafety.com. Your information resource for MRI safety, bioeffects and patient management. http://www.MRIsafety.com (accessed September 29, 2022).

Reilly, P.J. 1998. *Applied Bioelectricity. From Electrical Stimulation to Electropathology*. New York: Springer-Verlag.

SCENIHR [Scientific Committee on Emerging and Newly Identified Health Risks]. 2015. Opinion on potential health effects of exposure to electromagnetic fields (EMF). Luxembourg: European Commission. https://ec.europa.eu/health/scientific_committees/emerging/docs/scenihr_o_041.pdf (accessed September 29, 2022).

Wilén, J, K. Hansson Mild, L.E. Paulsson, and G. Anger. 2001. Induced current measurements in whole body exposure condition to radio frequency electric fields. *Bioelectromagnetics* 22(8):560–567. DOI: 10.1002/bem.84.

WHO [World Health Organization]. 2005. *Environmental Health Criteria 232: Static Fields*. China: WHO Press. https://www.who.int/peh-emf/publications/reports/ehcstatic/en/ (accessed February 27, 2020).
WHO [World Health Organization]. 2010. *Research Agenda for Radiofrequency Fields*. Geneva: WHO. https://apps.who.int/iris/bitstream/handle/10665/44396/9789241599948_eng.pdf?sequence=1&isAllowed=y (accessed September 29, 2022).
Zradziński, P. 2013. The properties of human body phantoms used in calculations of electromagnetic fields exposure by wireless communication handsets or hand-operated industrial devices. *Electromag Biol Med* 32(2):226–235. DOI: 10.3109/15368378.2013.776434.
Zradziński, P. 2015. Difficulties in applying numerical simulations to an evaluation of occupational hazards caused by electromagnetic fields. *Int J Occup Saf Ergon* 21(2):213–220. DOI: 10.1080/10803548.2015.1028233.
Zradziński P., J. Karpowicz, K. Gryz, and W. Leszko. 2018. Evaluation of the safety of users of active implantable medical devices (AIMD) in the working environment in terms of exposure to electromagnetic fields – Practical approach to the requirements of European Directive 2013/35/EU. *International Journal of Occupational Medicine and Environmental Health*, 31(6), 795–808. DOI: 10.13075/iljomeh.1896.0783.

3 Estimating Uncertainty in Assessments of Human Exposure to Radiofrequency Electromagnetic Fields

Vitas Anderson
Two Fields Consulting and University of Wollongong

CONTENTS

DOI: 10.1201/9781003020486-3

3.1 INTRODUCTION

Estimating the uncertainty of measured or calculated quantities is often one of those things that everyone agrees is a good idea, but most are hesitant to undertake. This seems to apply particularly to the evaluation of human exposure to radiofrequency electromagnetic fields (RF-EMF), which are typically subject to complicated and substantial levels of variability.

However, uncertainty estimates are generally required by standards or guidelines setting out good practices for RF-EMF exposure assessments [CENELEC 2019, IEC 2017, ITU-T 2020], so there is no escaping this obligation. Moreover, developing uncertainty estimates always engenders better and deeper understanding of the assessments, something which should be a matter of pride for all good RF-EMF metrologists. Uncertainty estimates are also useful in providing a common gauge for comparing the quality of assessments, even between the different modalities of measurement and calculation.

3.2 WHAT IS UNCERTAINTY?

3.2.1 Uncertainty Is the Quantification of Random Variation in Assessments

Every assessment of RF-EMF exposure will always entail a certain amount of random error. This is partly a consequence of natural limitations in accurately measuring physical quantities, as well as incomplete understanding or specification of how the RF-EMF levels are truly assessed or even defined. With careful thought, the dispersion of possible assessed levels due to this random variability, that is, uncertainty, can generally be estimated. If this were not so, then how could we have any confidence in the accuracy of the assessments?

Because uncertainty deals with random processes and incomplete knowledge, it can only be quantified as probability distributions. An uncertainty estimate does not tell you *exactly* how far away the result of an assessment is from the true value but rather indicates a probabilistic range within which the true value is likely to lie. When many sources of uncertainty contribute to an assessment, then by the central limit theorem the overall combined uncertainty tends towards a *normal* probability distribution.

3.2.2 Systematic Errors

Error in assessments can also arise from systematic biases that deflect the assessed level from its true value by a known consistent amount. For instance, some RF-EMF measurement instruments require adjustment for frequency-dependent calibration settings. For calculated assessments, transmission losses between the RF source and the antenna could be considered as a systematic bias requiring appropriate correction. In general, corrections for known systematic biases should be applied to the measurand in order to obtain the best estimate result. If the correction itself has a significant degree of random error then this should be considered as an input into the overall uncertainty.

3.2.3 Blunders

Apart from the known corrections, errors can also occur due to mistakes or poor assessment technique such as using an RF field probe outside of its rated frequency range or entering incorrect data into an RF-EMF calculation. This type of error is called a *blunder*, and should be addressed and mitigated under a quality assurance program. Blunders are not considered in an uncertainty estimate, since it is assumed that the assessment has been conducted correctly according to its stated scope or context.

3.2.4 Improving the Accuracy of an Assessment

The three panels in Figure 3.1 illustrate how the accuracy of an assessment can be improved by addressing uncertainty and known systematic errors. The first panel displays how the assessed value (triangle marker) is separated from the true value (round marker) by the summed contributions of known systematic biases as well as random uncertainty error dispersed within a probability distribution. In the second panel, the assessed value is improved by eliminating or compensating for any systematic biases. Finally, in the third panel diligent study of the random errors has revealed ways to reduce them, leading to narrower uncertainty bounds and hence a more accurate result.

3.3 SPECIAL CHALLENGES FOR RF-EMF UNCERTAINTY ASSESSMENTS

There are many good general references for estimating uncertainty, most notably the uncertainty guides from the *Joint Committee for Guides in Metrology (JCGM)*, commonly referred to as the *GUM* (*Guide to Uncertainty in Measurement*). The GUM guides are freely available on the internet, and the reader is wholeheartedly recommended to consult them (JCGM 2008a, b, 2009). However, as mentioned earlier in this chapter, uncertainty estimates for RF-EMF assessments present some special challenges not usually encountered in other fields of metrology, which will be a particular focus of this chapter.

Firstly, the probability distributions of the component contributions to an RF-EMF uncertainty assessment, that is, the input quantities, tend to follow *lognormal* distributions rather than the more commonly encountered normal distribution. This is a consequence of the typically logarithmic characteristics of power transmission through RF circuit components and physical media, as for instance seen in the logarithmic decay of an RF signal along a transmission line or an RF wave penetrating the lossy tissues of the human body.

Accordingly, the standard uncertainty of RF equipment parameters is usually expressed as a dB estimate, which indicates the $\log_{10}$ ratio of the energy or power content of the input quantity (P_1) relative to its expectation value (P_0)[1]:

$$\mathrm{dB}(P) = 10\ \log_{10}\left(\frac{P_1}{P_0}\right) \tag{3.1}$$

[1] Note: $\log_{10}(y)$ is the common logarithm to the base 10, i.e. $x = \log_{10}(y)$ is equivalent to $y = 10^x$

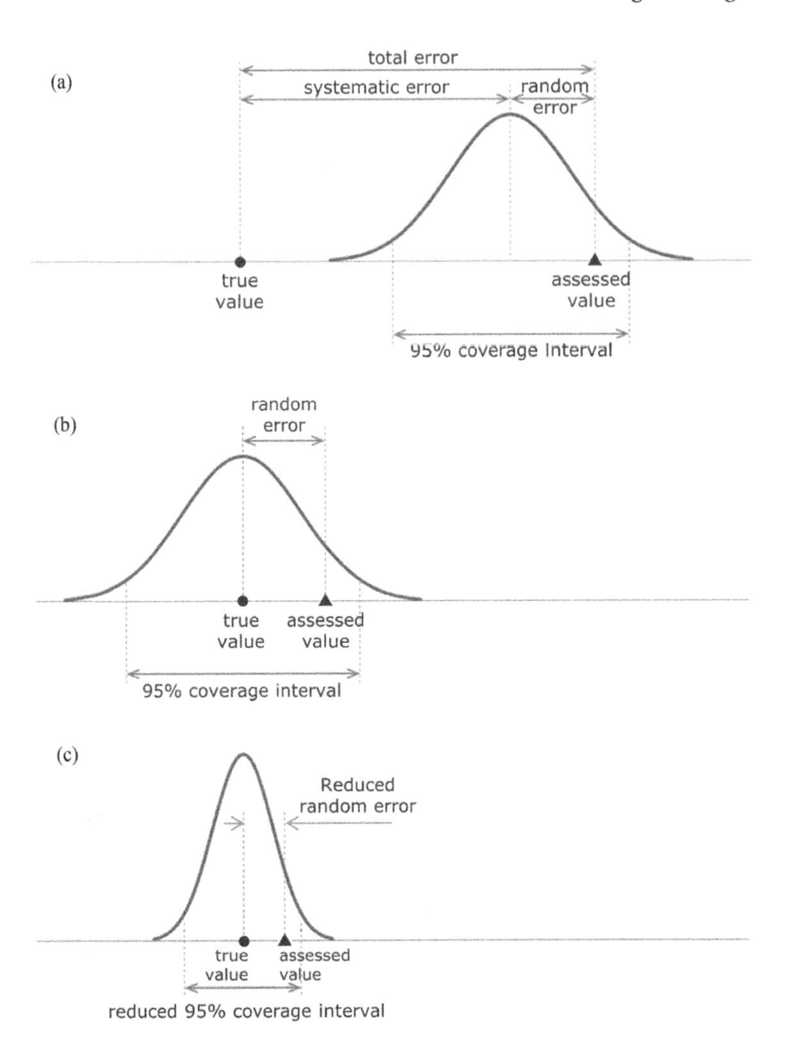

FIGURE 3.1 Strategies for improving the accuracy of an assessment. Panel (a) displays how the total error of an assessment is the sum of systematic and random error. In panel (b), the accuracy of the assessment is improved by eliminating or adjusting for systematic error. In panel (c), the accuracy is further improved by reducing the random error, that is, the uncertainty, of the assessment.

For instance, for power flux density: $dB(S) = 10\ \log_{10}(S_1/S_0)$, and for the electric field: $dB(E) = 10\ \log_{10}(E_1^2/E_0^2) = 20\ \log_{10}(E_1/E_0)$.

Figure 3.2 compares normal and lognormal dB distributions on a common linear scale. When the extent of the distribution is small, that is, when its standard deviation σ is less than approximately ±10% (approximately ±0.44 dB), then the difference between a normal and lognormal distribution is fairly trivial. However, the differences for wider distributions can become quite significant, as can be seen in Figure 3.2b. This panel also illustrates how a normal distribution with wide extents can contain non-physical *negative* values in the lower tail of the distribution.

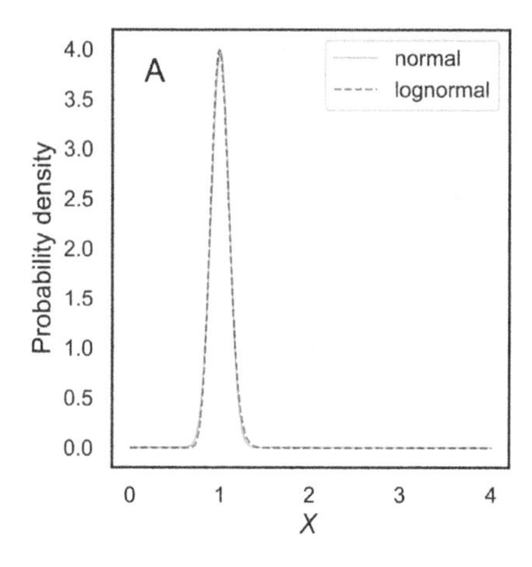

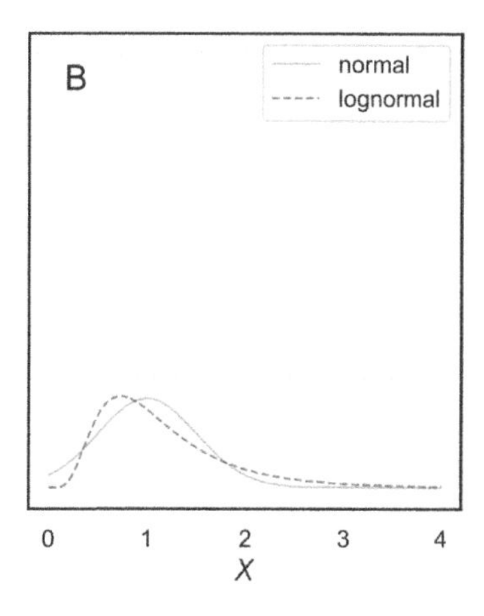

FIGURE 3.2 A comparison of normal and lognormal PDF distributions, each with mean values of 1 and presented on a common linear scale. In panel A, the standard deviation of the normal and lognormal distributions are 0.1 (10% of the mean) and 0.44 dB, respectively. In panel B, they are 0.5 (50% of the mean) and 2.43 dB, respectively.

The second distinctive characteristic of RF-EMF assessment uncertainties is that the functional relationship between the measurand, *Y*, and the various factors that affect the uncertainty of its assessment, that is, its input quantities *X*, can be complex and hard to define. Typically though, the mathematical model that defines this relationship is assumed to take a simplified multiplicative form, i.e:

$$Y = X_1 X_2 \cdots X_n \tag{3.2}$$

For this model, the use of a dB scale transforms the multiplicative relation between *Y* and the X_i components to a summative one, since $\log_{10}(ab)$ is $\log_{10}(a) + \log_{10}(b)$. This will be illustrated in more detail later in the chapter.

Finally, the extent of the uncertainty distributions of RF-EMF input quantities tends to be relatively large, often in the order of ±1 to ±3 dB, which on a linear scale equates to a range of [−21% to +25%] and [−50% to +200%], respectively. The classical GUM approach to calculating uncertainty entails linearising the mathematical model on the assumption that second and higher order terms are negligible. However, this assumption may not hold if the uncertainty errors of the input quantities are large.

All of these issues will be addressed in the following sections.

3.4 PROCEDURE FOR ASSESSING THE UNCERTAINTY OF RF-EMF ASSESSMENTS

The estimation of the overall uncertainty of an assessment can be divided into two sequential stages:

1. The *formulation* stage where the basic characteristics of the mathematical model and its parameters are defined.

2. The *calculation* stage where this information is processed using either classical or numerical (Monte Carlo) techniques to calculate the combined uncertainty of the assessment.

The following sub-sections illustrate how these stages are applied to estimating RF-EMF uncertainties.

3.4.1 Formulation Stage

3.4.1.1 Define the Measurand

The very first step is to define the measurand for the assessment. Common measurands of RF-EMF assessments are: specific energy absorption rate (SAR) in W/kg; ambient electric field strength (E) in V/m RMS and magnetic field strength (H) in A/m RMS; and incident power flux density (S) in W/m^2.

To make comparisons between E and H exposure limits easier, they can be specified in the common metric of equivalent plane wave power flux density, S_{eq} (in W/m^2), where:

When based on the electric field, S_{eq} is calculated as: $S_{eq}(E) = |E|^2/Z_0$

When based on the magnetic field, S_{eq} is calculated as: $S_{eq}(H) = Z_0|H|^2$

Z_0=377 Ohm and is the wave impedance of free space and E and H are RMS (rather than peak) values.

For free space conditions in the radiating far field of an RF source, the actual wave impedance, $Z = |E|/|H|$, trends asymptotically towards the free space impedance value, Z_0, so that $S_{eq}(E) = S_{eq}(H)$ at these locations. Moreover, at frequencies above 10–30 MHz the exposure limits for $S_{eq}(E)$ and $S_{eq}(H)$ in standards and guidelines are typically the same and so may be specified in the single metric of S_{eq}. This arrangement implies that compliance can be determined by conformance with either the E or the H limits in free space far field conditions.

However, this convenient outcome does not hold when the $|E|/|H|$ ratio significantly deviates from Z_0, as occurs close to the RF source in its near field or in areas where there is substantial field scattering from large nearby objects (e.g. ground, walls, large vehicles and other metallic structures, etc.). In such cases, compliance is determined by comparing the maximum value of $S_{eq}(E)$ and $S_{eq}(H)$ to the applicable S_{eq} limit, S_{lim}. In these circumstances, the measurand, Y, for assessing compliance with E and H exposure limits for any particular RF source is better defined as:

$$Y = \frac{\max\left[S_{eq}(E), S_{eq}(H)\right]}{S_{lim}} \tag{3.3}$$

3.4.1.2 Define the Context

Imagine you were told that 'the weather will be fine and sunny'. This statement is not particularly informative if the *time* and *location* of the forecast were not also provided. Likewise, an uncertainty estimate is also of little use if it is not presented within a defined scope or context, since the level of uncertainty may change substantially for different circumstances of assessment.

TABLE 3.1
A List of Common Contextual Factors for Uncertainty Estimates of RF-EMF Assessments

Contextual Factor	Typical Assessment States for the Context
Mode of assessment	• Measured or calculated
The transmitter output state of the RF source	• Operating at the maximum power • Operating during a certain time period, e.g. day or night • Operating at a certain activity level, e.g. low or high
Time sampling	• Instantaneous measurements • Peak hold measurements • Time averaging applied; this will decrease uncertainty when the source output power level is variable, since random variability is generally reduced by averaging
Spatial sampling	• Point spatial assessments • Spatial peak assessments • Spatial averaging applied; this will decrease uncertainty due to the averaging of any uncorrelated random errors of the sample points
Assessment bandwidth	• Narrowband • Broadband
Field scattering for calculated assessments	• Field scattering calculated in the assessment • Field scattering *not* calculated in the assessment
Field scattering for measured assessments	• Field scattering from large moving objects (e.g. motor vehicles) near the assessment location • Field scattering from the body of a person conducting the measurements
Cumulative RF source contributions	• Assessment of a single RF source • Cumulative assessment of many and possibly diverse RF sources

For instance, equipment calibration certificates usually specify a well-defined context for the calibration environment and inputs, recording any quantities that might affect the result such as laboratory air temperature, exposure field level and frequency modulation. This information provides a baseline reference for considering the bias or uncertainty effects of these quantities when assessments are made out in the field.

The context also encompasses the specification of the methodology for obtaining the measurand. If a different methodology is used to that defined by the assessment context, then the uncertainty introduced by this variation should be considered. For instance, if S_{eq} is recorded as a point spatial measurement but the measurand is defined as a spatial average (e.g. as for the whole body S_{eq} reference levels of the ICNIRP 2020 guidelines) then the error distribution between these two different methods of assessment should be considered in the overall uncertainty.

A list of common contextual factors for RF-EMF assessments is provided in Table 3.1.

3.4.1.3 Identify the Input Quantities

Having defined the context, the next task is to identify all of the possible factors that may influence the level of the assessed measurand, that is, the input quantities. A list of common input quantities for the measured and calculated assessment of ambient S_{eq} is provided in Table 3.2.

TABLE 3.2
Typical Influence Quantities for Measured or Calculated Assessments of S_{eq}

Measured Assessments	Calculated Assessments
• Instrument calibration • Frequency response of field probe and device • Isotropy of the field probe • Sensitivity of the field probe • Temperature response of field probe and device • Linearity deviation of field probe • Transmission line mismatch between instrument components • Personal bias in reading instrument readouts when the signal level is fluctuating with time • Field probe location, especially in high-gradient fields • Coupling of probe element with a nearby radiator • Field scattering from the assessor's body • Field scattering from substantive movable objects in the assessment environment • Internal instrument noise at low assessment levels	• Transmitter power • System losses • Antenna gain • Antenna dimensions • Antenna location and bearing • Field scattering • Assessment methodology variations relative to the stated assessment context (e.g. time and spatial assessment)

3.4.1.4 Estimate the Probability Distribution Functions of the Input Quantities

After identifying the input quantities, the *probability density functions* (PDF) of their uncertainties must be evaluated. This entails collecting data or making judgements to determine the appropriate type (normal, rectangular, triangular, etc.) and extent of each PDF from which its *expectation* and *standard uncertainty* may be calculated. The GUM identifies two general approaches for doing this: Type A and Type B evaluation.

Type A evaluation of an input quantity X is the determination of its PDF by a statistical analysis of repeated recordings of the input quantity. Often, the individual observations, q_k, of X are distributed normally (i.e. Gaussian) or as a t-distribution when the sample size is small. In these cases, the expectation of X is the average of the n observed values, $\overline{q}$, and the standard uncertainty is estimated as the standard deviation of the average, $s(\overline{q})$, where

$$\overline{q} = \frac{1}{n}\sum_{k=1}^{n} q_k \tag{3.4}$$

$$s^2(q_k) = \frac{1}{n-1}\sum_{j=1}^{n}\left(q_j - \overline{q}\right)^2 \tag{3.5}$$

$$s(\overline{q}) = \sqrt{s^2(q_k)/n} \tag{3.6}$$

Type B is a 'fuzzier' approach to determining the uncertainty PDFs of input quantitates that relies on sources of a priori knowledge. It is the most common approach applied for RF-EMF input quantities and entails incorporating data from 'expert sources', such as uncertainties in a calibration certificate or from the

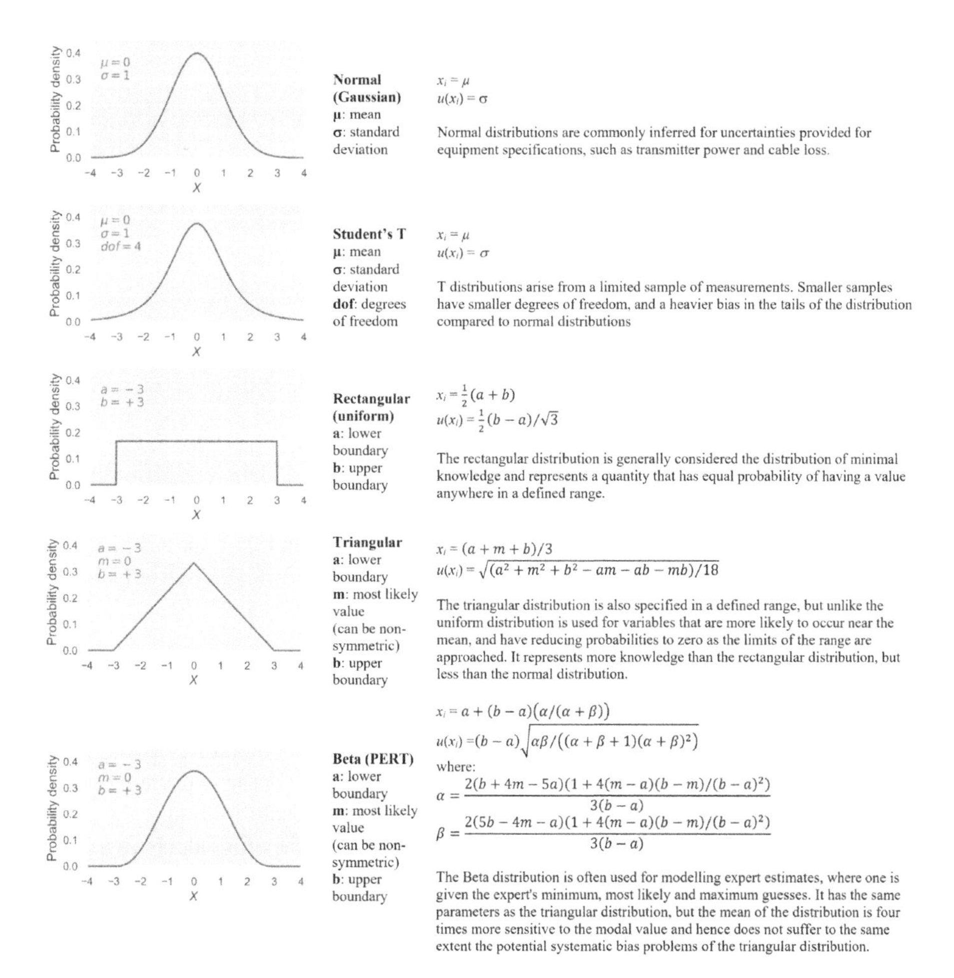

FIGURE 3.3 Useful probability density functions (PDFs) for RF-EMF input quantities. The characteristic parameters are listed for each PDF, as well as formulas for the PDF expectation, x_i and standard uncertainty, $u(x_i)$.

manufacturer's specifications, reference tables and books, and previous measurement data. It can also entail sound scientific and engineering calculations to determine worst-case limits and estimation of limits by suitably experienced people.

Some useful PDF types with notes about their usage and defining parameters are shown in Figure 3.3.

3.4.1.5 Develop the Mathematical Model

The final step of the formulation stage is to develop a model that defines the measurand as a mathematical function of the influence quantities. A useful approach for developing the model is to first represent the relationship between the input quantities and the measurand in a graphical system model. Such a model for calculated assessments of S_{eq} using a ray tracing technique is displayed in Figure 3.4 and will be referred to in a later example in this chapter.

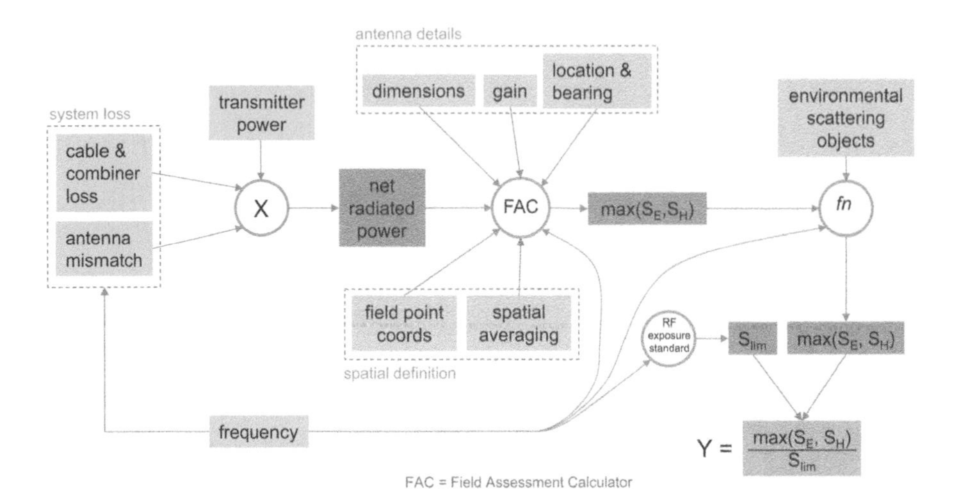

FIGURE 3.4 System diagram relating input quantities to measurand, Y, for complex field assessment calculations of power flux density.

3.4.2 Calculation Stage

With the characteristics and parameters of the uncertainty assessment defined from the formulation stage, the combined uncertainty of the measurand, Y, can now be calculated. This is achieved by propagating the PDFs of the input quantities through the mathematical model to obtain: (1) the combined PDF of Y; (2) the expectation of Y; (3) the coverage interval containing Y within a specified probability range.

Classical analytical and numerical Monte Carlo approaches for calculating these outputs are discussed in the following sections.

3.4.2.1 Classical GUM Approach

The 'classical' analytical approach to calculating uncertainty is well described in the GUM (JCGM, 2008a). This section provides a quick recap of the GUM approach with notes on how it might be best applied for RF-EMF uncertainty assessments. After establishing the PDFs of the input quantities and the mathematical model in the form $Y=f(X_1, X_2, \ldots X_n)$, the GUM stipulates the following steps for concluding the uncertainty calculation:

1. Determine x_i, the expectation of each input quantity X_i.
2. Evaluate the standard uncertainty $u(x_i)$ of each input estimate x_i.
3. Evaluate the covariances associated with any input estimates that are correlated.
4. Calculate the result of the measurement, that is, the best estimate y of the measurand Y, from the functional relationship f using for the input quantities X_i, the estimates x_i obtained in step 1.
5. Determine the combined standard uncertainty $u_c(y)$ of the measurement result y from the standard uncertainties and covariances associated with the input estimates.

6. Calculate the expanded uncertainty with the purpose of providing an interval from $(y - U)$ to $(y + U)$ that may be expected to encompass a defined fraction of the distribution of values that could reasonably be attributed to the measurand Y.

Before considering these steps in more detail, it is useful to briefly restate the three distinguishing (and unusual) features of RF-EMF uncertainty assessments, that is: (1) the input quantities tend to follow lognormal distributions; (2) the mathematical model can be quite complex but is often represented in a simplified multiplicative form ($Y = X_1 X_2 \cdots X_n$); and (3) the standard uncertainties of the input quantities tend to be relatively large.

In **step 1**, the expectation x_i of an input quantity X_i is simply the mid-point of its PDF if it is symmetric. For potentially non-symmetric PDFs, such as the triangular and beta distributions, general formulas for calculating x_i are provided in Figure 3.3.

Regarding **step 2**, Figure 3.3 also provides formulas for calculating the standard uncertainty $u(x_i)$ of useful PDFs. For RF-EMF input quantities, it is usual practice to specify the parameters of the PDF in dB units, for example, a rectangular distribution with lower and upper bounds of [−2, +2] dB. This approach satisfies the typically logarithmic characteristics of the RF-EMF input quantities. An alternative approach is to specify the PDFs in terms of percentage changes rather than in dB. However, as indicated earlier, this approach can introduce significant error for distributions with larger extents ($\sigma > \approx \pm 10\%$) due to the widening difference between its implicit normal distribution and the actual lognormal distribution (Figure 3.2b).

When uncertainty estimates are obtained from third-party reports, it is important to develop a clear understanding of the nature of the estimate. For instance, calibration certificates will generally provide an expanded uncertainty U for the calibration with a coverage factor k for a specified coverage interval (e.g. 95%). This implies a Student's t-distribution with $u(x_i) = U/k$ and degrees of freedom that can be deduced from the coverage interval for k. Note that calibration certificates usually also specify a scope for the calibration, recording any quantities that might affect the calibration such as laboratory air temperature, exposure field level and frequency modulation. This information provides a baseline reference for considering the bias or uncertainty effects of these quantities when assessments are made out in the field.

Unlike calibration reports, uncertainty estimates for the attributes of measuring equipment (e.g. probe isotropy, linearity, temperature response) can often be ambiguously presented by the manufacturer as just a ± estimate without further specification of the distribution type. Thus, this could be interpreted in various ways, such as the limits of a rectangular distribution, or perhaps alternatively as a standard uncertainty. In such cases, it is best to confirm the nature of the estimate with the manufacturer.

Step 3 entails calculating covariances between input quantities that may be correlated with each other. The input quantities for measured RF-EMF assessments in Table 3.2 are usually assumed to be uncorrelated, that is, independent of each other. For the calculated assessments, there is a possibility of correlation when calculating combined exposures from multiple RF sources if the sources share common elements such as antennas, transmitters or cabling.

Step 4 is straightforward when only a single observation is made. For n repeated observations, the result may be calculated as $y = f(\bar{X}_1, \bar{X}_2, \cdots, \bar{X}_n)$, if f is a linear function and $\bar{X}_i = \frac{1}{n}\sum_{j=1}^{n} X_{i,j}$. Otherwise, y is generally calculated as the *arithmetic mean* of the repeated estimates of y, as indicated below:

$$y = \bar{Y} = \frac{1}{n}\sum_{j=1}^{n} f(X_{1,j}, X_{2,j}, \cdots, X_{n,j}) \tag{3.7}$$

If the uncertainty assessment has been conducted in dB units, then it is important to note that this implies that the measurand is dB(Y) rather than just Y. In that case, the expectation value for Y is the arithmetic mean of the dB(PDF) for Y.

In **step 5**, the combined standard uncertainty $u_c(y)$ of Y is the positive square root of the combined variance $u_c^2(y)$, which is calculated from the standard uncertainties for X by applying what the GUM calls the *law of propagation of uncertainty*. This entails reducing the mathematical function $f(X_1, X_2, \ldots X_n)$ to a Taylor series approximation around the expectations of X, x_i. The resulting uncertainty equation is shown below, where only the first- and second-order Taylor expansion terms were retained.

$$u_c^2(y) = \sum_{i=1}^{N}\left(\frac{\partial f}{\partial x_i}\right)^2 u^2(x_i) + \sum_{i=1}^{n}\sum_{j=1}^{n}\left(\frac{1}{2}\left(\frac{\partial^2 f}{\partial x_i \partial x_j}\right)^2 + \frac{\partial f}{\partial x_i}\frac{\partial^3 f}{\partial x_i \partial x_j^2}\right) u^2(x_i) u^2(x_j) \tag{3.8}$$

If f is reasonably linear (i.e. having negligible second or higher order Taylor expansion terms) *and* the input quantity PDFs are symmetric, then the second-order term indicated above can be omitted, and the combined variance is simply calculated as:

$$u_c^2(y) = \sum_{i=1}^{n}\left(\frac{\partial f}{\partial x_i}\right)^2 u^2(x_i) \tag{3.9}$$

The partial derivative in this equation, $\partial f / \partial x_i$, is evaluated at the expectation x_i of X_i and is often called the *sensitivity coefficient*, c_i. It essentially describes how the output estimate y varies with changes in the values of the input quantities $x_1, x_2, \ldots, x_n$.

The multiplicative form commonly used for RF-EMF assessments is non-linear, but can be easily linearised by a dB $\log_{10}$ transformation. For instance, a three-term multiplicative function $(Y = X_1 X_2 X_3)$ can be re-expressed in dB units, as shown below, where the lower-case x and y variables represent the expectation values of X and Y:

$$\frac{Y}{y} = \frac{X_1 X_2 X_3}{x_1 x_2 x_3} \tag{3.10}$$

$$10\log_{10}\left(\frac{Y}{y}\right) = 10\log_{10}\left(\frac{X_1}{x_1}\frac{X_2}{x_2}\frac{X_3}{x_3}\right) = 10\log_{10}\left(\frac{X_1}{x_1}\right) + 10\log_{10}\left(\frac{X_2}{x_2}\right) + 10\log_{10}\left(\frac{X_3}{x_3}\right) \tag{3.11}$$

$$\mathrm{dB}(Y) = \mathrm{dB}(X_1) + \mathrm{dB}(X_2) + \mathrm{dB}(X_3) \tag{3.12}$$

This dB formulation of the multiplicative equation is an *exact* linearisation with no second or higher order Taylor expansion terms, and so can accommodate arbitrarily large values for the standard uncertainties of the input quantities without incurring higher order errors.

An alternative approach offered by the GUM for multiplicative functions is to recast the combined variance $u_c^2(y)$ as a *relative* combined variance $\left[u_c(y)/y\right]^2$ with the estimated variance $u^2(x_i)$ associated with each input estimate expressed as an estimated relative variance $\left[u(x_i)/x_i\right]^2$. Thus, for the general mathematical model of $Y = cX_1^{p_1}X_2^{p_2}\ldots X_n^{p_n}$, the relative combined variance can be calculated as shown below where the exponents p_i become the sensitivity coefficients:

$$\left[u_c(y)/y\right]^2 = \sum_{i=1}^{n}\left[p_i u(x_i)/x_i\right]^2 \tag{3.13}$$

It should be noted that this formula is a first-order *approximation* where higher order Taylor series terms have been neglected. In that case, it may significantly *underestimate* the relative combined uncertainty $u_c(y)/|y|$ when the relative standard uncertainties $u(x_i)/|x_i|$ are large, that is, approximately >10%.

The final task of the uncertainty assessment, **step 6**, is to calculate the expanded uncertainty U, which defines a coverage interval, $y - U$ to $y + U$, of the assessment result that may be expected to encompass a large fraction of the distribution of values that could reasonably be attributed to the measurand. U is obtained by multiplying the combined standard uncertainty $u_c(y)$ by a coverage factor, k:

$$U = ku_c(y) \tag{3.14}$$

If the combined PDF for y is symmetric and approximately normal, and the effective degrees of freedom of $u_c(y)$ is of significant size ($\nu_{eff} > 30$), then k can be simply looked up in a standard normal table as the z statistic for the upper bound of the cumulative probabilities of the coverage interval. For example, a two-sided 95% coverage interval spans between the cumulative probabilities of 0.025 (i.e. 2.5%) and 0.975 (i.e. 97.5%). The k value is thus the z statistic at the upper bound 0.975 cumulative probability, which is 1.96. For the upper bound of a one-sided 90% coverage interval, k is the z statistic at 0.90 cumulative probability, which is 1.28. For readers unfamiliar with looking up statistical tables, z can also be easily obtained using the Microsoft Excel NORM.INV function, for example, NORM.INV(0.975,0,1) for 0.975 cumulative probability.

If ν_{eff} is not of significant size, then k should be estimated as the t statistic for the upper bound of the cumulative probabilities of the coverage interval, with ν_{eff} degrees of freedom. The GUM recommends calculating an approximation of ν_{eff} using the Welch–Satterthwaite formula:

$$\nu_{eff} = \frac{u_c^4(y)}{\sum_{1=1}^{N}\frac{u_i^4(y)}{\nu_i}} \tag{3.15}$$

where $u_i(y) = |c_i|u(x_i)$, and ν_i denotes the degrees of freedom for $u(x_i)$.

For Type A evaluations of $u(x_i)$ from n independent observations, ν_i is simply $n-1$. For some Type B evaluations, the GUM suggests an approximation for ν_i based on the relative uncertainty of $u(x_i)$, that is, $\Delta u(x_i)/u(x_i)$:

$$\nu_i \approx \frac{1}{2}\left[\frac{\Delta u(x_i)}{u(x_i)}\right]^{-2} \tag{3.16}$$

So, for instance, if the width of a rectangular PDF of an input quantity is judged to be reliable at 25%, this may be taken to mean that the relative uncertainty of $u(x_i) = 0.25$. In that case, ν_i is estimated to be $\frac{1}{2}0.25^{-2} = 8$. For relative uncertainties of 2%, 5%, 10%, 20% and 50%, the corresponding estimated values of ν_i are 1250, 200, 20, 13 and 2, respectively.

3.4.2.2 Monte Carlo Method

If the classic GUM methodology seems overly complicated, there is an alternative simpler way to calculate uncertainty using Monte Carlo (MC) simulations (JCGM, 2008b). This numerical approach is also more flexible and accurate, and it is recommended by the GUM for complex and non-linear models, as well as for validating calculations conducted by the classical methodology.

Essentially, the MC method propagates uncertainties by repeated calculation of Y from the mathematical model for samples of random variates selected from the PDFs of the input quantities, X_i, over a large number of trials, generally up to 1 million. The lower and upper bounds of the specified coverage interval are easily determined as the appropriate percentile values of the resulting Y distribution for the designated coverage interval. For instance, the 2.5th and 97.5th percentile values define a two-sided 95% coverage interval. The MC method does not require calculation of a coverage factor.

The MC method avoids most of the simplifications and approximations of the classic GUM approach, and can be easily implemented on modern computers with scientific/statistical programming languages such as Python (2020), R (2020) or MATLAB (2020). For RF-EMF uncertainty evaluations, it is particularly appropriate when:

1. The mathematical model cannot be expressed in the simple multiplicative form, for example, when evaluating the uncertainty for cumulative field assessments.
2. The probability distribution of a dominant X_i is not represented as a normal or t-distribution.
3. One or more X_i has a non-symmetric or complicated PDF.
4. The X_i are represented in a mixture of log and linear scales.
5. The extents of the standard uncertainties are large, and the mathematical model contains significant higher order Taylor expansion terms that have been ignored.

3.5 REPORTING UNCERTAINTY

As a general rule, an uncertainty estimate should be provided with any formal report of an RF-EMF safety assessment. For short form reports, the statement on uncertainty should include at least:

1. A clear description of the measurand, Y, and the units it is reported in, for example, 'ambient power flux density exposure in units of W/m²'.
2. The best estimate(s) of the measurand, that is, the expectation of Y.
3. The context of the uncertainty assessment, for example, 'S_{eq} measured in the far field of the source, spatially averaged over 2 m at ground level, adjusted for the maximum source transmission levels and neglecting variability due to reflected fields from nearby large movable objects'.
4. The level of confidence associated with the uncertainty coverage interval, for example, 'a two-sided 95% coverage interval'.
5. The expanded uncertainty for the coverage interval, including the value of the coverage factor, k, if the classical GUM approach was applied.

On the last point, the expanded uncertainty for RF-EME assessments are indicated as either a dB or percentage range relative to the expectation value. If the expanded uncertainty is symmetric, then the range can be represented as a ± estimate, for example, $U_{90} = \pm\ 18\%$. Otherwise, it can be reported as a range, for example, $U_{95} = [-2.0, 2.8]$ dB.

For future reference, the methodology of evaluating the uncertainty estimate should be comprehensibly documented to a level of detail that would allow a third-party reader to update the estimate with new information. The GUM advises metrologists to:

a. Describe clearly the methods used to calculate the measurement result and its uncertainty from the experimental observations and input data.
b. List all uncertainty components and document fully how they were evaluated.
c. Present the data analysis in such a way that each of its important steps can be readily followed and the calculation of the reported result can be independently repeated if necessary.
d. Give all corrections and constants used in the analysis and their sources.

It is, particularly, important to record the context and mathematical model for the uncertainty evaluation.

3.6 EXAMPLES OF UNCERTAINTY ASSESSMENTS

This section works through various uncertainty assessments to help illustrate the preceding theory. We begin with a relatively simple example where the measurand S_{eq} is determined from the following far field formula:

$$S_{eq} = \frac{PG}{4d^2} \tag{3.17}$$

where:

S_{eq} is the equivalent plane wave power flux density (W/m²)
P is the antenna-radiated power (W)
G is the antenna gain (non-dimensional)
d is the distance of the field evaluation point from the antenna (m)

Equation 3.17 represents the mathematical model for our assessment with P, G and d as its input quantities. Since the model is in multiplicative form, we can exactly linearise it via a dB transformation as described previously in this chapter, leading to the uncertainty equation below. From this equation we see that the sensitivity coefficient, c_i, is 1 for P and G, and 2 for d.

$$\mathrm{dB}\left(S_{\mathrm{eq}}\right) = \mathrm{dB}(P) + \mathrm{dB}(G) - 2\ \mathrm{dB}(d) \tag{3.18}$$

Let us pretend that the antenna manufacturer has specified an expanded uncertainty of $U_{95} = \pm 1.5$ dB for G with a coverage factor $k = 2.1$. We estimate its standard error as $u_G = U_{95}/k = \mathbf{0.714}$ dB. From a Student's t-distribution table, we find that the corresponding degrees of freedom, ν_G, for $k = 2.1$ is **18**. We can verify this with the Excel function T.INV.2T(0.05,18), which yields 2.10 as expected.

Next, we assume that the antenna-radiated power P varies uniformly between −0.5 and 0.5 dB (i.e. a rectangular distribution), with a reliability of approximately 10% in this estimate. From Figure 3.3 we see $u_P = \frac{1}{2}(0.5-(-0.5))\Big/\sqrt{3} = 0.289$ dB. We calculate the degrees of freedom from equation 3.16 as $\upsilon_i = 1/2[0.1]^{-2} = 50$.

Finally, for d let us say the estimated distance is expected to vary as a triangular probability distribution around ± 0.1 m. From Figure 3.3, we see the uncertainty of d expressed in metres is:

$$\begin{aligned} u_d &= \sqrt{\left(0.1^2 + 0 + 0.1^2 - 0 - \left(-0.1^2\right) - 0\right)\Big/18} \\ &= \sqrt{3\left(0.1^2\right)/18} = \sqrt{0.1^2/6} = 0.1/\sqrt{6} = 0.041 \end{aligned} \tag{3.19}$$

Since for this example we are very confident of this estimate, we assume that ν_d is infinite. We also note that the estimate for d is in *absolute* units of m, rather than a relative variation in dB (or percentage units), creating a difficulty for combining its standard uncertainty estimate with the other two input quantities. However, since the far field in this fictitious example generally starts further than 5 m from the antenna, then the relative uncertainty will always be less than 0.041/5 × 100 = 0.82% (0.035 dB) and may hence be omitted from the uncertainty calculations due to its negligible contribution to the combined uncertainty.

With the uncertainty equation and standard uncertainty estimates for all input quantities, we can now apply the classical GUM approach to estimate the combined and expanded uncertainties for a two-sided 95% coverage interval as tabulated below (Table 3.3). We find that U_{95} is a *symmetric* range of ±1.59 dB, which corresponds to a *non-symmetric* percentage range of [−30.7%, 44.2%].

We can repeat this uncertainty calculation using relative quantities in percentage units, instead of dB, with the variances combined as per equation 3.18. The sensitivity coefficients, c_i, and the degrees of freedom, ν_i, remain the same as for the dB calculation. We convert the dB values for u to percentage values by taking the mean of the absolute percent values for the plus and minus dB range. For example, $u_G = (17.9\% + 15.2\%)/2 = 16.5\%$. The values for this percentage calculation of U_{95} is tabulated below (Table 3.4) and indicates $U_{95} = \pm 36.8\%$, an estimate that lies between the converted percentage values, [−30.7%, 44.2%], for the more accurate dB calculation.

TABLE 3.3
Calculation of Expanded Uncertainty in dB Scale

Input Quantity	Unit	Distribution Type	Degrees of Freedom, v_i	u	c_i	$u_i = \lvert c_i \rvert * u$	u_i^2	u_i^4/v_i
P	dB	t	18	0.714	1	0.714	0.5098	0.01444
G	dB	Uniform	50	0.289	1	0.289	0.0835	0.00014
						Suma	**0.5933**	**0.01458**

Considered components of the expanded uncertainty expressed in dB scale:

Combined standard uncertainty, $u_c(y)$ 0.770

Effective degrees of freedom, v_{eff} 24.1

Coverage factor, k 2.06

Expanded uncertainty, $U = k\, u_c$ 1.59 dB

TABLE 3.4
Calculation of Expanded Uncertainty in Percentage Scale

Input Quantity	Unit	Distribution Type	Degrees of Freedom, v_i	u	c_i	$u_i = \lvert c_i \rvert * u$	u_i^2	u_i^4/v_i
P	%	t	18	16.51	1	16.515	272.7326	4132.39394
G	%	Uniform	50	6.66	1	6.659	44.3474	39.33381
						Suma	**317.08**	**4171**

Considered components of the expanded uncertainty expressed in percentage scale:

Combined standard uncertainty, $u_c(y)$ 17.81

Effective degrees of freedom, v_{eff} 24.1

Coverage factor, k 2.06

Expanded uncertainty, $U_{95} = k\, u_c$ 36.8 %

We can also make comparison to uncertainty predictions generated by the MC method. For this example, we conduct the MC uncertainty calculations in the Python programming language (see python.org), as shown in Figure 3.5, making use of the open source NumPy, SciPy and Matplotlib packages (see scipy.org/). The previous calculations in dB units are easily replicated in the MC method by the Python code below. Random variate samples for P and G are generated with the Student's t (t) and trapezoidal (trapz) modules from the scipy.stats package. A trapezoidal distribution was used for G to better replicate the 10% variability in the extents of the uniform distribution, with the base of the trapezoid extending from 0.55 to +0.55 dB and its top extending from −0.45 to +0.45 dB. Many other statistical distributions (e.g. normal, uniform, beta, triangular, chi, etc.) are also available in the scipy.stats package. The P and G distributions are stored as numpy vector arrays containing a million elements and can be easily combined into a new S_{eq} array by applying the uncertainty equation (3.18). The last step is to utilise a numpy function for extracting the 2.5th and 97.5th percentiles of the S_{eq} array to obtain the U_{95} range. The code executes in approximately 210 ms on a standard desktop computer and is listed as Example #1 in Figure 3.5.

The output of the code indicates a range for U_{95} of [−1.60 dB, 1.60 dB], which aligns closely with the dB estimate using the classical GUM approach. It is a good idea to visually check the MC distributions, as, for instance, in the histogram plot generated by the Example #2 Python code at Figure 3.5 and displayed in Figure 3.6. The plot shows that the combined S_{eq} distribution is mostly dominated by contributions from the P distribution.

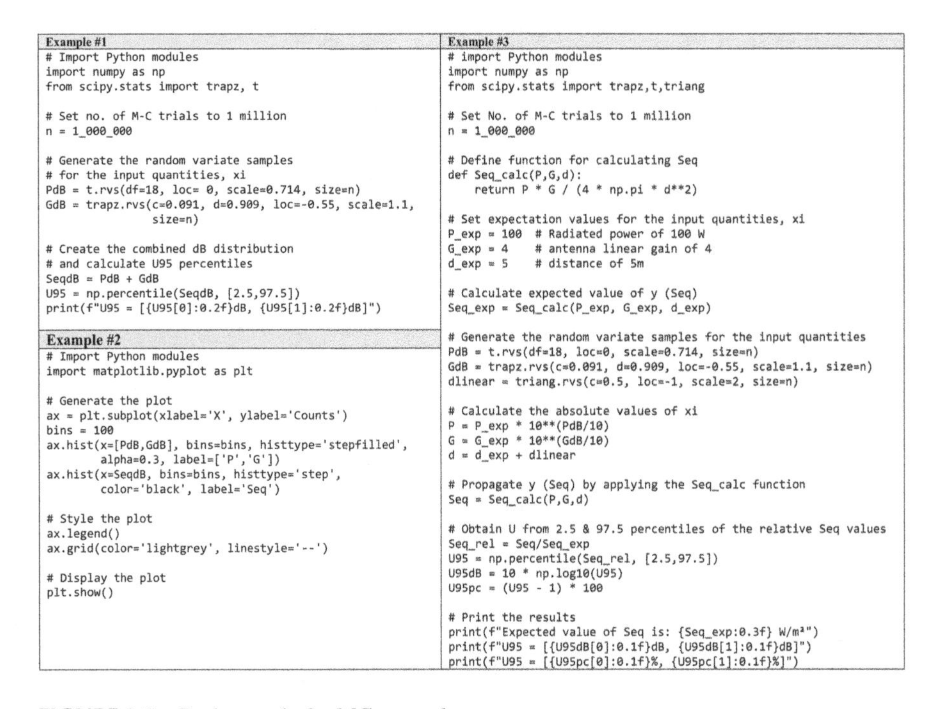

Example #1

```
# Import Python modules
import numpy as np
from scipy.stats import trapz, t

# Set no. of M-C trials to 1 million
n = 1_000_000

# Generate the random variate samples
# for the input quantities, xi
PdB = t.rvs(df=18, loc= 0, scale=0.714, size=n)
GdB = trapz.rvs(c=0.091, d=0.909, loc=-0.55, scale=1.1,
                size=n)

# Create the combined dB distribution
# and calculate U95 percentiles
SeqdB = PdB + GdB
U95 = np.percentile(SeqdB, [2.5,97.5])
print(f"U95 = [{U95[0]:0.2f}dB, {U95[1]:0.2f}dB]")
```

Example #2

```
# Import Python modules
import matplotlib.pyplot as plt

# Generate the plot
ax = plt.subplot(xlabel='X', ylabel='Counts')
bins = 100
ax.hist(x=[PdB,GdB], bins=bins, histtype='stepfilled',
        alpha=0.3, label=['P','G'])
ax.hist(x=SeqdB, bins=bins, histtype='step',
        color='black', label='Seq')

# Style the plot
ax.legend()
ax.grid(color='lightgrey', linestyle='--')

# Display the plot
plt.show()
```

Example #3

```
# import Python modules
import numpy as np
from scipy.stats import trapz,t,triang

# Set No. of M-C trials to 1 million
n = 1_000_000

# Define function for calculating Seq
def Seq_calc(P,G,d):
    return P * G / (4 * np.pi * d**2)

# Set expectation values for the input quantities, xi
P_exp = 100  # Radiated power of 100 W
G_exp = 4    # antenna linear gain of 4
d_exp = 5    # distance of 5m

# Calculate expected value of y (Seq)
Seq_exp = Seq_calc(P_exp, G_exp, d_exp)

# Generate the random variate samples for the input quantities
PdB = t.rvs(df=18, loc=0, scale=0.714, size=n)
GdB = trapz.rvs(c=0.091, d=0.909, loc=-0.55, scale=1.1, size=n)
dlinear = triang.rvs(c=0.5, loc=-1, scale=2, size=n)

# Calculate the absolute values of xi
P = P_exp * 10**(PdB/10)
G = G_exp * 10**(GdB/10)
d = d_exp + dlinear

# Propagate y (Seq) by applying the Seq_calc function
Seq = Seq_calc(P,G,d)

# Obtain U from 2.5 & 97.5 percentiles of the relative Seq values
Seq_rel = Seq/Seq_exp
U95 = np.percentile(Seq_rel, [2.5,97.5])
U95dB = 10 * np.log10(U95)
U95pc = (U95 - 1) * 100

# Print the results
print(f"Expected value of Seq is: {Seq_exp:0.3f} W/m²")
print(f"U95 = [{U95dB[0]:0.1f}dB, {U95dB[1]:0.1f}dB]")
print(f"U95 = [{U95pc[0]:0.1f}%, {U95pc[1]:0.1f}%]")
```

FIGURE 3.5 Python code for MC examples.

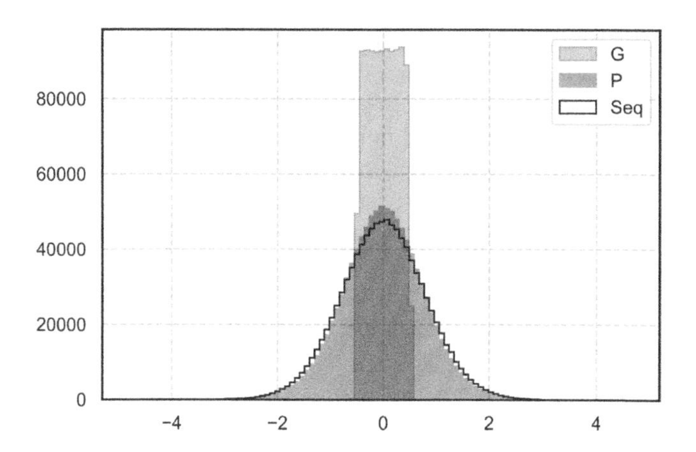

FIGURE 3.6 Histogram plot of distributions for input quantities and S_{eq}.

If the uncertainty of d were much larger than we first assumed, say a ±1 m triangular distribution, we would then be obliged to consider it in our uncertainty calculations. This would not be possible using the classical GUM approach, since it cannot accommodate the mix of relative dB units for P and G, and the absolute unit (m) for d. However, it is possible to combine d with P and G in the MC method by converting all distributions to the common form of absolute units. This entails the inclusion of expectation values for P, G and d, as illustrated in the Python code, for example, #3 at Figure 3.5. The mathematical model for calculating the expectation and distribution of S_{eq} is specified in a function at the top of the code.

The output from the code indicates that U_{95} increases to [−2.0 dB, 2.2 dB] = [−37.6%, 64.8%] for the much larger ±1 m distribution for d. It also demonstrates how U_{95} changes for different expectations of d, for instance reducing to [−1.7 dB, 1.8 dB] when the expectation of d is increased from 5 to 10 m. In other words, the combined S_{eq} uncertainty diminishes at further distances from the antenna due to the declining relative uncertainty of d. The MC method is a powerful and flexible approach for testing uncertainty influences!

In the next extension of this example, we examine a more complex RF-EMF assessment where we consider transmission losses between the antenna and its RF source, field scattering effects, near field errors in the field assessment calculator (FAC) and the applicable RF safety exposure limit (S_{lim}), as graphically modelled in the systems diagram of Figure 3.4.

First we note that P can be refined in equation 3.17 to incorporate the combined effect of the component transmission losses:

$$P = L_{tx}\ P_{tx} \tag{3.20}$$

where

L_{tx} is the transmission loss factor (non-dimensional) due to cable/combiner losses and impedance mismatch between the transmission line and antenna

P_{tx} is the transmitter power (W)

The effects of calculation error and field impedance (which affects max[S_E, S_H]) are interrelated in the complex algorithms of the FAC and so are not amenable to simple mathematical expression. In that case, a general omnibus input quantity, N_{FAC}, is proposed for representing the combined influences of these input quantities. Similarly, uncertainty due to field scattering is a complicated function, which will be approximated in the model as another multiplicative factor, F_s. Both N_{FAC} and F_s are affected by contextual factors such as frequency, assessment point location and the choice of spatial averaging scheme, which should accordingly be noted in the stated context for the uncertainty assessment.

Combining all of the influence quantities identified above into equation 3.17 yields the following model equation:

$$S_{eq} = \frac{L_{tx}\ P_{tx}\ G\ N_{FAC}\ F_s}{4d^2} \tag{3.21}$$

and the measurand can now be defined as:

$$Y = \frac{S_{eq}}{S_{lim}} = \frac{L_{tx}\ P_{tx}\ G\ N_{FAC}\ F_s}{4d^2\ S_{lim}} \tag{3.22}$$

Assuming no random variability in d and S_{lim}, the application of a log transformation converts the model equation to a linear form, which can be conveniently expressed in dB units:

$$\mathrm{dB}(Y) = \mathrm{dB}(L_{tx}) + \mathrm{dB}(P_{tx}) + \mathrm{dB}(G) + \mathrm{dB}(N_{FAC}) + \mathrm{dB}(F_s) \tag{3.23}$$

Estimating the uncertainty distributions for the input quantities requires some careful thought, especially for N_{FAC} and F_S. One possible approach for characterising these quantities is to numerically generate error distributions for the difference between FAC field level predictions in the near field compared to 'gold standard' values.

For instance, in regard to N_{FAC} the gold standard values might be the field solution of a radiating antenna using a full wave modelling technique such as the method of moments (MoM) or the finite difference time domain (FDTD) technique. The error distribution in N_{FAC} may be obtained by sampling the difference between the S_{eq} outputs of the FAC and the max[$S_{eq}(E)$, $S_{eq}(H)$] levels predicted by the full wave method at the same sampling points in the near field area. In order to ensure a valid 'apples with apples' comparison, the inputs to FAC solution would be drawn from the inputs to the full wave solution (e.g. antenna-radiated power, frequency, antenna dimensions) as well as its outputs (such as its predicted antenna pattern). A process chart illustrating this approach is shown in Figure 3.7.

The error distribution obtained this way for N_{FAC} will vary according to the context of the uncertainty assessment. The context may, for instance, specify assessment point locations inside a near field bounding box around the antenna, with the sides of the box distant by at least one wavelength (λ) from the antenna. Or it might specify points that lie near or within the RF-EMF hazard zone of the antenna for a standard operational configuration. The context of the error distribution will also vary according to the type of antenna model(s) chosen for the assessment. Ideally, these should be a reasonably

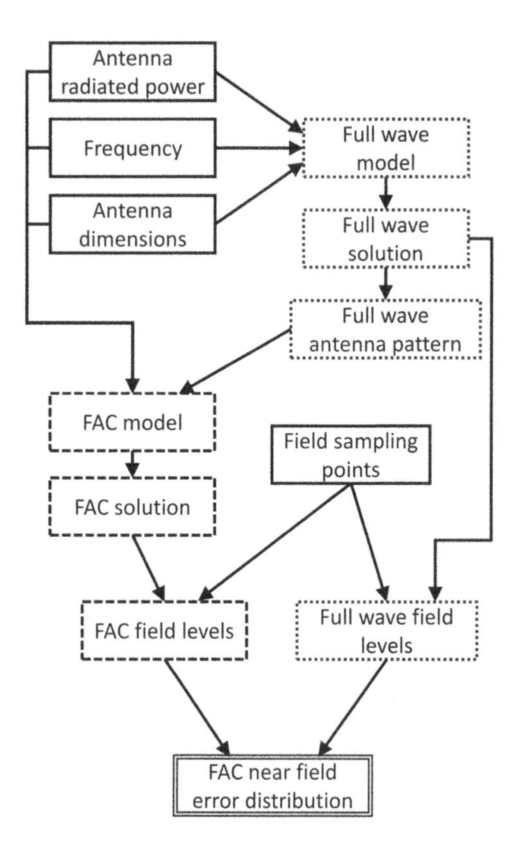

FIGURE 3.7 Process chart for generating an error distribution for N_{FAC}.

representative sample for the stated context, for example, six different types of mobile base station panel antennas when assessing the N_{FAC} error for a generic panel antenna.

The N_{FAC} error distribution obtained by this method will likely have a somewhat irregular shape, which will not be well fitted by a standard analytical PDF. In that case, it should be applied in an MC estimation of uncertainty by randomly sampling from the distribution. In Python, this can be achieved by using the numpy.random.choice function.

3.7 CONCLUSION

Although estimating the uncertainty of RF-EMF assessments might seem daunting, it is nonetheless a task that is important for representing the quality and reliability of the assessment, and for better understanding its limitations.

From the preceding parts of this chapter, the reader will hopefully have acquired a clear understanding of the fundamental mechanics of conducting an uncertainty assessment and the special issues that typically arise for RF-EMF assessments.

This chapter does not offer 'cookbook recipes' for particular types of RF-EME assessments, such as measurements around mobile base stations, since standardised approaches cannot adequately encompass the myriad and nuanced differences that can arise between independent assessments of even the same thing. Moreover, a standardised approach can stifle the development of new insights into how RF-EMF uncertainty should be practised, which would be pity for an area that is still relatively unexplored.

Thus, the challenge to you, dear reader, is to extend the learnings of this chapter with a finer understanding of the various components that affect RF-EMF assessment uncertainty. This applies particularly to how the measurand is defined, how the assessment was conducted, the physical equipment or computational tools that were used to make the assessment, and finally the formulation of the mathematical model that defines the relationship between the input quantities and the measurand.

The MC technique is recommended as a powerful, flexible and intuitive approach for calculating and exploring uncertainties. It can be easily implemented in scientific program languages such as Python, R and MATLAB, which also provide convenient notebook containers (e.g. see jupyter.org and rmarkdown.rstudio.com) for live code, equations, visualisations and narrative text.

Indeed, detailed documentation of the uncertainty assessment is essential for enabling incremental improvement by yourself or by members of your team. It also provides an evidence base for sharing insights about RF-EMF uncertainty with the rest of your professional community.

So, now it is over to you!

REFERENCES

EN 50413:2019. 2019. *Basic Standard on Measurement and Calculation Procedures for Human Exposure to Electric, Magnetic and Electromagnetic Fields (0 Hz – 300 GHz).* Brussels: CENELEC [European Committee for Electrotechnical Standardization].

IEC 62232:2017. 2017. *Determination of RF Field Strength, Power Density and SAR in the Vicinity of Radiocommunication Base Stations for the Purpose of Evaluating Human Exposure.* Geneva: IEC [International Electrotechnical Commission].

ITU-T 2020. 2020. *Recommendation ITU-T K.91 Guidance for Assessment, Evaluation and Monitoring of Human Exposure to Radio Frequency Electromagnetic Fields.* Geneva: ITU-T [Telecommunication Standardization Sector of the International Telecommunication Union].

JCGM 100:2008. 2008a. *Evaluation of Measurement Data — Guide to the Expression of Uncertainty in Measurement.* Sèvres: JCGM [Joint Committee for Guides in Metrology].

JCGM 101:2008. 2008b. *Evaluation of Measurement Data – Supplement 1 to the "Guide to the Expression of Uncertainty in Measurement" – Propagation of Distributions using a Monte Carlo Method.* Sèvres: JCGM [Joint Committee for Guides in Metrology].

JCGM 104:2009. 2009. *Evaluation of Measurement Data — An Introduction to the "Guide to the Expression of Uncertainty in Measurement" and Related Documents.* Sèvres: JCGM [Joint Committee for Guides in Metrology].

MATLAB. 2020. Version 9.9 (R2020b). Natick: The MathWorks Inc.

Python Software Foundation. 2020. *Python Language Reference, version 3.8.* Beaverton: Python Software Foundation. https://www.python.org.

R Development Core Team. 2020. *The R Project for Statistical Computing.* Vienna: R Foundation for Statistical Computing. https://www.R-project.org.

4 Evaluation of Electromagnetic Exposure during Workers' Activities near High-Voltage Electricity Grids

Krzysztof Gryz and Jolanta Karpowicz
Central Institute for Labour Protection—
National Research Institute (CIOP-PIB)

Karol Zajdler
Polskie Sieci Elektroenergetyczne S.A.—
transmission system operator (PSE S.A)

CONTENTS

4.1 BACKGROUND

Access to electricity requires a widespread system of devices for its generation, transmission and distribution. The supply of electricity from generating sources (conventional, coal or gas, nuclear or water power plants, wind or photovoltaic farms, etc.) to consumers is carried out using three-phase alternating currents (AC) of 50 Hz frequency (in all European countries) or 60 Hz (in America and Asia). The electricity

DOI: 10.1201/9781003020486-4

production and distribution system supplying electricity-consuming equipment consist of power plants and transmission and distribution grids. The structure of electricity systems over the world is quite uniform (CIGRE, 1980, 2020a) and is very stable in the physical structure over years; it is not unusual for electric power lines or substations to be used for well over 50 years. Electricity grids are divided into transmission and distribution grids based on the voltage level used. Electricity from the power plants is first transferred to a transmission grid covering the whole country using the highest voltage overhead power supply lines in order to reduce energy transmission losses. The voltage of overhead power lines may be different depending on the country. In the authors' home country (Poland), the grids, transmission lines and substations have the following electric structure (Marzecki, 2013; PSE, 2020; Szuba et al., 2016):

- 220 and 400 kV (EHV, extremely high voltage) used in the case of the longest transmission distances over a country or crossing borders between countries
- 110 kV (HV, high voltage) in the case of transmission distances of up to several dozen kilometres
- 10–30 kV (MV, medium voltage), usually 15 or 20 kV, used for local distribution lines.

Additionally, direct current (DC) lines are used to connect countries that do not have synchronised electricity systems, which makes it possible to import/export electricity between countries (e.g. under-sea 450 kV DC connection between Poland and Sweden) (PSE, 2020).

EHV and HV transmission lines are designed and carried out over the field using standardised support structures (towers) that determine the geometric layout of phase conductors (Figure 4.1a–c).

Electricity is supplied to users through a distribution grid divided into underground cables and overhead cables depending on the installation method. In cities and towns, distribution grids are frequently built using underground cables. In rural areas, overhead lines are generally used. The overhead cables are attached to the HV towers with brackets. Cables run through cable ducts, cable trays or are laid directly on land or water.

The transmission and distribution grids also include electrical substations used to convert or transform electricity for transmission in the system, the distribution of electricity in distribution grids and lowering the voltage to the required level. There are electrical substations on open ground (outdoors), underground and in specific premises. EHV and HV electrical substations consist usually of outdoor and indoor switchyards, transformers and control rooms (Figure 4.1d and e), but in the urban area indoor compact installations (SF_6 insulated) may prevail. Access to the fenced areas of substations is not available to non-workers; additionally, only authorised personnel have access (Figure 4.1f and g). Outdoor switchyards are typically operated at EHV and HV, and indoor switchyards are typically operated at low voltage (LV) and MV, sometimes at EHV and HV.

The transmission grid is connected to the distribution grid at distribution substations from which electricity passes through the MV grid. For ordinary electricity users, the voltage is converted from MV to LV (<1000 V) by distribution

FIGURE 4.1 Examples of structures of metal HV and EHV towers (a: 110 kV; b: 220 kV; c: 400 kV), outdoor switchyards (d: 400 kV; e: 110 kV) and examples of EMF-exposed locations exclusions from the working space by physical barriers (f: 110 kV switchgears in indoor switchyard; g: 15/0.4 kV transformer chamber) used in Poland. (Authors' collection)

transformers. Distribution transformers tend to be pole transformers, park transformers or 'substations' connected to buildings for distribution through the property. From distribution transformers, electricity is transferred to customers via LV lines. In all European countries, the voltage AC current of a LV grid is usually approximately 230 V (1-phase) or 400 V (3-phase).

4.2 ENVIRONMENTAL FACTORS AFFECTING WORKERS NEAR TO HIGH-VOLTAGE ELECTRICITY GRIDS

Various environmental factors affect the workers performing various tasks related to the use of high-voltage electricity grids (HV and EHV power lines and substations) (Karpowicz (ed.), 2013a; Szuba et al., 2016):

- Electric shock hazardous for those working in the vicinity of energised objects, that is, exposed to contact with electrical equipment;
- Variable microclimate while working in an open area where there are no natural protective barriers, for example from the low or high temperature, low or high air humidity, snow and rain;
- Sun optical radiation (visible, ultraviolet and infrared), which can cause, for example, sunburn and also the reflection of light from the metallic structures, which can cause glare in workers;
- Injuries to and loads on the musculoskeletal system during work requiring physical activity (dynamic or static physical effort, often forced work position);
- Psychological burden and stress—related to the need to be available, often difficult terrain, and the need to use personal protective equipment and awareness of working in the vicinity of live (electrically energised) devices;
- Biological factors—associated with the possibility of insect and animal bites;
- Hazardous chemical substances and mixtures, thereof, such as sulphur hexafluoride—a gas used as an insulation working medium, for example, in high-voltage circuit breakers (SF_6 is six times heavier than air, which makes it possible to accumulate, for example, in cavities such as cable ducts.);
- Extremely low frequency (ELF) electromagnetic fields (EMF), mainly of the power frequency 50/60 Hz, due to the presence of voltages and currents in all components of high-voltage electrical grids, which are sources of EMF affecting the environment and people present in their vicinity;
- Radiofrequency (RF) EMF (ranging usually 0.7–5.5 GHz in frequency), where HV towers are used also as the support for the antennas of mobile communication (phone/internet wireless access) networks, or RTV broadcasting or mobile communication antennas are located in their close vicinity (see Figure 4.1a).

4.3 EVALUATION OF ELF-EMF EXPOSURE—METRICS AND CRITERIA

Exposure to ELF-EMF may be considered in the context of compliance with the guidelines providing exposure limitation to protect against immediate effects of EMF influence (Directive, 2013; ICNIRP, 1998, 2010; IEEE, 2019; Recommendation, 1999) or with respect to the hypothesis of possible adverse health effects due to chronic (lasting many years) exposure (IARC, 2002; Schüz and Ahlbom, 2008; Huss et al., 2009; Hug et al., 2006).

On the basis of the limited evidence available from epidemiological studies (i.e. performed in the vicinity of EHV and HV power lines), the International Agency for Research on Cancer classified ELF magnetic field (MF) as a possible carcinogen for human (2B classification) (IARC, 2002). ELF electric field (EF) was not classified as a carcinogen for humans (Group 3). The pooled data indicated increased health hazards (increased cancer risk) in the case of chronic (recognized also to be long-term, i.e. years lasting) exposure to MF at yearly average level exceeding the magnetic flux density (B) of 0.4 μT (Greenland et al., 2000; Ahlbom et al., 2000). Newer reports from the World Health Organisation (WHO, 2007) and the Scientific Committee on Emerging and Newly Identified Health Risks (SCENIHR, 2009, 2015) did not question that opinion. These reports also indicated a possible increase in Alzheimer's disease related to chronic ELF-MF exposure. Based on the abovementioned conclusions, the WHO advised low-budget preventive measures to reduce exposure to ELF-MF (WHO, 2007).

Further research on health hazards due to exposure to ELF-EMF belongs to the research recommended by the WHO and SCENIHR, including studies on the carcinogenetic mechanisms, neurodegenerative diseases and exposure assessment for studying dose–response relationship in health hazards.

The minimum requirements aimed at protecting only against short-term safety and health hazards caused by EMF exposure were published in several international guidelines. Short-term hazards from exposure to EMF are recognised there to be the harmful direct biophysical effects in the human body—non-thermal effects, such as the stimulation of muscles, nerves or sensory organs in exposure to low-frequency EMF, and thermal load in tissues exposed to RF-EMF (Directive, 2013; ICNIRP, 1998, 2010, 2020; IEEE, 2019; Recommendation 1999). The main metrics considered with respect to evaluation of direct biophysical effects of EMF exposure are the EF induced in body tissues (E_{in}) or the density of electric current induced in body tissues (j)—used directly in evaluating hazards from low-frequency exposure (applicable up to several MHz) or converted to the specific energy absorption rate (SAR) when exposure comes from RF-EMF (applicable above 100 kHz). Exposure to EMF emitted by elements of the power system may also cause contact current (A kind of indirect effect caused by EMF influence – simultaneously on the humans and material objects.). Contact current flows through the body of an exposed person and the point of contact with a conductive object also affected by EMF, and may cause painful shocks or even burns (similarly to the case of electric shock when touching energised electric circuit). The EMF also causes other indirect hazards, for example caused by the unexpected perception of contact current or interference with the functioning of electronic devices, including medical implants, both of which may trigger hazardous spontaneous malfunctions in tasks performed by affected workers (Zradziński et al., 2018).

In considerations related to EMF exposure near high-voltage electricity grids, the key role has the limits of exposure to EMF at a power frequency of 50 Hz, established to protect general public and workers (Table 4.1) and the limits of contact current (Table 4.2).

Taking into account the evidence mentioned above on health hazards from chronic exposure, some countries (e.g. Switzerland, Italy, Belgium and the Netherlands) have introduced more restrictive supplementary guidelines to implement various measures

TABLE 4.1
Limits of Exposure to EMF of Power Frequency 50 Hz (Unperturbed Field)

	General Public		Occupational Exposure—Workers	
Requirements	**Magnetic Field Density *B*, μT**	**Electric Field Strength *E*, kV/m**	**Magnetic Field Density *B*, μT**	**Electric Field Strength *E*, kV/m**
ICNIRP, 1998	100	5	500	10
ICNIRP, 2010	200	5	1000	10
Recommendation, 1999	100	5	NA	NA
Directive, 2013	NA	NA	– Low AL: 1000 – High AL: 6000	– Low AL: 10 – High AL: 20
IEEE, 2019	904	5[a]	2710	20

[a] Within areas designated as power line rights-of-way (or similarly designated areas, e.g. easement or corridor): 10 kV/m.

Note: Hazards related to indirect effects of EMF exposure (such as caused by perception of contact currents or malfunctions of electronic medical implants) are observed in exposed persons also at EMF exposure weaker than exposure limits specified in the Table 4.1.

NA, not applicable.

TABLE 4.2
Limits of Contact Current of Power Frequency 50 Hz

Requirements	**Contact Current (mA)**	
	General Public	**Occupational Exposure – Workers**
ICNIRP, 1998, 2010	0.5	1.0
Recommendation, 1999	0.5	NA
Directive, 2013	NA	1.0
IEEE, 2019	0.5[a]	1.5[a] 3.0[b]

[a] Touch contact (area of contact between body and metallic structure exposed to EMF assumed to be 1 cm^2).

[b] Grasping contact (area of contact assumed to be 15 cm^2).

NA, not applicable.

to reduce public exposure up to a level of MF not exceeding 1–10 μT (EAHC, 2010; Stamm, 2011).

With respect to the indirect EMF hazards, ACGIH recommends that, when lacking information on immunity to electromagnetic interference from the manufacturer of electronic devices, the exposure to EMF at a power frequency of 50/60 Hz of users of cardiac pacemaker or similar medical electronic device should be lower than 100 μT or 2 kV/m (ACGIH, 2022).

4.4 EVALUATION OF EXPOSURE TO EMF EMITTED BY HV AND EHV POWER GRIDS

4.4.1 Measurements of EMF Near to Power Grids

The level of exposure to ELF-EMF caused by high-voltage power lines and at substations can be determined by measurement and by a relatively simple calculation of EMF from power lines.

The worker whose exposure is being assessed, and the person performing the measurements of ELF-EF, may significantly affect the spatial distribution of the EF. It may be explained that, due to the greater conductivity of the human body in relation to the air, the EF force lines are compressed in the vicinity of the human body. Consequently, it may cause an increase or decrease in the EF strength at measurement point, depending on the geometric configuration between: 'the human body–the EMF meter the EMF source'. Changes in the ELF-EF strength resulting from the presence of the worker or the measuring person near the measuring probe, and their impact on the results of the measurement, are impossible to predict for a particular configuration (They can be positive or negative.) and impossible to balance them by applying appropriate correction factors when interpreting the measurement results. Therefore, it is necessary to strictly follow the formalised rules (e.g. in measuring protocols or standards) for performing investigations in order to obtain measurement results corresponding to EF strength unperturbed by a human presence known also as the 'primary field'.

In order to minimise the impact of the measuring person on the measurement result, it is recommended that the measuring probe, or the entire meter (in the case of its integrated design), be moved away from the person performing the measurements at a distance of at least 1.8 m (IEC 61786-2, 2014). To meet this requirement, it is necessary to use proper measurement devices that not only have a sufficiently wide dynamic measuring range (up to at least 20 kV/m) but also are equipped with EF probes separated at an appropriate distance from the monitor, or EF probe is integrated with the monitor equipped with large-size indicator readable from an appropriate distance. Separation with a fibre optic connection ensures a sufficiently high impedance between the probe and monitor, so that the measurement process does not interfere with the distribution of the primary EF.

It is important to notice that ELF-MF is not deformed by the human body, and its measurements do not require such restrictions. Exposure to ELF-MF may be sufficiently evaluated by handheld measurement devices or even by MF data loggers carried in the pocket of exposed person.

The EMF investigations discussed in this chapter to show typical characteristics of workers exposure near HV and EHV power grid were performed using measurement devices sensitive to root mean square (RMS) value of EF strength and magnetic flux density:

- EFA-300 (Narda Safety Test Solutions, Pfullingen, Germany): Isotropic EF and MF meter with a frequency range of 5 Hz–30 kHz (flat) or selective at 50 Hz; measurement range of MF: 0.01 μT–32 mT and resolution 0.01 μT; measurement range of EF: 10 V/m–100 kV/m and resolution 1 V/m; accuracy ±3%;

- EMDEX II Standard (Enertech Consultans, Campbell, CA, USA): Isotropic pocket-sized data logger of MF with a frequency range of 40–800 Hz; measurement range 0.01–300 μT and resolution 0.01 μT; accuracy ±1%; sampling rate 1.5 s.

A reliable assessment of exposure to complex EMF is among the main tasks of epidemiological investigations and environmental hygiene inspections carried out in the context of environmental safety and health hazards. Where RF antennas operate near HV installations, both the components of EMF exposure may need to be evaluated. In this case, ELF-EF and -MF meters should be not sensitive to RF-EMF, and RF-EF and -MF meters should likewise not be sensitive to ELF-EMF. Such immunity of measurement devices needs to be experimentally proved in the laboratory using sources of strong EMF (Karpowicz et al., 2013b, 2016, Szuba et al., 2016). The discussed unexpected behaviour of EMF measurement devices used in the environment near sources of strong EMF exposure (such as HV power installations or RF broadcasting facilities) may create an important source of uncertainty in assessment of exposure to EMF. When the measurement devices used in environment with complex EMF components are not sufficiently immune, the results of their malfunctions (i.e. false indications) may also cause huge public/workers' concern—when exposure evaluation is misclassified to be much stronger than in reality.

The scale of unexpected sensitivity of EMF measurement devices to EMF of out-of-band frequencies may be very far from their declared frequency measuring range. Examples of out-of-band sensitivity, which were found in the laboratory studies, are showed at Figure 4.2. The sensitivity of the tested measurement devices have been defined as follows:

$$KE = E(RF)/E(50\,Hz) \tag{4.1}$$

$$KH = H(RF)/E(50\,Hz) \tag{4.2}$$

where:

E(RF): An indication of the RF-EF meter

H(RF): An indication of the RF-MF meter

E(50Hz): The EF strength of the ambient 50 Hz EF produced in the laboratory source

The sensitivity of RF-EMF measurement devices, declared to be sensitive in their measurement frequency ranges from 1 kHz to 38 GHz, to the influence of sinusoidal time-varying EF of 50 Hz frequency was tested in EF of 5–30 kV/m strength (Gryz and Karpowicz, 2013a, 2013b; Karpowicz et al, 2013b). The results were analysed in the context of the requirements on the protection of workers and the general public against the influence of EMF, and the characteristics of ambient EMF that may exist in the vicinity of HV electric power lines. In the EF of 5 kV/m at 50 Hz (i.e. general public exposure limit from ICNIRP), which are quite common in Poland near HV and EHV power grids, false indications of RF-EF of 1.5–12 V/m and RF-MF of 0.001–0.1 A/m were found. In the 10 kV/m at 50 Hz (i.e. workers' exposure limit from ICNIRP) false indications of up to RF-EF of 3–22 V/m and RF-MF of 0.002–0.1 A/m were found.

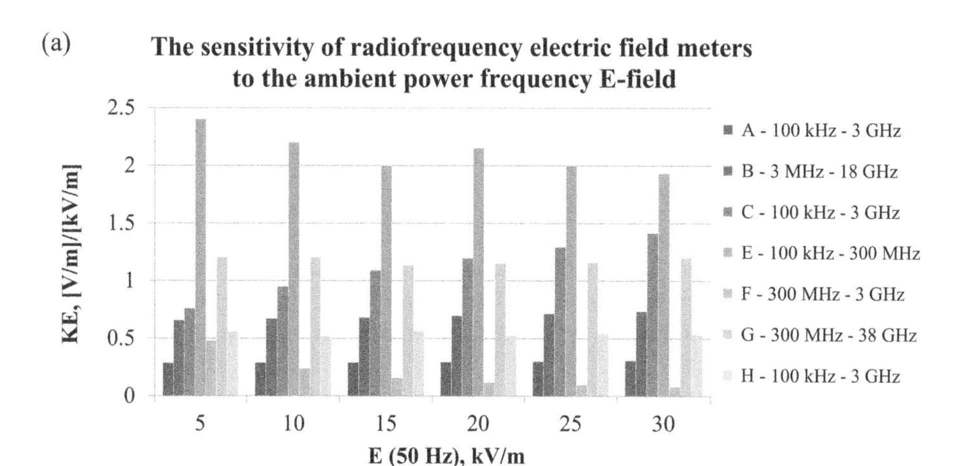

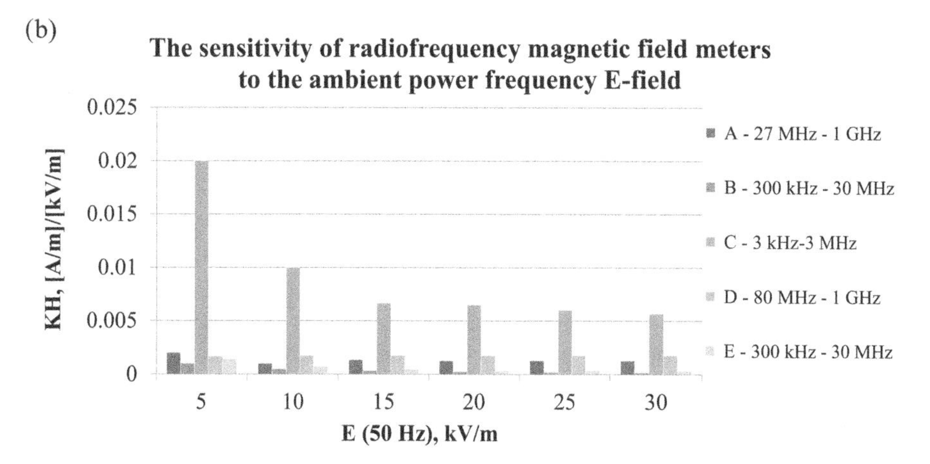

FIGURE 4.2 The sensitivity of measurement devices of RF-EMF to the 50 Hz frequency ambient EF. (Authors' collection)

Summarising, it was found that in the vicinity of HV and EHV electric power lines (where the real RF-EF exposure usually not exceed 3 V/m) the influence of 50 Hz EF on the RF-EMF measurement devices may cause a false identification of relatively strong RF-EF and -MF exposure, up to levels comparable to the general public exposure limits (which are set by ICNIRP guidelines within the frequency range explored by the mobile phone radiocommunication networks in the range: 27–61 V/m and 0.06–0.16 A/m).

A similar problem of possible false indications also requires the immunity of ELF-EMF meters to influences from RF-EMF. Discussed unexpected behaviour of EMF measurement devices used in the environment near the sources of strong EMF exposure (such as HV power grids or RF broadcasting facilities) may significantly contribute into the uncertainty in assessments of exposure to EMF. This problem has got expected increased significance, because the number of RF-EMF sources near power lines is increasing along enlarging of radio communication systems, expected, for example, because of spreading new-generation radiocommunication networks (knows as 5G networks for example).

4.4.2 Characteristics of Exposure to EMF of Power Grids

The transmission and distribution EHV and HV power lines are carried out over the fields using standardised support structures (towers) that determine the level of EF under the line and in its vicinity near the ground, because it mainly depends on the distance of the phase conductors from the ground, while the level of the MF also depends on the current load on the conductors (which may vary even more than 100 times over time).

The maximum levels of EF and MF occur in the middle between the towers, at the highest phase wire overhang (e.g. at high temperatures in summer). Approaching the tower, phase wires go up and EMF levels decrease proportionally—up to several times comparing to the level in the middle between adjacent towers (CIGRE, 2020a). The EMF exposure level also depends on the geometric structure of phase wires (See the examples mentioned by Hansson Mild in other chapter.). EHV and HV power lines are designed and built to comply with the exposure limits given in relevant requirements concerning general public exposure (Recommendation 1999; ICNIRP, 1998, 2010; or relevant national legislation). Near the multi-track lines, the EMF is usually weaker than near the single-track lines.

The highest EF and MF levels can occur under a single-track HV line with the highest voltage (In a majority of European countries, this would be approximately 400 kV line, though higher voltages are used in special installations, such as, for example Poland–Ukraine connector, which had a voltage of 750 kV.). In Poland in such 'worst-case' locations, EF somewhere reaches up to 10 kV/m at a height of 2 m above the ground under a 400 kV lines, when under a 110 kV line reaches only up to 3 kV/m (Figure 4.3) (Gryz and Karpowicz, 2013a).

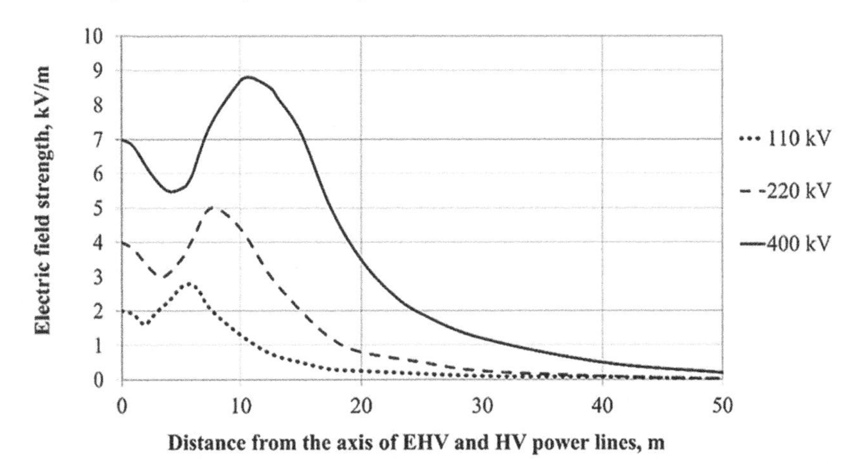

FIGURE 4.3 Typical spatial distribution of electric field strength below the HV and EHV power lines with a structure typically used in Poland and voltage of 110, 220, 400 kV, at height 2 m above the ground (Gryz and Karpowicz, 2013a). (Authors' collection)

In phase cables of 110 kV lines, the maximum current load are usually 500 A, and they are up to 1000 A in 400 kV lines. Under the wire, where the level of MF is the highest, under the 400 kV line somewhere MF reaches up to 10–30 μT, and under the 110 kV line, it is up to 5–10 μT (Szuba et al., 2016). About 30 m to the side of the wires of 400 kV lines, MF does not exceed 1–4 μT, when the maximum current lead appears (WHO, 2007); however, even at distances of up to a 100 m, MF can be found exceeding the level 0.4 μT—the earlier mentioned level of long-term (years lasting) average in time exposure, which was found to be possibly associated with adverse health effects of MF exposure (IARC, 2002). However, usually the current load is much lower than the mentioned maximum values for the current loads of particular lines, meaning that a better overview of average long-term MF exposure near the power lines can be obtained by using long-term (many hours, even daily lasting) MF monitoring by appropriate data logger or estimations based on calculations using the annual averages of cable currents.

In the cases of fault current, the MF near the power line also will be stronger and may exceed the mentioned values; but such short-term exposure has no significant contribution to the yearly averaged MF exposure level.

Problem of workers encountering much higher than the above-described exposure to EMF emitted by EHV and HV power lines concern specific cases of work tasks, while performing work under procedures known as 'live-line work'. During live-line work, the workers use personal protective equipment (a special suit, shoes, socks, gloves with metal threads) that shields them from EF (acting as a kind of Faraday cage) (CIGRE, 2020b). However, it needs attention that the shielding efficiency of ELF-MF by such personal protective equipment is negligible.

4.4.3 Characteristics of Exposure to EMF in Electrical Substations

Usually power equipment forms sources of strong EF and MF in outdoor switchyards. In indoor switchyards of LV and MV, there is weak EF and strong MF. EF is shielded by the metallic elements of substation construction. In modern indoor switchyards of HV, all live (energised) elements are insulated with SF_6 gas and enclosed in shielding metal structures. For this reason, the level of EF does not differ near such installations from the level present in a residential or office environment. Only significant MF is present there in the accessible area, especially in the vicinity of insulated HV cables or grounding installations of shielding structures, because metal shielding structures also prevent against the electric shock hazards and make close vicinity of HV elements accessible, what is prohibited in case of non-shielded (insulated by the air only) elements of the electric power grid at high or extremely high voltage.

The summary from the results of various studies, focussed on EMF in 400 and 110 kV electrical substations, showed that results of MF measurements do not exceeded 500 μT, that is, showed the MF levels lower than 1000 μT, given in the European Directive 2013/35/EU (2013) as the Low action level (Low AL) at 50 Hz. When considering the EF, the exposure of level up to 20 kV/m was found at switchyards, which exceeds the Low AL of 10 kV/m given in the mentioned directive. Both, MF and EF, the exposures are lower than the High ALs given in directive (1000 μT and 20 kV/m, respectively) (Table 4.1). As the example, the results of EMF

TABLE 4.3
Exposure to EMF in Outdoor 110, 220 and 400 kV Switchyards (106 Switchyards Managed by PSE S.A. in Poland)

	Exposure to EMF			
	Electric field strength, *E*, kV/m		Magnetic flux density, *B*, μT	
Switchyard Voltage	Median	Minimum–Maximum	Median	Minimum–Maximum
400 kV	16	12–20	24	4.4–395
220 kV	10	5.6–15	21	1.9–531
110 kV	7.4	4.0–14	42	11–244

Source: Derived from: Zajdler (2017).

measurements in 106 outdoor 110, 220 and 400 kV switchyards performed in 2018 and 2019 in places of workers' activities are summarised in Table 4.3.

Earlier investigations performed in 6, 15, 30, 110, 220 and 400 kV indoor and outdoor substations, in places where workers are present in the course of their routine activities (approx. 2000 locations of spot measurements), showed comparable measurement results to those given in Table 4.3 (Gryz and Karpowicz, 2001). In locations where the personnel spend usually the majority of their shift, MF did not exceed the value of 5–10 μT. The results of measurements in 6 kV substations showed that MF does not exceed 10 μT in 65% of locations. Only 1.3% of results exceeded 100 μT. In 15 kV substations, 68% of results were below 10 μT, and none exceeded 100 μT. In 30 kV substations, 85% of results were below 10 μT, and only 2% of results exceeded 100 μT. In 110 kV substations, 88% of results were below 10 μT, and only 1% of results exceeded 100 μT. In 220 kV substations, 79% of results were below 10 μT, and none of the results exceeded 100 μT. Finally, in 400 kV substations, 71% of the measurement results were up to 10 μT, and none of them exceeded 100 μT. An analysis of the entire obtained data showed that in (70%–90%) of locations where the spot measurements were taken, the magnetic flux density did not exceed 10 μT. Only 1% of all results exceeded 100 μT (Figure 4.4a) (Gryz and Karpowicz, 2001).

Near the investigated devices, in places accessible to workers, MF did not exceed 500 μT. Short lasting exposure to the highest MF in substations (at level: 200–300 μT) was found during patrols or maintenance of devices, when nearby devices are energised, and it may occur only near insulated single cables separated from others (Because the 3-phase bunch of cables produces MF decreased by the between-phase compensation phenomenon.). Relatively weak MF, despite a high current load, also occurs in the cable room, where usually the grouping of a larger number of three-phase cables running close to each other also means the efficient phenomenon of MF compensation coming from the currents flowing through individual cables.

We've also performed additional exposimetric studies on MF exposure, that is, a continuous over hours of work activities' measurements using pocket-sized MF data logger (i.e. recording of distribution of MF exposure over the working time and

(a)

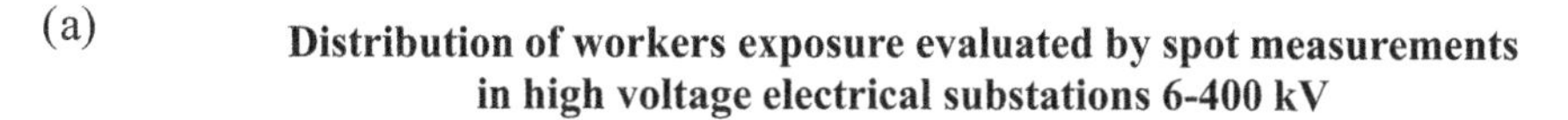

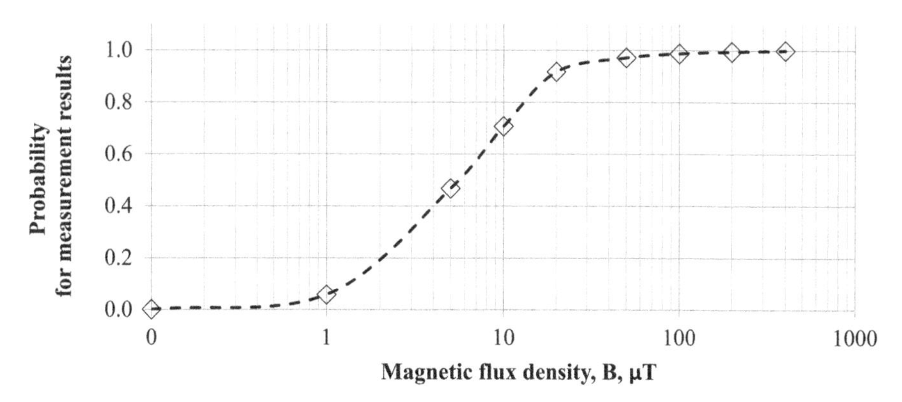

(b)

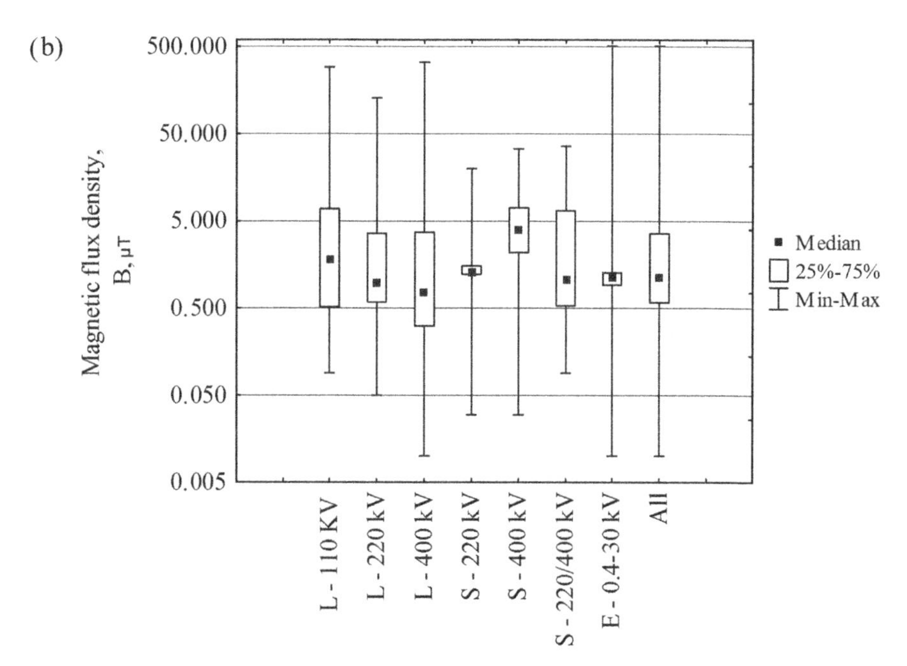

FIGURE 4.4 Magnetic field exposure in electrical substations: (a) results of spot measurements in approximately 2000 locations where workers are present in the course of routine activities in 6–400kV substations (*Derived from*: Gryz and Karpowicz, 2001); (b) results of exposimetric monitoring of exposure to MF during routine workers' activities in indoor 0.4–30kV and outdoor 220 and 400kV substations (L, laboratory staff; S, supervisory staff; and E, electricians, data logger EMDEX II carried by workers in the pocket on the chest or in the backpack). (Authors' collection)

along the working locations). These measurements were focussed on the MF affecting workers of different jobs in indoor 0.4–30 kV and outdoor 220 and 400 kV substations during routine activities carried out in the vicinity of power devices. From this study we've got confirmation for the conclusions discussed above, resulting from the study of MF spatial distribution by spot and exposimetric measurements; approximately 75% of the measurement results did not exceed approximately 10 μT, while the maximum level of MF reached 500 μT (Figure 4.4b).

Based on the presented data, it can be concluded that level of the workers' exposure goes to the level exceeding the EF Low AL set by the Directive 2013/35/EU at 50 Hz frequency, but tends to be lower than the High AL. This exposure occurs regardless of the voltage level at which the HV or EHV installation operates. Contrary, the levels of MF are well below both the relevant AL limits for workers' exposure. Exposimetric measurements suggest lower average MF exposure than obtained by analysis of spot measurements.

4.5 DISCUSSION

Electromagnetic influence on humans and other physical objects in the work environment can cause various types of safety and health hazards to workers, such as electric shocks or even burns, long-term adverse health effects, accidents and disturbance in the ability to work safely, and annoying unexpected perception of electric stimulation in exposed body (in some cases causing spontaneous reaction of workers, potentially hazardous to themselves of other personnel or devices) (Directive, 2013; IARC, 2002; IEEE 2019).

Levels of EMF affecting workers in the vicinity of power devices and associated hazards depend on:

- The operating electric voltage and current flowing in the current path (proportional relationship);
- The distance between workplaces and transmission conductors or live elements (inversely proportional relationship);
- The geometrical configuration of individual conductors of the power line or power equipment (complex relationship);
- The proportion of the current load of individual conductors of the power line or power equipment (Load symmetry reduces the level of MF in the vicinity of three-phase power objects by improving efficiency of compensation effects.).

The spatial distribution of the EF and workers' exposure in the vicinity of the working elements of the power system significantly depends on the size, distribution, location and electrical conductivity of the elements of the environment, such as transmission poles, trees and conductive structures located in the vicinity of lines (e.g. fences, building walls, etc.). The spatial distribution of the MF in the vicinity of power lines or power equipment, unlike the EF, is not subject to such spatial deformations.

If this is the case, the high exposure of workers needs to be reduced by applying relevant actions, such as improved work organisation by means for example, increased distances from energised infrastructure or electromagnetic shielding.

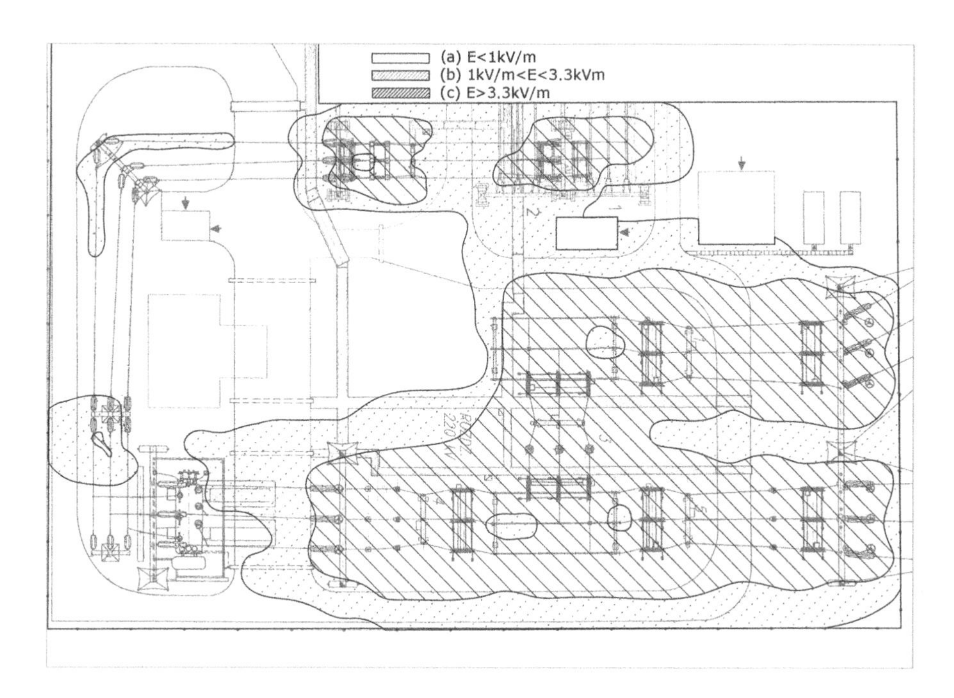

FIGURE 4.5 The spatial distribution of EF in an outdoor switchyard 110/220kV, as evaluated with respect to the labour law requirements. (Authors' collection)

The spatial distribution of EMF in outdoor switchyards has significant similarities between installations of similar technical structures—the strongest EMF may be found in small fraction of the switchyard area (Figure 4.5). Consequently, the level of workers' exposure to inhomogeneous EMF depends on where and how long they are performing activities in switchyards. Due to the potentially life-hazardous consequences of electric shock, work on the operation of electrical substations is carried out in accordance with relevant anti-shock safety procedures. The key element of such procedures is the spatial separation of worker from the high-voltage live conductors (as it was shown in Table 4.4), which also reduces the level of exposure to EMF. The example of such safety measures that aimed to decrease the risk of electric shock may be the use of physical barriers to prevent workers' access to the places where a strong EMF was found. An example of such exclusions from the working space are 110kV switchgears in indoor switchyard (Figure 4.1f) or the restriction of access to the 15/0.4kV transformer chamber (Figure 4.1g).

The practical consequence of mentioned anti-shock safety principles implemented in the work activities near high-voltage electric power installations is the significant reduction of the level, as well as the duration, of the strong EMF exposure of workers performing various activities there. The only exception when the EMF exposure may be strong, as well as long-lasting during the shift, may be the case when performing earlier mentioned procedures known as 'live-line work'—executed in some countries but usually by a small number of highly specialised work teams.

TABLE 4.4
Examples of the Minimum Safety Distances in the Air (with respect to Ergonomic Separation) for the Working Zones Near Electric Power Installations

Voltage Applied to the Installation	Minimum Distance of the Working Zone to the Energised Elements of Electrical Installations (in the Air)	
	Under Potential	Near Potential
kV	m	m
≤1	No touching	0.3
6	0.1	1.1
30	0.3	1.3
110	1.0	2.0
400	2.5	4.0
750	5.3	8.4

Source: Derived from: Zajdler (2017).

4.6 CONCLUSIONS

Evaluation of electromagnetic exposure during workers' activities belongs to research priority triggered by European Directive 2013/35/EU, which requires protection of workers against electromagnetic hazards or 2B carcinogenic classification issued by IARC with respect to EMF environmental exposures. High-quality study in that field is not achievable without sufficient application of relevant methods of evaluation of EMF exposure in the populations involved. Attention to EMF exposure of workers near high-voltage installations (such as electrical substations at potential exceeding 100 kV) belongs to key issues in that research field. We've analysed their EMF exposure using various measurement methods:

- Spot measurements of spatial distribution of EF strength and magnetic flux density in thousands of locations
- Monitoring of time variability of MF exposure by pocket-sized data loggers carried by workers during various tasks.

The results of studies performed in 110–400 kV substations in Poland showed:

- Over 10 times variability in EMF exposure during performing particular tasks
- The maximum level of exposure exceeding 10 kV/m and 100 μT, but significantly lower time-averaged level of exposure (1–20 μT in various subgroups)
- The possibility of significant over- or underestimation of EMF exposure level when only the type of workplace and 'job title' classification is considered.

The analysed results of MF monitoring by pocket-sized data loggers are compliant with the results of spot measurements in substations with respect to the range of exposure of workers, but the time-averaged level of workers' exposure estimated based on the results of spot measurements seems to be overestimated comparing to the exposure level during the real work practice (as recorded by pocket-sized data logger).

ACKNOWLEDGEMENTS

This paper has been based on the results of the National Programme 'Improvement of Safety and Working Conditions' partly supported in Poland by National Centre for Research and Development (within the scope of research and development), and by the ministry for labour issues (within the scope of state services), (research tasks: II.B.15, 1.G.12 and 2.SP.10). The CIOP-PIB is the programme's main co-ordinator. It is also based on the results of evaluation of electromagnetic field carried out within the system of managing hazards in working environment by Polskie Sieci Elektroenergetyczne S.A.—transmission system operator (PSE S.A.), Poland.

REFERENCES

ACGIH [American Conference of Governmental Industrial Hygienist]. 2022. *Threshold Limit Values for Chemical Substances and Physical Agents. Biological Exposure Indices.* Cincinnati: ACGIH.

Ahlbom, A., N. Day, M. Feychting et al. 2000. A pooled analysis of magnetic fields and childhood leukaemia. *Br J Cancer* 83(5):692–698. DOI: 10.1054/bjoc.2000.1376.

CIGRÉ [Conseil International des Grands Reseaux Electriques]. 1980. Electric and magnetic fields produced by transmission systems. description of phenomena and practical guide for calculation. *International Conference on Large High Voltage Electric Systems.* Paris: CIGRÉ.

CIGRÉ [Conseil International des Grands Reseaux Electriques]. 2020a. *C4 Power System Technical Performance. Extrapolation of Measured Values of Power-Frequency Magnetic Field in the Vicinity of Power Links*, Reference 795. Paris: CIGRÉ.

CIGRÉ [Conseil International des Grands Reseaux Electriques]. 2020b. *C3 Power System Environmental Performance. Responsible Management of Electric and Magnetic Field (EMF)*, Reference 806. Paris: CIGRÉ.

Council of the European Union. 1999. *Council Recommendation of 12 July 1999 on the Limitation of Exposure of the General Public to Electromagnetic Fields (0Hz to 300GHz) - (1999/519/EC). O.J.* No. L-199/59 of 30 July 1999, Brussels, Belgium. https://eur-lex.europa.eu/LexUriServ/LexUriServ.do?uri=OJ:L:1999:199:0059:0070:EN:PDF (accessed February 3, 2020).

Directive 2013/35/EU. 2013. Directive of the European Parliament and of the Council of 26 June 2013 on the Minimum Health And Safety Requirements Regarding The Exposure Of Workers To The Risks Arising From Physical Agents (Electromagnetic Fields) (20th Individual Directive within the Meaning of Article 16(1) of Directive 89/391/EEC). *Official Journal of the European Union* O.J. No. L-179 of 29 June 2013, 1–21, Brussels, Belgium.

EAHC [Executive Agency for Health and Consumers]. 2010. *Report 2010. Promoting Healthy Environments with a Focus on the Impact of Action on Electromagnetic Fields.* Paris: EAHC.

Greenland, S., A.R. Sheppard, W.T. Kaune, C. Poole, and M.A. Kelsh. 2000. A pooled analysis of magnetic fields, wire codes, and childhood leukemia. Childhood leukemia - EMF study group. *Epidemiology* 11(6):624–634. DOI: 10.1097/00001648–200011000–00003.

Gryz, K., and J. Karpowicz. 2001. Occupational to magnetic fields in 6–400 kV substations. In: *Proceedings of the Ebea 2001: 5th International Congress of the European Bioelectromagnetics Association (Ebea): 6–8 September 2001, Marina Congress Center*, eds: M. Hietanen, K. Jokela, and J. Juutilainen. Helsinki: FIOH [Finish Institute of Occupational Health], 2 pages.

Gryz, K., and J. Karpowicz. 2013a. Pole elektryczne i magnetyczne sieci elektroenergetycznych wysokiego napięcie. In: *Środowiskowe zagrożenia zawodowe przy obsłudze sieci elektroenergetycznych – profilaktyka*, eds: J. Karpowicz, and J. Bugajska, 149–182. Warszawa: CIOP [Central Institute for Labour Protection]. (In Polish).

Gryz, K., and J. Karpowicz. 2013b. The role of out-band sensitivity of measurement devices in the assessment of exposure to radiofrequency electromagnetic fields near high voltage power lines. *Bezpieczeństwo Pracy: Nauka i Praktyka* 9(504):6–8. (In Polish).

Hug, K., M. Röösli, and R. Rapp. 2006. Magnetic field exposure and neurodegenerative diseases--recent epidemiological studies. *Soz Praventivmed* 51(4):210–220. DOI: 10.1007/s00038-006-5096-4.

Huss, A., A. Spoerri, M. Egger, and M. Röösli. 2009. Residence near power lines and mortality from neurodegenerative diseases: longitudinal study of the Swiss population. *Am J Epidemiol* 169(2):167–175. DOI: 10.1093/aje/kwn297.

IARC [International Agency for Research on Cancer]. 2002. *IARC Monographs on the Evaluation of Carcinogenic Risks to Humans. Volume 80. Non-Ionizing Radiation, Part 1: Static and Extremely Low-Frequency (ELF) Electric and Magnetic Fields.* Lyon: IARC Press. https://publications.iarc.fr/Book-And-Report-Series/Iarc-Monographs-On-The-Identification-Of-Carcinogenic-Hazards-To-Humans/Non-ionizing-Radiation-Part-1-Static-And-Extremely-Low-frequency-ELF-Electric-And-Magnetic-Fields-2002 (accessed February 3, 2020).

ICNIRP [International Commission on Non-Ionizing Radiation Protection]. 1998. Guidelines for limiting exposure to time-varying electric, magnetic, and electromagnetic fields (up to 300 GHz). *Health Phys* 74(4):494–522.

ICNIRP [International Commission on Non-Ionizing Radiation Protection]. 2010. Guidelines for limiting exposure to time-varying electric and magnetic fields (1 Hz – 100 kHz). *Health Phys* 99(6):818–836. DOI: 10.1097/HP.0b013e3181f06c86.

ICNIRP [International Commission on Non-Ionizing Radiation Protection]. 2020. Guidelines for limiting exposure to electromagnetic fields (100 kHz to 300 GHz). *Health Phys* 118(5):483–524. DOI: 10.1097/HP.0000000000001210.

IEC 61786-2:2014. 2014. *Measurement of DC Magnetic, AC Magnetic and AC Electric Fields from 1 Hz to 100 kHz with Regard to Exposure of Human Beings - Part 2: Basic Standard for Measurements.* Geneva: IEC [International Electrotechnical Commission].

IEEE C95.1–2019. 2019. *IEEE Standard for Safety Levels with Respect to Human Exposure to Electric, Magnetic, and Electromagnetic Fields, 0 Hz to 300 GHz.* New York: IEEE [Institute of Electrical and Electronics Engineers].

Karpowicz, J., and J. Bugajska. 2013a. *Środowiskowe zagrożenia zawodowe przy obsłudze sieci elektroenergetycznych – profilaktyka.* Warszawa: CIOP-PIB [Central Institute for Labour Protection – National Research Institute]. (In Polish).

Karpowicz, J., K. Gryz, and W. Leszko. 2013b. The sensitivity of radiofrequency electric and magnetic field meters to the ambient electric field of power frequency. *Joint Meeting of the Bioelectromagnetics Society and the European BioElectromagnetics Association BioEM2013*, Thessaloniki, Greece, 2013.06.10–14, Abstract Collection - Complete Collection, 436–438.

Karpowicz, J., P. Bieńkowski, and J. Kieliszek. 2016. Model of the minimum requirements regarding electric and magnetic field strength measurement devices for use in the near-field occupational exposure in compliance testing with respect to the requirements of European Directive 2013/35/EU. In: *Proceedings 2016 International Symposium on*

Electromagnetic Compatibility - EMC EUROPE, Wrocław, Poland, 5–9 September 2016. 668–671. Danver: IEEE [Institute of Electrical and Electronics Engineers]. DOI: 10.1109/EMCEurope.2016.7739277.

Marzecki, J. 2013. Struktura sieci elektroenergetycznych wysokiego napięcia w Polsce. In: *Środowiskowe zagrożenia zawodowe przy obsłudze sieci elektroenergetycznych – profilaktyka*, eds: J. Karpowicz, and J. Bugajska, 11–44. Warszawa: CIOP [Central Institute for Labour Protection]. (In Polish).

PSE [Polskie Sieci Elektroenergetyczne]. 2020. Information about the power system, PSE, https://www.pse.pl/home.

SCENIHR (Scientific Committee on Emerging and Newly Identified Health Risks). 2009. Health effects of exposure to electromagnetic fields, The SCENIHR adopted this opinion at the 28th plenary on 19 January 2009.

SCENIHR (Scientific Committee on Emerging and Newly Identified Health Risks), (2015) Opinion on potential health effects of exposure to electromagnetic fields, SCENIHR adopted this Opinion at the 9th plenary meeting on 27 January 2015.

Schüz J., and A. Ahlbom 2008. Exposure to electromagnetic fields and the risk of childhood leukaemia: a review. *Radiation Prot Dosimetry* 132:202–211.

Stamm R. 2011. *Comparison of International Policies on Electromagnetic Fields (Power Frequency and Radiofrequency Fields)*. Bilthoven, Netherlands: National Institute for Public and the Environment. RIVM 118/2011 LSO Sta (13 pages). Available from: http://ec.europa.eu/health/electromagnetic_fields/docs/emf_comparision_policies_en.pdf.

Szuba M., I. Hasiec, P. Papliński, H. Śmietanka, K. Zajdler, M. Zmyślony, J. Karpowicz, and K. Gryz. 2016. Narażenie na pole elektromagnetyczne w przestrzeni pracy podczas użytkowania systemów elektroenergetycznych i elektrycznych instalacji zasilających prądu przemiennego w energetyce. *Podstawy i Metody Oceny Środowiska Pracy* 4(90):91–150. DOI: 10.5604/1231868X.1229515 (in Polish).

WHO (World Health Organization). 2007. *Environmental Health Criteria 238, Extremely Low Frequency Fields (ELF)*, Geneve. Available from: http://www.who.int/peh-emf/publications/elf_ehc/en/index.html.

Zajdler K. 2017. Protection of employees against exposure to 50 Hz electromagnetic fields, *Elektroenergetyka* 2(17):32–37 (In Polish).

Zradziński P., J. Karpowicz, K. Gryz, and W. Leszko. 2018. Evaluation of the safety of users of active implantable medical devices (AIMD) in the working environment in terms of exposure to electromagnetic fields – Practical approach to the requirements of European Directive 2013/35/EU. *International Journal of Occupational Medicine and Environmental Health*, 31(6): 795–808. DOI: 10.13075/ijomeh.1896.0783.

5 Long-Term Evaluation (2010–2018) of General Public and Occupational Electromagnetic Field Exposure in Radiocommunication Antenna Parks across Greece

Maria Christopoulou, Dimitris Koutounidis, Theodora Kyritsi, and Efthymios Karabetsos
Greek Atomic Energy Commission (EEAE)

CONTENTS

DOI: 10.1201/9781003020486-5

5.1 INTRODUCTION

World Health Organization (WHO) classifies the assessment of radiofrequency (RF) electromagnetic field (EMF) exposure levels as a research field of priority, due to the emerging and continuously evolving technologies (WHO, 2010). International literature abounds in publications that present the EMF exposure levels, assessing the large in-situ measurements data: (1) comparing urban, suburban and rural environments (Christopoulou and Karabetsos, 2015), (2) in schools, children playgrounds and parks (e.g. Christopoulou and Karabetsos, 2019; Birks et al., 2018; Struchen et al., 2016; Verloock et al., 2014a, b; Vermeeren et al., 2013) and (3) inside trains/metro and shopping malls (e.g. Gryz and Karpowicz, 2015, 2019; Sagar et al., 2018). Concerning the EMF exposure levels assessment in antenna park environments, international literature lacks in systematic presentation, and it is considered quite scarce, mainly due to the following reasons: (1) at the international level the antenna park areas are usually enclosed by protective fences and appropriate warning signage in well-defined regions, and they are not, by definition, accessible to the general public; (2) a group of radiating antennas is usually mounted onto a single high mast, and its position is accurately defined. Its position is redesigned only after a thorough and overall consideration of the EMF levels of the antenna park environment. Concerning the frequency composition of the exposure levels in antenna park environments, it should be noted that from the international perspective it is mainly composed of emissions by radio, television, mobile communications broadcasting antennas and radars, using similar frequency bands worldwide defined by International Telecommunication Union - ITU (ITU, 2020).

In Greece, the antenna park delimitation is governed by more relaxed considerations. An 'antenna park' is defined as a space on hills/mountains, away from urban and suburban environments, where there is a large number and density of active radio, television and mobile communications broadcasting antennas, radars, etc. The frequency bands allocated for frequency modulation (FM) radio and UHF TV (Ultra-High-Frequency television) services overwhelmingly determine the exposure levels in antenna parks and on building rooftops in municipalities close to where the main broadcast sites/antenna parks are located (Christopoulou and Karabetsos, 2015). In Greece, the antenna parks are not generally delimited by fences, and they are usually fully accessible by the general public. Additionally, the number and location of the antennas' supporting masts, the relative height where the antennas have been installed, and the number of the emitting antenna providers are not always clearly defined/declared; and they are being modified with relative ease, without informing the competent national authorities. Figure 5.1 illustrates characteristic views of antenna parks in Greece that correspond to (1) the largest one located in Athens (Mount Hymettus) and (2) the one in Corfu island (Mount Pantokratoras), where the road that leads to the nearby monastery almost crosses the antenna park area. More specifically, Figure 5.1b illustrates the antenna park view taken from the gate of the nearby monastery, surprisingly showing that the road that leads to the antenna parks serves as the parking area of the monastery and its shop. Due to the above-mentioned reasons, the constant and periodic inspections of the EMF exposure levels in antenna park environments, through in-situ measurements, is considered to be imperative, in

FIGURE 5.1 Characteristic view of antenna parks in Greece: (a) The largest one located in Athens (Mount Hymettus) and (b) The one in Corfu island (Mount Pantokratoras), where the road that leads to the nearby monastery almost crosses the antenna park area. (Authors' collection)

order to reassure compliance with the Reference Levels for both workers and general public exposure.

Concerning the recorded occupational EMF exposure in Greece, based on the published results (Gourzoulidis et al., 2018), a number of interesting issues were revealed, and they are indicatively summarized: (1) the exposure levels in the majority of the cases are essentially the same as the typical ones for general public exposure scenarios, and (2) there is a need to perform reliable measurements, as 'hot-spots' do exist at particular installations. According to the authors' knowledge, only one study has been published (Sahalos et al., 1995), and its scope was to present the extensive set of measurements for the purpose of mapping of the electromagnetic exposure in the vicinity of an antenna park. The present study is the first long-term presentation of the in-situ measurement data in antenna parks in Greece, during the period 2010–2018. The broadband and frequency selective in-situ audits of the RF-EMF exposure levels have been conducted by Greek Atomic Energy Commission (EEAE) personnel and other authorized accredited teams. According to Greek legislation, EEAE or other authorized laboratories/companies are monitoring EMF exposure levels by performing in-situ measurements, ex officio or within 20 working days after request of any interested party. The authorized teams are selected as the bidders of international calls for tenders according to the legislative rules, by the relevant EEAE evaluation committees. Based on these rules, EEAE as well as the authorized teams should be accredited according to the requirements of the EN ISO/IEC 17025 standard (ISO/IEC 17025, 2017). Furthermore, a detailed contract with a MoA (Memorandum of Agreement) also ensures the impartiality of the selected teams and the fact that they have no conflict of interest related to any business or other type of relations with the telecommunication service providers. The preliminary analysis of the in-situ measurement data, including the description of the active radio, TV and mobile telecommunications providers installed in the antenna park environment, the description of the measurement points, the data post processing and their comparison to the general public Reference Levels, as they are defined by the Greek legislation, are announced officially in the EEAE website (https://eeae.gr/en/), and they are freely accessible to all users (EEAE, 2020).

5.2 REFERENCE LEVELS

In 1999, the European Council issued the non-obligatory for Member States Recommendation 1999/519/EC (European Council, 1999) adopting International Commission on Non-Ionizing Radiation Protection (ICNIRP) Reference Levels and Basic Restrictions (ICNIRP, 1998) defining the limitation of exposure of the general public to EMF (from 0 Hz to 300 GHz). Here, it should be noted that it is a prerogative of each member state to apply lower reference limits compared to the European Council recommendation. Due to high density and emitted power of FM radio broadcasting installations operating in antenna parks, the European Council recommended Reference Levels (EC-RL) for general public exposure to time-varying electric and magnetic fields (unperturbed rms values) are indicatively presented for the frequency range 10–400 MHz: electric field strength (E) as 28 V/m and magnetic flux density (B) as 0.092 μT.

Based on the Recommendation 1999/519/EC, Greece has put into force two national legislative acts concerning the protection of general public concerning its exposure to EMF emitted by all kinds of land-based antenna stations providing telecommunication services (Act No.1105, 2000), (Law No 4635, 2019). The established Greek safety limits for general public exposure to EMF correspond to 70% of the 1999/519/EC Recommendation Basic Restrictions and Reference Levels values and to 60% of them for stations located closer than 300 m from the perimeter of schools, kindergartens, hospitals or eldercare facilities, thus introducing an additional safety factor. Therefore, it should be underlined that, according to legislation, Greece is one of the countries that have adopted the strictest reference limits across Europe. In Greece, antenna parks are located in rural environments, at distances larger than 300 m from the perimeter of schools, kindergartens, hospitals or eldercare facilities, as mentioned in Greek legislation. Therefore, within this study, the reference limits applied in Greece (GR-RL) correspond to the 70% of the EC-RL. More specifically, for the frequency range 10–400 MHz, the respective GR-RL for EF reaches 23.4 V/m. Table 5.1 summarizes the EF GR-RL compared to EC-RL ones calculated at indicative frequency values.

The assessment of the minimum health and safety requirements concerning occupational exposure to EMF is based on the European Parliament and Council Directive 2013/35/EU (Directive 2013/35/EU). Additionally, useful relevant information has been provided by the non-binding practical guides that accompanied the Directive (European Commission, 2015). The physical quantities, ELVs (Exposure Limit Values: to protect against thermal RF exposure effects) and ALs (Action Levels: to ensure by simplified assessment the compliance with the relevant ELVs) were laid down in this Directive. The 'real' ELVs correspond to the fields inside the human body, which cannot be directly measured, and compliance with them is ensured through the ALs. ALs have been derived from the ELVs through theoretical modelling. For the frequency range of 10–400 MHz, which is usually dominant in

TABLE 5.1
EF Values of the Greek Reference Limits (GR-RL) Compared to the Respective Ones Based on European Reference Levels (EC-RL), Calculated at Indicative Frequency Values

	EC-RL	GR-RL[a]	GR-RL(low)[b]
Frequency (MHz)	*E* (V/m)	*E* (V/m)	*E* (V/m)
10–400	28.00	23.43	21.69
460	29.49	24.67	22.84
600	33.68	28.18	26.09
800	38.89	32.54	30.12
876	40.70	34.05	31.52
900	41.25	34.51	31.95
1,710	56.86	47.57	44.04
1,800	58.34	48.81	45.19
1,905	60.01	50.21	46.49
2,000–300,000	61.00	51.04	47.25

[a] GR-RL: EMF limits set to be 70% of EC-RL applicable in the general environment.
[b] GR-RL(low): EMF limits set to be 60% of EC-RL applicable in environments where the radiating antennas are located closer than 300 m from the perimeter of schools, kindergartens, hospitals or eldercare facilities, thus introducing an additional safety factor.

antenna park environments, ALs coincide to ICNIRP reference levels for occupational exposure, that is, the AL for EF is 61 V/m, and the corresponding value for B field is 0.2 μT. It should be noted that broadcasting systems and devices (radio and TV: LF, low frequency; MF, medium frequency; HF, high frequency; VHF, very high frequency and UHF, ultra-high frequency) are explicitly stated as types of workplace or equipment where specific EMF assessment is required for all workers—workers not at particular risk, workers at particular risk (excluding those with active implants) and workers at particular risk because of the use of active implants (European Commission, 2015).

The European standard EN 50499 (EN 50499, 2019), developed for the Directive 2004/40/EC that was repealed by the 2013/35/EU, introduces the occupational EMF exposure zoning system approach (zones 0, 1 and 2), mainly as an administrative procedure, as it is the employer who shall define the workplace's zone area and the application of any corrective actions, according to the workplace's characteristics. Moreover, the employer has the right to limit the access of visitors to certain zones only if appropriate information about EMFs has been given (exposure levels, protection measures, etc.). More specifically, the exposure levels in zone 0 correspond to exposures that do not require actions different than those regarding the safety of workers with implants and during work practices involving contact currents, since compliance with the general public exposure limits exists and the available equipment is regulated by other legislation limiting emission to within permissible levels (i.e. screens, personal computers, Wi-Fi, etc.). In zone 1, the general public EC-RL may be exceeded, but not the occupational ALs. Finally in zone 2, the occupational limits may be exceeded, meaning that if this zone is accessible, corrective actions to reduce exposure or access limitation should be applied. In Gourzoulidis et al. (2019), a new flowchart system is proposed, concerning the occupational EMF exposure assessment survey in Greece, and it has proven to be a very useful tool. For RF fields, the zone 3 is introduced, in which the ALs and the ELVs are exceeded, demanding corrective Occupational Health and Safety (OHS) actions, such as clear boundaries, determination and access permission only to specialized personnel for specific time duration, for example, according to the maintenance needs of the installed equipment. Maintenance procedures have been identified during the occupational EMF exposure assessment to be of core importance. Even if the zoning approach is a valuable tool in order to control the occupational exposure and is already used for military installations (IEEE C95.1-2345, 2014), in Greece there is currently no related legislation. Figure 5.2 illustrates the zoning procedure flowchart that is proposed during RF-EMF occupational exposure assessment, based on Gourzoulidis et al. (2019).

In order to quantify the exposure for frequencies above 10 MHz, the exposure ratio λ is defined and is calculated as the ratio of the squared value of the electric field strength, E (V/m), to the corresponding squared exposure limit L_E:

$$\lambda = \frac{E^2}{{L_E}^2} \tag{5.1}$$

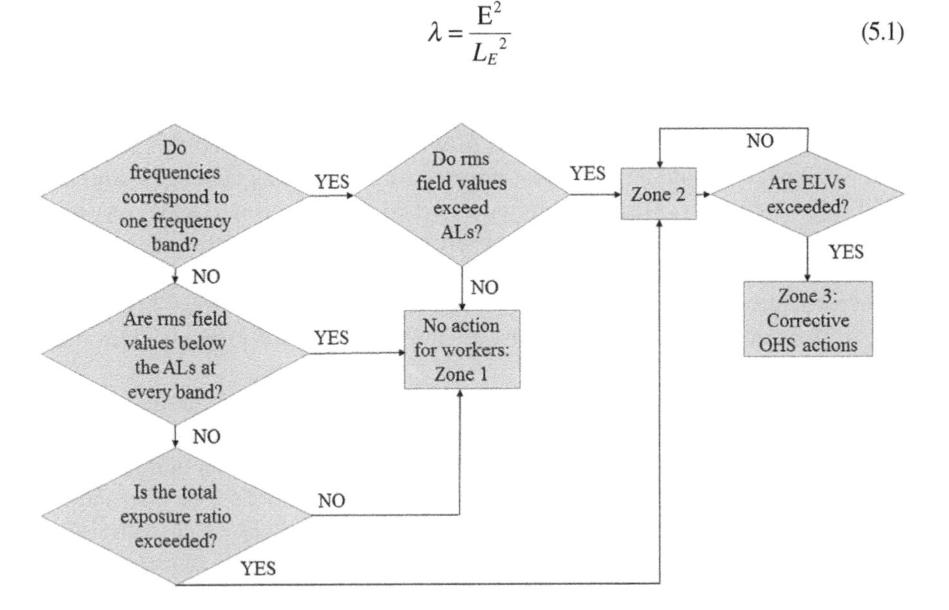

FIGURE 5.2 Modified (Gourzoulidis et al. 2019) flowchart of the high-frequency EMF measurements' evaluation, describing the zoning procedure for occupational EMF exposure, with respect to the need of applying corrective Occupational Health and Safety (OHS) actions. AL and ELV stand for Action Levels and Exposure Limit Values, respectively, concerning the characterization of occupational exposure. (Authors' collection)

5.3 MEASURING EQUIPMENT

For the frequency selective measurements, the SRM basic units (Narda Safety Test Solutions, Pfullingen, Germany) operating at frequency ranges from 100 kHz to 3 GHz (SRM-3000) and 9 kHz to 6 GHz (SRM-3006) are used. For each unit, a tri-axial (isotropic) EF antenna (Narda Safety Test Solutions, Pfullingen, Germany) is used (frequency range: from 27 MHz to 3 GHz; dynamic range: 0.2 mV/m to 200 V/m for SRM-3000, frequency range: from 420 MHz to 6 GHz or from 27 MHz to 3 GHz; dynamic range: from 0.14 mV/m to 160 V/m or from 0.2 mV/m to 200 V/m, respectively, for SRM-3006). In most cases, the expanded measurement uncertainty for the EF is calculated around ±2.5 dB (confidence level 95%). An RF extension cable (1.5 m long) can also be used, which is attached between the base unit and the antenna. A special tripod is used on which the measuring antenna is mounted and is appropriately labelled to position the antenna at selected heights.

5.4 MEASUREMENT METHODOLOGY

A survey is initially performed at each site under consideration using handheld broadband EF meter (e.g. Narda EMR-300) to identify the location or locations of spot maximum values. The selected measurement points correspond to the ones of higher exposure. The operator handles the basic unit of the SRM 3000 or SRM 3006, and the tri-axial EF antenna is attached at the top of a non-conductive extension onto a tripod at three successive heights: 170, 150 and 110 cm, in order to average over a typical human head and torso. For each height i ($i = 1, 2, 3$) and frequency band f that corresponds to a selected telecommunication service, the exposure ratio $\lambda_{i,f}$ is acquired, according to equation (5.1). The ratio $\lambda_{i,f}$ is the assessed exposure parameter at the specified height i, for each operating frequency f of the RF source, expressed as the fraction of the related limit value. The exposure ratio λ_f in the frequency band f, based on the measurements over the three successive heights of the point, is calculated as the mean value of the $\lambda_{i,f}$, as:

$$\lambda_f = \frac{1}{3}\sum_{i=1}^{3} \lambda_{i,f} \tag{5.2}$$

In order to calculate and weight the exposure in an environment with multiple EMF sources operating at various narrow frequency ranges, such as in an antenna park, the total exposure ratio Λ is used. The total exposure ratio Λ for the given point is calculated as the sum of the exposure ratios λ_f in each frequency band f (ICNIRP, 1998):

$$\Lambda = \sum_{f} \lambda_f \tag{5.3}$$

The value of Λ equal to 1 corresponds to 100% of the EC-RL. At each height, the maximum value for the EF, averaged over 6 minutes, is stored. The mean value of the EF over the three heights corresponds to the EF point value. For the higher exposure

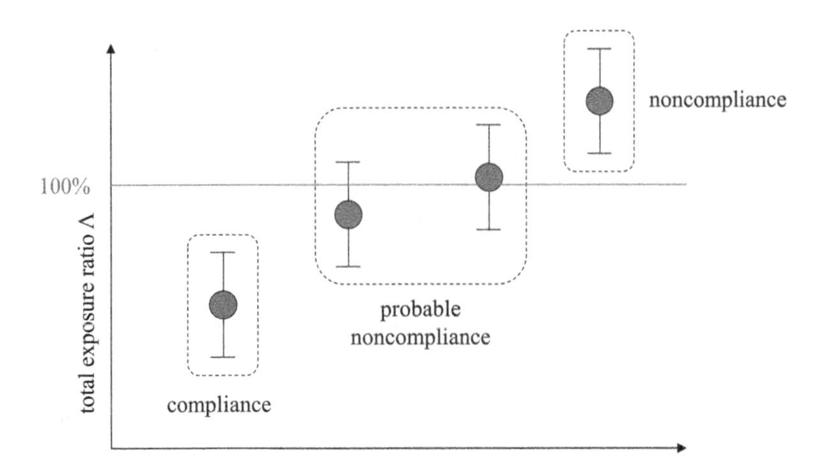

FIGURE 5.3 Illustration of compliance, probable non-compliance and non-compliance EMF exposure cases, taking into account the expanded measurement uncertainty of the total exposure ratio Λ. (Authors' collection)

point, the exposure ratio is calculated for each frequency band as well as the percentage contribution of each telecommunication service to the total exposure.

The expanded measurement uncertainty of the total exposure ratio U(Λ) is estimated, taking into account all types of uncertainty sources (measurement device, calibration, isotropy, linearity, influence of temperature and humidity on the measurement equipment, influence of the body of person performing measurements, perturbation by the environment, spatial averaging, etc.) and reaching even 50% in antenna park environments. The final outcome of the measurement is the 95% confidence interval ($\Lambda_{2.5\%} = \Lambda - U(\Lambda)$, $\Lambda_{97.5\%} = \Lambda + U(\Lambda)$). The comparison of this interval's limits to the maximum value of Λ (that is 1 or 100%) determines whether the exposure limits are not exceeded ($\Lambda_{97.5\%} < 100\%$), are probably exceeded ($\Lambda_{2.5\%} < 100\%$ and $\Lambda_{97.5\%} > 100\%$) or are exceeded ($\Lambda_{2.5\%} > 100\%$). Characteristic cases of compliance, probable non-compliance and non-compliance cases are illustrated in Figure 5.3.

The directly measured quantity is the EF from which the ratios of exposure to the pre-defined frequency bands are calculated, as well as the overall exposure ratio across the operating frequency range of the antenna probe is used (from 27 MHz to 3 GHz or from 420 MHz to 6 GHz). The pre-defined frequency bands have been introduced into the basic units (SRM 3000 and SRM 3006) and are called 'service tables'. In Tables 5.2 and 5.3, the applied frequency ranges with the corresponding telecommunication services operating in each range are presented. Depending on the used antenna probe, each service table summarizes the frequency ranges for which the measurements data are saved by each instrument (SRM 3000 or SRM 3006). Last but not the least, it should be mentioned that taking into account the characteristics of the dominant signals of each telecommunication service, the appropriate measurement settings for resolution bandwidth (RBW), video bandwidth (VBW), sweep time, etc. have been applied according to the settings proposed in the standards (EN IEC 62232, 2022 and ECC/REC/(02)04, 2007), at each frequency band.

TABLE 5.2
Frequency Ranges Commonly Used for Analyzing the Measured Field per Service Using the Isotropic EF Antenna Operating in from 27 MHz to 3 GHz

Frequency Range (MHz)		
From	To	Telecommunication Services
87.5	108	Radio broadcasting FM
110	272	VHF emissions TV
370	430	Private network intercommunications and TETRA system
460	875	Digital TV broadcasting (DVB-T in UHF band) and mobile phone base stations (LTE)
876	960	Mobile phone base stations (GSM, GSM-R & UMTS)
1,710	1,880	Mobile phone base stations (DCS & LTE)
1,905	2,160	Mobile phone base stations (UMTS)
2,160	3,000	Wi-Fi (802.11b), microwave antennas, radars

TABLE 5.3
Frequency Ranges Commonly Used for Analyzing the Measured Field per Service Using the Isotropic EF Antenna Operating in from 420 MHz to 6 GHz

Frequency Range (MHz)		
From	To	Telecommunication Services
420	430	TETRA system
460	875	Digital TV broadcasting (DVB-T in UHF band) and mobile phone base stations (LTE)
876	960	Mobile phone base stations (GSM, GSM-R & UMTS)
1,710	1,880	Mobile phone base stations (DCS & LTE)
1,905	2,160	Mobile phone base stations (UMTS)
2,400	2,497	Wi-Fi (802.11b)
3,410	3,600	Wi-Max (802.16)
5,150	5,875	Wi-Fi (802.11a), satellite communications
5,875	6,000	Microwave antennas, radars, satellite communications

The whole measurement methodology is based on the following standards (EN IEC 62232, 2022; ECC/REC/(02)04, 2007; EN 50420, 2006; EN 50413, 2019; and ITU-T K.91, 2022).

5.5 MEASUREMENT DATA

Measurement data are derived from 173 in-situ broadband and frequency selective audits in the environment of 57 antenna parks in order to check compliance to European EMF limits for general public (EC-RL) and occupational (AL) exposure.

Each audit in every antenna park environment includes in-situ measurements evaluating at least five (5) points of interest (that correspond to the highest exposure levels), and the total dataset includes more than 865 (5 × 173) points in antenna park environments, given the large number and high density of active broadcasting antennas. The measurement data are analyzed based on parameters that include: (1) the year (2010–2018), (2) the frequency bands of selected common telecommunication services (FM, VHF, TETRA-TErrestrial Trunked RAdio, UHF TV, GSM-Global System for Mobile Communications 900, DCS-Digital Cellular System 1800, UMTS-Universal Mobile Telecommunications System, Wi-Fi/radar) and (3) the percentage of antenna parks where there is compliance with the legislated limits of EMF exposure. During each audit, apart from the coordinates and time information, EF and total exposure ratio Λ are evaluated. Within this study, the point of the highest exposure is presented for each audit, resulting in a total of 173 measurements, corresponding to the highest exposure points in all audits. It is worth mentioning that of all 57 antenna parks, 11 parks (19%) have been inspected only once during the years 2010–2018, while the rest 46 (81%) more than once (from 2 to 7 times).

5.6 RESULTS AND DISCUSSION

5.6.1 Year and Frequency Analysis

In all the measurements, mean values of the EF and total exposure ratio Λ are calculated as: $E = 18.74$ (standard deviation σ: 11.05), V/m and $\Lambda = 0.63$ (σ: 0.73), respectively. Figure 5.4 summarizes the measured EF (V/m) values for the period of 2010–2018 by plotting the number of measurements that corresponds to pre-selected EF ranges, together with the percentage (%) cumulative distribution of the measured EF values in the pre-selected ranges: 0–5, 5–10, 10–15, 15–20, 20–25, 25–30 and

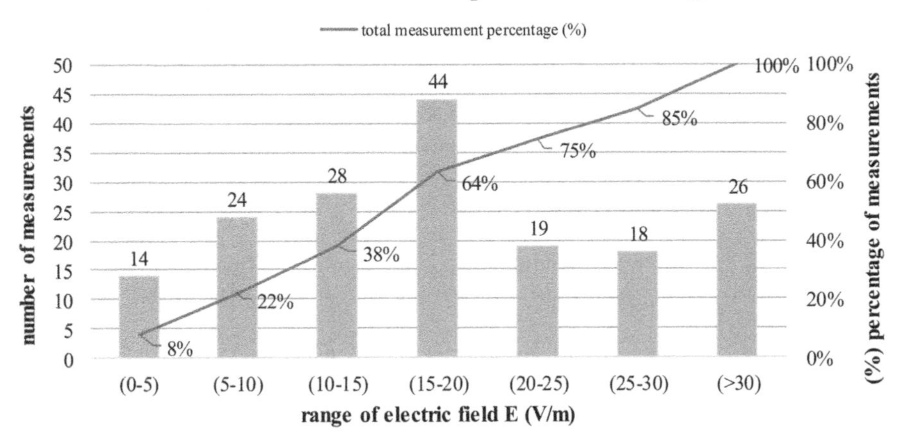

FIGURE 5.4 Illustration of the measurements number that corresponds to pre-selected EF (V/m) ranges, together with the percentage (%) cumulative distribution of the measured EF values. (Authors' collection)

>30 V/m. It is obvious that 75% of the measurements correspond to values lower than 25 V/m, which is a slightly lower than the lowest EC-RL for EF in the frequency range of 10–400 MHz (i.e. 28 V/m) that applies to the radio broadcasting service (FM radio), which is dominant in the antenna park environments. It should be noted here that FM radio contributes from 80% to 99% to the total field value at all the measurement points. However, taking into account the expanded measurement uncertainty, the EC-RL for general public and ALs for occupational exposure may be exceeded or probably exceeded in part of these measurements, as it will be analyzed subsequently. Additionally, it is obvious that comparing the selected ranges, the largest percentage (25%) of the measurement results (i.e. 44 of the 173) corresponds to the 15–20 V/m range.

In Figure 5.5, the total EF values are presented in comparison to the AL for EF for occupational exposure (i.e. 61 V/m) in the frequency range of 10–400 MHz. It is concluded that 87% of the measurement data corresponds to EF values lower than 50 V/m. The measurement data that corresponds to the highest EF value reaches 54 V/m, that is, 89% of the AL for occupational exposure in the frequency range of 10–400 MHz. Taking into account the expanded measurement uncertainty, ALs are probably exceeded (in spot regions) in 3 cases out of 173 audits (2%), corresponding to three different antenna parks in different years (i.e. 2010, 2014 and 2015).

Taking into account the EC-RL for the general public exposure, the annual presentation of the measurement results is summarized in Table 5.4, providing the minimum, maximum, mean, standard deviation and median values of total exposure ratio Λ by year. It is worth mentioning that the mean values of the total exposure ratio are not representative of the exposure levels. The wide distribution of the total exposure ratio sample, which is revealed by the relatively high standard deviation (comparable or greater than the mean value due to non-normal distribution of the data), leads to a mean value that corresponds to a worse exposure footprint comparing to the majority of data. Due to this characteristic, the median value or quartile 2 (Q2), that is, the value separating the higher half (50%) from the lower half of the measurements

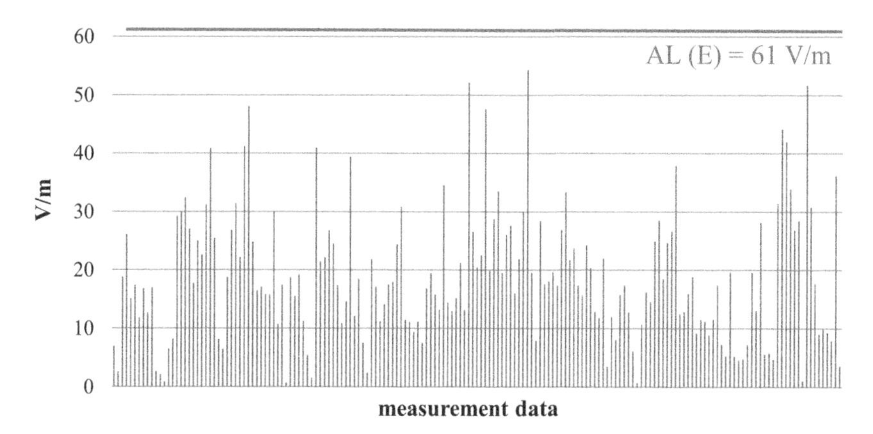

FIGURE 5.5 All the measurement data ($N = 173$) compared to the AL for electric field strength (E) for occupational exposure (i.e. 61 V/m) in the frequency range of 10–400 MHz. (Authors' collection)

TABLE 5.4
Annual Presentation of the Total Exposure Ratio Λ Values Based on the European Reference Levels (EC-RL) for General Public Exposure

Year	Number of Measurements	Λ (min)	Λ (max)	Λ (Mean ± SD)	Λ_m (Median)	Λ_w (Weighted Median)	IQR of Λ	Range Q1–Q3 of Λ
2010	23	<0.001	4.03	0.70 ± 0.99	0.35	0.05	0.97	0.03–1.00
2011	8	4.05×10^{-02}	1.65	0.56 ± 0.56	0.35	0.02	0.66	0.17–0.82
2012	15	1.15×10^{-03}	1.55	0.43 ± 0.47	0.36	0.03	0.46	0.08–0.54
2013	24	3.29×10^{-02}	2.47	0.48 ± 0.55	0.36	0.05	0.42	0.12–0.54
2014	32	<0.001	3.40	0.67 ± 0.77	0.41	0.08	0.76	0.17–0.93
2015	21	7.73×10^{-02}	3.76	0.87 ± 0.96	0.52	0.06	0.64	0.26–0.90
2016	21	6.16×10^{-02}	2.16	0.53 ± 0.54	0.38	0.05	0.34	0.20–0.53
2017	12	<0.001	2.14	0.52 ± 0.60	0.41	0.03	0.59	0.09–0.68
2018	17	1.44×10^{-03}	2.89	0.74 ± 0.71	0.39	0.04	0.76	0.33–1.09

Λ, total exposure ratio, value of Λ equal to 1 corresponds to 100% of the EC-RL.
SD, standard deviation.
Λ_m, median value of Λ.
Λ_w, weighted median value of Λ.
IQR, InterQuartile Range, calculated as the difference between the upper Q3 (75% of the values) and lower Q1 (25% of the values) quartiles.
Q1, lower quartile (25% of the values).
Q3, upper quartile (75% of the values).

sample, is presented. Additionally, for each year, the InterQuartile Range (IQR) is calculated as the difference between the upper Q3 (75% of the values) and lower Q1 (25% of the values) quartiles, corresponding to a measure of variability, based on dividing the data set into quartiles. Additionally, the range Q1–Q3 is also presented.

The number of measurements per year is 23 (for the year 2010), 8 (2011), 15 (2012), 24 (2013), 32 (2014), 21 (2015), 21 (2016), 12 (2017) and 17 (2018). Given the difference in measurements number per year, the results should be weighted with the ratio of the annual number of measurements to the total one, in order to illustrate the realistic exposure level per year. Let X be the total number of measurements and i be the corresponding number for a given year. The weighted median value Λ_w of the mean Λ_m exposure ratio is defined as:

$$\Lambda_w = \frac{i}{X}\Lambda_m \tag{5.4}$$

Figure 5.6 illustrates the annual presentation of the weighted median value of the total exposure ratio Λ_w, calculated based on the EC-RL. While the weighted median exposure ratio increases after the year 2011, it seems that this trend is suspended after 2015, which is the year when the transition from analog to digital television system has been completed in Greece. It is worth noting that the main contribution to the total exposure ratio is due to the FM radio broadcasting antennas, in the majority of the measurements. Therefore, in the future, after the completion of the transition to terrestrial digital audio broadcasting, a next step of significant reduction of the exposure levels is expected (Gkonis et al., 2017).

Concerning the used telecommunication services [FM, VHF TV, UHF TV, GSM, DCS, UMTS and LTE (Long-Term Evolution)], it is concluded that in the majority of the measurement audits, the main contributions in the total exposure ratio are due to the operation of firstly, the radio (FM) broadcasting transmitters for the

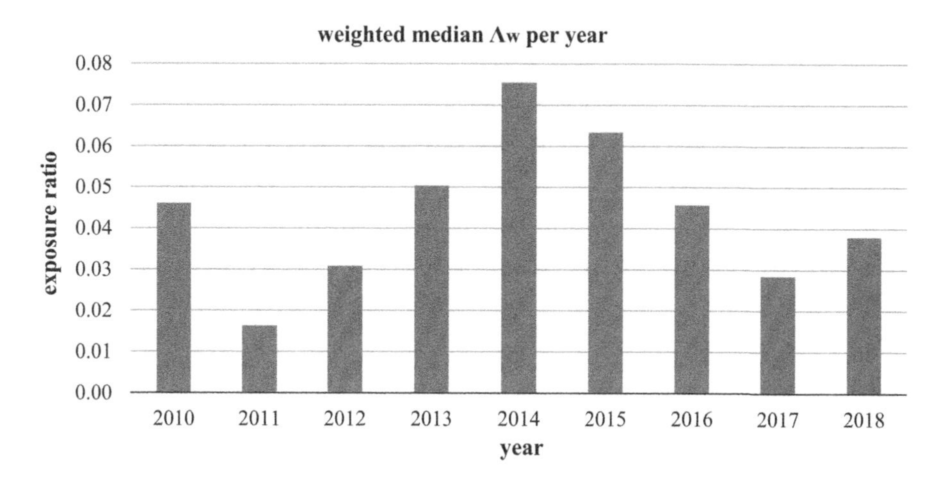

FIGURE 5.6 Annual presentation of the weighted median value of the total exposure ratio Λw based on the European Reference Levels for general public exposure (EC-RL). (Authors' collection)

corresponding frequency band of 87.5–108 MHz (with median exposure ratio at this frequency range based on EC-RL, 0.35) and, secondly, the television broadcasting transmitters in the UHF range, which is included in the frequency band of 460–875 MHz (with median exposure ratio 0.002 at the corresponding frequency range). The third highest contribution, with significant distance from the first two, is due to the operation of VHF transmitters, which has been significantly decreased after the year 2015, when the transition from analog to digital television system was completed in Greece.

5.6.2 Handling Cases Where the Reference Levels Are Exceeded or Probably Exceeded

The EC-RL for general public exposure are considered to be exceeded or probably exceeded when the total exposure ratio is calculated to be more than 1 (or more than 1/0.7 considering the EMF limits applied in Greece, GR-RL), taking into account the expanded measurement uncertainty. Therefore, the strictness of the Greek legislation results in 32 antenna parks out of the 57 (56%), where at least there is non-compliance or probable non-compliance with the GR-RL in one year. These antenna parks have been coded with the numbering #1–32 in order to be re-inspected by EEAE. Based on the EC-RL, the corresponding number of antenna parks with non-compliance or probable non-compliance reaches 21 of the 57 (37%). The following practice is applied by EEAE in order to verify whether there is compliance with the GR-RL in the free-access areas of the antenna parks. The regions where the GR-RL are exceeded (or probably exceeded) are explicitly defined after detailed measurements over the entire antenna park environment, and they are highlighted in colour in the appropriate satellite views of the antenna parks. Furthermore, certain technical measures are taken in order to mitigate exposure, including changes in the topology and/or the technical characteristics of the installed antennas. More specifically, in such regions (i.e. in delimited areas with black colour) it is proposed to: (1) prohibit/control public access and (2) post warning signs at prominent places around the regions in order to inform about the existence of high EMF levels. Additionally, EEAE officially informs EETT (Hellenic Telecommunications and Post Commission), which is the competent national authority for licensing the telecommunications providers. EETT then takes appropriate legal actions against the providers that present the higher contributions to the GR-RL non-compliance. In such cases, after a certain time period (i.e. 1 year), EEAE repeats the audit in the given antenna park in order to verify compliance with the GR-RL. Therefore, the majority of the antenna parks is inspected repeatedly. Figure 5.7 summarizes the practice that EEAE follows in order to verify that the GR-RL are not exceeded in the free-access areas in the antenna parks across Greece.

Figure 5.8 illustrates a characteristic example of an antenna park (#30) where the EMF limit values (GR-RL) have been exceeded. In the selected satellite view of Figure 5.8a, the measurement points are depicted in the antenna park environment (Point 2 corresponds to the point of the highest exposure,) for the year 2014, and the region where the GR-RL are exceeded is highlighted with black colour. This region consists

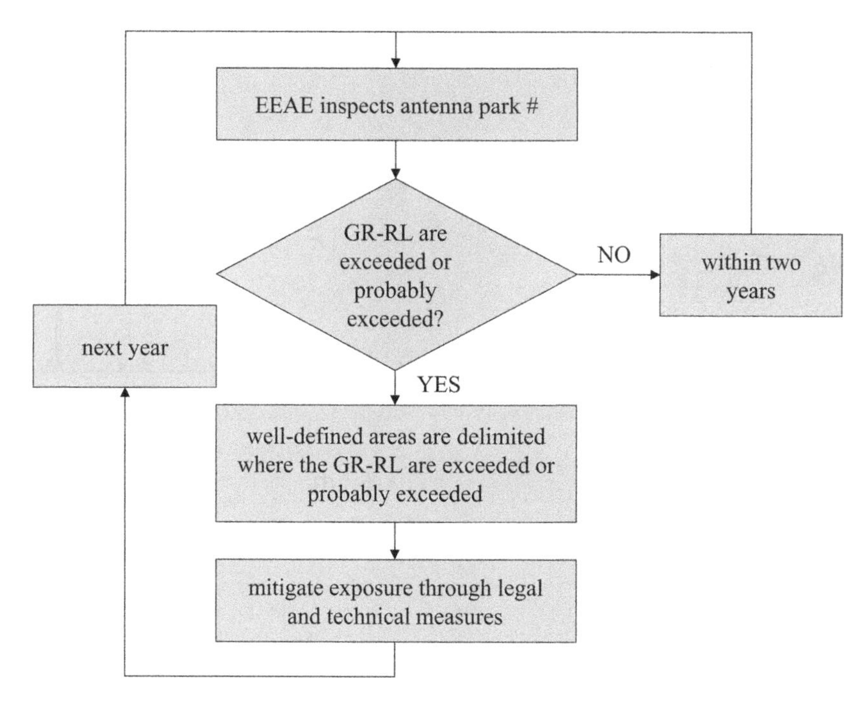

FIGURE 5.7 Flowchart of the practice that EEAE follows in order to verify that the reference limits adopted in Greece (GR-RL) are not exceeded or probably exceeded in the free-access areas in the antenna parks across Greece. (Authors' collection)

of a circular subregion of radius 8 m with central point 2, a circular subregion of radius 8 m with central point 1 and a circular subregion of radius 8 m with central point 3. At the point of the highest EF measured value, the spectrum analysis revealed that the radio FM frequency band contributes nearly 99% to total exposure levels. Therefore, focusing on radio FM spectrum analysis, it is illustrated that the main contributor of the high exposure levels is the radio station operating at 104.8 MHz (Figure 5.8b). The technical measures taken in order to mitigate exposure due to the 104.8 MHz radio provider, included: (1) reduction of the transmitted antenna's input power and (2) reinstallation of the radio provider's antennas at the top of the masts. According to the above-described practice, EEAE repeated the inspection in the antenna park #30 next year (2015). It was found that (1) the GR-RL were still exceeded, with point 3 as one of the highest exposure, and (2) the topology of the delimited regions (marked with black colour) was altered. This region consists of: the AC path with an approximate length of 29 m that connects the southern (A) mast and the northern (C) mast, the CD path with an approximate length of 35 m that connects the northern (C) mast to point D and the DA path with an approximate length of 40 m. At the point of the highest EF measured value, the spectrum analysis revealed that the radio FM frequency band contributes more than 99% to total exposure levels. In the spectrum analysis of Figure 5.8b and d, it is revealed that while the 104.8 MHz radio broadcasting provider complied with the proposed technical mitigation actions, after a year the GR-RL are still

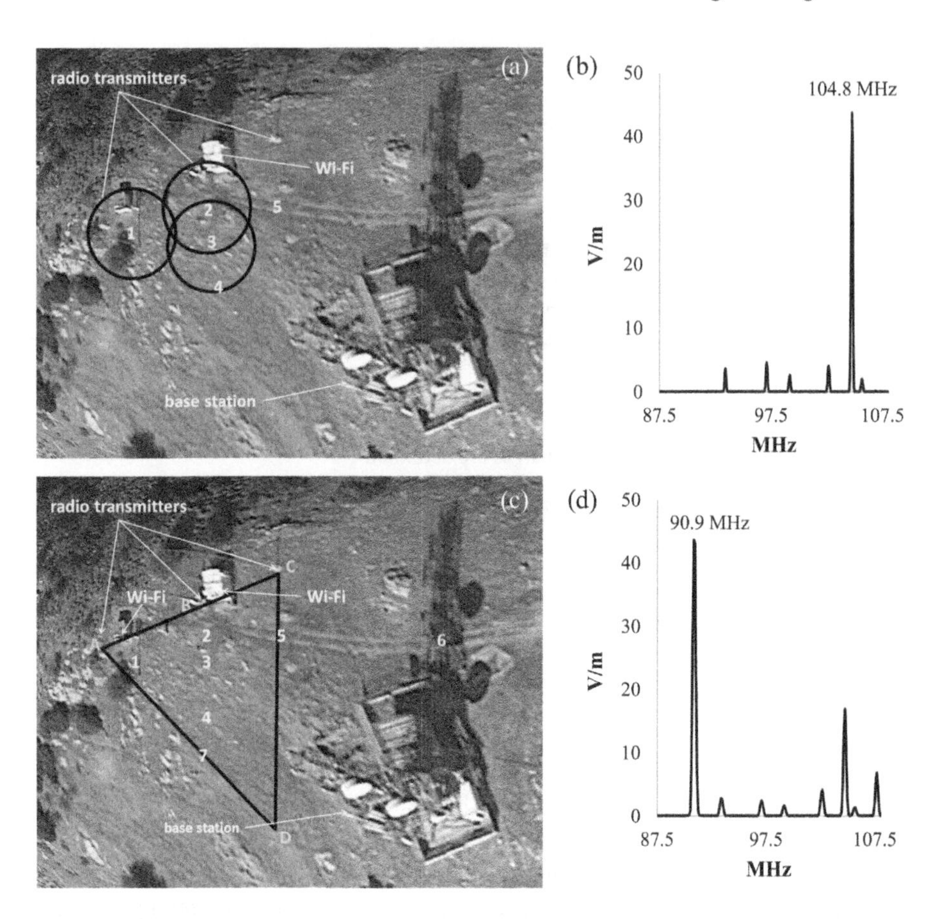

FIGURE 5.8 Satellite view of the antenna park #30 where the general public reference limits (GR-RL) have been exceeded for the years (a) 2014 and (c) 2015 inside the areas delimited by black colour. Spectrum analysis of the EF value in the radio frequency band (87.5–108 MHz), where the EF value corresponds to different emitted frequency values: 104.8 MHz (b) for the year 2014 and 90.9 MHz (d) for the year 2015, which are assigned to different radio providers. (Authors' collection)

exceeded (in an altered delimited region), and this non-compliance is due to a new radio broadcasting provider operating at 90.9 MHz. This non-compliance may have occurred due to the antenna installations at low heights (i.e. 2–3 m from the ground level) and/or to high antenna input power levels. It is noteworthy that in the specific antenna park (#30), the EC-RL have also been probably exceeded for both the years, that is, 2014 and 2015, in corresponding delimited areas.

Figure 5.9 illustrates another example of an antenna park (#26) where, in the year 2015, the GR-RL were probably exceeded in the delimited regions with black colour. These regions have the maximum dimension of 25 and 30 m, respectively. It is noteworthy that the EC-RL have also been probably exceeded in corresponding delimited areas in the specific antenna park (#26) for the year 2015. After the essential technical and legal measures taken by EEAE and EETT, the EMF exposure

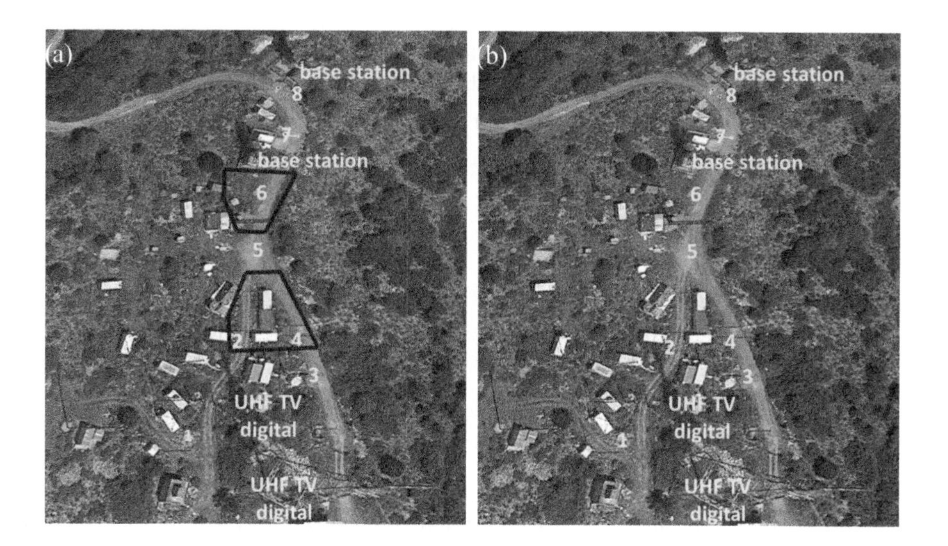

FIGURE 5.9 Satellite view of the antenna park #26 where there is (a) probable non-compliance with the general public reference limits (GR-RL) inside the areas delimited by black colour for the year 2015 and (b) compliance with the GR-RL for the year 2016. (Authors' collection)

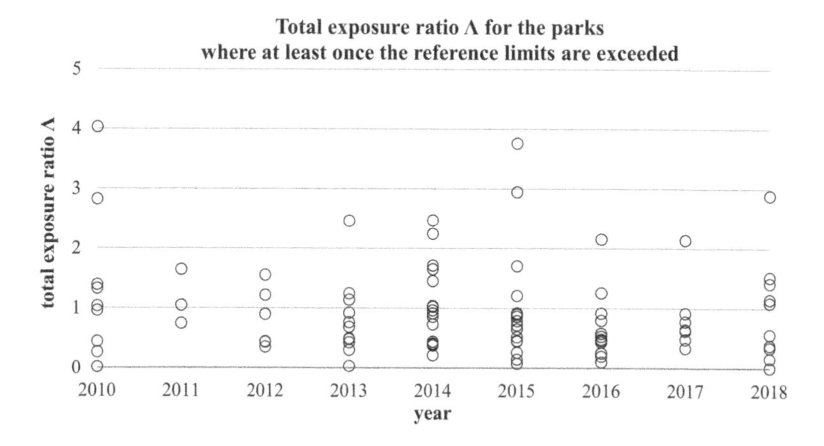

FIGURE 5.10 Annual distribution of total exposure ratio Λ for the 21 antenna parks where at least once the EC-RL for general public exposure are exceeded or probably exceeded. (Authors' collection)

inspection of the same antenna park environment has been re-performed by EEAE next year (2016), and, as the satellite view reveals, the probable non-compliance with the GR-RL and EC-RL disappeared (Figure 5.9b).

Figure 5.10 illustrates the annual distribution of the total exposure ratio Λ (without taking into account the expanded measurement uncertainty) for all the 21 antenna parks in which the EC-RL for general public exposure had been exceeded at least

(a)

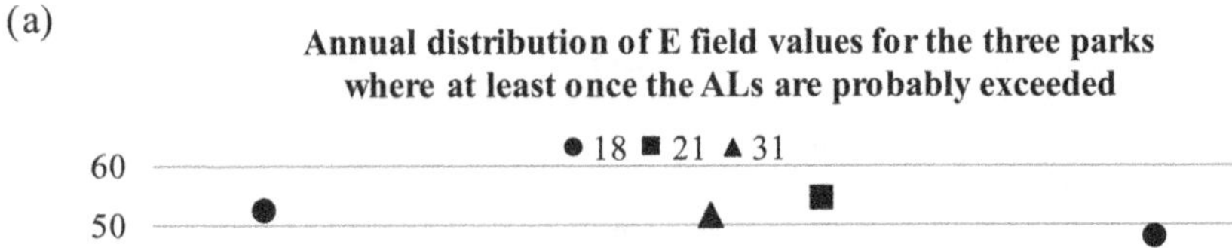

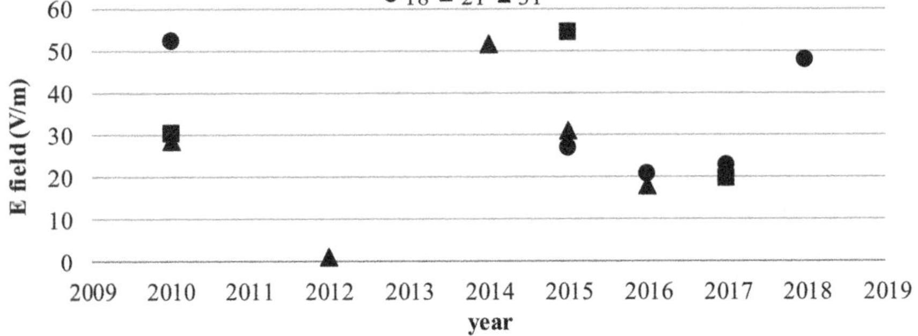

(b)

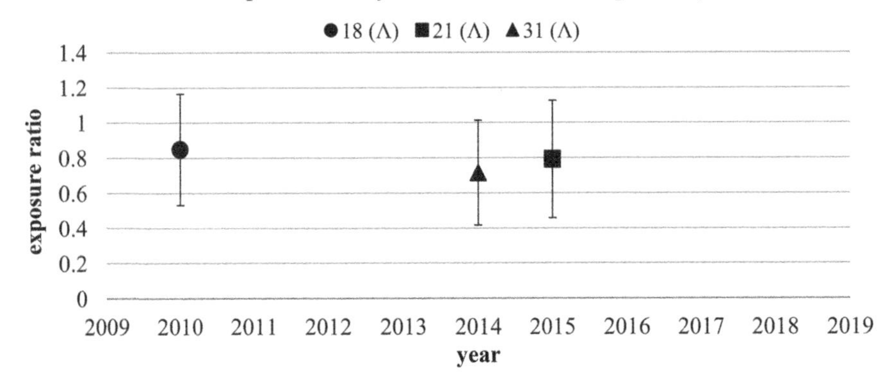

FIGURE 5.11 Annual distribution of (a) EF values and (b) total exposure ratio Λ with expanded measurement uncertainty based on the ALs for occupational exposure for the three parks where at least once the ALs were probably exceeded. (Authors' collection)

once for the period 2010–2018. Figure 5.11 summarizes the measurement results in the three antenna parks (i.e. #18, #21, #31) where the ALs for occupational exposure were probably exceeded at some test points. More specifically, the EF values are plotted in Figure 5.11a for the above-mentioned antenna parks for all the years that they have been inspected. In the years, when the ALs were probably exceeded, the corresponding values are given, that is, EF value equal to 52.1 V/m for the park #18 measured in 2010, 54.3 V/m for the park #21 measured in 2015 and 51.7 V/m for the park #31 measured in 2014. The total exposure ratio Λ is illustrated in Figure 5.11b, calculated from the above-mentioned audits, based on the ALs for occupational exposure and taking into account the expanded measurement uncertainty. The fact that the upper limit of the confidence interval exceeds the AL value for occupational exposure proves the probable non-compliance.

It is important to highlight that the areas where there is non-compliance with the GR-RL and EC-RL are strictly and clearly defined, and, almost in all cases, they are due to radio broadcasting antennas (FM). These antennas usually belong to local radio station providers, and they are installed/uninstalled onto masts of low height, not following any pre-defined spatial planning.

5.7 CONCLUSIONS

This study presents and analyses the results of the in-situ measurements conducted in the antenna parks across Greece from 2010 to 2018. It is concluded that in all the years under investigation, the main contribution to the total EMF exposure levels is due to the operation of the radio (FM) broadcasting stations. Concerning occupational exposures, the ALs were probably exceeded (at some test points) in 3 cases out of 173 audits (2%), recorded in three different antenna parks for the time period of 2010–2018. Additionally, it is concluded that 29.5% (44.5%) of the measurement data corresponds to non-compliance or probable non-compliance with the EC-RL (GR-RL) for general public exposure in well-defined areas set by the EMF inspection staff within antenna park environments. In such cases, EEAE officially informs EETT (Hellenic Telecommunications and Post Commission), which is the competent national authority for licensing the telecommunications providers and takes appropriate legal actions. In most cases, the inspection that follows the one that detected non-compliance proves that the legal and technical measures taken have resulted in compliance with the GR-RL and consequently with the EC-RL. However, in Greece, after the adoption of certain technical and legal measures, it is quite difficult to safely predict the future compliance to the GR-RL, since it is quite common that new radio antennas may be installed following a non-specified spatial plan, and thus periodic inspection is necessary. Last but not the least, following the observations of exposure levels during the transition to digital television broadcasting system (since the beginning of 2015), it is expected that the transition from analog to digital radio broadcasting system that will be performed in the next few years will drastically reduce the EMF exposure levels within the antenna park environments across Greece.

REFERENCES

Act No. 1105. 2000. *Protection Measures for the Exposure of General Public to All Land Based Antenna Stations.* Athens, Greece, Official Government Gazette, Articles 2–4, Vol. B/6–9–2000.

Birks, L. E., B. Struchen, M. Eeftens and L. van Wel. 2018. Spatial and temporal variability of personal environmental exposure to radio frequency electromagnetic fields in children in Europe. *Environ Int* 117:204–214.

Christopoulou, M., and Karabetsos, E. 2015. In situ measurements of radiofrequency exposure levels in Greece from 2008 to 2013: a multi-parametric annual analysis. *Bioelectromagnetics* 36:325–329.

Christopoulou, M., and Karabetsos, E. 2019. Evaluation of radiofrequency and extremely low-frequency field levels at children's playground sites in Greece from 2013 to 2018. *Bioelectromagnetics* 40:602–605.

Directive 2013/35/EU. 2013. Directive of the European Parliament and of the Council of 26 June 2013 on the Minimum Health And Safety Requirements Regarding The Exposure Of Workers To The Risks Arising From Physical Agents (Electromagnetic Fields) (20th Individual Directive within the Meaning of Article 16(1) of Directive 89/391/EEC). *Official Journal of the European Union* O.J. No. L-179 of 29 June 2013, 1–21, Brussels, Belgium.

EC [European Commission]. 2015. Non-Binding Guide to Good Practice for Implementing Directive 2013/35/EU. Luxembourg: Publication Office of the European Union.

ECC/REC/(02)04. 2007. Electronic communications committee (ECC) within the European conference of postal and telecommunications administrations (CEPT). ECC recommendation (02)04 (revised Bratislava 2003, Helsinki 2007). Measuring non-ionizing electromagnetic radiation (9 kHz-300 GHz). https://www.ecodocdb.dk/download/fa5b1c03-0a47/REC0204.PDF (accessed January 08, 2020).

EEAE [Greek Atomic Energy Commission], 2020. EEAE website, electromagnetic fields measurements. https://eeae.gr/en/ (accessed August 28, 2020).

EN 50413. 2019. Basic standard on measurement and calculation procedures for human exposure to electric, magnetic and electromagnetic fields (0 Hz-300 GHz). https://standards.iteh.ai/catalog/standards/clc/52672ee1-158b-442c-9982-6dad5f991869/en-50413-2019

EN 50420. 2006. Basic standard for the evaluation of human exposure to electromagnetic fields from a stand-alone broadband transmitter (30 MHz-40 GHz). https://standards.iteh.ai/catalog/standards/clc/b26e7364-b1dc-42fd-baed-0e46d5749332/en-50420-2006

EN 50499. 2019. Procedure for the assessment of the exposure of workers to electromagnetic fields. https://standards.iteh.ai/catalog/standards/clc/9e9a550f-3ff7-426d-88ce-8d7be3bb030d/en-50499-2019

EN IEC 62232. 2022. Determination of RF field strength, power density and SAR in the vicinity of radiocommunication base stations for the purpose of evaluating human exposure. https://standards.iteh.ai/catalog/standards/clc/74555741-db71-4146-b831-c3d41aaec6d3/en-iec-62232-2022

European Council. 1999. Council Recommendation 1999/519/EC on the limitation of exposure of the general public to electromagnetic fields (0 Hz to 300 GHz). *OJ L*, No. 199:59–70.

Gkonis, F., A. Boursianis, and T. Samaras. 2017. Electromagnetic field exposure changes due to the digital television switchover in Thessaloniki, Greece. *Health Phys* 113(5):382–386.

Gourzoulidis, G. A., C. Kappas, and E. Karabetsos. 2019. Development of a flowchart system for the risk assessment of occupational exposure to low and high frequency electromagnetic fields. *Hell J Radiol* 4(1):18–25.

Gourzoulidis, G., P. Tsaprouni, N. Skamnakis et al. 2018. Occupational exposure to electromagnetic fields: The situation in Greece. *Phys Med* 49:83–89.

Gryz, K., and J. Karpowicz. 2015. Radiofrequency electromagnetic radiation exposure inside the metro tube infrastructure in Warszawa. *Electromagn Biol Med* 34(3):265–273.

Gryz, K., and J. Karpowicz. 2019. Radiofrequency electromagnetic exposures during the use of wireless links of portable computers inside trains without internal WiFi services. In *Proc. of EMC EUROPE 2019 International Symposium on Electromagnetic Compatibility, EMC Europe*, 1030–1033. DOI: 10.1109/EMCEurope.2019.8872060.

ICNIRP [International Commission on Non Ionizing Radiation Protection]. 1998. Guidelines for limiting exposure to time varying electric, magnetic and electromagnetic fields (up to 300 GHz). *Health Phys* 74:494–522.

IEEE [Institute of Electrical and Electronics Engineers]. 2014. IEEE Std C95.1–2345™: IEEE standard for military workplaces—Force health protection regarding personnel exposure to electric, magnetic, and electromagnetic fields, 0 Hz to 300 GHz. https://ieeexplore.ieee.org/document/6766647?denied=

ISO [International Organization for Standardization]. 2017. ISO/IEC 17025: General requirements for the competence of testing and calibration laboratories. https://www.iso.org/publication/PUB100424.html

ITU [International Telecommunication Union]. 2020. *ITU Radio Regulations*, 119–120. ISBN number: 978-92-61-30317-4, ITU, Switzerland.

ITU [International Telecommunication Union]. 2022. Recommendation ITU-T K.91. Guidance for assessment, evaluation and monitoring of human exposure to radio frequency electromagnetic fields. https://www.itu.int/rec/T-REC-K.91-202201-I/en

Law No 4635, 2019. Chapter 1: Licensing and inspection of land-based antenna installations, Vol. A, 167/30.10.2019:4696-4712.

Sagar, S., S. M. Adem, B. Struchen et al. 2018. Comparison of radiofrequency electromagnetic field exposure levels in different everyday microenvironments in an international context. *Environ Int* 114:297–306.

Sahalos, J. N., E. E. Vafiadis, T. S. Samaras, D. G. Babas, and S. S. Koukourlis. 1995. EM field measurements in the vicinity of an antenna park for radiation hazard purposes. *IEEE Trans Broadcas* 41(4):130–135.

Struchen, B., I. Liorni, M. Parazzini, S. Gängler, P. Ravazzani, and M. Röösli. 2016. Analysis of personal and bedroom exposure to ELF-MFs in children in Italy and Switzerland. *J Expo Sci Environ Epidemiol* 26(6):586–559.

Verloock, L., W. Joseph, F. Goeminne, L. Martens, M. Verlaek, and K. Constandt. 2014a. Temporal 24-hour assessment of radio frequency exposure in schools and homes. *Measurement* 56:50–57.

Verloock, L., W. Joseph, F. Goeminne, L. Martens, M. Verlaek, and K. Constandt. 2014b. Assessment of radio frequency exposures in schools, homes, and public places in Belgium. *Health Phys* 107(6):503–513.

Vermeeren, G., I. Markakis, F. Goeminne, T. Samaras, L. Martens, and W. Joseph. 2013. Spatial and temporal RF electromagnetic field exposure of children and adults in indoor micro environments in Belgium and Greece. *Prog Biophys Mol Bio* 113(2):254–263.

World Health Organization (WHO). 2010. *Research Agenda for Radiofrequency Fields*, 1–42. ISBN 978 92 4 159994 8, WHO Library, Switzerland.

6 Pulsed Microwave Exposure of Humans

A Specific Analysis and Forms of Protection

Jarosław Kieliszek
Military Institute of Hygiene and Epidemiology

Roman Kubacki
Military University of Technology

CONTENTS

6.1 INTRODUCTION

Microwaves (MWs), defined as a part of the electromagnetic (EM) spectrum of 300–300,000 MHz (i.e. 0.3–300 GHz), are widely used in telecommunication systems as well as for military aims. This frequency range is also widely used by medical and industrial devices. Many types of these apparatuses emit an electromagnetic field (EMF) with pulsed modulation (PM)—at this frequency range known also as EM radiation. In this case, antennas emit EMF during the time period known as a pulse width. In between pulses, MWs are not generated. The typical pulse form is rectangular, but triangular or trapezoidal shapes are also used, especially in medical devices. From a biomedical point of view, pulsed radiation (when the EM energy

DOI: 10.1201/9781003020486-6

is not emitted constantly) and continuous wave (CW) can evoke different exposure effects in a living medium. The possibility of pulsed EMF to produce biological responses different from those caused by CW of the same average power has been conjectured since the early years of research into biological effects from such exposure. There are several reasons why pulse-modulated radiation affects living tissues in a specific manner:

a. A pulsed signal, especially when the pulse width is significantly shorter than the period of repetition, can be presented in the frequency domain as a series of harmonics whose fundamental components coincide with the modulation frequency (i.e. 1/repetition time). Given that electrical properties (the reflection coefficient and the absorption ability) depend on frequency, the biomedical effects in tissues will also depend on frequency. In fact, the frequency spectrum of radiation emitted in pulses of extremely short duration spans a wide frequency band around its central frequency of carrier. In the range of MWs, the higher order harmonics are strongly attenuated by biological tissues, while harmonics whose frequencies are lower than the sinusoidal carrier frequency will generally penetrate deeper than continuous waves.
b. Pulsed EMF energy can penetrate deeper into biological tissues than comparable EM CW energy. The electric field strength (E, expressed in volts per metre, V/m) inside exposed tissue decreases exponentially due to energy absorption. The gradient of EMF decreasing in tissues depends on complex values of tissue permittivity and, of course, on frequency. The parameter allowing an assessment of the decrement of absorption is 'penetration depth'. This parameter is defined as the depth in tissue at which the EF strength diminishes to 1/e, that is, to about 36.8% from its value at the initial boundary (i.e. body surface). For pulsed radiation, the value of an electric field strength incident to a tissue has a higher peak value compared with their average value, and this is why the penetration is deeper comparing CW of equal average in time electric field level.
c. Due to the higher value of the peak electric field strength inside the tissue, the forces influencing free charges or molecules in the biological tissue are higher. In the case of molecules, the stretching forces cannot be neglected. These higher forces cannot be proportionally scaled from CW to PM average power.
d. Small biological objects with a round shape, such as eyes and gonads, with dimensions comparable to the wavelength in the tissue, are more sensitive to radar radiation exposure. EMF can evoke what is known as a 'hot spot' inside such objects. After penetrating the interior of the object, EMF causes a 'standing wave' due to internal reflections. The round shape means that a standing wave of increased amplitude is generated in the middle of the object. For this reason, a radar worker's eyes, in particular, must be protected. The minimum protection is to use safety glasses, as discussed later on in this chapter.

The properties of pulsed EMF radiation, as presented above, yield to different biological effects comparing CW exposure. In some cases, the well-accepted thermal effects from EMF exposure are not sufficient to characterise the health risks related to occupational exposure to the PM radiation. The level of the differentiation between PM EMF exposure effects and CW ones depends on the duty factor. According to the definition, the duty factor is the ratio of pulse duration (with pulse width τ) to the pulse repetition period of a periodic pulse train (T). A duty factor of 1.0 corresponds to the CW signal. With a low duty factor value, the peak value of the field strength has a significantly higher value when compared to the average figure.

When analysing pulsed EMF in the context of biological effects, the duty factor allows four groups of devices to be determined:

a. Devices with a high duty factor, close to unity (exceeding 0.5), such as dielectric welding devices. In this case, the pulse width is large, and the average field strength (or power density) is the appropriate metric for the considered thermal effects of EMF influence in the context of observed bioeffects.
b. Signals used in wireless cellular systems of the second generation (base station antennas and terminals) have a medium duty factor that emits pulses at a width of 577 μs for each user of the wireless link. The duty factor is about 0.1 [from each handset (terminal) or higher from the base station, when many users are active]. The thermal effects of the EMF influence are the main effects considered in the context of observed bioeffects, but in some cases non-thermal effects can also be used to interpret health risks without a clear association with thermal effects.
c. Radars emit pulses with a width of 0.5–10 μs. A typical radar duty factor is of 0.001. In this case, the peak pulse can reach a value 1000 times higher than the average power density. Exposure to this type of pulsed radiation needs to take into account thermal as well as non-thermal exposure effects. Thermal effects are associated with average power density, while non-thermal effects can be related to the peak value of radiation [other metrics of non-thermal effects, for example those related to the parameters of modulation or the entire dose from exposure (time integrated exposure) may also be considered in studies on EMF environmental hazards].
d. Generators emitting high peak power ultra-short EM pulses. Such radiation is also known as HPMP (High-Power Microwave Pulses) and is characterised by extremely high peak power (gigawatts) and extremely short pulse duration of several nanoseconds. The HPMP are intended to inhibit or destroy electronic systems. Such systems can be used in military as well as in civilian (terrorist) actions. Many laboratories develop HPMP generators and investigate the influence on the electronics and on living systems. The duty factor of HPMP is extremely small (tends towards zero), and because of this the spectrum of harmonics is very broad, like in UWB (Ultra-Wide Band) signals. Nevertheless, the health risks of HPMP are still full of controversies. On the one hand, the very-high-power influences the strong forces between molecules, but on the other hand, taking into account the energy of HPMP, such short pulses may not have enough time to cause damage to biological living systems.

6.2 RADARS AS SOURCES OF STRONG MICROWAVES

In the MWs range, radiolocation devices, commonly known as radars, constitute the majority of sources of strong EMF pulses. The name RADAR comes from the term '*Radio Detection and Ranging*'. Radar devices, which were invented over 80 years ago, are widely used in navigation, aviation, national defence, and weather forecasting. Radars detect the position, direction of movement and range of planes, ships and other moving objects.

Radars operate by sending pulses of EMF, known as probe pulses, and retrieving pulses reflected by the target, known as echo pulses. Radars usually have only one antenna used for both transmitting and receiving. The device uses an antenna switch to distinguish between probing pulses and echo pulses, as seen in Figure 6.1a. The distance to the target is measured as the difference in time that elapses between sending a probe pulse and receiving an echo pulse.

The power emitted by radar antenna ranges from several milliwatts (police radars for speed control) to several kilowatts or single megawatts at peak (large airspace observation radars). Radars emit EMF in the form of pulses rather than CW. This means that the average power emitted by radars is much lower than the peak power in pulses.

The MWs radiation generated by radar antennas is characterised by pulse modulation, with the duration of a single pulse ranging between $\tau = 0.5$ and 10 μs, and the time of repetition for the pulses ranging between $T = 0.5$ and 5 ms. These times depend on the specific nature of the work and the purpose of the radar. The duration of pulses is limited by the need to turn the device off from the transmission mode so that it can receive the reflected echo. For a pulse duration of $\tau = 1$ μs, the minimum distance to a detected target is approximately 150 m. On the other hand, the maximum range of target detection is determined by the interval between successive pulses, because a reflected pulse must be received before the next probe can be sent. A pulse repetition time of $T = 1$ ms provides detection up to approximately 150 km from the antenna.

The MWs generated by radiolocation device is strongly attenuated in the atmosphere. Because of that, in order to achieve a high efficiency of radar operation, it is necessary to provide both a high value of MWs energy of the transmitted probe

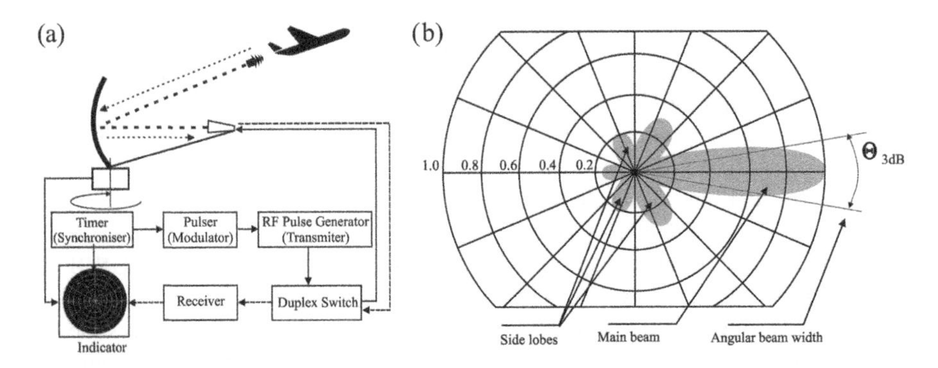

FIGURE 6.1 Block diagram of a radar system (a) and characteristic of the radar antenna (b). (Authors' collection.)

TABLE 6.1
Examples of Typical Air Traffic Control Radar Parameters

Typical Working Parameter	Value
Carrier frequency of the transmitter	3 GHz
Peak output power	450–600 kW
Average output power	400 W
Pulse width	0.7–1.0 μs
Pulse repetition rate	900 Hz
Antenna rotation speed	6–15 per min
Beam width in azimuth (horizontal)	1.5°
Beam width in elevation (vertical)	45°

signal as well as a proper concentration of radiation in a narrow sector of space. Radars always work in a fixed direction, and the emitted MWs energy is formed in very narrow beams similar to a spotlight beam. The level of MWs decreases rapidly when moving away from the main axis of the beam. In most cases, these levels of side radiation are thousands of times weaker than in the main beam. The characteristics of the radar antenna are shown in Figure 6.1b. Examples of the technical parameters of air traffic control radar are presented in Table 6.1.

In addition, many types of radars use antennas that rotate continuously or change their height with oscillating movement, thus changing the direction of radiation.

6.2.1 Types of Pulse Radar Devices

Some of the common types of radars found in everyday life include:

- **Air Traffic Control Radars** used to track and locate aircraft, and control their landing at airports, Figure 6.2a. They are usually located in elevated positions like masts or towers. Typical air traffic control radars can have a peak power of 100 kW or more and an average power of several hundred watts. Under normal operating conditions, these systems do not pose a threat to people around them.
- **Weather Radars** designed to detect atmospheric phenomena such as clouds, rainfall or storms, Figure 6.2b. Together with air traffic control radars, they are often located at the far ends of airports. They operate at higher frequencies, but generally have lower average and maximum radiation powers than traffic control radars. Like air traffic control radars, they normally do not pose a threat to the people around them.
- **Military Radars** constitute a large portion of radars, from very large installations that have a high peak power (1 MW or more) and medium power (kW) to small military fire control radars. Military radars can be divided into (Figure 6.3):
    - Surveillance radars
    - Rocket guidance radars

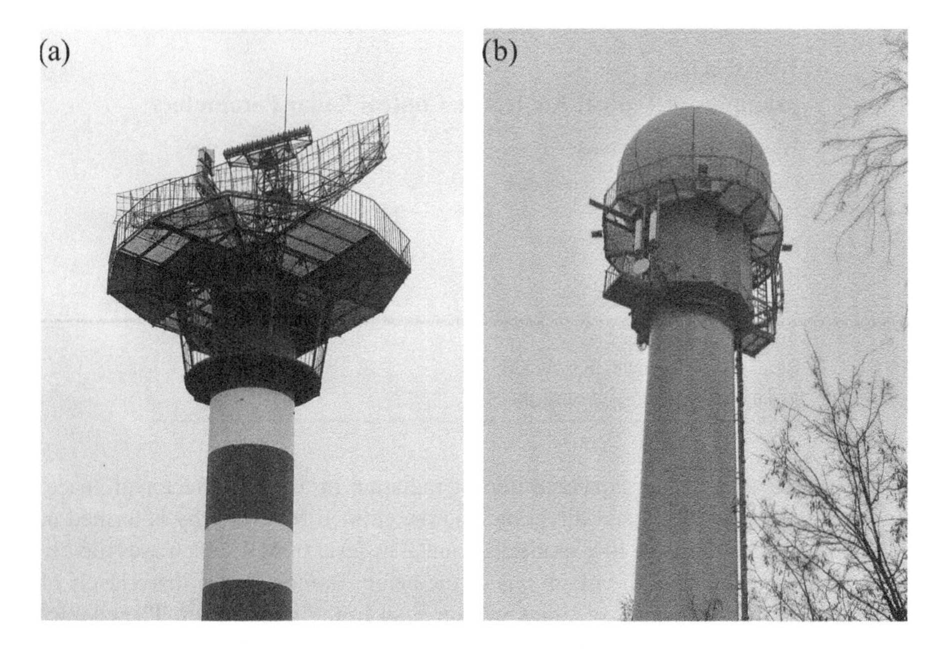

FIGURE 6.2 Air traffic control radar (a) and weather radar (b). (Authors' collection.)

FIGURE 6.3 Military radars: (a) Surveillance radar, (b) Rocket guidance radars, (c) 3D radar, (d) Battlefield observation radar, (e) Highfinder radar and (f) Radar landing system. (Authors' collection.)

FIGURE 6.4 Marine radars placed on the masts of a ship (a) and a cutter (b). (Authors' collection.)

  - Three-coordinate radars (3D)
  - Battlefield observation radars (also recognised as fire control radars)
  - Highfinder radars
  - Radar landing systems

  Both large-size radars and small fire control radars can pose a health risk to ground personnel.

- **Marine Radars** can be found on small boats, large ocean-going vessels and warships (Figure 6.4). The peak power of these devices can reach up to 30 kW, with average emitted power ranging from 1 to 25 W. In the areas available to the crews of most vessels, the levels of exposure to MWs are considerably below relevant limitation set to protect personnel against health and safety hazards from MW exposure.

6.3 EXPOSURE LIMITS FOR PULSED MICROWAVES

6.3.1 General Considerations

EMF emitted from radars is PM radiation, and the peak power can achieve high values. This kind of radiation has the potential to induce unique bioeffects. Nevertheless, the exposure limitation is usually set with respect to protection from the thermal exposure effect and refers to time-averaged parameter known as SAR (Specific Absorption Rate, expressed in Watts per kilogram, W/kg), which is a widely accepted quantity for relating adverse thermal effects with EMF exposure from the frequency range from at least 100 kHz to 10 GHz. Thus, the average value of the squared electric field strength or power density is necessary to determine the compliance with limit of radiation to protect people against the adverse health effects resulting from tissue heating. It is obvious that protection of workers against pulsed radiation based only on thermal effects is incomplete or even inadequate for setting safety guidelines. Guidance on protection against overexposure should consider the occurrence of other bioeffects caused by radiation emitted in the form of high peak powers. For example, the accidental exposure of a crew on the Norwegian naval ship described by Moen et al. (2013) documented those that exposed personnel had not experienced any major heating during the episode of exposure to MWs emitted from radar on the American destroyer.

Generally speaking, bioeffects induced by pulsed high-power radiation with a low average value may not be associated with thermal effects. This means that they may appear without any rise of temperature in tissues. This is why they are known as *non-thermal effects*. The non-thermal effects include the auditory effect (known as microwave hearing or the Frey effect, including tinnitus, whistling and crackling – experienced by humans exposed to the PM EMF), the blood–brain barrier effect, cardiovascular or behavioural changes depending on the values of peak power rather than the average radiation (DeLorge et al. 1989; Frey 1967; Guy 1975; Kubacki 2008; Thomas et al. 1994). Limitations on radar radiation should offer protection against thermal as well as non-thermal exposure effects. To reduce the health risks related to occupational radar exposure, all guidelines contain limitations on the average level of radiation (time-averaged E^2 or SAR) as well as limitations on their maximum level at peak.

However, there are differences in philosophy and values of exposure limits issued in different countries due to differing approaches to the safety principles, for example:

a) Exposure limits for the EMF developed by the International Commission for the Protection of Non-Ionising Radiation (ICNIRP) cover the frequency-dependent limitations on time-averaged EM radiation based on thermal effects (ICNIRP 1998), for the general public as well as for workers. Established higher values for workers are due to the fact that they can be exposed during a limited period of time in a day and health surveillance must be provided for them (ICNIRP 1998).
b) Directive 2013/35/EU of the European Parliament and of the Council of 26 June 2013 on the minimum health and safety requirements regarding the exposure of workers to the risks arising from physical agents (electromagnetic fields) includes frequency-dependent exposure limit values on time-averaged EM radiation based on ICNIRP 1998 guidelines on the protection of workers against thermal exposure effects. In addition, the directive sets out provisions whereby the employer must assess all risks for workers arising from EMF at the workplace and, if necessary, measure or calculate the levels of EMF to which workers are exposed, as well as establish a programme for implementing sufficient safety measures to protect workers against any health and safety risks (Directive 2013).
c) The occupational law in Poland also limits the time-average EM radiation in a way harmonised with a Directive 2013/35/EU. Legislation adopts also the provisions regarding application of non-averaged in time EM radiation in the managing of the safety measures required by the provisions of Directive 2013/35/EU (Dz.U. 2018).

Nevertheless, all these documents include safety limitations also for high peak values, as discussed later on in this chapter.

6.3.2 Peak Power Limitations

Taking into account the fact that a pulsed field, especially the one emitted by radar, can produce biological responses other than those of a CW field, it is necessary to specify limits to guard against potential hazards of pulsed EMF. Some organisations promulgated pulse limitations, underlining that there is still insufficient evidence that pulsed MWs of the type produced by radar transmitters cause biological effects not found under exposure to CW radiation at the same average power density. Nevertheless, the accumulation of experimental evidence on the biological effects of pulsed EMF justifies the need to set out such limitations. In the case of peak radiation limitations, the following exposure evaluation rules have been put in place by international guidelines (Table 6.2):

A/The ICNIRP'2020 guidelines (ICNIRP 2020).

Guidelines for exposure from any pulse, group of pulses or subgroup of pulses in a train, as well as from the summation of exposures (including non-pulsed EMFs), delivered in *t* seconds. Values of peak incident energy density must not exceed the frequency- and exposure duration-dependent reference level in Table 6.2 (reference levels for local exposure, integrated over intervals of between >0 and <6 minutes).

B/ The Directive 2013/35/EU (Directive 2013)

TABLE 6.2
Limits for Radar-Pulsed Radiation Issued in International Guidelines and Labour Legislation in Poland

			Limits for Peak Value of Pulsed Electric Field
	Guidelines	EMF Frequency	General Rules
1	ICNIRP 2020	>400–2000 MHz	$U_{inc} = 0.29 f_M^{0.86} \times 0.36\ [0.05 + 0.95\ (t/360)^{0.5}]$
		>2–6 GHz	$U_{inc} = 200 \times 0.36\ [0.05 + 0.95\ (t/360)^{0.5}]$
		>6–<300 GHz	$U_{inc} = 275/f_M^{0.177} \times 0.36\ [0.05 + 0.95\ (t/360)^{0.5}]$
		300 GHz	$U_{inc} = 100 \times 0.36\ [0.05 + 0.95\ (t/360)^{0.5}]$
2	Directive 2013/35/EU	100 kHz–6 GHz	$S_{peak} \leq (1000 \times S_{ave})$
3	IEEE Std C 95.1 2019	100 kHz–6 GHz	See equation (6.2)
		exceeding 30 GHz	See equation (6.3)
4	NATO Stg 2345 (Ed.3) 2003	exceeding 100 kHz	$E_{peak} \leq 200$ kV/m
5	Poland (Dz.U. 2018)	0.1–3 GHz	$E_{peak} < 4.5$ kV/m
		3–10 GHz	$E_{peak} < (3.2 + 0.43\, f_G)$ kV/m
		10–300 GHz	$E_{peak} < 7.5$ kV/m

f_G, frequency in GHz; f_M, frequency in MHz; *t*, time interval in seconds; U_{inc}, incident energy density (kJ/m²); E_{peak}, electric field strength RMS over pulse width; S_{peak}, peak power density averaged over pulse width and S_{ave}, power density averaged over 6 min (frequency-dependent limitations).

The directive set out additional limitations on the peak power density and SA:

a. For pulsed radiation, the peak power density (S_{peak}) averaged over the pulse width (S_{ave}) should not exceed 1000 times the respective limit of the averaged value of power density ($S_{peak} < 1000 \times S_{ave}$),
b. Spatial maximum power densities averaged over 1 cm^2 should not exceed 20 times the value of 50 W/m^2.

C/ The IEEE standard (IEEE Std C 95.1 2019)

The IEEE standard developed by the International Committee on Electromagnetic Safety set general rules of exposure evaluation as follow:

a. For exposures to pulsed RF fields in the range from 100 kHz to 300 GHz, peak power density limits are provided to prevent unintentionally high local exposure and to preclude high SA (specific absorption) in the frequency range from 100 kHz to 6 GHz or epithelial energy density above 6 GHz.

   The total incident energy density of a pulse train in any period of 100 ms is

$$\sum_{i=1}^{n}\left(S_{ipeak} \times \tau\right) \mathrm{J/m^2} \tag{6.1}$$

where:

n is the number of pulses within any period of 100 ms, $n = 1$ is for a single pulse

S_{ipeak} is the average (temporal) power density, averaged over τ, of the ith pulse (W/m^2)

τ is the width of the pulse (or a partial pulse width if any period of 100 ms captures only a portion of a pulse).

Compliance is established using equation (6.2).

$$\sum_{i=1}^{n}\left(S_{ipeak} \times \tau\right) \leq \frac{ERL_{local} \times t_{avg}}{5} \mathrm{J/m^2} \tag{6.2}$$

where:

t_{avg} is the duration of averaging time (6 min)

ERL_{local} is the ERL (exposure reference level) for local exposure at the given wavelength shown in Table 9, Table 10, and Table 11 in IEEE Std C 95.1 (2019).

The summation on the left side of the equation applies to any 100 ms of the exposure.

b. Incident energy density restrictions for intense pulses.

   For intense pulses (such as in certain military weapons systems) in the millimetre-wave frequency range (30–300 GHz), the maximum local incident energy density per pulse (fluence—incident power density integrated over the pulse duration, J/m^2) shall be limited to

$$< 1\tau^{1/2} \text{kJ/m}^2 \quad (6.3)$$

D/ NATO STANAG (NATO STANAG 2345, 2003).

The guidelines discussed above have been issued to protect against harmful high-power pulses with pulse durations in the range of 0.5–10 ms, which are typical in radar radiation. However, there are also sources of MWs emitting high peak power ultra-short pulses. They can be generated by a vircator or Marx generator emitting pulses of gigawatts in peak, but an extremely short pulse time duration of a few nanoseconds. For such a radiation, the limitation on the maximal peak value has been set at 200 kV/m.

In the guidelines mentioned above, there are not provided references to any scientifically justified biological or medical investigation that argue why a coefficient of 1000 has been set by these guidelines to protect against harmful exposure to pulsed MW radiation. The only reasonable explanation for this administrative proposal is that typical radar radiation with a pulse width of 1 μs and a time of repetition of 1 ms has duty cycles of 1:1000. For such a relationship ($S_{peak} = 1000 \times S_{ave}$), the average value of power density as well as the peak value can be scaled. Based on this limitation of peak power, it is possible to derive the limit for electric field strength, which is $E_{peak} = 32 \times E_{ave}$.

E/ Polish labour legislation (Dz.U. 2018).

Contrary to the above-mentioned approach, Polish labour legislation (Dz.U. 2018, Kubacki 2008) has set additional limitations of peak radiation regarding limitations on the maximum peak values based on well-accepted auditory effects. The values presented in Table 6.2 have been designed based on the adaptation of results of investigations into the auditory effect and on the extrapolation of the presented values to a broader frequency range, as well as, in some cases, scaling from cats to human. The auditory sensation evoked in a person exposed to pulsed MWs can be observed far below the threshold of thermal significance. This effect is caused by vibrations induced in the head of the exposed subject by a transient thermal expansion of tissue due to the rapid absorption of the pulsed MWs energy. This is why some people can hear pulsed MWs. Frey (1967) suggested that the intensity of the hearing effect is proportional to the maximum value of power density at peak. On the other hand, Guy et al. (1975) proved that this effect should rather be correlated with the energy of each pulse and found that the threshold for humans is of 0.4 J/m^2. This effect for a broader frequency range was documented by Guy et al. (1975) for guinea pigs and cats.

In Table 6.2, the example of limits values regarding pulsed EMF above 100 kHz are presented for comparison.

6.4 METROLOGY OF PULSED RADIATION EMITTED BY RADARS

Determining EMF emissions from radar antenna poses particular challenges for the measuring equipment. On the one hand, a radar signal is pulsed, highly directional and spatially variable, with the main beam illuminating the target or the measuring antenna (the metre's probe) for a short time. On the other hand, the metre for radar radiation must detect the entire harmonic spectrum existing due to the pulsed nature of the signal. Short radar pulses, with a high power density at peak and a long period of time between pulses, when MWs are not radiated, require special efforts in order to measure the pulse-modulated radiation.

The following measuring instruments are most commonly used to measure pulsed radar fields:

- Wide band spectrum analysers,
- Commercially available EMF metres with a dipole–diode probe, a thermocouple or thermistor probe.
- Specialised metres designed for measuring radar-pulsed radiation.

The use of each of these measuring instruments in evaluating human exposure requires different measuring techniques, together with additional actions and calculations. In particular, it is important to know the ratio between the peak value and the average value, in order to determine the factor needed to interpret the measuring instrument's indications (Bieńkowski et al. 2016).

For measuring the average value of non-rotating radar radiation power density (stationary kind of radiation), the thermocouple probe is the most suitable, because it works like a real averaging detector. For this reason, the thermocouple probe gives a real average value regardless of the waveform of the signal, even in the case of extremely pulsed radar signals. Some metres use dipole–diode detectors, but they must be equipped with specialised electronic elements to ensure the high time constant in the measuring circuit. Because of this, such measurements of radar radiation, especially with a short pulse duration, need correction factors, developed theoretically and experimentally with respect to the modulation of measured radiation and properties of the particular measuring apparatus in use (Kubacki and Szmigielski 1995).

For measuring the average value of radar radiation, the measuring detector should have a high value of time constant, which makes it impossible to detect the maximum value over the short peak.

Nevertheless, the evaluation of human exposure to pulsed radar radiation also requires checking the peak value. It should be noted that the average value of radar radiation can be low due to the pulse duration being as much as 1000 times shorter than the pulse repetition period. However, the peak value can be, in such a case, 1000 times higher than the average value. The important thing is to guarantee the same efficiency of measuring the low time-average value of exposure metrics as well as the high peak value in exposure pattern. The schematic view of a radar train of pulses for non-rotating radar radiation has been presented in Figure 6.5a.

It is possible to measure the radar signal, as presented in Figure 6.5a, using a dipole–diode detector. This kind of detector is not only 'quick' enough to measure the real value at peak, but it also encounters problems when averaging the measured signal. Nevertheless, dipole–diode detectors can be used in digital metres acquiring and probing the power density in time to create a time-averaged value in the digital post-processing of measurement results.

In order for radar equipment measurement to be successful, careful preparation for measurement and the use of appropriate measuring equipment is necessary.

Preparation for performing measurements includes obtaining information about the radar installation. Information about surroundings of the radar device is also important, in order to determine an appropriate representative measuring locations.

6.4.1 Measurement of a Non-Stationary Radar-Pulsed Radiation

When a radar antenna is scanning space, exposure to the pulsed signal occurs only for a fraction of the time. Such a case of exposure is known as 'non-stationary'. In this case, measured signals should be averaged twice. The first averaging, S_{ave} (see Figure 6.5b) should be as a result of the measurement of a short pulse with duration τ and the pulse repetition period T (PRP) (stationary field measurement). The second averaging is related to the change of the radar characteristics in space. The sequence of measured pulses is modulated by the shape of the characteristically changing antenna. A schematic presentation of this modulation is presented in Figure 6.5b. In this case, pulses are not detected by the metre all the time but can be acquired in the period of time when the antenna 'sees' the metre. The majority of the commercially available EMF metres cannot properly average such pulses. However, it is possible to measure this form of radiation by applying the proper correction factor. The correction factor can be determined experimentally in the known pulsed field. In the case of non-stationary exposure, metres with a thermistor probe are not applicable due to their insufficient dynamic range and the long, steady-state time of that type of metre.

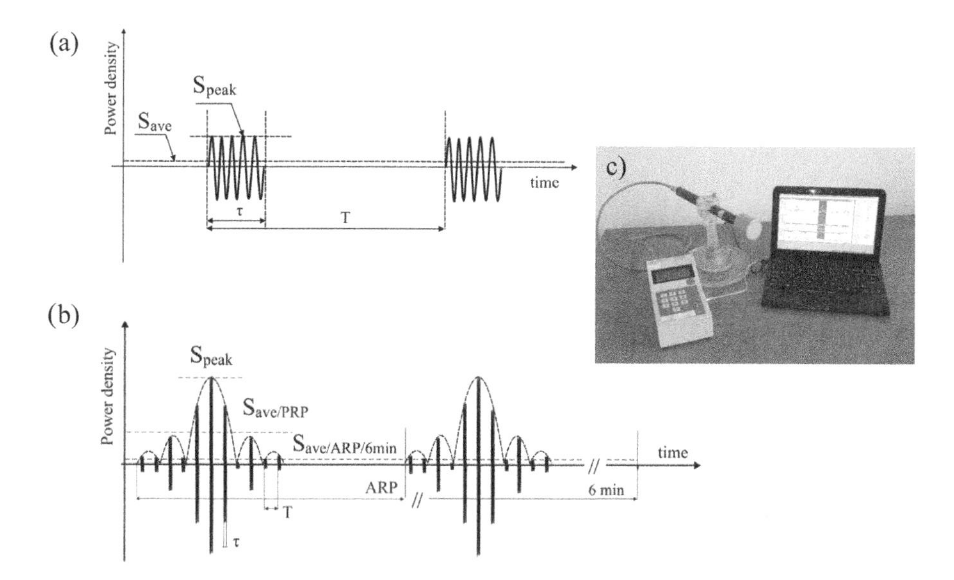

FIGURE 6.5 Parameters characterising pulsed radiation (a); the MWs modulated additionally by the rotation of radar antenna (b) and the view of device for measuring strong pulsed radar MWs (c); τ, pulse width; T, pulse repetition period (PRP); S_{peak}, peak power; S_{ave}, power time-averaged; $S_{ave/PRP}$, power averaged over PRP and $S_{ave/ARP/6min}$, power averaged over 6 minutes or antenna rotation period). (Authors' collection.)

A metre designed specifically to measure strong pulsed radar MWs, taking into account the demand of measurements of non-stationary MWs signals, should enable to evaluate three values of the measured EMF (Figure 6.5c), namely:

- S_{peak}: The peak power density value
- $S_{ave/PRP}$: The power density value averaged over the pulse repetition period (PRP)
- $S_{ave/ARP/6min}$: The power density averaged over 6 minutes or antenna rotation period (ARP)—total averaged pulse repetition and changing in time, a parameter especially provided for non-stationary radiation.

Each of the above-mentioned values characterises a spatially variable impulse radar field in a different way. $S_{ave/PRP}$ characterises a pulsed radar field that does not change its position in space. $S_{ave/ARP/6min}$ characterises a pulsed radar field that changes its position in space. The main challenge in evaluating of this parameter is that it is not always possible to stop a rotating antenna during measurements.

In addition, this metre would have the option to record and visualise the measured MWs over a given period of time, which would allow the variability of exposure at the measuring point to be demonstrated (Figure 6.6). This is particularly important when assessing the exposure for service personnel working in the vicinity of radars, in particular, when operating military radar equipment where the workstation may be located close to the antenna of strong operating radar.

Figure 6.6 shows three diagrams of electric field strength at three distances from the radar antenna, that is, quite close to the antenna (Figure 6.6c) as well as far away

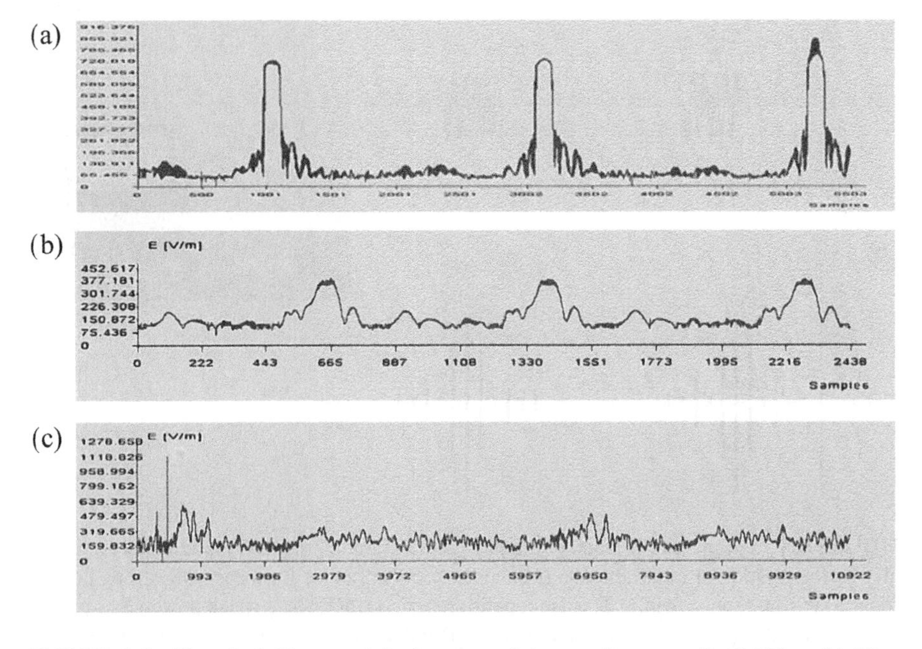

FIGURE 6.6 Electric field strength in function of time at distances of: (a) 100 m, (b) 20 m and (c) 7 m from radar antenna. (Authors' collection.)

(Figure 6.6a). When the exposure level is analysed near to the antenna (Figure 6.6c), the side lobes of the antenna pattern play a significant role, and radiation in time looks like a stationary case. The EMF metre located further away from the rotating antenna shows non-stationary exposure, that is, the highest level of radiation appears over time only when the main lobe of rotating antenna 'sees' the metre probe.

6.5 PROTECTIVE ACTIONS (MEASURES) AT EXPOSURES TO PULSED ELECTROMAGNETIC RADIATION

The purpose of protective actions is to keep the exposure level within the relevant requirements in the workplace. These include the following technical and administrative actions (Sobiech et al. 2017):

- Performing an analytical simulation to predict the radiation level of MWs before installing the radar
- Training workers about the potential health risks
- Measuring the level of MWs at each potentially exposed workplace
- Providing technical protection, including electronic blockades/shields, in the event of an unwanted leakage of radiation
- Introducing administrative restrictions at access [e.g. visual warning signs (Figure 6.7a,b) or barriers].

When technical and administrative restrictions are not sufficient, workers should employ personal protective equipment to ensure compliance with exposure limits. A number of protective suits, glasses, gloves, safety shoes and other personal protective equipment to reduce the level of MWs incident to the body are commercially available (Figure 6.7c,d).

Protective suits should be used with caution to ensure that the shielding efficiency of the barrier material fits the frequency of MWs affecting the work environment. They can only be reliably used if the attenuation properties of the protective equipment at a given frequency is known and sufficient with respect to the level of MWs in the location of the worker's planned activity and tested periodically.

6.6 SUMMARY

Pulsed MWs are a part of electromagnetic radiation that should be treated with special care. On the one hand, measuring pulsed radiation, especially that emitted by radar, needs measuring apparatus and procedures different than the ones used to measure the CW or slowly changing EMF. On the other hand, radar must be treated as a strong source of radiation with a significantly higher value of peak power density compared to the average value (with very high crest factor). This kind of radiation evokes not only thermal effects in the body but also some biological responses known as non-thermal effects. From this point of view, the safety guidelines must not only establish limits for the average level of radiation but also for the maximum peak value. Taking into account the fact that workers in the vicinity of these strong emitters can be exposed to unacceptable levels of radiation, special protective equipment

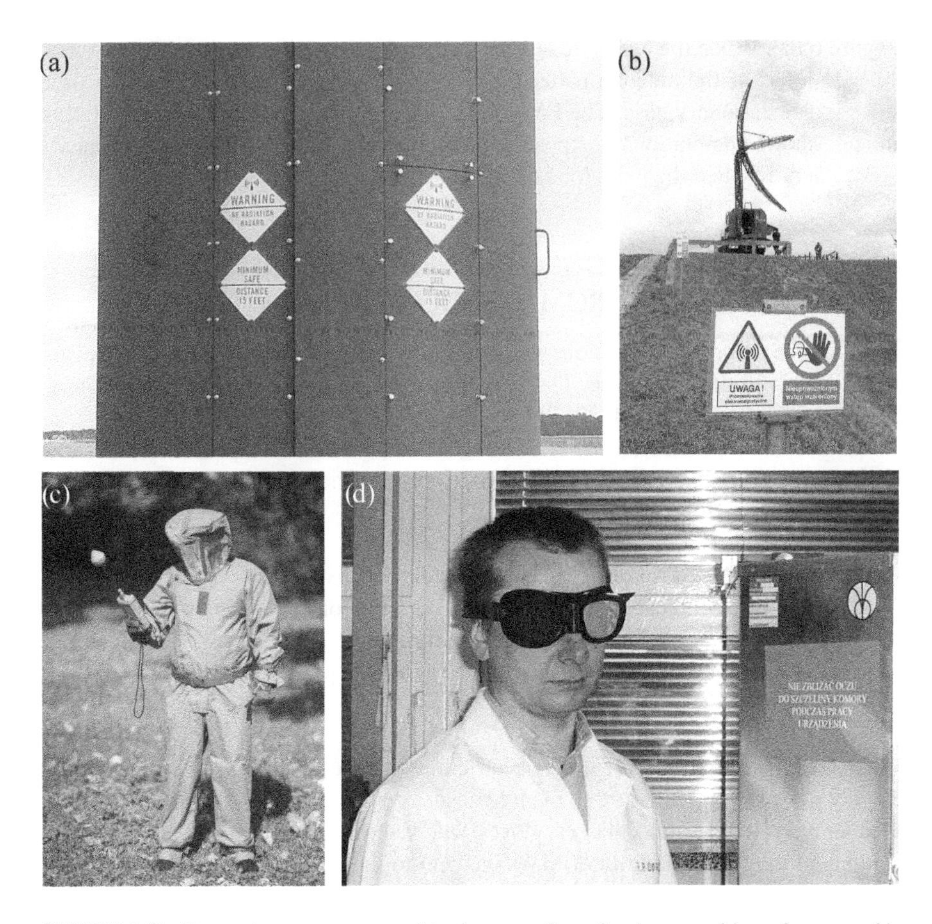

FIGURE 6.7 Protective measures used in the operation of radars: marking of sources (a), marking of protection zones for workers (b), personal protective suit (c) and personal safety glasses (d). (Authors' collection.)

and administrative restrictions should also be introduced in order to minimise the health risks.

Both the safety practices in the work environment as well as studies on the biomedical effects of the EMF exposure should address these specific properties of the PM MWs.

REFERENCES

Bieńkowski, P., J. Karpowicz, and J. Kieliszek. 2016. A review of the effects of exposure to a time-varying electromagnetic field and the metrological properties of measurement devices that have a significant influence when evaluating exposure in the work environment. *Podstawy i Metody Oceny Środowiska Pracy* 4(90):41–74 (in Polish). DOI: 10.5604/1231868X.1215436.

DeLorge, J.O., J.A D'Andrea, and B.L. Cobb. 1989. Lack of Behavioral Effects in the Rhesus Monkey: high peak microwave pulses at 1.3 GHz. *Bioelectromagnetics* 10(1):65–76. DOI: 10.1002/bem.2250100107.

Directive 2013/35/EU. 2013. Directive of the European Parliament and of the Council of 26 June 2013 on the Minimum Health And Safety Requirements Regarding The Exposure Of Workers To The Risks Arising From Physical Agents (Electromagnetic Fields) (20th Individual Directive within the Meaning of Article 16(1) of Directive 89/391/EEC). *Official Journal of the European Union* O.J. No. L-179 of 29 June 2013, 1–21, Brussels, Belgium.

Dz U 2018. Regulation of the Minister of Family, Labor and Social Policy of 12 June 2018 on the maximum allowable concentrations and intensities of factors harmful to health in the work environment (in Polish), Dz.U. 2018 poz. 1286. https://isap.sejm.gov.pl/isap.nsf/DocDetails.xsp?id=WDU20180001286

Frey, A.H. 1967. Brain evoked responses associated with low intensity pulsed UHF energy. *J Appl Physiol* 23(6):984–988. DOI: 10.1152/jappl.1967.23.6.984.

Guy, A.W., C.K. Chou, and J.C. Lin. 1975. Microwave-induced acoustic effects in mammalian auditory systems and physical materials. *Ann N Y Acad Sci* 247:194–218. DOI: 10.1111/j.1749–6632.1975.tb35996.x.

ICNIRP [International Commission on Non-Ionizing Radiation Protection]. 1998. Guidelines for limiting exposure to time-varying electric, magnetic, and electromagnetic fields (up to 300 GHz). *Health Phys* 74(4):494–522.

ICNIRP [International Commission on Non-Ionizing Radiation Protection]. 2020. Guidelines for limiting exposure to electromagnetic fields (100 kHz to 300 GHz). *Health Phys* 118(5):483–524. DOI: 10.1097/HP.0000000000001210.

IEEE C95.1–2019. 2019. *IEEE Standard for Safety Levels with Respect to Human Exposure to Electric, Magnetic, and Electromagnetic Fields, 0 Hz to 300 GHz*. New York: IEEE [Institute of Electrical and Electronics Engineers].

Kubacki, R. 2008. *Microwave Antennas; Technique and Environment*. Warszawa: Wydawnictwa Komunikacji i Łączności.

Kubacki, R., and S. Szmigielski. 1995. Methodological problems with RF pulse-power measurements. *Proceedings of the COST 244 on Method for Exposure Assessment Related to Standards*, 1: 42–47.

Moen, B.E., O.J. Møllerløkken, N. Bull, G. Oftedal, and K. Hansson Mild. 2013. Accidental exposure to electromagnetic fields from the radar of a naval ship: a descriptive study. *Int Marit Health* 64(4):177–182. DOI: 10.5603/imh.2013.0001.

NATO STANAG 2345 (Ed.3). 2003. *Evaluation and Control of Personnel Exposure to Radio Frequency Fields – 3 kHz to 300 GHz*. Brussels: NATO [North Atlantic Treaty Organization] Standardization Office.

Sobiech, J., J. Kieliszek, R. Puta, D. Bartczak, and W. Stankiewicz. 2017. Occupational exposure to electromagnetic fields in the Polish armed forces. *Int J Occup Med Environ Health* 30(4):565–577. DOI: 10.13075/ijomeh.1896.00696.

Thomas, T.G., Y. Akyel, F. Bates, M. Belt, and S.T. Lu. 1993. Temporal bisection in rats: the effects of high-peak-power pulsed microwave irradiation. *Bioelectromagnetics* 14(5):459–478. DOI: 10.1002/bem.2250140507.

7 The Occupational Health Surveillance of Workers Exposed to Electromagnetic Fields and the Problem of 'Workers at Particular Risk'

Alberto Modenese and Fabriziomaria Gobba
University of Modena & Reggio Emilia

CONTENTS

DOI: 10.1201/9781003020486-7

7.1 EXPOSURE TO EMF AND OHS OF WORKERS: PRELIMINARY CONSIDERATIONS

According to the International Labour Organization (ILO, 1998):

- **Occupational Health Surveillance (OHS)** is, in general, '*the ongoing systematic collection, analysis, interpretation, and dissemination of data for the purpose of prevention… essential to the planning, implementation and evaluation of occupational health programmes and to the control of work-related ill health and injuries, as well as to the protection and promotion of workers' health*'
- **Workers' Health Surveillance** is the '*…procedures and investigations to assess workers' health in order to detect and identify any abnormality*'
- **Work-Related Risk** is a factor related to the working activity potentially affecting the health of exposed workers.

OHS should be implemented in all situations where a recognised work-related risk exists and should include all the workers that are exposed to this risk due to their occupational activity.

Electromagnetic fields (EMF) are, undoubtedly, a recognised risk factor (ICNIRP, 2009, 2010, 2014, 2020; European Union, 2013). A problem here is that the definition of 'exposed worker' is a relevant (but not fully shared) problem to be considered when approaching the issue of individual worker OHS. As a matter of fact, EMF are virtually ubiquitous in all working environments (as are in the general environment). A consequence is that all (almost all) workers are exposed to EMF at work. Accordingly, all (almost all) workers should be considered as '*occupationally exposed*'. However, a similar approach seems unsatisfactory; in principle, specific preventive measures should be provided for the workers whose work-related EMF exposure can increase the risk for their health and/or safety; from this point of view, these are the workers that should be considered '*occupationally exposed*', hence deserving the implementation of OHS. But a clear definition of these workers is really problematic: for the biophysical short-term direct and indirect effects in workers not at particular risk (see Section 7.5) the relations with exposure levels are considered adequately known, thresholds were evaluated, and exposure limit values (ELVs) based on these effects are available, but these relations are not directly applicable to the *workers at particular risk*. Furthermore, up now, the causal association between quantitative characteristics of cumulative EMF exposure and long-term effects is not proven, as discussed in Section 7.3 ('The Adverse Health Effects in Workers Related to EMF Exposure and OHS'). As a consequence, up to now the definition of 'occupationally exposed workers' in the case of EMF probably cannot be considered entirely satisfactory. As a matter of fact, to the best of our knowledge, the most frequently applied criterion is the involvement of the worker in job task(s) inducing exposure levels potentially exceeding the limits for the general population, such as the ICNIRP limits (ICNIRP, 2009, 2010, 2020) and, in some European Member States, the values provided in the 'Council Recommendation of 12 July 1999 on the limitation of exposure of the general public to electromagnetic fields (from 0 Hz to 300 GHz), 1999/519/EC' (European Council, 1999). Nevertheless, different approaches have been proposed also, and we have to admit that, to date, no widely agreed definition of *'occupationally exposed worker'* seems to be available. One further point to be considered here is that the levels recommended for the general public cannot be seen as completely 'safe', for example, in the case of subjects with active implantable medical devices (AIMD) such as pacemakers, especially in the case of unipolar sensing (Napp et al., 2015). Taking this latter problem into consideration, to ensure more comprehensive prevention, all workers, including those exposed to 'low' levels of EMF, i.e. not exceeding the limits for the general population, should be at least informed about the exposure levels and on the potential hazards from EMF, in particular, on the conditions that may induce increased sensitivity to the risk, and trained on the appropriate health and safety procedures, including the usefulness to seek occupational medical advice if considered necessary/opportune.

Moving to the specific topic of health surveillance for EMF-exposed workers, a relevant example approach to be cited and considered comes from the European Directives on Occupational Health and Safety *'Framework Directive'* 89/391/EEC (European Council, 1989) and *'Directive 2013/35/EU of the European Parliament and of the Council of 26 June 2013 on the minimum health and safety requirements regarding the exposure of workers to the risks arising from physical agents (electromagnetic fields) (20th individual Directive within the meaning of Article 16(1) of Directive 89/391/EEC) and repealing Directive 2004/40/EC'* (European Union, 2013), currently implemented in European Member States (It should be noted here that these directives provide only minimum requirements, and, in the transposition into national legislation, each Member State can freely adopt more restrictive requirements.).

In this chapter, we mainly approach the topic of the OHS of EMF-exposed workers considering the example of the European Directives, as we believe that, overall, at least the general concepts, also including the problem of subjects at particular risk, can represent a good paradigm to be deemed useful also outside of Europe.

7.2 THE ASSESSMENT OF WORK-RELATED EMF RISK IN WORKERS WHEN IMPLEMENTING OHS, AND THE SIGNIFICANT EXPOSURES CAN BE EXPECTED DURING THEIR ACTIVITIES

The OHS of workers should be implemented based on the results of an evaluation of the risk related to the occupational exposure(s) typical of the specific job activity: risk evaluation is, usually, one of the obligations of the employers. For example, it is set out in the European legislation that employers have to *'assess all risks for workers arising from electromagnetic fields at the workplace and, if necessary, measure or calculate the levels of electromagnetic fields to which workers are exposed'* (European Union, 2013). A practical help to this (possibly complicated) task is the three-volume 'Non-binding guide to good practice for implementing Directive 2013/35/EU' of the European Commission. The first volume gives the employer the necessary information to understand what they will need to do to comply with Directive 2013/35/EU

(European Commission, 2014a). *Volume 2* presents examples of risk assessment and EMF exposure evaluation in office environments, in medical units, in industrial settings involving electrolysis processes, welding activities or the use of machinery, as well as in specific sectors such as automotive, metallurgy and airport facilities, in workplaces with rooftop antennas, where walkie-talkies are used and where radio-frequency plasma devices are operated (European Commission, 2014b). Finally, the third volume contains practical indications for the implementation of the directive in small and medium enterprises (SME). In this volume, Table 3.2 entitled '*Requirements for specific EMF assessments in respect of common work activities equipment and workplaces*' deserves particular interest, reporting a comprehensive (even if, inevitably, non-exhaustive) list of occupational sources potentially requiring an assessment of the EMF health risk and where, according to the results, OHS and/or specific measures are likely to be required. All the sources listed in Volume 2 are included, along with other additional examples, such as base station antennas, garden appliances, various electrical installations, generators, inverters, construction equipment and activities, electrically driven trains and trams and other (European Commission, 2014c). We can observe here that, due to the rapid advancement in technology, an update of the non-binding guides, covering the new exposures coming to the occupational environment, would be very helpful and welcome for enterprises.

Various other sources and databases useful in order to identify potentially relevant EMF occupational exposure important for evaluating the need for appropriate measures, including health surveillance, are available. Regarding the extremely-low-frequency (ELF) EMF, examples include the Job Exposure Matrix (JEM) promoted by the National Institute of Occupational Safety and Health (NIOSH), based on the results of power–frequency magnetic fields' (a part of ELF range of magnetic fields—ELF-MF) personal exposure assessment in 2,317 workers (Bowman et al., 2019), or the JEM proposed by Gobba et al. based on ELF-MF 2-days personal monitoring in 543 workers engaged in various industrial sectors (Gobba et al., 2011). Another available database, including measurements and complementary information for the most common sources of EMF exposure in the workplace and covering the entire EMF frequency was prepared by Vila et al. (2016), based on responses to a studies questionnaire by INTERPHONE (INTERPHONE Study Group, 2010) and INTEROCC (Turner et al., 2014). A further database is freely available online at the Italian 'Physical Agents Portal' (PAF) website, https://www.portaleagentifisici.it/?lg=EN (INAIL, 2020), including the results of EMF measurements for several industrial and medical sources, with indications for the evaluation of occupational risk. A comprehensive investigation into relevant EMF exposure sources at the workplace, with the identification of exposure levels by frequency ranges, was performed in the European project EMF-NET (Hansson Mild et al., 2009). Data was collected on specific exposure levels regarding MRI operators, for example, by Karpowicz and Gryz (2013), while other relevant exposure data on the emerging problem of occupational EMF exposure related to Ultra-High-Frequency Radiofrequency Identification (UHF RFID) Guns—an increasingly common and rapidly growing wireless technology, were recently published (Zradziński et al., 2020).

7.3 THE ADVERSE HEALTH EFFECTS IN WORKERS RELATED TO EMF EXPOSURE AND OHS

In a discussion on OHS of EMF-exposed workers, another fundamental preliminary point to consider is the definition of the health effects to be taken into account. The approach adopted by the European Directive 2013/35/EU is to prevent *'all known direct biophysical effects and indirect effects caused by electromagnetic fields'*. The *'suggested long-term effects'* are not addressed, *'since there is currently no well-established scientific evidence of a causal relationship'*, even if the European Commission explicitly makes a commitment to take into account the development of scientific research and new scientific data and, in case *'.... well-established scientific evidence emerges, the Commission should consider the most appropriate means for addressing such effects'*. (European Union, 2013).

Various long-term effects related to EMF exposure have been proposed, including cancer, neurodegenerative and cardiovascular diseases, as well as reproductive outcomes and others. A comprehensive overview of the scientific studies on this topic is well beyond the scope of this chapter and is not approached here; but it seems important to address at least some points. Regarding carcinogenic effects, EMF were evaluated by the International Agency for Cancer Research (IARC) which, in 2001, classified ELF-EMF as possibly carcinogenic to humans (2B) based on a statistical association of higher level residential ELF magnetic fields and an increased risk of childhood leukaemia (while ELF electric fields and static fields were classified as group 3, i.e. 'not classifiable as to its carcinogenicity to humans') (IARC, 2002). In 2011, the IARC included also radiofrequency (RF) EMF in the same group (2B) based on limited evidence in humans related to some positive epidemiological associations observed between exposure to RF radiation from wireless phones and glioma and acoustic neuroma, and limited evidence in experimental animals (IARC, 2013).

So far, despite thousands of scientific studies being published, including epidemiological studies in groups of exposed workers and studies on the time-trends of the incidence of various cancers in different countries, the overall result of several reviews prepared by authoritative international independent scientific experts groups is that a causal association between chronic EMF exposure and long-term effects, including cancer, is not proven (Advisory Group on Non-Ionising Radiation, 2012; Agence nationale de sécurité sanitaire de l'alimentation, de l'environnement et du travail, 2013; Australian Radiation Protection and Nuclear Safety Agency, 2014; Comité Científico Asesor en Radiofrecuencias y Salud, 2017; Health Council of the Netherlands, 2016; Health Council of the Netherlands, 2018; Istituto Superiore di Sanità, 2019; New Zealand Ministry of Health, 2018; Swedish Radiation Safety Authority's Scientific Council on Electromagnetic Fields, 2016). A similar position is also currently adopted by several important public authorities and summarised on their online websites (e.g. Agence nationale de sécurité sanitaire de l'alimentation, de l'environnement et du travail, 2017; American Cancer Society, 2020; Australian Radiation Protection and Nuclear Safety Agency, 2020; Federal Communications Commission, 2015; Food and Drug Administration, 2019; Public Health England, 2019, last accessed April 2023).

According to these premises, for practical purposes the approach of the EU Directive seems commendable, i.e. the EMF-related effects currently to be considered in exposed workers, and therefore in OHS, are the direct biophysical (‘*effects in the human body directly caused by its presence in an electromagnetic field*’) and the indirect effects (‘*effects caused by the presence of an object in an electromagnetic field, which may become the cause of a safety or health hazard*’) as, at present, they are the adverse effects for which there is adequately robust scientific evidence of a causal relation with occupational EMF exposure (European Union, 2013). A list of direct and indirect effects and safety risks of relevance for OHS of EMF-exposed workers considered by the EU Directive is presented in Table 7.1. In any case, as anticipated, when transposing Directive 2013/35/EU, each Member State may adopt different (more restrictive) requirements, which means the health surveillance is not completely unified following the Framework Directive provisions. As a result, OHS criteria may also differ within different European Member States.

Non-thermal direct effects can be induced by static and low-frequency fields, or by movements in the static field, while direct *thermal* effects are related to high-frequency EMF exposure; intermediate frequencies can induce both the direct effects. *Indirect effects* may involve all the frequency bands according to the specific characteristics of the object, environment and of the EMF.

A relevant aspect of the approach of European Directive 2013/35/EU to the direct biophysical effects of the various EMF frequencies on the human body is a further classification into ‘*sensory*’ (Table 7.2) and ‘*health effects*’ (Table 7.3).

TABLE 7.1
Direct Biophysical Effects and Indirect Effects and Safety Risks of Relevance for OHS of EMF-Exposed Workers (According to European Directive 2013/35/EU)

Direct Biophysical Effects	Indirect Effects
• Thermal effect • Non-thermal effects (*stimulation of muscles, nerves or sensory organs, inducing temporary annoyance or leading to a possible detrimental effect, e.g. affect cognition or other brain or muscle functions or induce safety risks)* • Other *(limb currents)*	• ***Interference*** *(with medical electronic equipment and devices, including cardiac pacemakers and other implants or medical devices worn on the body)* • ***Contact currents*** • ***Other*** (as the ‘projectile risk’ in static fields, the initiation of electro-explosive devices, fires and explosions)

TABLE 7.2
Summary of *Sensory Effects* Related to EMF Exposure

Type of EMF	Sensory Effects
Static magnetic fields	Vertigo, nausea, perception of a metallic taste in the mouth
Low-frequency fields	Magnetophosphenes, minor changes in brain function, tingling sensation due to the stimulation of the nerves
Intermediate-frequency fields	Effects of both high and low frequencies can be experienced
High-frequency fields	Microwave auditory effects, microwave stimulation of nerves/receptors in the skin

TABLE 7.3
Summary of the *Health Effects* Related to EMF Exposure

Type of EMF	Health Effects
Static magnetic field	Altered blood flow in limbs, altered brain function, altered heart function (e.g. altered blood flow or cardiac rhythm)
Low-frequency fields	Pain due to the stimulation of the nerves, involuntary contractions of the muscles, alterations of the cardiac rhythm
Intermediate-frequency fields	The effects of both high and low frequencies can be experienced
High-frequency fields	Excessive increase in temperature or thermal burns over the whole body or in specific areas, thermal damage at the eyes (possibility of thermal cataracts) or skin

Sensory effects can be considered somewhat 'minor' adverse effects, as their main characteristics are that they are transient and reversible, with no major direct consequences on the health status of the workers, if not associated with work accidents. These effects, mainly related to relevant static magnetic fields and ELF-EMF exposure (Table 7.2), are due to the stimulation of sensory organs based on the induction of current mechanisms, and may include '*sensory perceptions and effects in the functioning of the central nervous system in the head evoked by time varying magnetic fields*', for example, vertigo and magnetophosphenes, and '*static magnetic field effects, such as vertigo and nausea*' (European Union, 2013). A summary of the relevant sensory effects related to exposure to the various frequency regions of the EMF spectrum is reported in Table 7.2 (European Commission, 2014a).

The '*health effects*' are more severe effects that can imply an impairment of the health of workers. These effects are generally only induced by high levels of EMF, and they are related to non-thermal (e.g. heart arrhythmia) or thermal mechanisms (e.g. burns), respectively, in case of low-frequency/static fields exposure or in case of high-frequency fields. The body of data on the effective impact on workers' health is relatively limited, though transient and reversible alterations are often described. A summary of the relevant *health effects* related to EMF exposure according to the various frequency regions of the EMF spectrum is set out in Table 7.3 (European Commission, 2014a).

7.4 LIMITATION OF WORKERS' EMF EXPOSURE FOR THE PREVENTION OF POSSIBLE ADVERSE HEALTH EFFECTS

With the objective of preventing the appearance of EMF exposure direct effects, as well as (most of) the indirect effects (with some exceptions, as it will be discussed in detail in the next section of this chapter), the 2013 European Directive introduced specific ELVs and action levels (ALs). The bases for these limits are explicitly defined in the text of the directive, which sets out that ELVs are '*established on the basis of biophysical and biological considerations, in particular, on the basis of scientifically well-established short-term and acute direct effects, i.e. thermal effects and electrical stimulation of tissues*' (European Union, 2013). Two types of ELV are defined in the EU Directive: '*sensory effects ELVs*', defined as '*ELVs above which workers might be subject to transient disturbed sensory perceptions and minor changes in brain functions*', and '*health effects ELVs*', i.e. '*those ELVs above which workers might be subject to adverse health effects, such as thermal heating or stimulation of nerve and muscle tissue*' (European Union, 2013). In general, EMF exposures exceeding the ELVs are necessary to induce direct effects, as the induction of nerve stimulation and involuntary muscle contraction, and only at levels significantly above the ELVs is possible to observe direct '*health effects*' such as changes in blood flow in limbs and/or heart rate (ICNIRP, 2014; SCENIHR, 2015).

Direct effects of radio frequencies are related to thermal mechanisms: a temperature increase, localised or generalised, of more than 4°C can cause damage to the biological tissue, even if usually reversible, while the damage becomes irreversible for protein denaturation with a temperature increase of more than 6°C (i.e. localised or generalised body temperature >43°C). Workers' RF exposures sufficient to induce such thermal effects are currently considered rare/unlikely in the majority of well-organised workplaces, even if they were described in the past in case of accidental exposures, and also some cases of high RF exposures have been recently reported after work-related accidents (Moen et al., 2013). An underreporting cannot be excluded, as data are rare and sparse, and insufficient effort was devoted up now to investigate this problem. Especially in the low-MHz region, the resulting injuries can involve the tissues without obvious superficial burns, being easily underrated; keratitis and iritis were also described (Hocking and Gobba, 2011). In experimental studies on small-sized animals, serious adverse effects have been observed in case of exposures corresponding to whole-body SAR levels between 10 and 100 W/kg (i.e. 20–200 times multiple of the ELV), while minor effects (i.e. behavioural alterations) in case of exposures in the order of whole-body SAR levels between 1 and 4 W/kg have been reported (i.e. 2–10 times multiple of the ELV). Finally, local thermal effects such as skin burns and acute thermal cataract have been observed in animals for local SAR levels of 100 W/kg (10 times multiple of the corresponding head and neck ELV) (ICNIRP, 2020; SCENIHR, 2015).

Considering the importance of the respect of the ELVs for the prevention of direct effects related to EMF exposure, but on the other hand considering also the operational difficulties in evaluating individual EMF exposure warranting the compliance with the ELVs (assessable by numerical simulations only), the EU Directive also introduced '*action levels (ALs)*', which are '*operational levels established for the purpose of simplifying the process of demonstrating the compliance with relevant ELVs or, where appropriate, to take relevant protection or prevention measures*'. Two types of ALs are defined: '*low ALs*' and '*high ALs*', which, for magnetic fields, are, respectively, the '*levels that relate to the sensory effects ELVs*' and '*to the health effects ELVs*' (European Union, 2013).

7.5 THE PROBLEM OF THE '*WORKERS AT PARTICULAR RISK*' AND EMF EXPOSURE

The objective of any activity aimed at the prevention of occupational EMF risks is '*to ensure that risks arising from electromagnetic fields at the workplace are eliminated or reduced to a minimum*' (European Union, 2013). In this context, a relevant aspect to be considered is the possible occurrence of 'particularly sensitive workers'

(This group is expressly provided in a European directive – '*Framework Directive*' 89/391/EEC (European Council, 1989). Specifically, considering the occupational EMF health risk, the existence of subgroups of persons who are more vulnerable (or potentially more vulnerable) due to various physiological or pathological conditions is a known issue. As an example, these workers, defined '*workers at particular risk*', are specially recognised and taken into account in the EU Directive. This concept is introduced in Article 4 of the EU Directive: '*when carrying out the risk assessment ... the employer shall give particular attention to ... any effects on the health and safety of workers at particular risk ....*' (European Union, 2013). Accordingly, for a comprehensive assessment of the risks and for the development of adequate preventive interventions, the necessary actions to be implemented include not only an exhaustive inventory of all potentially relevant EMF sources and an evaluation of the occupational risk by comparison with occupational exposure limits, but also an exhaustive investigation on the potential presence of workers with conditions making them particularly susceptibility to risk, with the aim of evaluating specific areas on the working environment, which may be restricted for some users of AIMD, and with special needs concerning training and information on EMF risks (Zradziński et al., 2018). In such a way, providing an individual evaluation of the risk related to the specific task(s) for the worker equipped with particular AIMD and, in case, adequate restrictions, is possible, in order to avoid the exclusion of a subject with AIMD from workplaces where a potential (general) EMF risk can exist.

A practical example of managing and protecting '*workers at particular risk*' can result from EU Directive 2013/35, Article 5 of which, on the definition of adequate preventive measures, sets out that '*the employer shall devise and implement an action plan that shall include technical and/or organizational measures to prevent any risks to workers at particular risk ...* ' and in the following Article 6 on information and training of the workers, sets out that '*the employer shall ensure that workers who are likely to be exposed to risks from electromagnetic fields at work and/or their representatives receive any necessary information and training relating to the outcome of the risk assessment provided for in Article 4 of this Directive, concerning in particular... workers at particular risk*' (European Union, 2013).

However, one problem in this respect is that, to date, there is no exhaustive list of conditions inducing a *particular risk*. A partial definition is given in Article 5 of the EU Directive, where it is recommended to carry out '*individual risks assessments, in particular, in respect of workers who have declared the use of active or passive implanted medical devices, such as cardiac pacemakers, or the use of medical devices worn on the body, such as insulin pumps, or in respect of pregnant workers who have informed their employer of their condition*' (European Union, 2013). In Article 4, comma 5d, and Article 5 comma 4, the directive explicitly describes two types of conditions inducing '*... particular risk ...*': implanted (or body worn) medical devices, whether active or passive devices, and pregnancy, though these are cited only as examples. A more comprehensive list of conditions determining a particular sensitivity to the risk, categorised into four groups, is presented in the following Table 7.4, derived adapting the indications from the previously mentioned *non-binding guide* (European Commission, 2014a), and a 2016 UK guide published by the Health and Safety Executive (HSE, 2016).

TABLE 7.4
Non-Exhaustive List of Health Conditions Potentially Inducing a Particular Risk in EMF-Exposed Workers (From: European Commission, 2014a, modified)

Categories of *Workers at Particular Risk*	**Examples of the Health Conditions Potentially Inducing a Particular Risk in Relation to EMF Exposure in the Workplace**
Workers using active implantable medical devices (AIMD)	Workers with cardiac pacemakers, cardiac defibrillators, cochlear implants, brainstem implants, inner ear prostheses, neurostimulators, retinal encoders, implanted drug infusion pumps
Workers using passive implanted medical devices (especially when containing metal and ferromagnetic parts when exposure to static magnetic field)	Workers with artificial joints, pins, plates, screws, surgical clips, aneurism clips, stents, heart valve prostheses and other prostheses (including orthopaedic, eye/retinal and other), annuloplasty rings, metallic contraceptive implants
Workers using body-worn medical devices	Workers with external hormone infusion pumps, hearing aids, continuous glucose monitoring systems and metallised drug-delivery patches
Other categories (not including the use of medical devices)	Pregnant workers

7.5.1 Workers with Medical Devices

In all cases presented in Table 7.4 involving an implanted or body-worn device, the condition of particular susceptibility to the risk is due to a possible indirect effect of EMF exposure. More specifically, for all active devices the main effect is the possibility of interference with the functioning of the device, while for both active and passive devices, if there are metallic parts possibly interacting with EMF, there are other possible indirect effects to be considered: a mechanical effect possibly inducing the dislocation of the ferromagnetic device (mainly related to high inhomogeneous static magnetic field exposure or pulsed exposure static magnetic field) or the induction of contact or induced currents, possibly determining an inflammatory reaction of body tissue with different possible mechanisms (Hocking & Hansson Mild, 2008). These mechanisms are expected and are considered of concern only in the case of quite significant EMF exposure of subjects with devices containing a certain quantity of metal (e.g. prosthesis, vascular clips, stents or other devices containing electrically conductive materials). Also non-medical body inclusions (e.g. metal splinters, body piercings, metallic pigments used in tattoos, etc.) may possibly represent a risk in these cases.

On the other hand, EMF interference with active devices is also possible in the case of relatively low EMF exposure, below the ELVs defined in the 2013 EU Directive and, in some cases, possibly even below the limits recommended for the general public. Accordingly, this issue deserves particular consideration for the prevention of EMF risk at work and for the health surveillance of workers. Pacemakers and implantable cardiac defibrillators (ICD) are the most studied AIMD with regard to their possible interference with EMF. The first relevant consideration is that the number of workers with AIMD is currently significant, and has been constantly increasing in recent years, for two main reasons:

a. The development of technologies and their increased safety, which leads to a significant increase in the number of implants according to new clinical indications and new types of devices available;
b. The progressive ageing of the working population in the recent years, resulting in a higher prevalence of workers with AIMD.

The interference of EMF with AIMD may result in disturbances in the electric signals detected by the devices and/or in interference involving the electronic circuits of the devices directly. Both these conditions can cause alterations of the sensing functions of the devices, with possible consequences being inhibiting the stimulation or inappropriate stimulations, and in the worst cases permanent damage to the device requiring a reset or a replacement. The (scarce) available data suggest that, to a large extent, minor interferences with AIMD are completely reversible and clinically silent, so that the workers do not perceive any malfunction, and the problems are discovered only after a periodical check of the devices, if they are able to register their activities, when episodes of interference could be detected and analysed. Clinical manifestations could be severe in the case of interference occurring at the same time as a needed stimulation (e.g. an alteration in the sensing function of a pacemaker or an ICD, causing the device not to recognise a change in the cardiac rhythm that needs an appropriate and immediate electric stimulation), and any event that results in a permanent alteration of the sensing function or of the setting of the devices, or in a significant unrequested stimulation.

Fortunately, considering the published scientific literature on this topic, the reporting of in vivo malfunctions of AIMD of workers exposed to EMF is rare, and one of the reason may be the relatively low levels of exposure, when compared to the ELVs, detectable in the majority of real workplaces; among the few available examples in occupational settings, there is the study of Souques et al., describing a risk assessment protocol of three subjects with ICDs working in an electricity company and exposed to 50 Hz EMF, finding no interference problems (Souques et al., 2011). In another study by Tiikkaja et al., 24 volunteers, 11 with a pacemaker and 13 with an ICD, were exposed to various types of low-frequency magnetic fields (2–200 Hz) with flux densities up to 300 μT (representing a small percentage of the relevant ELV), in order to evaluate possible interference problems. Moreover, the subjects were also exposed to EMF emitted by an electronic article surveillance (EAS) gate, an induction cooktop and a metal inert gas (MIG) welding machine, again looking for possible interference problems. In all the exposure scenarios it was found that none of the pacemakers with bipolar settings and none of the ICDs experienced any interference. Three pacemakers with unipolar settings were affected by the highest fields of experimental exposure with magnetic fields at frequencies of 2–200 Hz, and one of them also by the EAS gate and the welding cable (Tiikkaja et al., 2013).

On the other hand, there are some studies based on mannequin models that were showing relevant interference problems of AIMD within static magnetic fields produced by MRI scanners (Mattei et al., 2015, 2016a, b), or were studying the interference risk of various types of cardiac pacemakers in work scenarios as workers affected by spark discharges (Korpinen et al., 2016) or immersed in the magnetic fields of shunt reactors at 400 kV substation (Korpinen et al., 2015). Other experimental studies evaluate possible interference in standard exposure conditions, for example of GSM mobile phones (Huang et al., 2015) and of walking-through metal detector security systems (Guag et al., 2017) with various AIMDs. In all these cases, the interference is most often detected in the case of older devices with unipolar configuration, while the most recent bipolar devices seem to be less affected by electromagnetic interference. Nevertheless, in the case of relevant EMF exposure, newer devices can also be susceptible to interference, and, as shown by examples, patients with AIMD classified as "MRI-conditional" when undergoing an MRI examination need an appropriate setting of the devices before accessing the scanner (Nazarian et al., 2017; Klein-Wiele et al., 2017). With regard to work-related EMF exposure, this *ad hoc* setting of the device cannot be applied, as it is not possible to temporarily adjust an individual medical device according to the needs of the working activities, so that the fitness to work of people with AIMD exposed to relevant EMF sources may represent a problem. If needed, an individual risk assessment can be performed, for example, according to the European Standard CENELEC-EN 50527-2-1:2016 for pacemakers (European Committee for Electrotechnical Standardisation, 2016) or the CENELEC-EN 50527-2-2:2018 for cardioverter defibrillators (CENELEC–EN, 2018). It has to be noted that for specific sources, such as mobile phones, properly informing the workers with AIMD and recommending the respect of the instructions for the use of the instruments (usually requiring a distance of 15–20 cm from the AIMD) should be considered usually sufficient.

Turning to other possible indirect effects involving non-active medical devices, it should be noted an Italian case report (Gobba et al., 2012), confirmed more recently by a Dutch cohort study in 381 female radiographers working with MRI scanners (Huss et al., 2018), showed an increase in the risk of abnormal uterine bleeding among women wearing Intrauterine Contraceptive Devices (IUDs). The mechanism(s) involved have not yet been elucidated.

7.5.2 Pregnant Workers

According to European Directive 2013/35/EU, another condition considered as potentially inducing a particular risk for EMF-exposed workers is pregnancy. In this case, the possibility of direct effects must be considered. In general, some data suggesting an increased susceptibility of the foetus to the thermal effect induced by exposure to high-frequency EMFs are available (Murbach et al., 2017), while scarce published scientific data show a definite increased occupational risk in pregnant women exposed to static or low-frequency EMF (IARC 2002; SCENIHR, 2015; WHO, 2005 2007). In some epidemiological studies performed in the past in video display units (VDU) users, a possible association with adverse pregnancy outcomes was suggested; due to some limits in these studies as the lack of EMF measurements, especially the oldest ones, (but measurements performed in other studies showed levels of EMF generally compliant with the general public exposure limits, or even significantly lower depending on the technology of VDU manufacturing) and the scarce coherence of the results (Brent et al., 1993; Delpizzo, 1994; IARC, 2002;

Juutilainen, 1991; Lindbohm et al., 1992; Schnorr et al., 1991; Parazzini et al., 1993; Shaw, 2001; Shaw and Croen, 1993), the evidence on association between adverse pregnancy outcomes and EMF work-related exposure is currently considered inadequate (IARC 2002, SCENIHR, 2015; WHO, 2005 2007). Some quite large epidemiological studies on cohorts of pregnant women exposed to ELF-EMF (Migault et al., 2018; Ren et al., 2019) and higher frequency EMF from other sources (Khan et al., 2018; Tsarna et al., 2019) have recently been published: no association between maternal work-related ELF-EMF exposure and an increased risks of moderate prematurity or of being small for the gestational age was observed, while a possible association between maternal cell-phone use during pregnancy and a shorter pregnancy duration, and increased risk of preterm birth was described, even though these preliminary data, especially the causal role of EMF, has still to be confirmed in further scientific studies, and also possible mechanisms should be elucidated. The main issue in discussing evidence-based data on the problem of the risk related to EMF exposure in pregnant worker is that in the large majority of the available studies (except, for example, some old studies on VDU workers), the exposures considered were low, mainly (largely) compliant with the general population limits, while the recent epidemiological results in pregnant workers exposed to levels exceeding, or in the order, of the current occupational exposure limits are lacking.

On the other hand, we have to consider here that the Directive 92/85/EEC (European Council, 1992) includes the exposure to non-ionising radiation among the activities liable to involve a specific risk for pregnant women, and that in the Directive 2013/35/EU '*pregnant workers*' are explicitly cited among '*workers at particular risk*', deserving '*particular attention*' and an '*individual risk assessment*', and that '*technical and/or organisational measures to prevent any risks to workers*' have to be adapted to the needs of these workers (European Union, 2013).

A last consideration that deserves to be mentioned here is that, even if the mother is a worker, and is consequently subjected, for example, to European Directives on exposed workers as the 35/2013 or 92/85, etc., this is not the case for the product of conception that, in principle, should be rather considered similar/comparable to a member of the general population.

Based on these considerations, compliance with the ELVs established by European Directive 2013/35/EU may not be considered sufficiently protective for pregnant workers (at least in Europe), and it would be advisable to refer to lower exposure limits, such as those set for the general public according to European Recommendation 1999/519/EC, and more recently updated for some EMF frequency bands by the International Commission on Non-Ionising Radiation Protection (ICNIRP 2009, 2010, 2014, 2020), or even lower than these limits in some countries, as France or Italy, for a '*quality objective*'.

7.5.3 Possible other Conditions Inducing a Particular Susceptibility to the EMF Risk

Discussing other possible conditions determining a particular risk for EMF-exposed workers, as stated above, no other conditions are listed, whether in European Directive 2013/35/EU or in the related '*non-binding guides*'. Furthermore, excluding the aforementioned problems of medical devices and pregnancy, scant and scattered sound scientific literature data currently exists on other groups of workers to be considered at particular risk. In principle, based on the recognised biophysical mechanisms of EMF interaction with human tissues and organs, two main situations may be considered:

a. For static and low-frequency fields, as the main known mechanism is the induction of current, an increased risk may be induced by para-physiological and/or pathological conditions inducing a possible reduction of thresholds in biological systems basing their function on electrophysiological signals (e.g. heart/cardiovascular function, neural and neuromuscular function, etc.);
b. For high-frequency EMF, as the biological effects are mainly based on thermal mechanisms, any possible para-physiological and/or pathological condition determining an increased susceptibility to changes in the temperature of the body, as, for example, alterations of the thermoregulatory function, may be of possible interest.

In the case of intermediate frequencies, as both mechanisms are possible, all the above-mentioned conditions may be of interest.

Despite these considerations, very few scientific data, if any, are currently available regarding the possible thresholds for the occurrence of static or low-frequency EMF-related effects in subjects affected, for example, by epilepsy or by a pathologic alteration of the cardiac rhythm, or similar, compared with healthy subjects. Similarly, no data are available on the possible threshold for the appearance of RF-related thermal effects in subjects with hyperthyroidism or other known conditions affecting thermoregulation compared to healthy subjects (SCENIHR, 2015; Swedish Radiation Safety Authority's Scientific Council on Electromagnetic Fields, 2016). The main causes of this scant knowledge are the difficulty in performing such studies in workers related to practical problems such as the selection of adequate study groups, an adequate evaluation of exposure, the control of possible interfering factors as well as obvious ethical issues, especially in case of exposure to significant levels of EMF. As a consequence, scientific evidence is mainly derived from experimental in vitro and animal studies, and from case reports or from (quite) small human studies performed in healthy volunteers groups exposed to EMF and investigated for possible electroencephalography alterations during sleep or for alterations in performance and cognitive tests (de Vocht et al., 2003, 2006, 2007; Heinrich et al., 2013; van Nierop et al., 2012, 2013, 2015). Recently, some additional research focused on the problem of possible alterations of the cardiovascular function after EMF exposure, mainly RF, using, for example, heart rate variability or elevated blood pressure as outcome parameters (Bongers et al., 2018; Malek et al., 2015; Misek et al., 2018; Devasani and Razdan, 2017; Ekici. et al., 2016). The results of these studies are still rather heterogeneous, supporting the opportunity for further well-designed research to replicate the results, and to better understand the possible mechanisms and the EMF exposures involved.

But besides the incompleteness of the data, another important issue to be considered in this context is the problem of biological sensitivity and variability in the setting of exposure limits. These factors affect the estimates of the thresholds for effects and dose–response relationships, and, consequently, they are also of great relevance in the setting of exposure limits (Bailey and Erdreich, 2007). For example, in the case of the perception of electric 50 Hz currents, an inter-individual variability of two orders of magnitudes was reported in different subjects, investigated with pairs of electrodes at the lower forearms. Moreover, women as well as children (up to about 10 y/o) were found to be more sensitive than men (Leitgeb et al., 2007). According to some authors, the ranges of individual sensitivity have not been adequately considered, nor assessed, in the current ICNIRP limits (Bailey and Erdreich, 2007).

This opens the problem of the possible existence of another group of subjects 'at particular risk', possibly not adequately protected by the current limits due to a higher individual sensitivity. The proportion of such subjects is unknown but presumably very small; in any case, considering the total number of EMF-exposed workers, the absolute number can be possibly not negligible. The effects possibly induced, presumably sensory and/or health effects, are unknown. As a consequence, a systematic, active seeking, and collection of the occurrence of any symptom and sign possibly related to EMF is fundamental in the OHS of these workers.

In conclusion, according to the results of scientific research on the conditions, and on mechanisms possibly inducing *particular risk* for workers in the event of their work-related EMF exposure, sufficient data are currently available for workers with medical devices, especially AIMD such as ICD and pacemakers in unipolar mode. Pregnant workers should also be considered to be at particular risk; in Europe, the inclusion of this group is provided by EU Directives 92/85/EEC and 2013/35/EU. Regarding other conditions possibly inducing a particular risk in the case of work-related EMF exposure, the scientific data are largely insufficient, even if some available data suggest the existence of an inter-individual variability with respect to personal sensitivity to EMF-related direct effects, which are possibly not adequately addressed in the definition of the ELVs and ALs. More systematic theoretical and experimental considerations of mentioned problems are needed within further EMF research, especially focused on the health or safety effects of EMF exposure at the high level.

According to these and other considerations, for preventive purposes, an active systematic seeking of symptoms and signs possibly related to EMF should be considered when approaching the problem of the health surveillance of EMF-exposed workers; and occupational physicians should look for and follow, in particular, the possible evolutions/changes in the course and/or in their clinical/symptomatic manifestations, possibly in relation with occupational exposure. The results of OHS performed in EMF-exposed workers should be especially important in the case of, among other, workers with conditions possibly inducing a particular risk. In this respect, interestingly EU Directive 2013/35/EU requires that the results of OHS '*shall be preserved in a suitable form that allows them to be consulted at a later date*' (Art. 8), and in the Preamble it involves the possibility for the commission to acquire *the appropriate information that it receives from Member States,* to keep the European Parliament and the Council informed about any new evidence on the possible health effects related to work-related EMF exposure.

7.6 GENERAL CRITERIA FOR THE OHS OF EMF-EXPOSED WORKERS

As anticipated, OHS of EMF-exposed workers is a legal obligation in Europe based on the Framework Directive (European Council, 1989) and on Directive 2013/35/EU (European Union, 2013), even though it is not harmonised across European Member States.

According to Article 8 of the Directive 2013/35/EU (European Union, 2013), OHS is aimed at the prevention and early diagnosis of any adverse health effects due to EMF exposure, i.e. mainly those that have been scientifically proven and biologically demonstrated. Accordingly, OHS of exposed workers chiefly address the direct biophysical effects and indirect effects of EMF exposure, i.e. the effects for which there are recognised, plausible biological mechanisms; these effects were discussed earlier in this chapter. Other effects, including the suggested long-term effects and others, as the *idiopathic environmental intolerance attributed to electromagnetic fields* (IEI-EMF), are not necessarily taken into account during the OHS, as a causal association with the occupational risk factor is not proven. Nevertheless, as reported in the Directive, in the event that scientific knowledge resulting from new research data and from appropriate information received from Member States supports a well-established evidence on such effects, The Commission should consider the most appropriate means for addressing these effects, possibly including the integration in OHS activities of EMF-exposed workers.

As defined at the beginning of this chapter, workers' OHS includes various actions for the assessment and protection of workers' health with respect to an occupational risk factor, and the procedures involved '*...may include, but are not limited to, medical examinations, biological monitoring, radiological examinations, questionnaires or a review of health records*' (ILO, 1998). In the definition of OHS programmes it must be considered that, according to the '*International code of ethics for occupational health professionals*' of the International Commission on Occupational Health (ICOH), '*Biological tests and other investigations must be chosen for their validity and relevance for protection of the health of the worker concerned, with due regard to their sensitivity, their specificity and their predictive value*', and '*Occupational health professionals must not use screening tests or investigations which are not reliable or which do not have a sufficient predictive value in relation to the requirements of the work assignment*' (ICOH, 2014).

As discussed in another part of this chapter, EMF exposure can induce indirect effects as well as direct effects, the latter of thermal and non-thermal type; the thermal ones are induced mainly by high-frequency EMF, while the non-thermal ones are induced mainly by static and low-frequency time-varying EMF. To date, no lab-tests or other medical investigations have been demonstrated as effective, or useful, for the monitoring of these EMF-related adverse effects for the purposes of prevention during an appropriate routine OHS of workers occupationally exposed. Even in the case of '*extraordinary*' health surveillance of workers, such as the situations explicitly cited in the Directive 2013/35/EU in the case that '*any undesired or unexpected health effect is reported by a worker*' or '*in any event where exposure above the ELVs is detected*', requiring that '*the employer shall ensure that appropriate medical examinations or individual health surveillance is provided to the worker(s) concerned*' (European Union, 2013), no authoritative and/or shared guidelines or operational instructions currently exist for these *medical examinations.* Various problems should be considered in this context, including differences in modality of exposure, frequency involved, body area(s) interested, etc. Furthermore, an exposure exceeding the ELVs does not necessarily result in the occurrence of adverse health effects in exposed workers (Gobba and Korpinen, 2018). Also, (especially) in case, overexposures, particularly to sensitive workers represent a somewhat special case.

In general, in case an extraordinary health surveillance is needed, an appropriate in-depth medical examination to the worker provided by an occupational physician with an adequate competence in the field, possibly integrated by specific medical consultation(s) and, in case, laboratory tests and/or diagnostic exams on an individual basis, is the approach recommended.

Current available experience suggests that, in the *health surveillance* of EMF-exposed workers, the occurrence of '*health effects*' (as defined in the European Directive 2013/35, referred in Table 7.3) is rarely or extremely rarely observed, and mainly in the case of accidents at work near the powerful sources of very high EMF (Hocking and Gobba, 2011). The reporting of certain '*sensory effects*' in EMF-exposed workers seems less unusual, especially in case of exposure to a strong static field in MRI activities. These effects are considered rapidly reversible after the interruption of EMF exposure and without significant clinical consequences. However, some of them, for example, acute vertigo and contact currents perception, may represent a risk of accidents of various types, including the possibility of the worker falling (Hartwig et al., 2021; Modenese and Gobba, 2021).

Another possibility when designing health surveillance programmes for groups of EMF-exposed workers is an adequate consultation of available scientific literature on possible effects reported in workers exposed in similar conditions, if available. Considering EMF exposure and the possible occurrence of sensory effects, in some specific groups of EMF-exposed subjects, such as during MRI activities, several scientific publications have reported an increased occurrence of minor and reversible alterations in performance, balance and cognitive tests, suggesting possible short-term changes in attention, concentration and other functions (de Vocht et al., 2003, 2006, 2007; Heinrich et al., 2013; van Nierop et al., 2012, 2013, 2015). An exhaustive analysis of these scientific findings is beyond the scope of this chapter, but it should be noted that these effects have usually been detected after intense exposure to static field in groups of volunteers, so the exposure cannot really be considered comparable to the usual exposure of MRI operators. Nevertheless, the possible impact on the work performance of workers, such as MRI operators, should be considered and monitored during OHS activities, at least for the prevention of possible work-related injuries. Interestingly, the topic of accidents, and, in particular, of car accidents and near-missed car accidents after work, has been recently reported in two quite large Dutch studies (approximately 500 subjects per study) performed by the same research group in cohorts of workers, respectively, engaged in a MRI scanners' production facility (Bongers et al., 2016) and as MRI operators (Huss et al., 2017). Even if in the case of the MRI scanners' production facility the EMF exposure was really peculiar and different from that of a large part of MRI operators, and in the case of the MRI operators study the increased risk was limited to subjectively reported near-missed accidents, the results reported, suggesting a possible increased risk of accidents, seem to deserve the opportunity of future research.

Another field that should be considered for the definition of an appropriate OHS programme is the one involving the reporting of sensory symptoms, again in subjects with high static field exposure, such as MRI operators. Various studies are available on this topic (Bravo et al., 2021; Schaap et al., 2014, 2016; de Vocht et al., 2015; Friebe et al., 2015; Zanotti et al., 2015, 2016; Wilén and de Vocht, 2011), showing a quite a high prevalence of several subjective symptoms, frequently collected through self-administrated questionnaires. These symptoms include some non-specific clinical signs that can be related to several medical conditions, for example, migraine, asthenia and memory loss, and it should be noted that their occurrence may be highly confounded by other occupational and non-occupational risk factors (e.g. distress, concomitant diseases and related therapies, etc.). On the other hand, other reported symptoms are more specific and are also in line with those cited in the European Directive. Recently, a group of five more specific symptoms were proposed as '*core symptoms*', to be possibly focused and monitored for their evolution during the health surveillance of MRI operators, and possibly of other workers with relevant high exposure to static and low-frequency EMF. These five symptoms are vertigo, nausea, head ringing, magnetophosphenes and a metallic taste (Schaap et al., 2014); all these symptoms may be related to a direct sensory effect, based on the induction of currents in the body, of the magnetic field exposure of the MRI operators, in particular, if they perform (rapid) movements within the field. An investigation of these symptoms could be important during health surveillance activities, at least of MRI operators; during OHS, physicians should periodically monitor the possible causes of these symptoms, changes in frequency/severity, the need for drug therapies and associations with a particular work organisation, in order to identify appropriate preventive initiatives, and, in particular, adequate information and training (e.g. on the need to avoid rapid movements close to a MRI scanner), to preserve the fitness for work of the operators.

The other type of effects to be considered in the OHS activities are the *indirect effects*. In particular, all workers with body-worn and/or implanted medical and/or non-medical devices should be appropriately considered in order to identify the *workers at particular risk*, for the prevention of possible interference problems. The identification of *workers at particular risk* is for sure one of the most important activities (possibly the most important from the practical point of view), during the OHS of EMF-exposed workers.

To identify such workers, a practical and useful tool is the collection of specific questionnaires listing all the significant conditions including the presence of the medical devices and other (as described in Table 7.4) and other non-medical body inclusions/implants such as metal splinters, piercings, tattoos (with metal-based pigments), etc. As such questionnaires collect medical data, obviously they must comply with medical confidentiality and can be acquired by authorised health personnel only in the respect of the privacy of the workers.

A specific problem is the possible occurrence of one of the above-mentioned conditions inducing a particular susceptibility to the EMF risk in a worker not included in an OHS program or in case of the occurrence during the period between two OHS interventions. In these cases a direct communication of the condition to the employer should be considered unethical, as medical information are covered under doctor–patient confidentiality. A practical possibility applied in some countries, as in Italy, according to the national legislation is that the worker asks for the need of occupational medical advice due to an occupation-related health problem, without any obligation to declare the specific problem. Of course, a necessary prerequisite is that, as anticipated in Section 7.1, the workers are informed about the exposure levels and on the conditions that may induce increased sensitivity to EMF risk, and trained on the appropriate health and safety procedures, including the need to seek occupational medical advice if considered necessary/opportune. Such information should be refreshed on a regular basis, possibly also during OHS.

In some cases, for example, in case of low EMF exposure related to the use of a mobile phone, a worker with an AIMD has only to be appropriately informed about the preventive measures to be applied (i.e. maintaining the device in a suitable distance from the source) and, in principle, no specific health surveillance is necessarily needed, as the use of these devices following the instructions of the manufacturer is sufficient to avoid any interference problem. In other cases, a communication of the occupational physician to the employer may be necessary in order to implement measures ensuring the prevention of the health and safety of the workers, possibly including a risk assessment and/or the delimitation of specific areas. In any case, the privacy of the involved individual must be preserved as far as possible, for example, preferring the communication of collective anonymous data.

Anyway, the fitness for work of subjects with particular susceptibility to EMF, especially in case of relevant risk, should be reconsidered and frequently monitored in order to highlight any occurrence of possibly related events, including those that could pass unnoticed.

As previously described, a case deserving specific attention is the presence of workers with AIMD, as adverse effects (such as interference) may occur even at exposure levels below the exposure limits recommended for the general public. Sometimes these effects may be not clearly perceived and recognised, and may be potentially dangerous. In these cases the possible relations of eventual electromagnetic interferences with the work tasks performed by the subjects could be carefully investigated during OHS activities, and the medical specialist responsible for the devices could be consulted. If needed, the procedures described in Section 7.5.1 (Workers with Medical Devices) can be applied.

7.7 CONCLUSIONS

In conclusion, the health surveillance of EMF-exposed workers is a legal obligation in Europe according to the Framework Directive and Directive 2013/35/EU.

An appropriate occupational health surveillance should include a list of actions aimed at evaluating workers' health, in order to perform an early detection and identification of any adverse effect related to an occupational risk factor (ILO, 1998).

As reported in the European Directive 2013/35/EU, specific OHS actions are needed to address the protection from the risks related to known short-term direct biophysical and indirect short-term effects caused by EMF, while the proposed long-term effects are not covered, as, at present, a causal relationship between exposure and this type of adverse effects is considered not adequately demonstrated by the available scientific evidence.

However, the European Commission monitors the advancements of research and new scientific knowledge, as well as appropriate information received from Member States; if any well-established evidence of a causal relationship of other effects will emerge, the commission will consider the most appropriate means for addressing such effects, and will keep the European Parliament and Council informed.

A relevant aspect of occupational EMF risk is the occurrence of groups of workers considered '*at particular risk*'. A comprehensive, shared list of physiological and pathological conditions inducing a particular risk related to EMF exposure is not defined, but at least those workers with implanted or body-worn medical devices (in particular, ICDs and cardiac pacemakers, especially those in unipolar mode), or other implanted or body-worn devices with metal components, and pregnant workers should be included. Knowledge on other possible conditions inducing a particular risk to EMF is currently insufficient due to the lack of adequately designed scientific studies as a result, among other, of the variability of individual sensitivity to EMF exposure and of the variability of exposure parameters.

Regarding the criteria and the contents of an 'adequate' health surveillance of EMF-exposed workers, up until now there is no agreement, and differences among the various European Member States are likely, though a specific objective should be, at least, the (early) detection of EMF-related adverse effects, such as the stimulation of muscles, nerves or sensory organs (including temporary annoyance or effects on cognition) and limb currents, or any thermal effects. In the case of strict compliance with the current ELVs, these effects are usually prevented, though it has to be noted that exceeding the ELV cannot be excluded or can be possibly expected, especially during certain occupational activities, such as MRI. Furthermore, ELVs may not be adequately protective in the case of '*workers at particular risk*'; for this reason, the identification of these workers is an essential component of an appropriate OHS programme for EMF-exposed workers.

Regarding possible tests and other monitoring procedures, to date, no specific single laboratory tests or other medical investigations have been demonstrated as effective for an appropriate routine OHS of all exposed workers, and even in the case of '*extraordinary*' health surveillance, no 'a priori' recognised valid contents have been identified and proposed. In general, in this case the approach recommended is an appropriate in-depth medical examination to the worker provided by an occupational physician with an adequate competence in the field, possibly integrated by specific medical consultation(s) and, in case, laboratory tests and/or diagnostic exams on an individual basis.

One last point to mention here is that, according to the EU Directive 2013/35/EU, the results of the OHS '*shall be preserved in a suitable form that allows them to be consulted at a later date*' (Article 8); this point seems relevant because the data, if properly collected and evaluated, may provide an important source of evidence on any possible health effects related to EMF occupational exposure. The problem here is that, to the best of our knowledge, to date no effort is ongoing and none is planned, at least at an international level, to provide any collection of these data. Furthermore, and equally important, the current unavailability of shared OHS programmes for EMF-exposed workers makes almost impossible or, in any case, of little benefit any similar collection. In our opinion these problems, likely to offer important answers in the field of the health and safety of workers that are EMF-exposed, would require an urgent and more adequate effort.

REFERENCES

ACS [American Cancer Society]. 2020. Cancer A-Z. What causes cancer? Sun and other types of radiation. US. http://www.cancer.org/cancer/cancer-causes/radiation-exposure.html (accessed April 19, 2023).

AGNIR [Advisory Group on Non-Ionising Radiation]. 2012. *Health Effects from Radiofrequency Electromagnetic Fields*. London: Health Protection Agency. https://assets.publishing.service.gov.uk/government/uploads/system/uploads/attachment_data/file/333080/RCE-20_Health_Effects_RF_Electromagnetic_fields.pdf (accessed April 19, 2023).

ANSES [Agence Nationale de Sécurité Sanitaire de l'Alimentation de l'Environnement et du Travail]. 2013. Radiofréquences et santé. Mise à jour de l'expertise. Maisons-Alfort: Agence Nationale de Sécurité Sanitaire de l'Alimentation de l'Environnement et du Travail. https://www.anses.fr/fr/system/files/AP2011sa0150Ra.pdf (accessed April 19, 2023).

ANSES [Agence Nationale de Sécurité Sanitaire de l'Alimentation de l'Environnement et du Travail]. 2017. *Extremely Low Frequency Electromagnetic Fields. Health Effects and the Work of ANSES*. France. https://www.anses.fr/fr/node/79598 (accessed April 19, 2023).

ARPANSA [Australian Radiation Protection and Nuclear Safety Agency]. Radiofrequency Expert Panel. 2014. *Review of Radiofrequency Health Effects Research – Scientific Literature 2000–2012*. Yallambie: Australian Radiation Protection and Nuclear Safety Agency. http://emfguide.itu.int/pdfs/tr164.pdf (accessed April 19, 2023).

ARPANSA [Australian Radiation Protection and Nuclear Safety Agency]. 2020. *Extremely Low Frequency Electric and Magnetic Fields*. Australia. https://www.arpansa.gov.au/understanding-radiation/what-is-radiation/non-ionising-radiation/low-frequency-electric-magnetic-fields (accessed April 19, 2023).

Bailey, W. H., and L. S. Erdreich. 2007. Accounting for human variability and sensitivity in setting standards for electromagnetic fields. *Health Phys* 92(6):649–57. DOI: 10.1097/01.HP.0000249741.31108.ce.

Bongers, S., P. Slottje, and H. Kromhout. 2018. Development of hypertension after long-term exposure to static magnetic fields among workers from a magnetic resonance imaging device manufacturing facility. *Environ Res* 164: 565–573 DOI: 10.1016/j.envres.2018.03.008.

Bongers, S., P. Slottje, L. Portengen, and H. Kromhout. 2016. Exposure to static magnetic fields and risk of accidents among a cohort of workers from a medical imaging device manufacturing facility. *Magn Reson Med* 75(5):2165–2174. DOI: 10.1002/mrm.25768.

Bowman, J. D., J. A. Touchstone, and M. G. Yost. 2019. *A Population-Based Job Exposure Matrix for Power-Frequency Magnetic Fields*. Cincinnati: National Institute of Occupational Safety and Health. https://www.cdc.gov/niosh/topics/emf/jem-powerfreq/jempowerfreq.html (accessed April 19, 2023).

Bravo, G., A. Modenese, G. Arcangeli, et al. 2021. Subjective symptoms in magnetic resonance imaging personnel: A multi-center study in Italy. *Front Public Health* 7(9):699675. DOI: 10.3389/fpubh.2021.699675.

Brent, R. L., W. E. Gordon, W. R. Bennett, and D. A. Beckman. 1993. Reproductive and teratologic effects of electromagnetic fields. *Reprod Toxicol* 7(6):535–580. DOI: 10.1016/0890-6238(93)90033-4.

CCARS [Comité Científico Asesor en Radiofrecuencias y Salud]. 2017. *Informe sobre Radiofrecuencia y Salud (2013–2016).* Las Rozas: Comité Científico Asesor en Radiofrecuencias y Salud. Informe-CCARS-Radiofrecuencia-y-Salud-2016.pdf (salud-ambiental.com) (accessed April 19, 2023).

de Vocht, F., B. van-Wendel-de-Joode, H. Engels, and H. Kromhout. 2003. Neurobehavioral effects among subjects exposed to high static and gradient magnetic fields from a 1.5 Tesla magnetic resonance imaging system – a case-crossover pilot study. *Magn Reson Med* 50(4):670–674. DOI: 10.1002/mrm.10604.

de Vocht, F., E. Batistatou, A. Mölter et al. 2015. Transient health symptoms of MRI staff working with 1.5 and 3.0 Tesla scanners in the UK. *Eur Radiol* 25(9):2718–2726. DOI: 10.1007/s00330-015-3629-z.

de Vocht, F., T. Stevens, B. van Wendel-de-Joode, H. Engels, and H. Kromhout. 2006. Acute neurobehavioral effects of exposure to static magnetic fields: analyses of exposure-response relations. *J Magn Reson Imaging* 23(3):291–297. DOI: 10.1002/jmri.20510.

de Vocht, F., T. Stevens, P. Glover, A. Sunderland, P. Gowland, and H. Kromhout. 2007. Cognitive effects of head-movements in stray fields generated by a 7 Tesla whole-body MRI magnet. *Bioelectromagnetics* 28(4):247–255. DOI: 10.1002/bem.20311.

Delpizzo, V. 1994. Epidemiological studies of work with video display terminals and adverse pregnancy outcomes (1984–1992). *Am J Ind Med* 26(4):465–480. DOI: 10.1002/ajim.4700260404.

Devasani, K., and R. Razdan. 2017. Exploring the impact of 900 and 1800 MHz radio frequency electromagnetic radiation on blood pressure and haematological parameters. *Toxicol Int* 24(2):150–156. DOI: 10.22506/ti/2017/v24/i2/162412.

Directive 2013/35/EU. 2013. Directive of the European Parliament and of the Council of 26 June 2013 on the Minimum Health And Safety Requirements Regarding The Exposure Of Workers To The Risks Arising From Physical Agents (Electromagnetic Fields) (20th Individual Directive within the Meaning of Article 16(1) of Directive 89/391/EEC). *Official Journal of the European Union* O.J. No. L-179 of 29 June 2013, 1–21, Brussels, Belgium.

Ekici, B., A. Tanındı, G. Ekici, and E. Diker. 2016. The effects of the duration of mobile phone use on heart rate variability parameters in healthy subjects. *Anatol J Cardiol* 16(11):833–838. DOI: 10.14744/AnatolJCardiol.2016.6717.

EN 50527-2-1:2016. 2016. *Procedure for the Assessment of the Exposure to Electromagnetic Fields of Workers Bearing Active Implantable Medical Devices. Part 2-1: Specific Assessment for Workers with Cardiac Pacemakers.* Brussels: CENELEC [European Committee for Electrotechnical Standardization]. https://standards.globalspec.com/std/10070544/en-50527-2-1 (accessed April 19, 2023).

EN 50527-2-2: 2018. 2018. *Procedure for the Assessment of the Exposure to Electromagnetic Fields of Workers Bearing Active Implantable Medical Devices. Part 2-2: Specific Assessment for Workers with Cardioverter Defibrillators (ICDs).* Brussels: CENELEC [European Committee for Electrotechnical Standardization]. https://standards.global-spec.com/std/10383402/en-50527-2-2 (accessed April 19, 2023).

European Commission, Directorate-General for Employment, Social Affairs and Inclusion. 2014a. *Non-Binding guide to Good Practice for Implementing Directive 2013/35/EU Electromagnetic Fields.* Volume 1: Practical Guide. European Union. https://op.europa.eu/en/publication-detail/-/publication/c6440d35-8775-11e5-b8b7-01aa75ed71a1 (accessed April 19, 2023).

European Commission, Directorate-General for Employment, Social Affairs and Inclusion. 2014b. *Non-Binding Guide to Good Practice for Implementing Directive 2013/35/EU Electromagnetic Fields*. Volume 2, Case studies. European Union. https://op.europa.eu/en/publication-detail/-/publication/e71e8b3f-8775-11e5-b8b7-01aa75ed71a1 (accessed April 19, 2023).

European Commission, Directorate-General for Employment, Social Affairs and Inclusion. 2014c. *Non-Binding Guide to Good Practice for Implementing Directive 2013/35/EU Electromagnetic Fields*. Guide for SMEs. European Union. https://op.europa.eu/en/publication-detail/-/publication/c5fb1d53-8775-11e5-b8b7-01aa75ed71a1 (accessed April 19, 2023).

European Council. 1989. Council directive 89/391/EEC of 12 June 1989 on the introduction of measures to encourage improvements in the safety and health. *OJEC* L 183:1. https://eur-lex.europa.eu/legal-content/EN/ALL/?uri=CELEX%3A31989L0391 (accessed April 19, 2023).

European Council. 1992. Council Directive 92/85 /EEC of 19 October 1992 on the introduction of measures to encourage improvements in the safety and health at work of pregnant workers and workers who have recently given birth or are breastfeeding. *OJ EC* L 348:1. https://eur-lex.europa.eu/legal-content/EN/TXT/?uri=celex%3A31992L0085 (accessed April 19, 2023).

European Council. 1999. Council recommendation of 12 July 1999 on the limitation of exposure of the general public to electromagnetic fields (0 Hz to 300 GHz) - (1999/519/EC). *OJEC* L 199/59, 30. 7. 1999. https://eur-lex.europa.eu/LexUriServ/LexUriServ.do?uri=OJ:L:1999:199:0059:0070:EN:PDF (accessed April 19, 2023).

FCC [Federal Communications Commission]. 2015. RF Safety FAQ. US. https://www.fcc.gov/engineering-technology/electromagnetic-compatibility-division/radio-frequency-safety/faq/rf-safety#Q5 (accessed April 19, 2023).

FDA [Food and Drug Administration]. 2019. Cell phones current research results. US. https://www.fda.gov/radiation-emitting-products/cell-phones/scientific-evidence-cell-phone-safety (accessed April 19, 2023).

Friebe, B., A. Wollrab, M. Thormann et al. 2015. Sensory perceptions of individuals exposed to the static field of a 7T MRI: A controlled blinded study. *J Magn Reson Imaging* 41(6):1675–1681. DOI: 10.1002/jmri.24748.

Gobba, F., G. Bravo, P. Rossi, G.M. Contessa, and M. Scaringi. 2011. Occupational and environmental exposure to extremely low frequency-magnetic fields: a personal monitoring study in a large group of workers in Italy. *J Expo Sci Environ Epidemiol* 21(6):634–645. DOI: 10.1038/jes.2011.9.

Gobba, F., N. Bianchi, P. Verga, G.M. Contessa, and P. Rossi. 2012. Menometrorrhagia in magnetic resonance imaging operators with copper intrauterine contraceptive devices (IUDS): a case report. *Int J Occup Med Environ Health* 25(1):97–102. DOI: 10.2478/s13382-012-0005-y.

Gobba, F., and L. Korpinen. 2018. What health surveillance of EMF exposed workers? *Occup Environ Med* 75(Suppl 2):A422. DOI: 10.1136/oemed-2018-ICOHabstracts.1205.

Guag, J., B. Addissie, and D. Witters. 2017. Personal medical electronic devices and walk-through metal detector security systems: assessing electromagnetic interference effects. *Biomed Eng Online* 16(1):33. DOI: 10.1186/s12938-017-0328-9.

Hansson Mild K., T. Alanko, G. Decat et al. 2009. Exposure of workers to electromagnetic fields. A review of open questions on exposure assessment techniques. *Int J Occup Saf Ergon* 15(1):3–33. DOI: 10.1080/10803548.2009.11076785.

Hartwig, V. G. Virgili, F.E. Mattei, et al. 2022. Occupational exposure to electromagnetic fields in magnetic resonance environment: an update on regulation, exposure assessment techniques, health risk evaluation, and surveillance. *Med Biol Eng Comput* 60(2):297-320. DOI: 10.1007/s11517-021-02435-6.

HSE [Health and Safety Executive]. 2016. *Electromagnetic fields at Work a Guide to the Control of Electromagnetic Fields at Work Regulations 2016*. Norwich: Health and Safety Executive. https://www.hse.gov.uk/pubns/books/hsg281.htm (accessed April 19, 2023).

Health Council of the Netherlands. 2016. *Mobile Phones and Cancer Part 3. Update and Overall Conclusions from Epidemiological and Animal Studies*. The Hague: Health Council of the Netherlands. https://www.healthcouncil.nl/documents/advisory-reports/2016/06/01/mobile-phones-and-cancer-part-3-update-and-overall-conclusions-from-epidemiological-and-animal-studies (accessed April 19, 2023).

Health Council of the Netherlands. 2018. *Power Lines and Health Part I: Childhood Cancer*. The Hague: Health Council of the Netherlands, 2018/08. https://www.healthcouncil.nl/documents/advisory-reports/2018/04/18/power-lines-and-health-part-i-childhood-cancer (accessed April 19, 2023).

Heinrich, A., A. Szostek, P. Meyer et al. 2013. Cognition and sensation in very high static magnetic fields: a randomized case-crossover study with different field strengths. *Radiology* 266(1):236–245. DOI: 10.1148/radiol.12112172.

Hocking, B., and F. Gobba. 2011. Medical aspects of overexposures to electromagnetic fields. *J Health Saf Environ* 27(3): 185–195. https://www.arpansa.gov.au/sites/default/files/legacy/pubs/rps/rps3_hocking.pdf (accessed April 19, 2023).

Hocking, B., and K. Hansson Mild. 2008. Guidance note: risk management of workers with medical electronic devices and metallic implants in electromagnetic fields, *Int J Occ Saf Ergon* 14(2), 217–222.

Huang, D., Z. F. Dong, Y. Chen et al. 2015. Interference of GSM mobile phones with communication between Cardiac Rhythm Management devices and programmers: a combined in vivo and in vitro study. *Bioelectromagnetics* 36(5):367–376. DOI: 10.1002/bem.21911.

Huss, A., K. Schaap, and H. Kromhout. 2017. MRI-related magnetic field exposures and risk of commuting accidents – A cross-sectional survey among Dutch imaging technicians. *Environ Res* 156:613–618 DOI: 10.1016/j.envres.2017.04.022.

Huss, A., K. Schaap, and H. Kromhout. 2018. A survey on abnormal uterine bleeding among radiographers with frequent MRI exposure using intrauterine contraceptive devices. *Magn Reson Med* 79(2):1083–1089. DOI: 10.1002/mrm.26707.

IARC [International Agency for Research on Cancer]. 2002. *IARC Monographs on the Evaluation of Carcinogenic Risks to Humans. Volume 80. Non-Ionizing Radiation, Part 1: Static and Extremely Low-Frequency (ELF) Electric and Magnetic Fields*. Lyon: IARC press. https://publications.iarc.fr/Book-And-Report-Series/Iarc-Monographs-On-The-Identification-Of-Carcinogenic-Hazards-To-Humans/Non-ionizing-Radiation-Part-1-Static-And-Extremely-Low-frequency-ELF-Electric-And-Magnetic-Fields-2002 (accessed April 19, 2023).

IARC [International Agency for Research on Cancer]. 2013. *IARC Monographs on the Evaluation of Carcinogenic Risks to Humans. Volume 102. Non-Ionizing Radiation, Part 2: Radiofrequency Electromagnetic Fields*. Lyon: IARC press. https://publications.iarc.fr/Book-And-Report-Series/Iarc-Monographs-On-The-Identification-Of-Carcinogenic-Hazards-To-Humans/Non-ionizing-Radiation-Part-2-Radiofrequency-Electromagnetic-Fields-2013 (accessed April 19, 2023).

ICNIRP [International Commission on Non-Ionizing Radiation Protection]. 2009. Guidelines on limiting exposure to static magnetic fields. *Health Phys* 96(4):504–514. DOI: 10.1097/01.HP.0000343164.27920.4a.

ICNIRP [International Commission on Non-Ionizing Radiation Protection]. 2010. Guidelines for limiting exposure to time-varying electric and magnetic fields (1Hz – 100kHz). *Health Physics* 99(6):818–836. DOI: 10.1097/HP.0b013e3181f06c86.

ICNIRP [International Commission on Non-Ionizing Radiation Protection]. 2014. Guidelines for limiting exposure to electric fields induced by movement of the human body in a static magnetic field and by time-varying magnetic fields below 1 Hz. *Health Physics* 106(3):418–425. DOI: 10.1097/HP.0b013e31829e5580

ICNIRP [International Commission on Non-Ionizing Radiation Protection]. 2020. Guidelines for limiting exposure to electromagnetic fields (100 kHz to 300 GHz). *Health Phys* 118(5):483–524. DOI: 10.1097/HP.0000000000001210.

ICOH [International Commission on Occupational Health]. 2014. International code of ethics for occupational health professionals. http://www.icohweb.org/site/multimedia/code_of_ethics/code-of-ethics-en.pdf (accessed April 19, 2023).

ILO [International Labour Organization]. 1998. *Occupational Safety and Health Series* number 72. *Technical and Ethical Guidelines for Workers' Health Surveillance.* Geneva. https://www.ilo.org/wcmsp5/groups/public/—ed_protect/—protrav/—safework/documents/normativeinstrument/wcms_177384.pdf (accessed April 19, 2023).

INAIL [National Institute for Insurance against Accidents at Work]. 2020. *Physical Agents Portal. Tuscany and Emilia-Romagna Regions.* https://www.portaleagentifisici.it/?lg=EN (accessed April 19, 2023).

INTERPHONE Study Group. 2010. Brain tumour risk in relation to mobile telephone use: results of the INTERPHONE international case-control study. *Int J Epidemiol* 39(3):675–694. DOI: 10.1093/ije/dyq079.

Istituto Superiore di Sanità (ISS). 2019. *Radiazioni a radiofrequenze e tumori: sintesi delle evidenze scientifiche. Rapporti ISTISAN 19/11.* Roma: Istituto Superiore di Sanità. http://old.iss.it/binary/publ/cont/19_11_web.pdf (accessed April 19, 2023).

Juutilainen, J. 1991. Effects of low-frequency magnetic fields on embryonic development and pregnancy. *Scand J Work Environ Health* 17(3):149–158. DOI: 10.5271/sjweh.1716.

Karpowicz, J., and K. Gryz. 2013. The pattern of exposure to static magnetic field of nurses involved in activities related to contrast administration into patients diagnosed in 1.5 T MRI scanners. *Electromagn Biol Med* 32(2):182–191. DOI: 10.3109/15368378.2013.776428.

Khan, M. W., P. Roivainen, M. Herrala et al. 2018. A pilot study on the reproductive risks of maternal exposure to magnetic fields from electronic article surveillance systems. *Int J Radiat Biol* 94(10):902–908. DOI: 10.1080/09553002.2018.1439197.

Klein-Wiele, O., M. Garmer, G. Barbone et al. 2017. Deactivation vs. asynchronous pacing – prospective evaluation of a protocol for rhythm management in patients with magnetic resonance conditional pacemakers undergoing adenosine stress cardiovascular magnetic resonance imaging. *BMC Cardiovasc Disord* 17(1):142. DOI: 10.1186/s12872-017-0579-1.

Korpinen, L., H. Kuisti, H. Tarao et al. 2016. Possible influences of spark discharges on cardiac pacemakers. *Health Phys* 110(1):1–10. DOI: 10.1097/HP.0000000000000373.

Korpinen, L., H. Kuisti, H. Tarao, J. Elovaara, and V. Virtanen. 2015. Cardiac pacemakers in magnetic fields of a shunt reactor at a 400 kV substation. *Int J Occup Saf Ergon* 21(2):229–232. DOI: 10.1080/10803548.2015.1029286.

Leitgeb, N., Schröttner, J., and R. Cech. 2007. Perception of ELF electromagnetic fields: excitation thresholds and inter-individual variability. *Health Phys* 92(6):591–5. DOI: 10.1097/01.HP.0000243128.29337.aa.

Lindbohm, M. L., M. Hietanen, P. Kyyrönen et al. 1992. Magnetic fields of video display terminals and spontaneous abortion. *Am J Epidemiol* 136(9):1041–1051. DOI: 10.1093/oxfordjournals.aje.a116569.

Malek, F., K. A. Rani, H. A. Rahim, and M. H. Omar. 2015. Effect of short-term mobile phone base station exposure on cognitive performance, body temperature, heart rate and blood pressure of Malaysians. *Sci Rep* 5:e13206. DOI: 10.1038/srep13206.

Mattei, E., E. Lucano, F. Censi, L. M. Angelone, and G. Calcagnini. 2016a. High dielectric material in MRI: numerical assessment of the reduction of the induced local power on implanted cardiac leads. *Conf Proc IEEE Eng Med Biol Soc* 2016:2361–2364 DOI: 10.1109/EMBC.2016.7591204.

Mattei, E., F. Censi, G. Calcagnini et al. 2016b. Pacemaker and ICD oversensing induced by movements near the MRI scanner bore. *Med Phys* 43(12):6621. DOI: 10.1118/1.4967856.

Mattei, E., G. Gentili, F. Censi, M. Triventi, and G. Calcagnini. 2015. Impact of capped and uncapped abandoned leads on the heating of an MR-conditional pacemaker implant. *Magn Reson Med* 73(1):390–400. DOI: 10.1002/mrm.25106.

Migault L., C. Piel, C. Carles et al. 2018. Maternal cumulative exposure to extremely low frequency electromagnetic fields and pregnancy outcomes in the Elfe cohort. *Environ Int* 112:165–173 DOI: 10.1016/j.envint.2017.12.025.

Misek J., I. Belyaev, V. Jakusova, I. Tonhajzerova, J. Barabas, and J. Jakus. 2018. Heart rate variability affected by radiofrequency electromagnetic field in adolescent students. *Bioelectromagnetics* 39(4):277–288. DOI: 10.1002/bem.22115.

Modenese, A., and F. Gobba. 2021. Occupational Exposure to Electromagnetic Fields and Health Surveillance According to the European Directive 2013/35/EU. *Int J Environ Res Public Health* 18(4):1730. DOI: 10.3390/ijerph18041730.

Moen B.E., O.J. Møllerløkken, N. Bull, G. Oftedal, K. and K. Hansson Mild. 2013. Accidental exposure to electromagnetic fields from the radar of a naval ship: a descriptive study. *Int Marit Health* 64(4):177–182. DOI:10.5603/imh.2013.0001.

Murbach, M., E. Neufeld, T. Samaras et al. 2017. Pregnant women models analyzed for RF exposure and temperature increase in 3T RF shimmed birdcages. *Magn Reson Med* 77(5):2048–2056. DOI: 10.1002/mrm.26268.

Napp, A., D. Stunder, M. Maytin, T. Kraus, N. Marx, and S. Driessen. 2015. Are patients with cardiac implants protected against electromagnetic interference in daily life and occupational environment? *Eur Heart J* 36(28):1798–1804. DOI: 10.1093/eurheartj/ehv135.

Nazarian, S., R. Hansford, A. A. Rahsepar et al. 2017. Safety of Magnetic Resonance Imaging in Patients with Cardiac Devices. *N Engl J Med* 377(26):2555–2564. DOI: 10.1056/NEJMoa1604267.

New Zealand Ministry of Health. 2018. *Interagency Committee on the Health Effects of Non-Ionising Fields – Report to Ministers.* Wellington: Ministry of Health. https://www.health.govt.nz/system/files/documents/publications/interagency-committee-health-effects-non-ionising-fields-report-ministers-2018.pdf (accessed April 19, 2023).

Parazzini, F., L. Luchini, C. La Vecchia, and P. G. Crosignani. 1993. Video display terminal use during pregnancy and reproductive outcome – a meta-analysis. *J Epidemiol Community Health* 47(4):265–268. DOI: 10.1136/jech.47.4.265.

Public Health England. 2019. *Collection: Electromagnetic Fields. Advice on Exposure to Electromagnetic Fields in the Everyday Environment, Including Electrical Appliances in the Home and Mobile Phones.* UK. https://www.gov.uk/government/collections/electromagnetic-fields (accessed April 19, 2023).

Ren, Y., J. Chen, M. Miao et al. 2019. Prenatal exposure to extremely low frequency magnetic field and its impact on fetal growth. *Environ Health* 18(1):6. DOI: 10.1186/s12940-019-0447-9.

SCENIHR [Scientific Committee on Emerging and Newly Identified Health Risks]. 2015. *Opinion on potential Health Effects of Exposure to Electromagnetic Fields (EMF).* Luxembourg: European Commission. https://ec.europa.eu/health/scientific_committees/emerging/docs/scenihr_o_041.pdf (accessed April 19, 2023).

Schaap, K., L. Portengen, and H. Kromhout. 2016. Exposure to MRI-related magnetic fields and vertigo in MRI workers. *Occup Environ Med* 73(3):161–166. DOI: 10.1136/oemed-2015-103019.

Schaap, K., Y. Christopher-de Vries, C. K. Mason, F. de Vocht, L. Portengen, and H. Kromhout. 2014. Occupational exposure of healthcare and research staff to static magnetic stray fields from 1.5–7 Tesla MRI scanners is associated with reporting of transient symptoms. *Occup Environ Med* 71(6):423–429. DOI: 10.1136/oemed-2013-101890.

Schnorr, T. M., B. A. Grajewski, R. W. Hornung et al. 1991. Video display terminals and the risk of spontaneous abortion. *N Engl J Med* 324(11):727–733. DOI: 10.1056/NEJM199103143241104.

Shaw, G. M. 2001. Adverse human reproductive outcomes and electromagnetic fields: A brief summary of the epidemiologic literature. *Bioelectromagnetics* 22(Suppl 5):S5-S18. DOI: 10.1002/1521-186x(2001)22:5+<::aid-bem1020>3.3.co;2-c.

Shaw, G. M., and L. A. Croen. 1993. Human adverse reproductive outcomes and electromagnetic field exposures: review of epidemiologic studies. *Environ Health Perspect* 101(Suppl. 4):107–119. DOI: 10.1289/ehp.93101s4107.

Souques, M., I. Magne, and J. Lambrozo. 2011. Implantable cardioverter defibrillator and 50-Hz electric and magnetic fields exposure in the workplace. *Int Arch Occup Environ Health* 84(1):1–6. DOI: 10.1007/s00420-010-0599-y.

Swedish Radiation Safety Authority's Scientific Council on Electromagnetic Fields. 2016. *Research Report number 2016:15. Recent Research on EMF and Health Risk. Eleventh report from SSM's Scientific Council on Electromagnetic Fields, 2016.* Stockholm: Swedish Radiation Safety Authority. https://www.stralsakerhetsmyndigheten.se/contentassets/98d67d9e3301450da4b8d2e0f6107313/201615-recent-research-on-emf-and-health-risk-eleventh-report-from-ssms-scientific-council-on-electromagnetic-fields-2016 (accessed April 19, 2023).

Tiikkaja, M., A. L. Aro, T. Alanko et al. 2013. Electromagnetic interference with cardiac pacemakers and implantable cardioverter-defibrillators from low-frequency electromagnetic fields in vivo. *Europace* 15(3):388–394. DOI:10.1093/europace/eus345.

Tsarna, E., M. Reedijk, L. E. Birks et al. 2019. Associations of maternal cell-phone use during pregnancy with pregnancy duration and fetal growth in 4 birth cohorts. *Am J Epidemiol* 188(7):1270–1280. DOI: 10.1093/aje/kwz092.

Turner, M. C., G. Benke, J. D. Bowman et al. 2014. Occupational exposure to extremely low-frequency magnetic fields and brain tumor risks in the INTEROCC study. *Cancer Epidemiol Biomarkers Prev* 23(9):1863–1872. DOI:10.1158/1055-9965.EPI-14-0102.

van Nierop, L. E., P. Slottje, H. Kingma, and H. Kromhout. 2013. MRI-related static magnetic stray fields and postural body sway: a double-blind randomized crossover study. *Magn Reson Med* 70(1):232–240. DOI: 10.1002/mrm.24454.

van Nierop, L. E., P. Slottje, M. J. van Zandvoort, and H. Kromhout. 2015. Simultaneous exposure to MRI-related static and low-frequency movement-induced time-varying magnetic fields affects neurocognitive performance: a double-blind randomized crossover study. *Magn Reson Med* 74(3):840–849. DOI: 10.1002/mrm.25443.

van Nierop, L. E., P. Slottje, M. J. van Zandvoort, F. de Vocht, and H. Kromhout. 2012. Effects of magnetic stray fields from a 7 tesla MRI scanner on neurocognition: a double-blind randomised crossover study. *Occup Environ Med* 69(10):759–766. DOI: 10.1136/oemed-2011-100468.

Vila, J., J. D. Bowman, L. Richardson et al. 2016. A source-based measurement database for occupational exposure assessment of electromagnetic fields in the INTEROCC study: a literature review approach. *Ann Occup Hyg* 60(2):184–204. DOI: 10.1093/annhyg/mev076.

WHO [World Health Organization]. 2005. *Environmental Health Criteria 232: Static Fields.* China: WHO Press. https://www.who.int/publications/i/item/9241572329 (accessed April 19, 2023).

WHO [World Health Organization]. 2007. *Environmental Health Criteria 238: Extremely Low Frequency Fields.* Spain: WHO Press. https://wedocs.unep.org/handle/20.500.11822/29527 (accessed April 19, 2023).

Wilén, J., and F. de Vocht. 2011. Health complaints among nurses working near MRI scanners – a descriptive pilot study. *Eur J Radiol* 80(2):510–513. DOI: 10.1016/j.ejrad.2010.09.021.

Zanotti, G., G. Ligabue, and F. Gobba. 2015. Subjective symptoms and their evolution in a small group of magnetic resonance imaging (MRI) operators recently engaged. *Electromagn Biol Med* 34(3):262–264. DOI: 10.3109/15368378.2015.1076442.

Zanotti, G., G. Ligabue, L. Korpinen, and F. Gobba. 2016. Subjective symptoms in magnetic resonance imaging operators: prevalence, short-term evolution and possible related factors. *Med Lav* 107(4):263–270.

Zradziński, P., J. Karpowicz, K. Gryz., and V. Ramos. 2020. An evaluation of electromagnetic exposure while using ultra-high frequency radiofrequency identification (UHF RFID) guns. *Sensors* 20(1):202. DOI: 10.3390/s20010202.

Zradziński, P., J. Karpowicz, and K. Gryz. 2018. In silico modelling of influence from low or intermediate frequency magnetic fields on users of wearable insulin pumps. *Int J Radiat Biol* 94(10):926–933. DOI: 10.1080/09553002.2017.1419305.

8 Evaluating Current Induced in Limb When Managing Electromagnetic Hazards Caused by Operating Electrosurgical Units

Jolanta Karpowicz, Krzysztof Gryz, and Patryk Zradziński
Central Institute for Labour Protection—National Research Institute (CIOP-PIB)

CONTENTS

8.1 INTRODUCTION

8.1.1 Electromagnetic Properties of Electrosurgical Units Usage

Electrosurgical units (ESUs), also referred to as the electric knives, are used to reduce the amount of blood lost during surgical treatment performed using a traditional,

DOI: 10.1201/9781003020486-8

laparoscopic or endoscopic method. ESUs are mainly used for cutting soft tissue (CUT mode) or coagulating blood vessels (COAG mode), made possible due to heating the tissue by radiofrequency (RF) electric current flowing between active and passive electrodes (Eggleston and Von Maltzahn, 2000). This current may pass through the air (even forming a visible arc discharge) near an active small-sized electrode, when a sufficiently high electric potential exceeding 200 V is applied to an active electrode. Each time it passes through the patient's tissue to a passive (large-sized) electrode, a heating effect is produced in the tissue proportional to RF current density, with the highest values near the active electrode position. The handle of the active electrode and the cables connecting electrodes to the power supply unit (the ESU generator) are covered by insulating plastic. A frequency exceeding 0.3 MHz is used for surgical treatment, with the aim being to avoid the electrical stimulation of the patient's nervous or muscle tissues. The application of various types of ESU results in the emergence of surgical current, which time waveforms vary between various modes of operation (Figure 8.1). The CUT mode usually involves applying pure sinusoidal or quasi-sinusoidal continuous waves voltage at the active electrode (with a crest factor of U_{peak}/U_{RMS} of 1.4–2.1, where, peak is the peak value and RMS is the root mean square value), whereas the COAG mode involves applying amplitude-/pulse-modulated waves (with a crest factor of 2.1–20) (Eggleston and Von Maltzahn, 2000).

Electromagnetic field (EMF) emissions are caused by high voltage at the power supply surgical electrodes (usually for 200–12000 V peak-to-peak, depending on the operation mode). The EMF sources include the active electrode and cables (usually

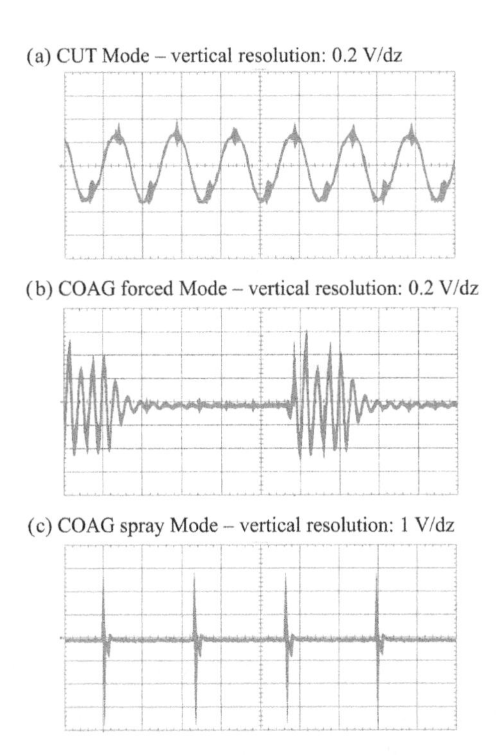

FIGURE 8.1 An example of a time wave of EMF emitted in various ESU operation modes.

3–5 m long) connecting both the electrodes with the ESU generator (later referred to as ESU cables). This EMF complies with the RF range (usually of 0.3–1.8 MHz, depending on the operation mode and ESU generator type). The assessment should entail undertaking various parameters that will relate to worker exposure to ESU-sourced EMF to ensure the compliance with the applicable occupational health and safety guidelines and/or regulations. The research priorities still focus on following the changes to emerge in the pattern of the workers' exposure to EMF resulting from the development of RF-EMF emission-related technologies (Hansson Mild et al., 2009; WHO, 2010). It is also important to broaden the understanding of the exposure that various professionals face when performing epidemiological research and studies prepared thereon, as well as when managing environmental hazards in the workplace.

A surgical current does not usually exceed 1 A. This suggests that the electric field (EF) has a predominant role in the EMF emitted by ESUs affecting workers near its source (recognised to be the near-field region of EMF). The RF EF induced in an electrically conductive object (E_{in}) exposed to RF-EMF causes the flow of RF currents and heating in this object, as well as in the worker's body. The spatial distribution of healthcare workers' exposure to an EF of various polarisations depends upon the spatial configuration of the ESU cables and material objects in the vicinity. When a surgeon or nurse is grasping a handle or cables of an ESU electrode, the localised exposure of their hand always emerges (Figure 8.2a). Where, sometimes, the cable

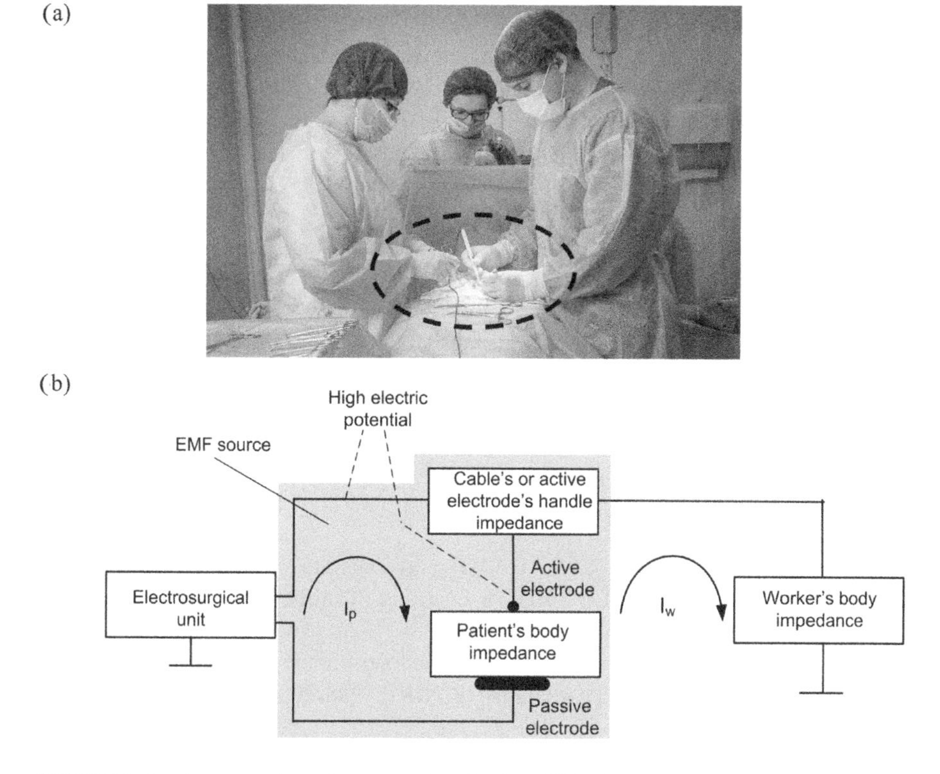

FIGURE 8.2 An example of the scenarios of using ESUs for surgical treatment (a) and the scheme of the EMF exposure while using ESUs (b). (Photo: romavin/Bigstockphoto.)

hangs over the shoulder along the torso and leg, almost the whole of the worker's body may be subject to exposure. However, the most typical position of healthcare professionals conducting a surgical procedure is the first one, that is, where the hand receives the highest and local EMF exposure and RF current. Figure 8.2 presents the scheme of RF-EMF and RF current flow near an ESU.

The RF electric current that affects an exposed worker may be an effect of direct interaction between the EMF and the worker's body (usually referred to as the 'induced current'). This may also be caused by an indirect interaction between the EMF and electrically conductive objects, namely something metal or any other person, along with a current flow when touching these objects (usually referred to as the 'induced contact current'). These currents produce thermal effects in the human body and are of a particular concern when it comes to limbs (especially over the wrist or ankle), due to their relatively small cross-section with low content of muscles there. Limb currents may be the cause of an increased body temperature and even thermal damage to tissue (referred to as RF burns) or pain sensations within the contact area where nerve excitation occurs (referred to as an electric shock).

8.1.2 Principles on Evaluating Exposure to an Electromagnetic Field at 0.1–10 MHz

The international guidelines on exposure evaluation (ICNIRP, 1998, 2010, 2020; IEEE, 2005, 2019) regarding the exposure to RF-EMF with frequency of 0.1–10 (5) MHz, including the frequency range of EMF emitted by the ESU, concern not only the prevention of acute thermal effects (which are the most frequently dominant effect of exposure to EMF of this frequency range) but also the prevention against EMF-induced electrical neuroexcitation, both of which may be caused by E_{in} induced in the body.

8.1.2.1 Criteria to Evaluate EMF Exposure

The metric used to evaluate the exposure effect appeared in the body during the EMF exposure – referred to as the 'Specific Absorption Rate', *SAR* (W/kg) – represents the spatial distribution of EMF energy absorbed into the tissue, causing a thermal load of tissues. *SAR* is a function of the external EMF level and spatial distribution, as well as the grounding conditions of an exposed person, for example, contact with electrically conductive metallic structures nearby (Reilly, 1998; Zradziński, 2015).

The following are the internationally recommended limits of *SAR* values provided to evaluate workers' EMF exposure at 0.1–10 MHz frequency (which need separate considerations):

- A whole body averaged $SAR = 0.4$ W/kg, averaged over any 6-minute interval (ICNIRP 1998, IEEE 2005) or over any 30-minute interval (ICNIRP 2020, IEEE, 2019),
- A local *SAR* averaged over 10 g of tissue and a 6-minute interval: 10 W/kg (in head and trunk) or 20 W/kg (in limbs) (ICNIRP, 1998, 2020; IEEE, 2005, 2019).

For electrical neuroexcitation during the EMF exposure, the exposure metric corresponds to the maximum value of electric field induced in the body, E_{in}, that is not averaged in time. For the frequency of 0.1–10 (5) MHz, it is linearly proportional to the frequency f_{MHz} denoted in MHz:

- E_{in} [V/m] = 270 f_{MHz}; in all tissues, with a value of 135 V/m @ 0.5 MHz (ICNIRP, 2010, 2020).
- E_{in} [V/m] = 630 f_{MHz}; in the limbs only, with a value of 315 V/m @ 0.5 MHz (IEEE, 2005, 2019).

The secondary limit values for evaluating exposure to environmental EMF (Table 8.1) have been derived, taking into account the relation between the E_{in} in the human exposed to an unperturbed homogenous EMF affecting humans, and the electric field (EF) strength (E) and the magnetic field (MF) strength (H) (The model of exposure to unperturbed EMF is valid at the workplace located far from an EMF source, with no workers present there.).

Following the general principles regarding the electromagnetic health hazards assessment, the limits of SAR and E_{in} determine the ceiling levels for worker's exposure provided by international guidelines. An assessment of the EF and the MF at the workplace is to be considered just the first step in the EMF hazard assessment. When the E or H measured at the workplace are likely to exceed the limits specified in Table 8.1, then more thorough assessment procedures are required, including the evaluation of parameters that directly relate to the exposure effects (SAR, E_{in}). These are actually assessed through measurements or calculations. In the EMF that are significantly different than the unperturbed homogeneous case, the EF and MF limits (as specified in Table 8.1) usually develop significantly more restrictive exposure limits than the SAR and E_{in} limits. The fact goes that assessing the exposure effects (SAR, E_{in}) is time consuming and cannot be performed in a particular workplace, due to the need to use a laboratory or numerical human body phantoms and EMF sources models that adequately mimic exposure conditions at the workplace (including EMF spatial distribution, insulation and grounding conditions), as well as the need for sophisticated computation software (Figure 8.3).

For localised limb exposure to RF-EMF, like for the ESU operation, in between both the strategies specified above, applied to assess the EMF hazards, it is possible to assess current induced in limbs that represents an exposure effect being more related to E_{in} than to EMF at the workplace, and, in fact, it can be measurable there in exposure scenarios nearly identical to the regular use of the EMF sources.

8.1.2.2 Criteria to Evaluate Limb Currents

The evaluation of current induced in limbs allows for better control over compliance with the SAR limits in limbs (i.e. protecting limbs against harmful local thermal effects). Therefore, particular guidelines provide that the limits of induced current values pertain to each foot (IEEE, 2005, 2019) or both feet (IEEE, 2005); when following other guidelines, the limits set pertain to each limb, and the evaluation of induced current is required only for cases where the human body is not electrically insulated from a ground plane (ICNIRP, 2020). It should be noted here that almost all materials are better electric conductors for RF currents than for power frequency ones (50/60 Hz).

TABLE 8.1
International Guidelines on Limits of Exposure to the Electromagnetic Field

The Criteria to Evaluate the Measured Values of Electric Field Strength (*E*) and Magnetic Field Strength (*H*) of Unperturbed EMF		Frequency Range	
		0.1–1 MHz	**1–10 MHz**
ICNIRP 1998[a]	E, V/m	610	$610/f_{MHz}$
[*E* and *H* are RMS values – averaged within any 6 minutes of exposure]	H, A/m	$1.6/f_{MHz}$	
ICNIRP 2010[b]	E, V/m	170	
[*E* and *H* are the maximum in-time values]	H, A/m	80	
ICNIRP 2020[c]	E, V/m	$660/f_{MHz}^{0.7}$	
whole body exposure [*E* and *H* are RMS values – averaged within any 30 minutes of exposure]	H, A/m	$4.9/f_{MHz}$	
ICNIRP 2020[c]	E, V/m	$1504/f_{MHz}^{0.7}$	
local exposure [*E* and *H* are RMS values – averaged within any 6 minutes of exposure]	H, A/m	$10.8/f_{MHz}$	
IEEE 2005[d]	E, V/m	1842	$1842/f_{MHz}$
[*E* and *H* are RMS values – averaged within any 6 minutes of exposure; up to 5 MHz only]	H, A/m	$16.3/f_{MHz}$	
IEEE 2019[e]	E, V/m	1842	$1842/f_{MHz}$
whole body exposure [*E* and *H* are the maximum in-time RMS values; up to 5 MHz only]	H, A/m	$16.3/f_{MHz}$	
IEEE 2019[e]	E, V/m	4119	$4119/f_{MHz}$
local exposure [*E* and *H* are RMS values – averaged within any 6 minutes of exposure; up to 5 MHz only]	H, A/m	$36.4/f_{MHz}$	

f_{MHz}, frequency in MHz; *E*, electric field strength; *H*, magnetic field strength.

[a] with averaging of E^2 and H^2 measured over the worker's body position; limits for non-sinusoidal EMF regarding peak *E* or *H* values are calculated by multiplying the relevant limit of RMS values by the frequency-dependent coefficient (i.e. multiplied by approx. 1.5 @ 0.1 MHz, 2.1 @ 0.3 MHz, 3.0 @ 0.6 MHz, 7.3 @ 2 MHz) (ICNIRP, 1998).

[b] With *E* and *H* measured with respect to the spatial extension of the human body (ICNIRP, 2010).

[c] With averaging of E^2 and H^2 measured over the whole body for whole-body exposure; and over the relevant projected body space for local exposure (ICNIRP, 2020).

[d] With averaging of E^2 and H^2 measured over an area equivalent to the vertical cross-section of the worker's body (projected area); and the limit for non-sinusoidal EMF regarding the instantaneous peak EF strength is 100 kV/m (IEEE, 2005).

[e] With averaging of E^2 and H^2 measured over the projected area of the body measured for whole-body exposure or for local exposure (IEEE, 2019).

The European Directive 2013/35/EU on workers protection in European Union Member States (Directive, 2013) considers the maximum values of EF and MF measured over the worker's body position, to be evaluated with respect to limits based on selected previously published international guidelines (ICNIRP, 1998, 2010).

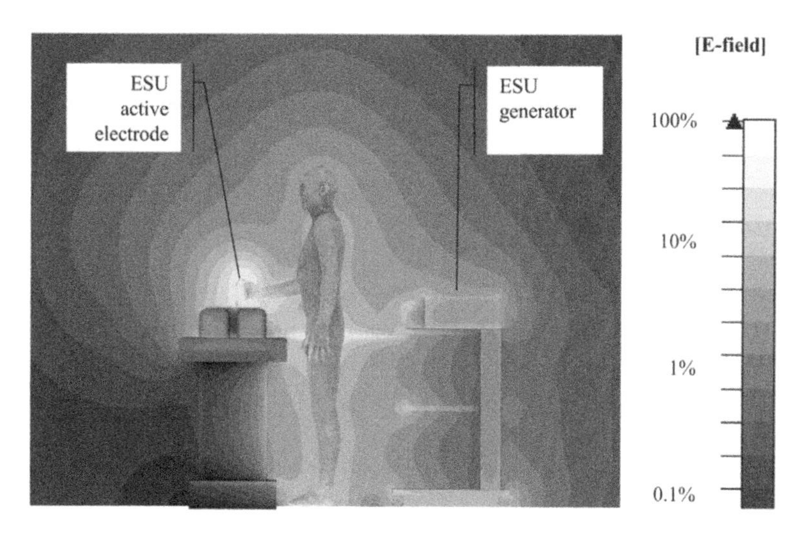

FIGURE 8.3 An example of spatial distribution of the EF modelled in the vicinity of ESU cables and electrodes.

The limits of the induced contact current have been split with respect to the conditions of contact between the hand and the object exposed to EMF. The limits for a grasp are higher than for a finger touch (a single-point contact) due to a larger contact area and the lower risk of excitation of nervous or muscle tissue that may cause pain, or even RF burns, due to excessive current density in the skin. Particular guidelines differ in details regarding the considered contact conditions with a conducting structure exposed to EMF, for example considering (IEEE, 2005, 2019):

- The contact area of 1 cm^2 for the touch contact (commonly using a finger),
- The contact area of 15 cm^2 for the full-palm grasp on the construction.

Other guidelines may be less precise, for example, providing that point contact current is limited, but without specifying the contact area (ICNIRP, 1998, 2010, excluding the 2020 edition). The limits specified in Table 8.2 are references to induced current evaluation in the human body within exposure that cover the RF-EMF produced by an ESU.

As for the 0.1–10 MHz (5 MHz) frequency range, the limits of current induced in limb refer to both the main EMF exposure effects, that is, electrostimulation and thermal effects. Therefore, the assessment is conducted for the time-averaged squared RMS value (related to protection against thermal effects and *SAR* limits) and the maximum in-time value (related to protection against electrostimulation and E_{in} limits). The tests of compliance with a localised *SAR* limit are carried out for the square root of the squared induced current which was time averaged over any six-minute interval. The assessment of the induced contact current is conducted based upon the peak in-time value.

TABLE 8.2
International Guidelines on Limits of the Induced Current at the Frequency Range of 0.1–10 MHz

	Induced Current, *I*, mA			
	Contact Current		Limb Current	
ICNIRP 1998, 2010	40 (Hand)		Not Specified	
ICNIRP 2020	Not Specified[a]		100 (Each Limb)	
	Touch	Grasp	Each Foot	Both Feet
IEEE 2005	50	100	100	200
IEEE 2019	$500 f_{MHz}$	$1000 f_{MHz}$	$1000 f_{MHz}$	Not specified

f_{MHz}, frequency in MHz.

[a] No limits on the contact current are specified, though the hazards related to accidents that may be caused by the unexpected perception of contact current during a touch longer than 10 seconds is mentioned (ICNIRP, 2020), together with a note regarding a wide discrepancy in the perception threshold in the frequency range 0.1–10 MHz (see also Karpowicz et al., 2016; Karpowicz & Gryz, 2016)
To this extent, the provisions of the EU Directive on the protection of workers in European Union Member States (Directive, 2013) comply with the selected previously published by international guidelines (ICNIRP, 1998, 2010).

As far as the exposure to continuous EMF is concerned, the limits based upon protection against thermal effects are more restrictive, but the protection against electrostimulation turns to provide stronger restrictions when exposure changes to the pulse-modulated EMF. It should also be noted that the limits for the induced contact current have been established to ensure protection against burns caused by the RF current (ICNIRP 1998). As for the small contact areas, sensitive individuals may experience a perception of a small electric shock, even when currents do not exceed the limits of the touch contact. The spontaneous reaction to such perception may be a cause of accidents in the work environment (ICNIRP, 2020).

It needs attention that providers of 'the occupational exposure limits' applicable in the work environment (of the levels exceeding the ones applicable to the general public exposure cases), usually are also defining the safety measures, which have to be already applied in case when mentioned occupational limits are taken to evaluate EMF exposure of anyone.

8.2 ELECTROMAGNETIC FIELD EMITTED BY THE ELECTROSURGICAL UNITS

In the recent decades, extensive research on EMF exposure near ESUs have been performed in various countries (Liljestrand et al., 2003; Gryz and Karpowicz, 2006; De Marco and Maggi, 2006; Wilén, 2010, Karpowicz, 2015, Karpowicz et al., 2021). It has been evoked based upon the already published measurement result that a surgeon's localised exposure to the EMF near ESU electrodes and cables may exceed

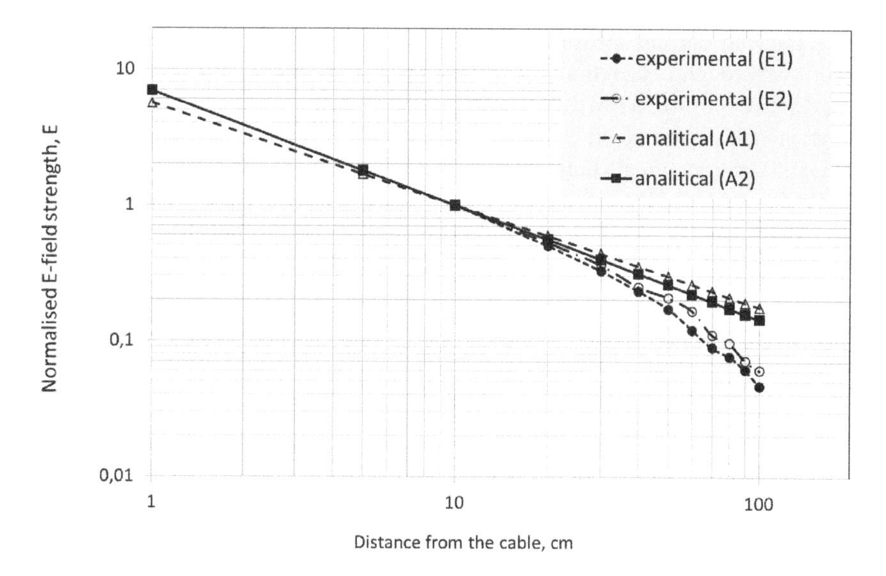

FIGURE 8.4 The normalised EF distribution near the ESU cables, according to calculation formulas for the EF @ 30 W (A1) and @ 50 W (A2) output power (Liljestrand et al., 2003) and according to measurement results for a vertical (E1) or horizontal (E2) location of the electrode cable @ 120 W output power (Gryz et al., 2008).

the limits specified in Table 8.1. At various output power and configurations of the electrode used, EF near the electrode and cable (at a distance of a ten or less cm) ranged: 400–1800 V/m, as reported by Liljestrand et al. (2003), 294–380 V/m as reported by De Marco and Maggi (2006), 720–1400 V/m as reported by Wilén (2010) or 300–1660 V/m and 130–1200 V/m as reported by Gryz and Karpowicz (2006) and Karpowicz et al. (2021). The EF level decreases rapidly along with the distance from the ESU cable, as evidenced based upon the data obtained during relevant experiments (Liljestrand et al., 2003; Gryz et al., 2008) and presented in Figure 8.4.

A more thorough assessment of the hazards caused by the EMF exposure is recommended for the worker's localised exposure, for example, in the opinion provided by the relevant international guidelines - at a distance shorter than 20 cm from the EMF source (ICNIRP, 2010). The induced currents assessment is advised to be applicable when the vertically polarised EF affecting the worker exceeds 8–25% of the EF limits (provided for the whole body homogeneous exposure), that is, exceeds approximately 150–450 V/m with the frequency range where EMF emitted by ESUs were found (IEEE, 2005, 2019). No specific guidelines are available with regard to the induced current assessments concerning EMF exposure to the non-vertically polarised EF which is spatially non-homogeneous, like the spatial distribution of the exposure near ESUs. Therefore, the reported EF values that have been measured near ESUs and the short distance observed between healthcare workers and EMF sources are jointly taken as evidence, that is the induced current measurements need to be involved in our study to assess the electromagnetic hazard caused by the EMF emission during the use of ESUs.

The induced current measurements at ESU operators limbs have not yet been subject to thorough research and analysis. There is rather a paucity of data on RF work-related exposure to EMF and the practical application of body-induced currents assessment within the healthcare environment. Nevertheless, the results of experimental and computational studies regarding the assessment of EF-based hazards, for example, in electric substations (Tarao et al., 2013; Korpinen et al., 2009; Karpowicz et al., 2017), have shown that the induced contact current and the maximum EF affecting the palm (not subject to spatial average value determination) have proven to be good indicators of EMF hazards caused by an induced EF (and current stream caused by it) in limb. Such evidence supports the idea applied in our endeavours, that is, with regard to the use of currents measured at limb (CML), together with the EF in the palm position, to assess the ESU operators' exposure.

8.3 METHOD OF EVALUATING ELECTROMAGNETIC EXPOSURE

Based upon the arguments that have been presented in detail in the previous section, the purpose of the undertaken efforts was to examine exposure to EMF while using an ESU, applying the EMF and induced current measurements, and also analysing the data obtained therefrom, in order to consider when our EMF exposure assessment method may be applied for the purpose of assessing the workers' exposure during surgical treatment.

The relevant research activities were performed at 19 medical centres located in various regions of Poland, using 259 ESUs, denoted as of a various commonly used type, manufactured by globally renowned brands, that is, Aesculap, Berchtold, Bovie, Conmed, ERBE, Martin, Olympus, Storz and Valleylab, to name a few, as well as local brands manufactured in Poland, for example, EMED and Famed.

The induced current was measured at limb during regular inspections (conducted in compliance with the provisions of labour law in Poland) conducted in the work environment affected by EMF, while the authors of this research were grasping the insulated handle (*IH*) or an insulated supply cable (*IC*) of an active electrode. The research was authorised by the managers of the medical centres and performed under real working conditions (i.e. in operating rooms) with the location of ESUs, cables and electrodes that usually exists there during surgical treatment, and the researchers wearing clothing and shoes (with wooden or plastic sole) that are commonly used in that operating room. During the research, the settings of output power complied with the usual settings, as reported by representatives of the user of each ESU assisting the measurements reported here, the patient's body was replaced with a 'phantom' (fresh apples) as, due to the patient's safety precautions, EMF measurements are not authorised during actual surgical procedures. The phantom type was selected based upon the previously performed laboratory tests using various options for volume or electronic structure (e.g. 100–1000 ohm electronic load), with regard to the EMF level near the ESU cables and electrodes. It has been found that the use of fresh apples is usually recognised by the ESU automatic control of output circuit to be equivalent to a regular load by the patient's body, which means that the ESU operates in a stable manner and provides an opportunity to evaluate the EMF nearby.

The research conducted here also involved the relation of the induced CML at an upper limb and at a leg. The data obtained from the 16 tests performed evidenced that the ratio of CML at an upper limb of a person grasping a handle of an ESU device to the one measured at a leg has been set for 2.3–3.5 (median value of 2.8). These results show that an upper limb CML should be considered as a dominant measure of hazards from induced current (in limbs) when operating an ESU. This does not prove true when the work is performed close to radio broadcasting installations, where foot current proves to be a better indicator of hazards caused by quasi-vertically polarised EF, as the major current stream flows via the feet to the ground. As for the EMF exposure near an ESU, the exchange of RF currents may flow over various areas of the body that are nearest to conductive objects, for example, the operating table or another person, so the CML at upper limb is usually stronger than at lower leg, because it is situated closer to an electrode and cable emitting EMF.

The CML was measured using a HI-3702 device, with a HI-4416 System Readout (Holaday Industries, Inc., Eden Prairie, MN, USA). The HI-3702 is a clamp-on CML meter measuring the electromotive force induced in the coil, being proportional to the current passing through the limb. The coil of the clamp-on meter plays the role of the output circuit of the current transformer created together with the limb current circuit. The frequency response of the meter is 0.009–110 MHz, with the measurement values of 1–1000 mA and an approximate uncertainty of ±0.5 dB. The procedure of the research provides for the coil of the clamp-on meter being placed on the wrist of the person grasping the handle (*IH*) or the supplying cable (*IC*) of the active electrode (Figure 8.5).

The EMF (both *E* and *H* strength) were measured at a fixed distance of 10 cm from the cables supplying the active electrode and were considered as representing palm exposure. The Narda EMR-300 EMF meter (Narda Safety Test Solutions, Pfullingen, Germany) was used; for this purpose it was equipped with two isotropic probes 6 cm in diameter: the EF measurement range 0.6–800 (1300) V/m with a frequency response of 0.1–3000 MHz and an approximate uncertainty of ±2 dB; the MF

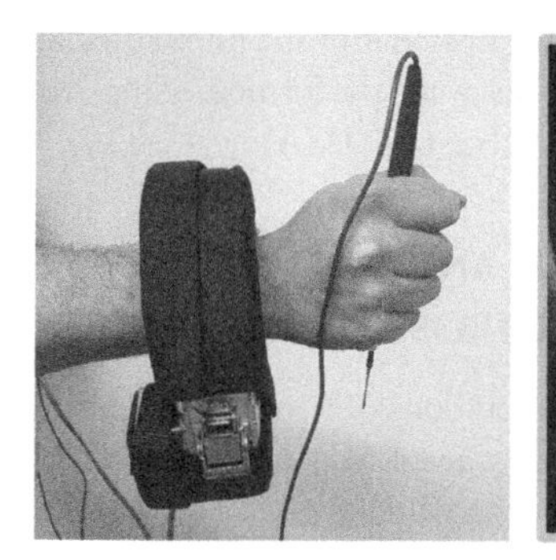

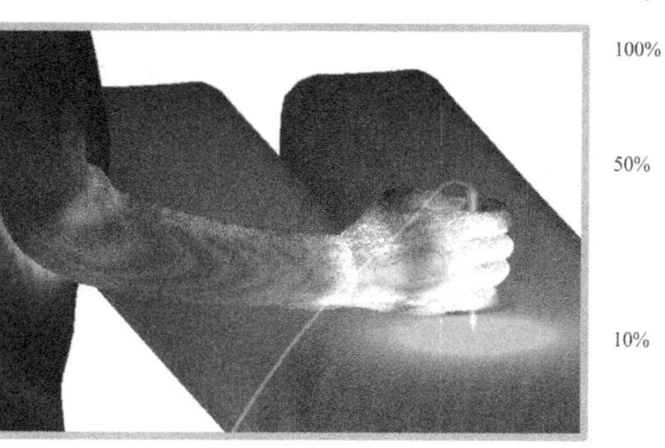

FIGURE 8.5 The EMF exposure of palm grasping an ESU cable: (a) the measurements of current induced in limb (current measured at limb) using a Holaday clamp-on CML meter; (b) numerical simulations of the induced EF.

measurement range 0.017–17 A/m with a frequency response of 0.3–30 MHz and an approximate uncertainty of ±2 dB.

The 10 cm distance from the cable has been fixed to prevent any damage that could possibly be caused by the probe overload within a strong EF near the cable, where it may exceed 1000 V/m, and to prevent against increased uncertainty of measurement results in the EMF with a highly inhomogeneous spatial distribution over the probe volume located at the cable, and where direct coupling between the EMF sensors and the source may also significantly contribute to the uncertainty of measurements.

The used EMF and clamp-on current meters are RMS-value sensitive. This means that, for a pulsed modulated EMF (such as is emitted during the use of ESUs in the COAG mode), the temporal maximum EMF (as applicable to the evaluation of the neuroexcitation hazards) should be estimated on the basis of applying individual correction factors to the RMS indications of the meter, as established on the basis of the analysis of the EMF waveform in time (Gryz and Karpowicz, 2006; Wilén, 2010).

The frequency and waveform of EMF emitted by a particular ESU has been identified by the use of an EMCO EF probe 904 (EMCO, Austin, TX, USA) and a digital oscilloscope Scopemeter 199C (Fluke, Everett, WA, USA).

The measurement results have been characterised by statistical parameters, that is, by minimum (min), maximum (max) and median (med) values, as well as the inter-quartile range (25–75, IQR) (i.e. the range between the values to which 25% or 75% of the results are lower), and for the EF, respectively: E_{min}, E_{max}, E_{med}, E_{25-75}.

The results from our study were gathered from 2007 to 2022, which means that both the old-fashioned ESUs and the modern ESUs have been included into the set of the data reported. To this extent, the measurement results have been divided into two subsets, that is, concerning the old-fashioned (O-) devices (operating at 1.8 MHz) and the modern (M-) devices (operating at approximately 0.32–0.62 MHz), in order to analyse the variability of exposure caused by changes in electrosurgical technology.

The statistical correlation between CML (*IH* and *IC*) and EF strength (*E*), and the ESU's output power (*P*) characterising conditions during particular measurements were subject to a non-parametric Spearman test. The statistical significance was set at $p < 0.01$, and the statistical differences between the tested subsets of the measurement result (for the O-ESU and the M-ESU) were subject to a non-parametric Mann–Whitney U test (applicable to data without a Gaussian distribution). The statistical significance was set at $p < 0.01$. The statistical analyses were performed using the software package Statistica, Version 8.0PL (StatSoft, Tulsa, OK, USA).

8.4 RESULTS OF ELECTROMAGNETIC FIELD AND INDUCED CURRENT MEASUREMENTS NEAR ELECTROSURGICAL UNITS

The measurement results were collected during CUT operations of a monopolar knife (a monopolar electrode). The frequencies of the investigated EMF, as identified by oscilloscopic observations, were mostly in the range of approximately 0.32–0.62 MHz, whereas they were aproximately 1.8 MHz for the 17 ESUs (the old type, O-ESUs).

The statistical parameters of the ESU output power (*P*), the values determined during particular measurements and the EF values measured at a distance of 10 cm from the cable supplying the active electrode are summarised in Tables 8.3 and 8.4.

TABLE 8.3
Output Power of Investigated ESUs Set during the Reported Measurements

	Statistical Parameters of ESU Output Power in the CUT Mode of Operation *P*, W		
Parameter	**All ESUs (n=259)**	**O-ESUs (n=17)**	**M-ESUs (n=242)**
Minimum value	20	44	20
Median/IQR	120/70–150	165/120–200	120/70–150
Maximum value	360	360	360

IQR, Inter-quartile range: 25th–75th percentile.

TABLE 8.4
Results of Measurements of the Electric Field Strength at a Distance of 10 cm from the Cable Supplying an Active Electrode

	Statistical Parameters of the Electric Field Strength *E*, V/m		
Parameter	**All ESUs (n=259)**	**O-ESUs (n=17)**	**M-ESUs (n=242)**
Minimum value	29	160	29
Median/IQR	235/160–315	330/320–432	226/156–300
Maximum value	830	710	830

IQR, Inter-quartile range: 25th–75th percentile.

The maximum output power of the investigated ESUs was up to 500 W; however, according to user reports, a lower output power is commonly applied during the patients' surgical treatment (median (IQR)): in monopolar modes, in CUT—120 (70–150) W, in COAG—60 (55–90) W and in bipolar modes—54 (40–60) W. The output power during the discussed investigations in the CUT mode was in the range of 20–360 W. The option to conduct the research during the CUT mode of the ESU's operation was decided due to the quasi-sinusoidal emission and the use of a higher output power at this mode of operation.

The strength of the MF within a distance of 10 cm from the electrodes and the cables was measured within the range of 0.1–1.3 A/m (median value of 0.2 A/m), and the EF was measured within the range of 29–830 V/m (median value of 235 V/m).

The statistical parameters that characterise the distribution of the CML results near various ESUs are summarised in Table 8.5 to depict the moment when the handle of the active electrode is grasped (*IH*), that is, a case of exposure equivalent to the one experienced by the surgeon or when the cable supplying the active electrode is grasped (*IC*), that is, a case of exposure equivalent to the one experienced by assisting personnel, such as the nurse. Figure 8.6 depicts the distribution of the (*IH*)/(*IC*) ratio in the measurement results.

TABLE 8.5
Results of Measurements of the Upper Limb CML (Current Measured at Limb)

	Statistical Parameters of the Upper Limb CML *I*, mA					
	All ESUs ($n = 259$)		O-ESUs ($n = 17$)		M-ESUs ($n = 242$)	
Parameter	*IH*	*IC*	*IH*	*IC*	*IH*	*IC*
Minimum value	1.0[a]	1.0[a]	4.0	7.0	1.0[a]	1.0[a]
Median/IQR	3.5/2.0–6.0	5.0/3.5–7.5	29/10–48	35/18–72	3.0/2.0–5.0	5.0/3.0–7.0
Maximum value	58	100	58	100	49	23

IQR, Inter-quartile range: 25th–75th percentile; *IH*, Upper limb CML when grasping an active electrode handle; *IC*, upper limb CML when grasping a cable supplying an active electrode.

[a] Sensitivity of the used current metre.

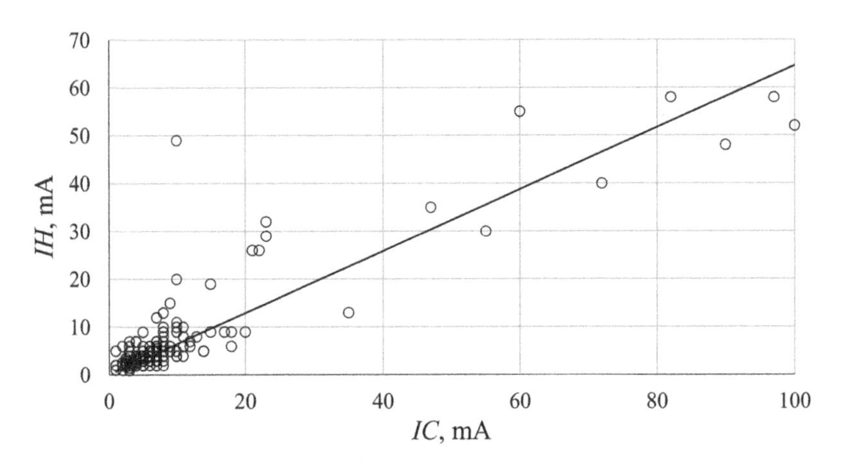

FIGURE 8.6 The relation between the upper limb CML when grasping a handle (*IH*) or the cable (*IC*) of the active electrode – the (*IH*)/(*IC*) ratio has been found in the range: 0.25–5.0, median value: 0.75, IQR: 0.56–1.0.

The CML at workers' upper limb are characterised by the median value of 3.5 mA or 5.0 mA and the range of 1.0–58 mA or 1.0–100 mA, when grasping a handle or a cable of an active electrode, respectively. It has been determined from the results reported that the linear correlation between the upper limb CML and the EF strength ($p < 0.01$) measured at a distance of 10 cm from the cable supplying the active electrode are specified using the following formulas:

$$\text{for O-ESUs:} \quad IH\,(\text{mA}) \approx 0.070\,E(\text{V/m}) \tag{8.1}$$

$$\text{for M-ESUs:} \quad IH(\text{mA}) \approx 0.018\,E(\text{V/m}) \tag{8.2}$$

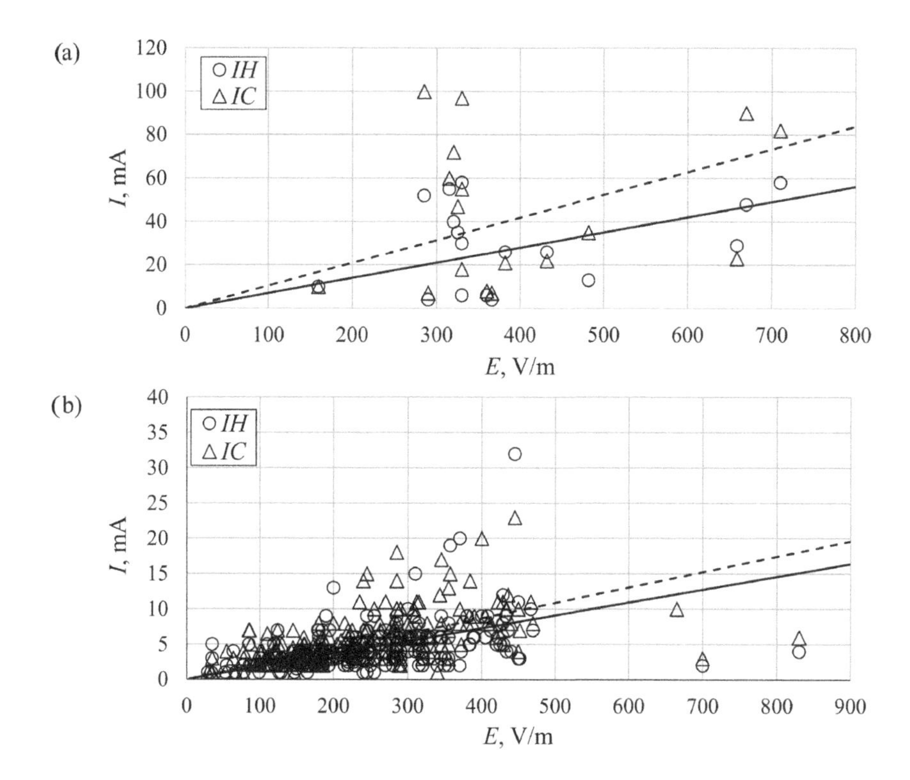

FIGURE 8.7 The upper limb CML when grasping a handle (*IH*) or a cable (*IC*) of an active electrode as a function of the EF emitted by: (a) old-fashioned devices (O-ESUs) or (b) modern devices (M-ESUs).

$$\text{for All-ESUs}: \quad IH(\text{mA}) \approx 0.026E(\text{V/m}) \tag{8.3}$$

$$\text{for O-ESUs}: \quad IC(\text{mA}) \approx 0.110E(\text{V/m}) \tag{8.4}$$

$$\text{for M-ESUs}: \quad IC(\text{mA}) \approx 0.022E(\text{V/m}) \tag{8.5}$$

$$\text{for All-ESUs}: \quad IC(\text{mA}) \approx 0.035E(\text{V/m}) \tag{8.6}$$

No correlations between upper limb CML (or the squared CML values) and the output power of the ESU and between the EF (or the squared EF values) and output power were found ($p<0.01$). Statistically significant differences ($p<0.01$) were identified between the subsets of the measurement results obtained for O-ESUs and M-ESUs (Figure 8.7).

8.5 DISCUSSION

The upper limb CML during the CUT mode of the ESU's operation @ 20–360 W output power settings, when grasping the handle or the cable of an active electrode, exceeds 11 mA (M-ESU) and 90 mA (O-ESU) with regard to as few as 5% of the analysed cases. An upper limb CML during the CUT mode that exceeded 50 mA was measured near O-ESUs only (commonly referred to be at least 15 years old).

The literature lacks data on the relation between the EF and the limb current when using an ESU. Nevertheless, it may be found that the stream of induced current through the grounded feet (*IF*) of a human exposed to a homogenous vertically polarised EF may be estimated [in mA] using the following formula:

$$IF = K f_{\mathrm{MHz}}\, h^2 E \tag{8.7}$$

Where, K is the current ratio, which depends on the exposure conditions; f_{MHz}, frequency [in MHz]; h, height of the exposed person [in m] and E, EF strength [in V/m].

The current ratio K reported from various research, regarding the frequency range of 0.01–40 MHz, lies within the range of 0.073–0.121 [mA (m^{2}MHz V/m)$^{-1}$] (e.g. Hill and Walsh, 1985; Korniewicz, 1995; Jokela et al., 1994; Wilén et al., 2001). While assuming the central value from this range, that is, $K = 0.1$ [mA (m^{2}MHz V/m)$^{-1}$], for a human of $h = 1.8$ m height and $f = 0.5$ MHz, the formula (8.7) can be simplified to:

$$IF(\mathrm{mA}) = 0.16\,E(\mathrm{V/m}) \tag{8.8}$$

Following our reported findings (Formulas 8.1–8.6), it was proven that, in the case of healthcare workers operating ESUs and exposed to EF evaluated near the palm position (measured within a distance of 10 cm from the handle or cable of an active electrode), it is justified to assume limb currents at least four times as low as when determined using formula (8.7) and based on an EF within the radio broadcasting environment (which is vertically polarised and quasi-homogeneous). For all the ESUs, the ratio CML/$E = 0.04$ [mA/(V/m)] may be considered the worst case when assessing the limb current based on the EF spot measurements at the palm position, but for the M-ESUs a much lower ratio CML/$E = 0.02$ [mA/(V/m)] may represent the worst case of exposure scenario.

Taking into account the experimentally set range of 2.3–3.5 for the ratio of the upper limb CML divided by the leg CML, the presented results show that, when estimating induced currents through legs, following Formula (8.7) and the results of the EF measurements at the palm position (10 cm from the cables), the leg current is overestimated by at least 10 times, because localised nature of the exposure to ESU's EF and its non-vertical polarisation, whereas for the application of Formula (8.7), the assumption for a vertical polarisation of exposure to a uniform EF has been made as typical for the radio broadcasting environment.

Still, what needs to be pointed out in this respect is the fact that, where an ESU is used in a non-standard manner, when long cables are wrapped over the worker's body, for example, the exposed worker may be found to be exposed to induced RF currents many times stronger than reported in this paper.

There are still no appropriate detailed measurement procedures or assessment standards developed for CML investigations. The discrepancies reported in the interpretation of international guidelines (Tables 8.1 and 8.2) include questions on how to distinguish whether the CML should be assessed based on criteria regarding the induced contact current or the limb current. The variety of options that may need to be considered in practical tasks to assess the exposure of healthcare workers include the following:

- When to assess CML through upper or lower limb?
- When, how and by what parameters of CML the assessment should be performed – using the steady state currents only or including transients (peak, peak-to-peak or RMS values—instantaneous or time averaged)?
- What contact area should be considered when taking CML measurements?
- How to assess an induced current flowing through part of worker's body other than the limb, being near the source of the EMF-induced currents?
- Whether the limits of induced currents applied to the evaluation of the effects of EMF exposure in upper limbs, legs and other parts of a worker's body should differ?

It should also be pointed out that the devices for the CML measurements available today are characterised by the RMS-value sensitivity. Therefore, any assessment of the deeply modulated induced contact current proves complicated and is only capable of roughly estimating the RMS value of the measured parameter based on the use of correction factors appropriate for the waveform of the exposure in question. As for the CUT mode, the EMF and currents induced in limb are usually sinusoidal or quasi-sinusoidal, varying in frequency for various types of ESU; therefore, the CML values do not need to be corrected before their interpretation, that is, both maximum in-time and RMS averaged in-time values can be directly derived from the results of reported measurement. In the COAG mode, various ESUs produce signals that vary considerably in terms of frequency and modulation. This proves to be a significant challenge when interpreting the measurement results, as the EMF and CML meters applied for this study are RMS-value sensitive, and do not match the EMF and induced contact current limitations regarding the maximum in-time value. To manage this discrepancy, it may be necessary to provide for a new type of CML meter equipped with an analogue output signal allowing for the direct use of the oscilloscopic method of the maximum in-time current assessment.

While analysing the measurement results regarding quasi-sinusoidal signals in the CUT mode (covered in our study reported in this paper), a quasi-normalised protocol was achieved to be directly applicable to an individual type of ESU device.

It has been suggested, following the obtained CML values, that, when using the deeply modulated COAG mode, it would be necessary to assess CML: (i) for both the old-fashioned ESUs and the modern ESUs, (ii) with the first step of any assessment undertaken to this extent being focused on the upper limb (where currents are higher than in the legs), (iii) when grasping the cable supplying the active electrode (usually higher than when grasping the electrode handle). The assessment of the CML as regarded the induced contact currents limits (with the maximum in-time value) emerges as the first task for the COAG mode, due to the expected crest factor in the waveform (peak/RMS values) in the range of 2–20, and with the 6-minute averaging, which lowers the RMS value, used for the assessment of the CML considered as the induced limb currents (Karpowicz et al., 2021).

However, it must also be pointed out that when the cables touch the worker's body, the localised exposure nearby is stronger than reported in Table 8.4, up to approximately seven times stronger within a distance of 1 cm from the cable (Figure 8.4). Given that the EF is significantly stronger at the cable or the handle cover as compared to the presented EF measured at a distance of 10 cm, it may be expected that not only is the localised EF over the palm and fingers much higher than the results delivered in this paper, but also that the localised induced EF there (in the palm and fingers) and the thermal effects prove to be much higher than has been assumed based on the delivered CML (spatially averaged over the wrist or ankle cross-section). When reviewing the obtained CML, the conclusion goes that, while measuring the current stream over the ankle or the wrist, the only option is to obtain an integrated parameter representing the exposure effect over entire limb cross-section. This is why the SAR and E_{in} parameters need further analysis using numerical simulations with regard to the localised effects of exposure in the palm.

The CML values should be interpreted against the dimensions of a cross-section of various parts of a body exposed to the stream of induced current (e.g. the size of an ankle cross-section corresponds to the twice the wrist size) (Gryz et al., 2008). Therefore, it seems to be more justified to apply the lower limits on induced currents in the upper limbs than in the lower limbs. While examining the practical aspects of assessing the currents induced in limb at the workplace against the criteria provided for the two different parameters characterising the adverse effects of exposure, that is, the thermal load and electrostimulation risk in exposed body, it appears more reasonable to develop a new practical approach for the future, based on combined parameters, but with a more detailed interpretation of the assessment protocol to be delivered, as well as the interpretation of the relevant measurement results.

The obtained CML prove that the level of currents stream upon the design of the ESU, and that for modern ESUs the limits provided by international guidelines to evaluate the current induced in limb are not exceeded when used in the CUT mode. As regards to the old-fashioned ESUs, exposures have been reported that have exceeded the limits of induced current. The differences in the ESU design include modifications in the electronic output current circuit, introduced in order to obtain better control of output power, with the aim being to prevent excessive burns in patients' tissue (Friedrichs et al, 2011; Schneider and Abatti, 2008). The other difference can be found in the grounding of the ESU generator and plastic materials used for covering the handles and cables of the active electrode.

Further developments are required as regards to the assessment of CML in the workplace, with the aim being to provide assistance for the practical implementation of the labour legislation on the protection of workers against direct and indirect electromagnetic health and safety hazards in exposure situations similar to those discussed here—cases of using ESUs for medical treatments.

For epidemiological research, it is recommended to retrospectively examine the exposure of surgeons and nurses to the EMF while using ESUs for a surgical procedure, as they are considered a group that works in a setting characterised by high EMF exposure, which may at the same time induce a RF current in the body (as comparable to or even exceeding relevant limits), specifically when applying highly modulated COAG modes. Further research is necessary to assess the localised exposure inside the fingers and the palm, as well as any health consequences of long-term exposure (taking years sometimes).

8.6 CONCLUSIONS

The relevant assessment regarding EMF exposure in the workplace, when an ESU is used for surgical treatment, should include induced currents flowing through the workers' bodies, with attention to the currents in the surgeon's or nurse's wrist through the contact with the handle or the cable of ESU electrodes.

The upper limb-induced RF current was found to be correlated with the spot EF at the palm. In the CUT operating mode of ESU, an upper limb current comparable to the relevant limit values is expected only when operating the O-ESU at 1.8 MHz frequency; but for all the devices the induced contact current needs special attention when using the ESU deeply modulated COAG mode.

The limits on induced currents (time-averaged or peak in-time values), as well as the assessment procedures under the international guidelines, need further clarification, specifically for their implementation in a healthcare workplace, where compliance with the provisions of labour regulations may be binding.

It is also necessary to develop new measurement devices to measure the maximum value in time of deeply modulated limb currents, as these need to be assessed against the induced contact current limits.

Medical personnel involved in medical treatments using ESUs need to be considered in the epidemiological studies among those that are highly exposed to EMF in the work environment.

ACKNOWLEDGEMENTS

This chapter has been based on the results of the research tasks that have been carried out in Poland within the scope of the National Programme 'Improvement of safety and working conditions' (CIOP-PIB is the Programme's main co-ordinator), partly supported by the National Centre for Research and Development (within the scope of research and development), and by the ministry for labour issues (within the scope of state services), (tasks 2.SP.10, 1.G.12 and 04.A.03, and project II.PB.17).

REFERENCES

De Marco, M., and S. Magi. 2006. Evaluation of stray radiofrequency radiation emitted by electrosurgical devices. *Phys Med Biol* 51(14):3347–3358. DOI: 10.1088/0031-9155/51/14/004.

Directive 2013/35/EU. 2013. Directive of the European Parliament and of the Council of 26 June 2013 on the Minimum Health And Safety Requirements Regarding The Exposure Of Workers To The Risks Arising From Physical Agents (Electromagnetic Fields) (20th Individual Directive within the Meaning of Article 16(1) of Directive 89/391/EEC). *Official Journal of the European Union* O.J. No. L-179 of 29 June 2013, 1–21, Brussels, Belgium.

Eggleston, J.L., and W.W. Von Maltzahn. 2000. Electrosurgical devices. Chapter 81. In: *The Biomedical Engineering Handbook*. Second Edition, ed. J.D. Bronzino. Boca Raton: CRC Press.

Friedrichs, D.A., R.W. Ericson, and J. Gilbert. 2011. A new system architecture improves output power regulation in electrosurgical generators. *Annu Int Conf IEEE Eng Med Biol Soc* 2011:6870–6873 DOI: 10.1109/IEMBS.2011.6091694.

Gryz, K., and J. Karpowicz. 2006. Electromagnetic hazards from electrosurgery – assessment of occupational exposure to electromagnetic field and currents induced in the body. *Rocz Panstw Zakl Hig* 57(2):165–175 (in Polish).

Gryz K, Karpowicz J, Zradziński P. 2008. Electromagnetic fields produced by electrosurgical devices – occupational risk assessment. *Bezpieczeństwo Pracy* 5(440):16–21 (in Polish). http://archiwum.ciop.pl/27734 (accessed September 29, 2022).

Hansson Mild, K., T. Alanko, G. Decat et al. 2009. Exposure of workers to electromagnetic fields. A review of open questions on exposure assessment techniques. *Int J Occup Saf Ergon* 15(1):3–33. DOI: 10.1080/10803548.2009.11076785.

Hill, D.A., and J.A. Walsh. 1985. Radio-frequency current through the feet of a grounded human. *IEEE Trans Electromagn Compat* 27(1):18–23. DOI: 10.1109/TEMC.1985.304241.

ICNIRP [International Commission on Non-Ionizing Radiation Protection]. 1998. Guidelines for limiting exposure to time-varying electric, magnetic, and electromagnetic fields (up to 300 GHz). *Health Phys* 74(4):494–522.

ICNIRP [International Commission on Non-Ionizing Radiation Protection]. 2010. Guidelines for limiting exposure to time-varying electric and magnetic fields (1 Hz – 100 kHz). *Health Phys* 99(6):818–836. DOI: 10.1097/HP.0b013e3181f06c86.

ICNIRP [International Commission on Non-Ionizing Radiation Protection]. 2020. Guidelines for limiting exposure to electromagnetic fields (100 kHz to 300 GHz). *Health Phys* 118(5):483–524. DOI: 10.1097/HP.0000000000001210.

IEEE C95.1–2005. 2005. *Standard for Safety Levels with Respect to Human Exposure to Radio Frequency Electromagnetic Fields, 3 kHz to 300 GHz*. New York: IEEE [Institute of Electrical and Electronics Engineers].

IEEE C95.1–2019. 2019. *IEEE Standard for Safety Levels with Respect to Human Exposure to Electric, Magnetic, and Electromagnetic Fields, 0 Hz to 300 GHz*. New York: IEEE [Institute of Electrical and Electronics Engineers].

Jokela, K., L. Puranen, and O.P. Gandhi. 1994. Radio frequency currents induced in the human body for medium-frequency/high-frequency broadcast antennas. *Health Phys* 66(3):237–244. DOI: 10.1097/00004032-199403000-00001.

Karpowicz, J. 2015. Environmental and safety aspects of the use of EMF in medical environment. Chapter 21. In: *Electromagnetic Fields in Biology and Medicine*. ed. M. Markov, 341–362. Boca Raton: CRC Press. DOI: 10.1201/b18148-22.

Karpowicz, J., and K. Gryz. 2016. The practical application of limb contact current limits in the safety programme at electromagnetically exposed workplace. *2016 International Conference on Applied and Theoretical Electricity (ICATE)*, Craiova, Romania, 2016.10.06–08. DOI: 10.1109/ICATE.2016.7754695.

Karpowicz, J., K. Gryz, and P. Zradziński. 2016. The experimental study on the limb contact current (the perception and the current load) at the electromagnetically exposed workplace – the study focused of the intermediate- and radio-frequency exposures. *2016 International Conference on Applied and Theoretical Electricity (ICATE)*, Craiova, Romania, 2016.10.06–08. DOI: 10.1109/ICATE.2016.7754696.

Karpowicz, J., P. Zradziński, and K. Gryz. 2021. Surgical diathermy – primary source of health care workers' exposure to elekctromagnetic fields. *Inżynier i Fizyk Medyczny* 3(10): 253–260 (in Polish).

Karpowicz, J., P. Zradziński, J. Kieliszek, K. Gryz, J. Sobiech, and W. Leszko. 2017. An in situ and in silico evaluation of biophysical effects of 27 MHz electromagnetic whole body humans exposure expressed by the limb current. *BioMed Res Int* Article Number 5785482. DOI: 10.1155/2017/5785482.

Korniewicz, H. 1995. The first resonance of a grounded human being exposed to electric fields. *IEEE Trans Electromagn Compat* 37(2):295–299.

Korpinen, L.H., J.A. Elovaara, and H.A. Kuisti. 2009. Evaluation of current densities and total contact currents in occupational exposure at 400 kV substations and power lines. *Bioelectromagnetics* 30(3):231–240. DOI: 10.1002/bem.20468.

Liljestrand, B., M. Sandstrom, and K. Hansson Mild. 2003. RF exposure during use of electrosurgical units. *Electromagn Biol Med* 22(2–3):127–132. DOI: 10.1081/JBC-120024622.

Reilly, P.J. 1998. *Applied Bioelectricity. From Electrical Stimulation to Electropathology*. New York: Springer-Verlag.

Schneider, B., and P.J. Abatti. 2008. Electrical characteristics of the sparks produced by electrosurgical devices. *IEEE Trans Biomed Eng* 55(2):589–593. DOI: 10.1109/TBME.2007.903525.

Tarao, H., L.H. Korpinen, H.A. Kuisti, N. Hayashi, J.A. Elovaara, and K. Isaka. 2013. Numerical evaluation of currents induced in a worker by ELF non-uniform electric fields in high voltage substations and comparison with experimental results. *Bioelectromagnetics* 34(1):61–73. DOI: 10.1002/bem.21738.

Wilén, J. 2010. Exposure assessment of electromagnetic fields near electrosurgical units. *Bioelectromagnetics* 31(7):513–518. DOI: 10.1002/bem.20588.

Wilén, J, K. Hansson Mild, L.E. Paulsson, and G. Anger. 2001. Induced current measurements in whole body exposure condition to radio frequency electric fields. *Bioelectromagnetics* 22(8):560–567. DOI: 10.1002/bem.84.

WHO [World Health Organization]. 2010. *Research Agenda for Radiofrequency Fields*. Geneva: WHO. https://apps.who.int/iris/bitstream/handle/10665/44396/9789241599948_eng.pdf?sequence=1&isAllowed=y (accessed September 29, 2022).

Zradziński, P. 2015. Difficulties in applying numerical simulations to an evaluation of occupational hazards caused by electromagnetic fields. *Int J Occup Saf Ergon* 21(2):213–220. DOI: 10.1080/10803548.2015.1028233.

9 Electromagnetic Safety and Smart Wireless Solutions

Mikel Celaya-Echarri and Leyre Azpilicueta
Public University of Navarre (UPNA)

Patryk Zradziński and Jolanta Karpowicz
Central Institute for Labour Protection—
National Research Institute (CIOP-PIB)

Victoria Ramos
Instituto de Salud Carlos III

CONTENTS

DOI: 10.1201/9781003020486-9

9.1 INTRODUCTION

The notion of Smart (wireless) Solutions as a full connected paradigm, based on the aid of Smart Technologies as: (1) Smart Cities, (2) Smart Factories (Industry 4.0), (3) Smart Homes, (4) Internet of Things (IoT), (5) Smart Healthcare Systems (e-Health) and (6) Intelligent Transportation Systems (ITS), forming Contextual Environments has been a vigorous research topic in the last decade. The use and presence of wireless technologies (functioning mediated by emitting and receiving non-ionising radiation, mostly from the radiofrequency (RF) range of electromagnetic field (EMF), between various components of the networks) have increased exponentially at the same time, extending the technological advances and developments to a large number of applications and services. With more than half of the population living in cities (United Nations, 2018) and an average (constantly increasing) of more than 2.4 devices per user connected to the internet in 2018 (Cisco, 2020), billions of devices and wireless technologies, interconnected by Heterogeneous Networks (HetNet), are and will be coexisting as complex heterogeneous environments. As a result, the concept of IoT and smart solutions are pivotal in order to achieve the goal of global connection by means of sensing and actuation leading to applications over multiple worldwide services, ranging from wearables and end-user devices, to beacons, controllers and collector sensors embedded in complex wireless systems. These solutions depend on the interaction of a large number of transceivers with multiple indoor and outdoor cells coexisting in heterogeneous communications networks where many challenges must be addressed. Smart solutions for medical purposes (e-Health) are one of the earliest and already the most widely worldwide implemented smart solutions. Therefore, the model for assessing electromagnetic hazards is presented in the following sections, mainly taking e-Health smart solutions as an example.

9.1.1 SMART WIRELESS SOLUTIONS

Smart wireless solutions have made a dramatic increase in a huge variety of services and applications. One of the uses is in Wireless Sensor Networks (WSN) for ITS and vehicular communications to improve safety and transportation, water and gas monitoring, smart lighting, energy-saving sensors, smart parking solutions, home automation, industry and business (Bradshaw, 2006; Zeiler et al., 2011). They are also used to monitor various bodily functions, (often e-Health solutions with medical applications, though they are also applicable in other fields, such as the safety of firefighters, the military and industry workers, and even monitoring sports activities). In this scope, they are usually recognised as crucial healthcare treatment relying on remote medicine safety, wellness or location control, and the tracking of personnel, patients, biological materials and medical devices (Dickerson et al., 2011; Carranza et al., 2010, 2011; Marquez et al., 2019; Reiner and Sullivan, 2005; Hebert et al., 2006). WSN and IoT are also used to monitor a number of harmful factors in the work environment (e.g. noise) and to reduce the subsequent health hazards to workers (Morzyński, 2021). Other uses include the latest personal alert safety system (PASS) devices that detect firefighter movements (NFPA, 1982) or devices to monitor health parameters of soldiers, tracking their position, detecting nearby bombs and predicting the warzone environment (Gondalia et al., 2018).

These powerful applications have a huge impact in the way that society functions and on the safety of their users. At the same time, the rise of wireless technologies such as Bluetooth, Zigbee, Wireless Fidelity (Wi-Fi) and recently also new-generation networks known as fifth- or sixth- generation (5G/6G) networks, along with technical improvements in miniaturisation, the development of novel, smart, small-sized wireless wearable sensors for biomonitoring and sensing applications, popularly known as short-range devices (SRDs), have been enabled for general use (Zheng et al., 2011; Hanson et al., 2009).

9.1.2 EMF Safety

EMF safety is a research topic focused on multiple influences on human lives due to EMF exposure, such as the one caused by the development of wireless technologies and its coexistence with human beings. Since the beginning of the wireless era, there have been growing concerns from the general public and workers about the adverse effects of EMF exposure directly on human health. Indeed, it is well known that exposure to high-intensity EMF produces biological effects in human tissues, potentially leading to adverse health consequences (WHO, 1993, 2006; IARC, 2013; SCENIHR, 2015; ICNIRP, 1998, 2020; IEEE 1999, 2019). There are multiple factors to consider with respect to the biophysical effects of EMF influence, and their significance with respect to the safety and health of the population: human body characterisation is a complex task, where the behaviour of human tissues is based on the frequency of affecting EMF under analysis, and, hence, there is a vast range of frequencies to study; biological interactions may be thermal from tissue being physically heating by absorbed electromagnetic energy, or more complex non-thermal bioelectromagnetic effects involving various biochemical or bioelectrical processes (ICNIRP, 2020; Kim et al., 2019; SCENIHR, 2015; Sánchez-Hernández, 2009; Wust et al., 2020; Zradziński, 2015a,b; Jalilian et al., 2019; Leach et al., 2018).

The most commonly accepted metrics to characterise direct biophysical thermal effects, considered in the evaluation of exposure to EMF with respect to the minimum safety requirements are (Directive 2013/35/EU, 2013; ICNIRP, 1998, 2020; IEEE, 1999, 2019):

- in the case of exposure to EMF at a frequency from 100 kHz up to 6 GHz: the specific energy absorption rate (SAR, in watts per kilogram, W/kg– body averaged or locally averaged over 1- or 10-g values),
- in the case of exposure to EMF at a frequency exceeding 6 GHz: various sets of the body-averaged SAR or absorbed power density (S_{ab}, in W/m^2) values, depend on the EMF frequency and safety guidelines considered.

Compliance with SAR or S_{ab} limits may be evaluated by compliance with the operational exposure limits provided for incident electric field strength (E, in V/m) and incident magnetic field strength (H, in A/m); and at far-field RF-EMF are replaceable by incident power density values (S_{inc}, in W/m^2), usually evaluated based on one of parameters of affecting EMF (*E* or *H*) and the fixed value of far-field impedance (377 ohms). The newest RF guidelines for the whole-body exposure suggest using *E* and *H* for frequencies up to 30 MHz; *E*, *H* or S_{inc} for frequencies from 30 MHz up to 2 GHz, while for higher frequencies using S_{inc} (ICNIRP, 2020). Localised exposure from nearby small-size EMF sources needs to be evaluated by the use of local SAR values.

Wireless devices are usually used in close proximity to the human body; in such cases, in accordance with international safety guidelines, a SAR or S_{ab} compliance assessment is required, even when incident EMF has already been evaluated as compliant with relevant limits.

Moreover, exposure to EMF can also cause indirect effects, meaning effects caused by the presence of an object in an EMF, which may become the cause of a safety or health hazard, such as interference with medical electronic equipment and devices (including implants or medical devices worn on the body) (Directive 2013/35/EU, 2013).

9.2 AN OVERVIEW OF WIRELESS COMMUNICATION SYSTEMS OF SRDs

9.2.1 Wireless Communication Networks

Short-range (SR) technology has been considered a very promising option for monitoring bodily functions. In this subsection, a technology overview of the most relevant SR wireless communication systems involved in e-Health or IoT applications is presented.

The classification of wireless communications networks (Goldsmith, 2005) most commonly used in the literature is based on the communication range, as presented in Figure 9.1a. Nowadays, a 100–200 m range distance is considered to be the standard boundary between SR and long-range (LR) communications systems. Based on a theoretical approach, SR systems include: Wireless Body Area Networks (WBANs), Wireless Personal Area Networks (WPANs) and Wireless Local Area Networks (WLANs). On the other hand, LR systems include Wireless Metropolitan Area Networks (WMANs) and Wireless Wide Area Networks (WWANs). The connections between wireless communications networks and the internet became the beginning of the IoT, that is, the network in which objects, devices and machines, etc. communicate with each other without human intervention.

A WBAN (Figure 9.1b) is a wireless system where communications are entirely and directly associated to the immediate proximity of the human body (though not limited to humans) (IEEE 802.15.6–2012, 2012; IEEE 802.15.6–2017, 2017). This means that it provides connectivity in a very limited coverage nearby the impact area from the person body. WBANs are normally deployed, for example, in medical environments and specifically for real-time human health applications such as biophysical monitoring or e-Health services where the smart device (even body wearables) is located on, in or in the vicinity of the body as an ad-hoc wireless connected network (Movassaghi et al., 2014). Their main performance features are low transmission power, miniaturised devices, strong security for sensitive data and minimum

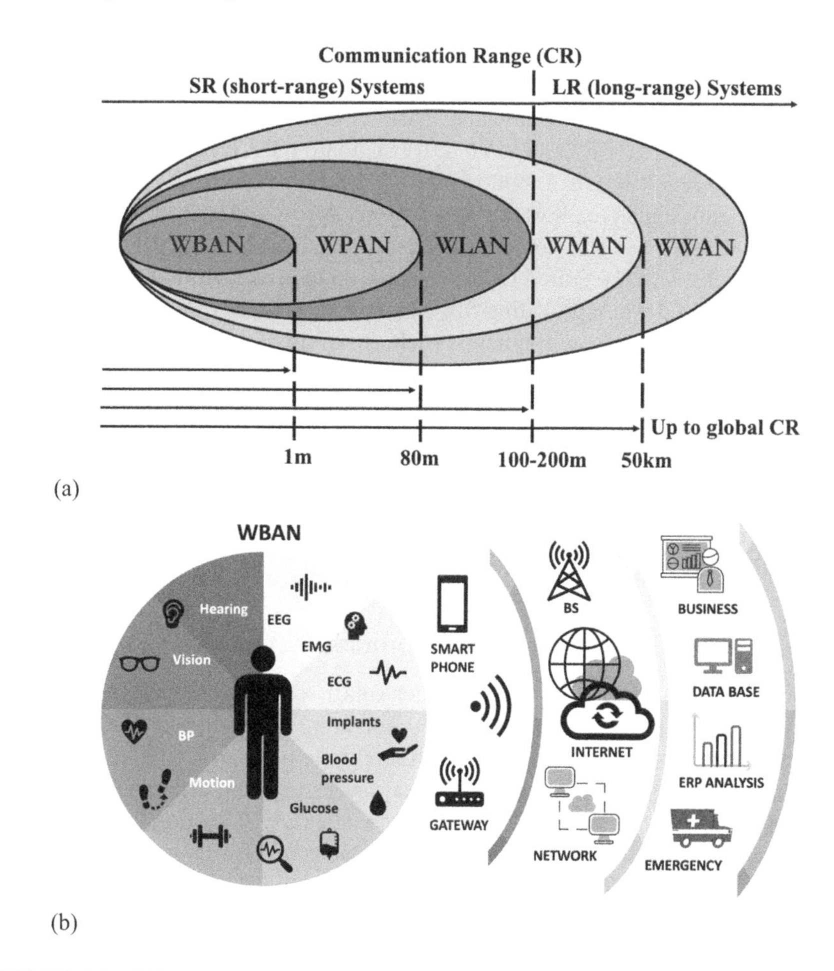

FIGURE 9.1 Wireless communication networks: (a) Classification based on operational communication range (CR): WBAN, Wireless Body Area Network (CR < 1 m); WPAN, Wireless Personal Area Network (CR < 80 m); WLAN, Wireless Local Area Network (CR < 100–200 m); WMAN, Wireless Metropolitan Area Network (CR covering the city and suburbs); WWAN, Wireless Wide Area Network (CR covering broad geographic area, up to the global coverage); and (b) WBAN architecture scheme. (Authors' collection)

biophysical impact on the body from EMF emitted by fixed or wearable devices (parametrised by SAR caused by EMF energy absorbed in the body).

A WPAN typically allows communications in a range of up to approximately 10 m. Nowadays, this kind of technology is capable of providing services in higher and wider coverage areas, up to 50–80 m or even more under optimal conditions. Their usual deployment has notable increase from close indoor environments, usually within a person's workspace, to efficient solutions for open indoor–outdoor environments (i.e. Bluetooth or ZigBee), becoming one of the most promising opportunities in the near future. Their main features are less infrastructure required from the established link, energy harvesting and easy full connectivity in a wide range of popular devices such as smartphones, Personal Digital Assistants (PDAs) and laptops. It is relatively common for WBANs to be included into a WPAN, due to both having multiple features in common and sharing the same Institute of Electrical and Electronics Engineers (IEEE) 802.15.6–2012 standard ((IEEE 802.15.6–2012, 2012) and IEEE 802.15.6–2017 (IEEE 802.15.6–2017, 2017).

A WLAN is designed to allow wireless internet access and high-speed data transfer between devices such as computers, laptops, smartphones, PDAs, etc. in relatively large areas with a featured radio coverage up to around 100–200m. They are commonly deployed when providing full connectivity and user mobility capacity in indoor and outdoor local environments, such as buildings, malls, offices, libraries, manufacturing halls, residences or urban open areas like parks, school yards or university campuses, among others. WLANs are based on IEEE 802.11–2016 standard (2016) and are popularly known as Wi-Fi. Their main features are general worldwide adoption, fast deployment, unlicensed radio frequency bands, mobility allowed, high-speed connectivity and interoperability between different technology suppliers. All these advantages and widespread user popularity have made WLANs the most popular SR system around.

9.2.2 Wireless Communication Technologies, Systems and Standards

E-Health and IoT solutions, as well as other smart solutions, rely on many different wireless communication systems, often operating simultaneously, for complex indoor and outdoor applications. Most of these systems share some common features, such as their spectral location, physical layer operation or higher layer functionalities. The most popular SR wireless technologies are Bluetooth, ZigBee, Wi-Fi, Radio Frequency Identification (RFID) and cellular systems.

9.2.2.1 Bluetooth

Bluetooth technology was created out of a partnership between communications companies with huge synergies in common, to unify, harmonise and innovate in a vast range of connected devices formalised under the IEEE 802.15.1–2005 standard (2005). Bluetooth enables SR communications operating in the 2.4GHz unlicensed industrial, scientific, and medical (ISM) frequency band. It was originally designed for simple, point-to-point (P2P) connections, but the recent updates in terms of structure and topology allow broadcast and mesh connections, empowering actual WPANs, WSNs or IoT, and, consequently, the global smart concept. Its main features are supported for multiple radio options, low-power consumption, reliability and scalability (self-healing networks and industrial message-oriented performance), industrial-grade security and a trusted standard for wireless communications.

Different kinds of Bluetooth technologies are available: Bluetooth Basic Data Rate/Enhanced Data Rate (BDR/EDR) and Bluetooth Low Energy (BLE) (Table 9.1). The BDR/EDR technology was first released (Bluetooth, 2020) to replace cable in audio products (audio streaming over a P2P network) and computer peripherals. Over the years, in response to market requirements for low-power operation, high data transfer rate and an Adaptive Frequency Hopping (AFH) approach, Bluetooth

TABLE 9.1
Characteristics of Common Wireless Technologies

Type of Wireless Technology	Frequency Band	Maximum Operational Communication Range (m)	Maximum Sensitivity (dBm)[a]	Maximum Data Rate (Mbps)	Effective Radiated Power (ERP) (mW)[a]	Network Topologies
Bluetooth Basic/ Enhanced Data Rate (BDR/EDR)	2.4 GHz	100 – Class 1 10 – Class 2 1 – Class 3	(−90)	3	100 (20 dBm) – Class 1 2.5 (4 dBm) – Class 2 1 (0 dBm) – Class 3	P2P
Bluetooth Low Energy (BLE)	2.4 GHz	1,000 outdoor 400 indoor	(−93)	2	100 (20 dBm) – Class 1 10 (10 dBm) – Class 1.5 2.5 (4 dBm) – Class 2 1 (0 dBm) – Class 3	P2P Broadcast Mesh
ZigBee 3.0	2.4 GHz 915 MHz 868 MHz	300 (line of sight) 100 indoor	(−101)	0.250 @2.4 GHz 0.010 @915 MHz 0.100 @868 MHz	100 (20 dBm)	P2P Tree Star Broadcast Mesh
Wi-Fi	900 MHz 2.4 GHz 5 GHz 60 GHz	1000 outdoor 70 indoor	(−95)	347 @900 MHz 600 @2.4 GHz 3,500 @5 GHz 6,800 @60 GHz	10 (10 dBm) @900 MHz 100 (20 dBm) @2.4 GHz 1,000 (30 dBm) @5 GHz 10,000 (40 dBm) @60 GHz	P2P Ring Tree Star Broadcast Mesh
RFID	125 kHz 13.56 MHz 433 MHz 860–965 MHz 2.4 GHz 5.8 GHz	0.1 @125 kHz 1–1.5 @13.56 MHz 800 @433 MHz 32 @860–965 MHz 100 @2.4 GHz & 5.8 GHz	(−80) with active tags (−20) with passive tags	0.064 @125 kHz 0.848 @13.56 MHz 0.250 @433 MHz 0.640 @860–965 MHz 2 @2.4 GHz 100 @5.8 GHz	1 (0 dBm) @125 kHz 3.16 (5 dBm) @13.56 MHz 16 (12 dBm) @433 MHz 4,000 (36 dBm) @860–965 MHz & 2.4 GHz 2,000 (33 dBm) @5.8 GHz	P2P Tree Star Mesh

[a] In the dB notation, the lower values indicate better sensitivity of communication, but lower level of emitted power.

performance has increased (12 Bluetooth standards from 1.0 up to 6.0). It has multiple setup options based on the usage requirements, in term of security options, data transmission channels, and rates and power operation levels. The BLE technology is a new approach for solutions based on energy harvesting (energy efficiency can be 50 times higher or even more) (Bluetooth, 2020). It provides wireless connectivity anywhere, anytime, while being interoperable, flexible, portable and efficient. BLE is widely adopted in smartphones, tablets and wearables (such as smartwatches and health, security, sports and fitness devices). The main advantages of BLE are low-power solutions and multiple network topologies (P2P, broadcast and mesh options) to enable WSNs and IoT solutions, as shown in Table 9.1.

The majority of e-Health devices, peripherals and accessories use some kind of Bluetooth technology for data transfer, such as blood pressure, heart rate, glucose or temperature (ring) monitors, spirometers or oximeters. Nowadays, it has also been relevant for the monitoring of positive cases of SARS-CoV-2 (i.e. Radar COVID application). Intensive use of this technology is also presented in sports and leisure environments.

9.2.2.2 ZigBee

ZigBee is a SR wireless communication technology developed in 2002 (ZigBee, 2020). It was developed mainly for WSN and IoT solutions (also in intelligent buildings and homes, or industrial control systems) as a simpler alternative to the Bluetooth technology. ZigBee is defined by the IEEE 802.15.4 standard and operates in the 868 MHz, 915 MHz and 2.4 GHz unlicensed ISM frequency bands (IEEE 802.15.4–2020, 2020). It allows devices to communicate in a variety of network topologies, as shown in Table 9.1. The most relevant characteristics of the ZigBee standard are open standard, high reliability, high security, low energy consumption and low data transmission rate. The latest ZigBee 3.0 protocol was developed to help unify the IoT solutions. It provides mesh networks, secure layers and an application framework, and allows interoperable capabilities for network joining, reliable and robust self-hailing, and scalable networks, and the minimisation of error transmission packets. It is perfectly optimised for large networks with thousands of devices, in complex environments, such as industrial or commercial ones.

ZigBee Green Power is an open-energy harvesting technology (piezoelectric elements or dynamo-mechanic converters) for IoT–Zigbee networks integration (Williams, 2019). Its main features are interoperability between smart devices from different families (from the first ZigBee to new Green Power technologies), maintenance free, support for smart, batteryless beacons, energy-saving capabilities (up to five times or more), simple components, high security and multiple location possibilities. ZigBee e-Health solutions include blood pressure, heart rate, electrocardiogram (ECG)/electroencephalograms (EEG) monitors and body fat analysers.

9.2.2.3 Wi-Fi

Wireless Fidelity (Wi-Fi) is a SR wireless communication technology using WLAN based on IEEE 802.11 standards since 1997. In 1999, the 802.11. High Rate standard (known as IEEE 802.11b) was approved, providing new user data rate capabilities up to 11 Mbps in contrast to the original 2 Mbps.

Since the beginning (Wi-Fi, 2020), this technology has allowed wireless data transfer between devices in relatively large areas such as a campus or a building. Devices usually connect using unlicensed RF bands to an access point that provides the internet. The adoption of Wi-Fi continues to grow worldwide, with the aim of connecting everyone and everything, everywhere with a high-quality user experience. Over time, the standard has evolved, introducing different modulations, frequencies, higher data rates and upgraded characteristics. Four different frequencies are considered in the standards, 2.4, 3.6, 5 and 60 GHz. A new Wi-Fi iteration called Wi-Fi 6 (IEEE 802.11ax: The Sixth Generation of Wi-Fi, 2017) has arrived to increase capacity and performance (data rate up to 4.8 Gbps) required by next-generation connectivity.

The evolution of Wi-Fi has delivered new devices with improved network performance and has enhanced the user experience with lots of new developments and solutions in both consumer and enterprise environments. Wi-Fi innovation has allowed an increase in the flexibility to work, be entertained, or connect to friends and family in a growing variety of places, particularly in dense RF environments, with a high density of devices intensively sharing bandwidth and latency-sensitive solutions. The main popular Wi-Fi e-Health solutions include blood pressure or heart rate monitors, among others.

9.2.2.4 RFID

Radio frequency identification (RFID) is the most common and the fastest growing wireless technology of automatic identification and data capture, which identifies and tracks RFID sensors (tags) attached to objects. RFID technology dates back to the 1970s (some sources mention even the 1950s). Over time, RFID technology has evolved, introducing different frequencies, ranges, higher data rates and upgraded characteristics. RFID technology may be integrated with various wireless communication networks such as WSNs or WLANs.

The most commonly used RFID systems in the world are low frequency (LF band: 30–300 kHz; operating typically at 125 kHz), high frequency (HF band: 3–30 MHz; operating typically at 13.56 MHz frequency), ultra-high frequency (UHF band: 300–1000 MHz; operating in the frequency range 860–965 MHz (in Europe, 865–868 MHz) for passive tags and 443 MHz for active tags), and super-high frequency (SHF bands: 2.400–2.4835 GHz and 5.725–5.875 GHz; operating typically at 2.45 and 5.8 MHz frequency) (Finkenzeller, 2010).

RFID devices are used for various purposes, for example, aimed at the identification, monitoring, controlling or managing of objects in libraries, shops, enterprises, etc.; the marking of animals, prisoners, or dangerous substances to control them in a public environment; contactless payment (cards, public transport cards, toll collection on highways and bridges); in near-field SRDs, and in control access to buildings, rooms or even vehicles. RFID-based smart healthcare devices are used to monitor, control or manage medical devices, pharmaceuticals, biological samples and even patients.

9.2.2.5 Cellular Systems—Towards 5G

Cellular communication technology has become one of the most common artificial EMF exposure sources to which a large population is exposed in working, public and healthcare environments.

Mobile networks have evolved, starting with the analogue or first-generation (1G) networks (the 1980s), moving on to the digital second-generation (2G) networks (early 1990s), third-generation (3G) networks (2000) and the fourth-generation (4G) networks (since 2010). The wireless mobile network has undergone a huge transformation from a pure telephony system (voice communication) to a network that can transport rich multimedia contents via mass data transfer. The 4G networks were designed to meet the requirements of the International Mobile Telecommunications-Advanced (IMT-A) requirements using Internet Protocol (IP) for all services (Del Peral-Rosado et al., 2018). They can support data rates of up to 1 Gbps (giga bit per second) for low mobility, such as nomadic/local wireless access, and up to 100 Mbps for high mobility, such as mobile access.

One of the main problems with 4G networks is that they have almost reached the theoretical limit on the data rate with current technologies, and, therefore, they are not sufficient to accommodate the aforementioned challenges. The next generations, known as 5G and 6G networks, are promising in these respects. The 5G network will provide higher data rates, regardless of the user's location. The aim is to connect the entire world and achieve seamless and ubiquitous communications between anybody (people to people), anything (people to machine, machine to machine), wherever they are (anywhere), whenever they need (anytime), using whatever electronic devices/services/networks they wish (anyhow). It should achieve 1000 times the system capacity, 10 times the spectral efficiency, energy efficiency and data rate (i.e. peak data rate of 10 Gbps for low mobility and peak data rate of 1 Gbps for high mobility), and 25 times the average cell throughput.

The 5G network will introduce life-changing services, providing users with significantly increased capacity and real-time responsiveness. It also has the potential to revolutionise the e-Health and IoT mobile experience with massive numbers of connected devices communicating in real time with each other. The main 5G use cases are Enhanced Mobile Broadband (EMBB), Ultra-Reliable and Low Latency Communications (URLLC), and Massive Machine Type Communications (Massive MTC). Table 9.2 presents various possible use cases of 5G for e-Health applications.

TABLE 9.2
Examples of 5G e-Health Smart Solution Applications of Short-Range Wireless Communication Systems

Destination	Application
Patient applications	Precision medicine (patient's individual characteristics); Remote Specialty Treatment; AR/VR/MR[a] Adaptative Treatment; 24/7 Continuous Health & Wellness Monitor and Address Conditions;
Hospital applications	AR/VR-assisted surgery; video-based check-ups; Telemetry; Remote-assisted surgery; robotic surgery
Medical data management	Collaborative Care; Real time delivery of data sets; e-Health records
Other	Connected ambulances; 3D printing – bioprinting (real time, personalised, on-demand); Emergency drones

[a] AR, augmented reality; VR, virtual reality; MR, mixed reality.

Finally, next-generation 6G networks are expected to provide further improvements in terms of quality of service, data rate, real-time and low latency, allowing future cutting-edge applications and services.

9.3 ACTIVE IMPLANTABLE MEDICAL DEVICES

The continuous development of biomedical engineering has made it possible to effectively compensate for various types of body dysfunctions through the use of active medical implants, and their users can be anyone, including workers.

Various dysfunctions of the human body, especially chronic ones, may be compensated by implants or medical devices worn on the body containing electronic circuits considered to be Active Implantable Medical Devices (AIMDs) (Zradziński et al., 2018a,b). A large variety of organism dysfunctions have led to a large variety of implants being used. Medical implants can be divided into two groups:

- Passive: mechanical implants not containing electronic components
- Active: electronic implants, that is, AIMDs.

The most frequently used passive implants include endoprostheses, plates, rods or screws to compensate for orthopaedic dysfunctions (e.g. endoprostheses of the hip or knee joint, endoprostheses for the reconstruction of the craniofacial bones), eye or dental implants, or cardiovascular stents.

According to EU Directive 90/385/EEC, an AIMD is 'any active medical device that is intended to be totally or partially introduced, surgically or medically, into the human body or by medical intervention into a natural orifice, and which is intended to remain after the procedure' (Council Directive 90/385/EEC). AIMDs include devices supporting the proper functioning of the circulatory system (e.g. pacemakers, cardioverter-defibrillators), supporting the hearing impaired or deaf people (e.g. bone conduction implants, cochlear or middle ear implants, auditory brainstem implants), eye implants and supporting the functioning of the nervous system (brainstem implants). Devices for the continuous monitoring of glucose levels, and insulin or infusion pumps are also used.

9.4 AIMD MALFUNCTIONS CAUSED BY EMF EXPOSURE

The use of AIMD significantly differentiates people's sensitivity to the influence of EMF, regardless of their formal status—worker, patient, public, etc. Hence, the EMF safety issues of AIMDs users apply equally to the entire population. The safety of AIMDs users is one of the key issues of electromagnetic safety required by international labour law, safety recommendations and standards. Particularly noteworthy are cases where the AIMD user is also a smart wireless solutions user (e.g. E-health SRD solutions).

Medical devices are especially sensitive to possible indirect effects caused by EMF interference, which can even lead to fatal consequences in critical health cases. As a possible example, a lack of electrical cardiac stimulation in a patient fully dependent on an AIMD, due to a hypothetical high level of EMF interference, could be a potentially life-threatening situation (Tiikkaja et al., 2013; Hauser and Kallinen, 2004; Abubakar et al., 2017; Mattei et al., 2021). Accordingly, commercial deployments of healthcare SRD systems require strict health security measures and control in terms of Electromagnetic Compatibility (EMC), as a guarantee of user safety, before they are released.

Electric potentials induced through conductive materials can cause thermal effects/damage to biological tissues, and dysfunctions can be presented in the body's nervous system due to electrostimulation (Directive 2013/35/EU, 2013). Moreover, AIMDs can present malfunctions due to thermal effects caused by induced currents directly applied over the implant structure and/or the embedded electronic components, or even collateral indirect thermal affections when adjacent tissues are exposed to the mentioned elevated heating caused by absorption of electromagnetic energy in AIMD structures. Such effects depend on numerous EMF factors and conditions, including frequency, level, polarisation or distribution in space and time (Zradziński et al., 2018b). Thus, all these potential EMF safety hazards must be identified and evaluated for the user's safety, and that is not a trivial process.

The various wireless communication systems alongside the current technological advances mean that EMF exposure in workers, the general public and particularly in medical personnel, patients and AIMD users, cannot be avoided.

The EMF exposure impacts involving AIMDs can be roughly divided into the following categories:

- Electrical and magnetic impact (i.e. over the multiple embedded electric circuit components on board the AIMD).
- Mechanical impact (i.e. over the device elements/replacement parts or the integral structure).
- Thermal impact (i.e. over the device materials or human tissues in the vicinity of the implant).
- Performance impact (i.e. lack of implant activities, implant malfunctions causing inadequate activities, software-reset or halt-uncontrolled situations).

Regarding SRD technologies, this EMF exposure threat leads to possible health effects that can induce or provoke potential hazards directly to the own users or indirectly to other persons present nearby (in particular, when EMF exposure in the work environment is considered). This situation is particularly crucial when considering AIMDs, such as pacemakers, implantable cardioverter-defibrillators (ICDs), hearing implants and insulin pumps, as shown in Table 9.3.

9.4.1 AIMD User Safety Legislation and Regulations

International Standards and Guidelines cover AIMD user safety in terms of EMC interference management manufacturing and general or occupational EMF exposure.

European requirements, such as from the EN 60601-1-2, implementing the IEC 60601-1-2 (EN 60601-1-2:2015/A1:2021, 2021), have been developed in order to control the design and specifications of healthcare equipment, concerning EMC in frequencies from 80 MHz to 2.7 GHz (the most heavily used part of the frequency range

TABLE 9.3
Examples of AIMDs' Malfunctions Observed through EMF Exposure

Observed Malfunctions of AIMD	Exposure Conditions	References
	Implantable Cardiac Pacemakers' (CP)	
Pacing inhibition (complete or temporary stop of pacing)	(a) EAS; (b) GSM handsets; (c) BTS; (d) MD; (e) RFID	(a) McIvor and Sridhar (1998); (b) Hekmat et al. (2004); Tandogan et al. (2005); (c) Alanko et al. (2008); Toivonen et al. (2009); (d) Kainz et al. (2005); Guag et al. (2017); (e) Mattei et al. (2016)
Triggering of rapid or premature pacing	(a) EAS; (b) GSM handsets; (c) BTS; (d) MD	(a) McIvor and Sridhar (1998); Groh et al. (1999); (b) Tandogan et al. (2005); (c) Alanko et al. (2008); Toivonen et al. (2009); (d) Guag et al. (2017)
Reversion to noise mode	(a) EAS; (b) GSM handsets (c) BTS	(a) McIvor and Sridhar (1998); (b) Tandogan et al. (2005); (c) Alanko et al. (2008); Toivonen et al. (2009)
Activation of magnetic switch	Portable headphones	Lee et al. (2009)
	Implantable Cardioverter-Defibrillators (ICD)	
Triggering of rapid or premature pacing	(a) EAS; (b) GSM handsets	(a) Groh et al. (1999); (b) Barbaro et al. (1999)
False arrhythmia detection	EAS	Groh et al. (1999)
Reversion to noise mode	BTS	Alanko et al. (2008); Toivonen et al. (2009)
Activation of magnetic switch. Tachycardia detection and treatment is switched off.	Portable headphones	Lee et al. (2009)
	Insulin Pumps and Glucose Monitoring Devices	
Pump delivers insulin inaccurately or behaves erratically	(a) GSM handsets; (b) RFID	(a) Zhang et al. (2010); (b) Christe (2009); Calcagnini et al. (2006)
Failure of electronic components	GSM handsets	Zhang et al. (2010)
Temporary stoppage with restart with the basic factory preset	GSM handsets	Zhang et al. (2010)
	Hearing, Cochlear Implants	
Sound quality problems	Mobile handsets	Cray et al. (2004); Levitt (2001)
Hearing distorted sound	EAS; MD	Tagnola et al. (2007)

Note: EAS, electronic article surveillance systems; BTS, vicinity of antenna of mobile phone base station; RFID, radiofrequency identification devices; MD, walk-through metal detectors gates.

for SRDs) and is also applied to AIMDs. This is the harmonised standard for medical devices drafted in support of Council Directive 93/42/EEC, contained in and repealed by Regulation 2017/745 of the European Parliament and of the Council. It basically requires that, in order to be released into the European Union market, the functioning of medical devices for professional or home healthcare environments should be immune (resistant) to the influence of a radiofrequency electric field (EF) with a strength of up to 3 or 10 V/m, respectively, and additionally in selected narrow bands immune to EF with a strength of up to 9 V/m (104–787 MHz and 5100–5800 MHz), 27 V/m (380–390 MHz) and 28 V/m (430–470 MHz, 800–960 MHz, 1700–1990 MHz, 2400–2570 MHz) (EN 60601-1-2:2015/A1:2021, 2021).

Furthermore, the assessment of potential hazards caused by EMF exposure to the AIMD user is covered by Appendix A of standard EN 50527-1:2016 (2016) harmonised with the directive 2013/35/EU. Though this non-binding standard recommends that AIMDs for use in the European Union be immune to EMF-exposure-related malfunctions up to the level equal to the general public exposure limits provided by the European Council Recommendation 1999/519/EC (European Council, 1999). However, this recommendation itself says (Article 13) that AIMD malfunctions need attention in EMF exposures that are weaker than the exposure limits set by this recommendation.

Another important aspect in the analysis of the safety of AIMD users exposed to EMF is that the exposure level of 28–61 V/m, which is compliant at the frequency range 80 MHz – 2.7 GHz with the European Council Recommendation (1999), may be several times stronger than the level of basic test EMFs used in the mentioned EMC immunity evaluation following the requirements of EN 60601-1-2:2015/A1:2021.

There is also European Directive 2013/35/EU (Directive 2013/35/EU, 2013), which was issued to set out the minimum requirements for the protection of workers' health and safety with respect to a particular set of direct and indirect biophysical effects of EMF exposure at frequencies ranging from 0 to 300 GHz, covering hazards for AIMD users within the set of hazardous indirect EMF exposure effects. However, the directive does not prohibit the EMF exposure for AIMD users. Otherwise, AIMD users would be considered in the directive to be 'workers at particular risk' to which special protection (i.e. based on the individual EMF risk assessment) must be provided in order to prevent potential health hazards and the management of AIMD interference with EMF exposure. The EMF exposure data characterising the EMF hazards for AIMD users are rather limited. Examples may be found in the form of the general safety distances related to the EMF emitted from medical and industrial devices evaluated based on the measurements at various workplace (Zradziński et al, 2018a). The results of the survey showed that the risk of AIMD malfunctions needs to be considered and labelled at a distance of tens of cm (up to 1.5 m) from medical devices (such as physiotherapeutic devices and electrosurgery units), and up to several metres from industrial devices (such as welding devices, dielectric sealers and induction heaters). Fortunately, the literature suggests that the immune to EMF influence of many particular AIMD is sufficient to ensure the safety of users even at significantly shorter distances from an EMF source. Only when detailed safety data provided by the manufacturer of the particular AIMD used by worker is available, such individual safety considerations may be performed, without the test of EMF exposure to the AIMD user, which may be hazardous for workers' health or even lives.

Nevertheless, the immunity of implants to EMF exposure varies significantly and is determined by multiple factors: the implant model design and operation settings, location in the body, duration of exposure, transmitted power and spatial distribution of the EMF near its source, among other things (Napp et al., 2014). This makes it necessary to keep detailed records regarding applied AIMD for every user, especially worker, as well as to properly label EMF hazards at the workplace. Any considerations on the EMF safety of AIMD users need to pay attention to the fact that EMC requirements, applicable to the safety of SRDs and AIMD users (EN 60601-1-2:2015/A1:2021 or the IEC 60601-1-2:2014/A1:2020), require basic immunity from AIMDs against the influence of weak RF-EMF only (3, 9, 10 or 28 V/m), whereas requirements applicable to human exposure accept much stronger EMF in the general public (the European Council, 1999: 28–61 V/m) or workplace (Directive 2013/35/EU, 2013: 60–140 V/m) environments.

It must be pointed out that there is unharmonised policies worldwide, as well as there are different cases where legal standards and regulation cannot be applied. Some examples of these presented problems or gaps could be the following ones: In some cases, declaration of compliance with the EMC requirements may be issued by the manufacturer of AIMDs based on theoretical analysis only (i.e. without experimental verification), or older AIMDs could be compliant with outdated less restrictive requirements (i.e. exposure to radiofrequency EMF of EF exceeding 3 V/m may be hazardous for some AIMD users).

It also needs special attention that when in the vicinity of AIMD user many EMF sources are used simultaneously, the level of exposure needs to be assessed (potentially as high as the total sum of all the components of all sources).

Finally, other electronic devices may also be the subjects of electromagnetically induced malfunctions and the reason of related safety hazards in the workplace. But EMC requirements regarding their immunity to EMF influence may be less formalised and less restrictive than the previously mentioned ones applicable to AIMDs, with exception to devices specially designed to be free from EMF-induced malfunctions (for example for the use in highly exposed industrial or military environments).

9.5 EVALUATION OF ELECTROMAGNETIC HAZARDS ASSOCIATED WITH THE USE OF SRDs

Alarm devices are one example of medical SRDs, such as small devices used, for example, in telecare monitoring activities, which can be hung over the neck or attached to the wrist (alarm buttons) or fixed to a wall or furniture [wireless access points, in this case recognised to be a social alarm device (SAD)].

The general operation of the device can be described as follows: during a potentially hazardous situation, the SAD user can push the emergency button, and an emergency call is provided to the monitoring centre by a wireless signal, for example, a healthcare emergency unit. This wireless transmission typically consists of a three-pulse signal (depending on the device specification) using a frequency of 869.21 MHz. These emissions could increase the EMF exposure levels of the SAD user and nearby individuals (e.g. medical personnel or the general public), and could enable electromagnetic interference over other electronic devices, which in turn could potentially result in serious injuries, inappropriate treatment or even fatal outcomes. Therefore, the environmental impact of EMF in the vicinity of the devices is often included in the research topics considering SRDs, SADs or similar devices usage (García-Fernández et al., 2016; Lopez-Iturri et al., 2015).

9.5.1 Environmental EMF Measurements

To have a clear insight into the interaction between the considered SAD and potential AIMD users, a campaign of laboratory measurements has been performed in order to verify compliance with current international regulations, standards and guidelines. Measurements have been carried out without the presence of anyone operating the devices (measurements of unperturbed fields) and under normal operating conditions of EMF sources (De Miguel-Bilbao, 2013; Directive 2013/35/UE, 2013; ICNIRP, 1998, 2020; European Council, 1999). In short, the EF strength was measured using a protocol based on the EMC regular practice, in the direction of the maximum interaction with the AIMD, assuming the worst EF strength case, as a function of distance in steps of 10 cm, from 0.2 m to 1.7 m, considering horizontal and vertical polarisation in the near field region—below 5λ, where λ is the wavelength (Salous, 2013). To determine the exact distances, an automatic positioning device FSM 016, together with a HD10 controller, was used. By means of a Rohde & Schwartz ESIB26 EMI Test Receiver, with a frequency range from 20 Hz to 26.5 GHz, the EF strength, considering the antenna factor and the cable attenuation, was calculated.

Figure 9.2 shows the EF measured (arithmetic mean and range) in the vicinity of five example SADs: AMIE+ Tunstall, Neat Atom, TX4 Bosch, S37 TeleAlarm and System 5000 SmartCall, considering their normal transmission power conditions at 869.21 MHz operating frequency. All the obtained measurement results at the considered distances (identified as safe distances) are far below the general public International Commission on Non-Ionizing Radiation Protection (ICNIRP) limits for 869.21 MHz, which are fixed at 40 V/m (ICNIRP, 1998, 2020). As introduced in the previous subsection, the minimum prevention basis for EMC immunity testing of medical equipment in EMF from 80 MHz to 2.7 GHz was set at the level of 3 V/m (EN 60601-1-2:2015/A1:2021, 2021).

From the obtained results at a distance of 20 cm from the individual tested SADs, the maximum measured EF values are much lower than this aforementioned limit ($E < 0.8$ V/m). Nevertheless, it must be remarked that significant variations of EF levels near particular tested SADs were found, at least 4 times difference between the lower and higher exposure near various SADs, most probably, due to variations in the communication distances of the specific devices. Additionally, logarithmic prediction on the basis of the measured EF, extrapolating experimental data for shorter vicinity of tested SADs, indicates the possibility of twice higher EF values for distances of several centimetres from the SADs. In order to test this possibility, EMF measurements using small-dimensions near-field probes or full-wave numerical simulations can be helpful in order to predict in advance near field EF levels.

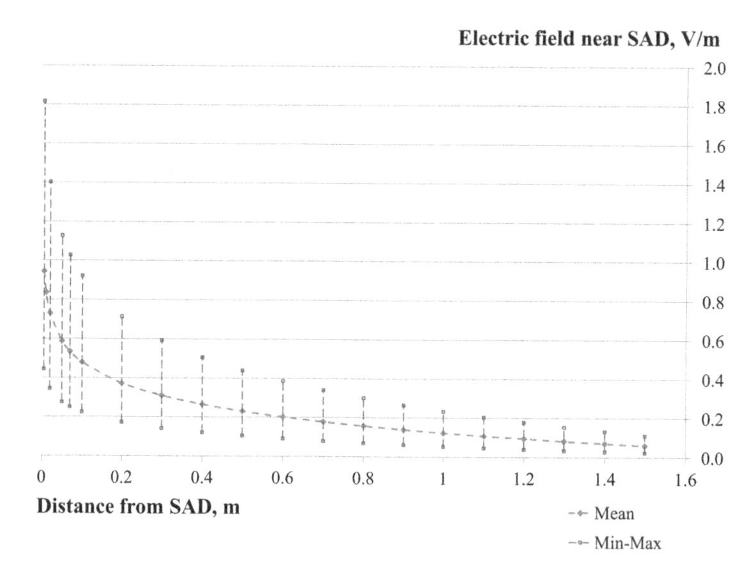

FIGURE 9.2 Variation of the EF as a function of distance, evaluated based on measurements near five examples of various SADs at distances exceeding 0.2 m. Extrapolation of experimental results for distances of 0.005 m and 0.1 m; dots, the arithmetic mean (mean) of measurement results ($N = 5$); whiskers, range between the minimum and the maximum values obtained from measurements (Minimum–Maximum). (Authors' collection)

Finally, other SRDs' technical features (SADs among others) must be taken under consideration when analysing specific e-Health environments. Restrictions in terms of total emissions due to the power control system apply may affect directly the communication range between devices. In this sense, e-Health solutions are designed to be compliant with the precautionary exposure thresholds, limiting the communication range as well as the corresponding total emissions in the worst-case conditions. Considering all these technical issues, its communication range is expected in the order of 1–3 m approximately (i.e. compliance with Bluetooth Class 3 Standard limited to 1 mW), based on the morphology and topology of the scenario under evaluation. Nevertheless, safety analyses must include the worst-case scenarios (upgraded technology versions with higher powers or less restrictions and/or considerations of the simultaneously use of many devices, among others) where expected emissions in the vicinity—near field conditions, could be potentially higher than the measured ones, with the maximum EF levels close by the aforementioned limits. Thus, the application of safety precautionary actions when e-Health systems are designed is pivotal in order to warrant compliance with relevant international exposure regulations as well as the EMC technical rules.

9.5.2 Environmental EMF Simulations

In order to provide clear insight of the potential EMF hazards for AIMD users in realistic case scenarios (of exposure near various physical objects), deterministic simulations using virtual human body models and multiple EMF sources can be applied. For that purpose, a propagation model—a set of mathematical expressions, diagrams and algorithms used to represent the RF-EMF propagation characteristics of an environment—is needed. When selecting a suitable propagation channel model, three main aspects must be taken into consideration: (1) the type of application (system-wide analysis or critical-safety application), (2) the availability of geographical information and (3) the influence of the velocity. One of the deterministic approaches (other approaches include theoretical, empirical or stochastic) is the Ray Launching (RL) technique (Azpilicueta et al., 2016; Walfisch and Bertoni, 1988; Yin et al., 2015; Li et al., 2018). The RL technique achieves a good trade-off between precision and simulation time. Its principle is based on launching thousands of test rays in a solid angle where the true path is determined by looking for the rays arriving at the receiver. These methods are precise but time-consuming due to inherent computational complexity. Nevertheless, in combination with the Uniform Theory of Diffraction (UTD) (Kouyoumjian and Pathak, 1974), they are the most frequently applied to wireless communication coverage prediction (Yun and Iskander, 2015; Zhang and Yu, 2013). Hence, RL models potentially represent the most accurate and versatile methods for outdoor and indoor, multipath propagation characterisation or prediction in far-field conditions. This means that deterministic methods such as RL can be an appropriate propagation model approach for complex heterogeneous environments, such as the RF characterisation in healthcare scenarios, which makes it suitable for use when simulating case studies.

An indoor realistic case of exposure scenario was considered, in order to analyse EMF exposure levels within the complete volume of the scenario at far-field conditions (Salous, 2013) due to the emissions caused by an SRD [considering an 869.21 MHz, monopole antenna, with a transmission power of 1 mW (0dBm), that is, Bluetooth Class 3 EMF source used in devices of intended communication range of 1 m] in realistic exposure use case conditions placed on the user's body. In this case, the transmitter was located at a height of 1.2 m, emulating a SAD hanging around the neck of a standing person in the middle of the room, as shown in Figure 9.3a. By means of the chosen user position within the considered scenario, all the possible interactions with an AIMD user at every location can be assessed.

The highest EF strength values (calculated with a resolution of 0.05 m for all the volume of the scenario) are clearly obtained in the immediate vicinity of the transceiver position, decreasing rapidly as we move away from the transmitter location, based on the geometry of the obstacles of the scenario, as shown in Figure 9.3b. It must be pointed out that an exclusion area of 5λ has been applied, avoiding unreliable near-field results (Salous, 2013). In addition, the path loss absorption caused by the human body is notable due to the body shielding effect (Celaya-Echarri et al., 2019). In analysing the results of simulation of discussed type, it also needs attention that emission from SRDs considered in the real workplace may be at a very different levels, for example, Bluetooth device of Class 1 with 100 m communication range may be 10-fold stronger than the emission from device of Class 3 modelled in presented example of simulations.

These results can improve the understanding and prevention of potential hazards to an AIMD user caused by environmental EMF exposure. The user's density, as well as the configuration of the scenario and the number of active transceivers (AIMD,

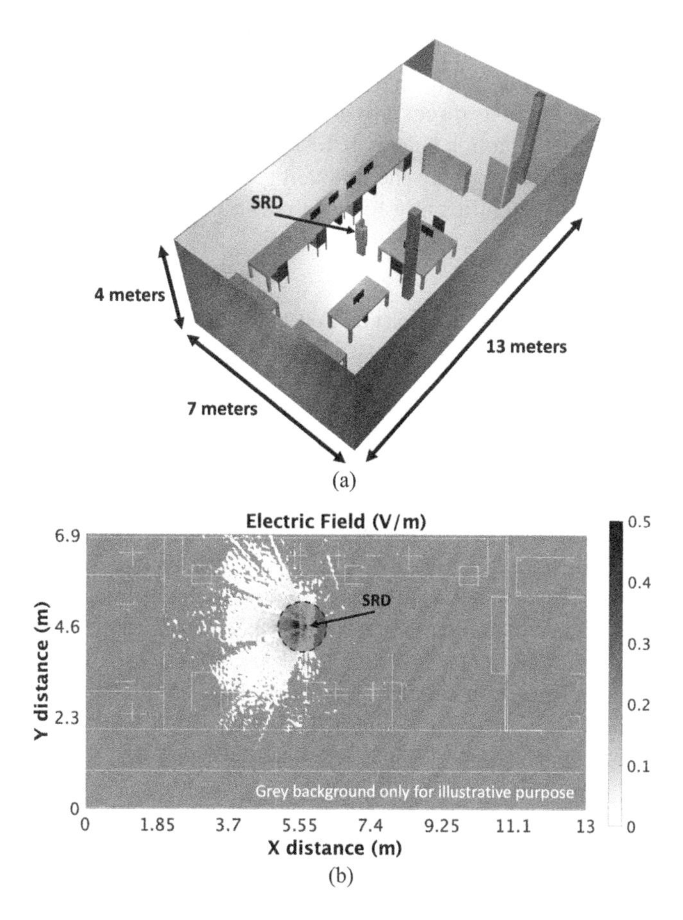

FIGURE 9.3 Ray launching simulations of EMF from SRD @ 1 mW emission level (i.e. Bluetooth device Class 3-1 m communication range) considering an exclusion area of 5λ to avoid uncertainty in near-field conditions: (a) schematic view of the exposure scenario; (b) estimated received EF strength within the complete volume of the scenario. (Authors' collection)

SRD or any wireless communication system presented in the scenario), can impact the EF levels in the considered space, which plays a relevant role when analysing compliance with safety exposure limits and evaluating EMF-related hazards for AIMD users.

The presented SRD simulation example complements the previous EMF measurements' results of various SADs, providing a full understanding of the potential RF-EMF impact in a real complex scenario.

As it has been previously discussed, it must be remarked that malfunctions of AIMDs or other various electronic devices (i.e., caused by the EMF influence during the activation of SADs, the use of SADs designed for longer communication ranges, the simultaneous use of many EMF sources in the vicinity or by the differences in the EMC immunity of particular electronic devices, especially older ones, or re-designed or repaired using substitute electronic components, different than the intentional ones specified by the designer of the device, among other potential triggers) cannot be excluded in its direct proximity. Therefore, this kind of EMF indirect hazards require special attention (adequate EMF exposure assessment), especially in the healthcare environment, where the probability of the presence of users of various kinds of AIMDs is significantly higher than in the general public or in work environments.

9.5.3 Simulations of Specific Energy Absorption Rate in Exposed Human Body

According to Directive 2013/35/EU, in the case of '*a very localised source at a distance of several centimetres from the body* (e.g., the e-Health devices that are often used in or in the vicinity of the body), *compliance with exposure limit values* (expressed as SAR values for frequencies of EMF emitted by SRDs) *must be determined dosimetrically* (e.g. by numerical simulations in near-field conditions), *on a case-by-case basis*' (Directive 2013/35/EU, 2013). This is important, especially for AIMD users, because SAR values in the vicinity of an implanted device may be several times higher in comparison to regular people under the same conditions of EMF exposure. For example, investigations carried out on exposure of users of two different bone conduction hearing implants to EMF emitted from an RFID HF (13.56 MHz) reader showed up to 2.1 times higher localised SAR in the vicinity of the implants, in comparison to SAR in these tissues in a non-user's head (Zradziński et al., 2019).

To obtain reliable results for a worker's exposure through evaluation by numerical simulations of SAR, it is necessary to use models adequately representing exposure situations (known as exposure scenarios) and specific parameters of numerical models as the shape, dimensions and posture of numerical models of the worker's body and the conditions of their contact to the ground (or other grounded objects), the shape and dimensions of individual elements of the EMF source, as well as the shape and dimensions of environmental objects in the vicinity (electrically conductive objects affecting the electric field distribution (Zradziński, 2015a,b). Generally, various numerical methods may be applied in evaluating of SAR, for example, Finite Difference Time Domain (FDTD), Finite Integration Technique (FIT), Method of Moments (MoM) and similar algorithms of Boundary Element Method (BEM) or Impedance Method (IM).

9.6 CONCLUSIONS

The continuous growth of wireless communications has led to the development and standardisation of various smart wireless solutions, such as medical e-Health SRDs and AIMDs. The present trend shows that various smart services and applications will continue growing exponentially, based on numerous wireless communication services, including the new-generation wireless networks (known as 5G/6G networks), or the full interaction of intelligent systems (known as the IoT). Therefore, this massive increase in wireless communication solutions implicitly involves a common electromagnetic exposure also affecting humans, even if they are not aware or do not use any of the aforementioned systems.

The quality of life of humans can be improved through the use of SRDs in assisted environments, for example, medical care, where SRDs bring a great range of advantages, such as the monitoring of patients and the elderly, among others. Depending on the model and purpose of use of the SRDs, various wireless technologies in different frequency bands can be used, such as Bluetooth, Wi-Fi or ZigBee. Similar systems may be applied in other environments, such as hazardous workplace, sports and fitness, or military environment.

In order to prevent any electromagnetic hazard to the AIMD user, at least the following aspects must be understood: the technical aspects of any SRDs that can coexist with the AIMD and the EMF exposure in the environment, which can arise from all the wireless devices surrounding the user.

There is certainly no doubt that, with a more precise characterisation of the interaction between RF-EMF and the human body, user safety as well as future smart systems (applications and services) will develop enormously.

ACKNOWLEDGEMENTS

This chapter has been based on the results of the research tasks that has been carried out in Poland within the scope of the National Programme 'Improvement of Safety and Working Conditions' (CIOP-PIB is the Programme's main co-ordinator), partly supported by the National Centre for Research and Development (within the scope of research and development – project II.PB.15).

This work was also supported in part from Spain by the Instituto de Salud Carlos III Project "Electromagnetic Characterization in Smart Environments of Healthcare, and their Involvement in Personal, Occupational, and Environmental Health" under Grant PI14CIII/00056, and in part by the Sub-Directorate-General for Research Assessment and Promotion through the Project "Metrics Development for Electromagnetic Safety Assessment in Healthcare Centers in the Context of 5G [(PI19CIII/00033) TMPY 508/19]."

Authors would like to acknowledge also the networking support by European COST Action BM1309 (COST EMF-MED).

REFERENCES

Abubakar, I., J. Din, M. Alhilali, and H. Y. Lam. 2017. Interference and electromagnetic compatibility challenges in 5G wireless network deployments. *Indones J Electr Eng Comput Sci* 5(3):612–621. DOI: 10.11591/ijeecs.v5.i3.

Alanko, T., M. Hietanen, and P. von Nandelstadh. 2008. Occupational exposure to RF fields from base station antennas on rooftops. *Ann Telecommun* 63(1–2):125–132. DOI: 10.1007/s12243-007-0001-6.

Azpilicueta, L., C. Vargas-Rosales, and F. Falcone. 2016. Intelligent vehicle communication: deterministic propagation prediction in transportation systems. *IEEE Veh Technol Mag* 11(3):29–37. DOI: 10.1109/MVT.2016.2549995.

Barbaro, V., P. Bartolini, F. Bellocci et al. 1999. Electromagnetic interference of digital and analog cellular telephones with implantable cardioverter defibrillators: In vitro and in vivo studies. *Pacing Clin Electrophysiol* 22(4 Pt. 1):626–634. DOI: 10.1111/j.1540-8159.1999.tb00504.x.

Bluetooth. 2020. https://www.bluetooth.com (accessed February 3, 2020).

Bradshaw, V. 2006. *The Building Environment: Active and Passive Control Systems*. New Jersey: John Wiley & Sons, Ltd.

Calcagnini, G., M. Floris, F. Censi, P. Cianfanelli, G. Scavino, and P. Bartolini. 2006. Electromagnetic interference with infusion pumps from GSM mobile phones. *Health Phys* 90(4):357–360. DOI: 10.1097/01.hp.0000183559.25124.5d.

Carranza, N., V. Ramos, F.G. Lizana et al. 2010. A literature review of transmission effectiveness and electromagnetic compatibility in home telemedicine environments to evaluate safety and security. *Telemed J E Health* 16(7):530–541. DOI: 10.1089/tmj.2010.0036.

Carranza, N., V. Febles, J.A. Hernández et al. 2011. Patient safety and electromagnetic protection: A review. *Health Phys* 100(5):530–541. DOI: 10.1097/HP.obo13e3181focad5.

Celaya-Echarri, M., L. Azpilicueta, P. Lopez-Iturri et al. 2019. Spatial characterization of personal RF-EMF exposure in public transportation buses. *IEEE Access* 7:33038–33054 DOI: 10.1109/ACCESS.2019.2903405.

Christe, B. 2009. Evaluation of current literature to determine the potential effects of radio frequency identification on technology used in diabetes care. *J Diabetes Sci Technol* 3(2):331–335. DOI: 10.1177/193229680900300214.

Cisco. 2020. Cisco annual internet report (2018–2023). https://www.cisco.com/c/en/us/solutions/collateral/executive-perspectives/annual-internet-report/white-paper-c11-741490.pdf. (Accessed October 7, 2020).

Council Directive 90/385/EEC of 20 June 1990 on the approximation of the laws of the Member States relating to active implantable medical devices. https://eur-lex.europa.eu/LexUriServ/LexUriServ.do?uri=CELEX:31990L0385:en:HTML (accessed 3 February 2020).

Cray, J.W., R.L. Allen, A. Stuart, S. Hudson, E. Layman, and G.D. Givens. 2004. An investigation of telephone use among cochlear implant recipients. *Am J Audiol* 13(2):200–212. DOI: 10.1044/1059-0889(2004/025).

de Miguel-Bilbao, S., J. García, M. D. Marcos, and V. Ramos. 2013. Short range technologies for ambient assisted living systems in telemedicine: New healthcare environments. *InTech 2013* DOI: 10.5772/57020.

Del Peral-Rosado, J. A., R. Raulefs, J.A. López-Salcedo, and G. Seco-Granados. 2018. Survey of cellular mobile radio localization methods: From 1G to 5G. *IEEE Commun Surveys Tuts* 20(2):1124–1148. DOI: 10.1109/COMST.2017.2785181.

Dickerson, R., E. Gorlin, and J. Stankovic. 2011. Empath: A continuous remote emotional health monitoring system for depressive illness. *WH '11: Proceedings of the 2nd Conference on Wireless Health, San Diego*, 2011.10.10–13. New York: Association for Computing Machinery. DOI: 10.1145/2077546.2077552.

Directive 2013/35/EU. 2013. Directive of the European Parliament and of the Council of 26 June 2013 on the Minimum Health And Safety Requirements Regarding The Exposure Of Workers To The Risks Arising From Physical Agents (Electromagnetic Fields) (20th Individual Directive within the Meaning of Article 16(1) of Directive 89/391/EEC). *Official Journal of the European Union* O.J. No. L-179 of 29 June 2013, 1–21, Brussels, Belgium.

EN 60601-1-2:2015/A1:2021. 2021. *Medical electrical equipment – Part 1–2: General Requirements for Basic Safety and Essential Performance – Collateral standard: Electromagnetic Disturbances – Requirements and Tests*. Brussels: CENELEC [European Committee for Electrotechnical Standardization].

EN 50527-1:2016. 2016. *Procedure for the Assessment of the Exposure to Electromagnetic Fields of Workers Bearing Active Implantable Medical Devices – Part 1: General.* Brussels: CENELEC [European Committee for Electrotechnical Standardization].

European Council. 1999. Council recommendation of 12 July 1999 on the limitation of exposure of the general public to electromagnetic fields (0 Hz to 300 GHz) - (1999/519/EC). OJEC L 199/59, 30. 7. 1999. https://eur-lex.europa.eu/LexUriServ/LexUriServ.do?uri=OJ:L:1999:199:0059:0070:EN:PDF (accessed February 3, 2020).

Finkenzeller, K. 2010. *RFID Handbook. Fundamentals and Applications in Contactless Smart Cards, Radio Frequency Identification and Near-Field Communication.* Chichester: John Wiley & Sons, Ltd.

García-Fernández, M. Á., Y. Percherancier, I. Lagroye et al. 2016. Dosimetric characteristics of an EMF delivery system based on a real-time impedance measurement device. *IEEE Trans Biomed Eng* 63(11):2317–2325. DOI: 10.1109/TBME.2016.2527927.

Goldsmith, A. 2005. *Wireless Communications.* New York: Cambridge University Press.

Gondalia, A., D. Dixit, S. Parashar et al. 2018. IoT-based healthcare monitoring system for war soldiers using machine learning. *Procedia Comput Sci* 133:1005–1013. DOI: 10.1016/j.procs.2018.07.075.

Groh, W.J., S.A. Boschee, E.D. Engelstein et al. 1999. Interactions between electronic article surveillance systems and implantable cardioverter-defibrillators. *Circulation* 100(4):387–392. DOI: 10.1161/01.CIR.100.4.387.

Guag, J., B. Addissie, and D. Witters. 2017. Personal medical electronic devices and walk-through metal detector security systems: assessing electromagnetic interference effects. *Biomed Eng Online* 16, Article Number: 33. DOI: 10.1186/s12938-017-0328-9.

Hanson, M.A., H.C. Powell Jr, A.T. Barth et al. 2009. Body area sensors networks: Challenges and opportunities. *Computer* 42(1):58–65. DOI: 10.1109/MC.2009.5.

Hauser, R.G., and L. Kallinen. 2004. Deaths associated with implantable cardioverter defibrillator failure and deactivation reported in the United States Food and Drug Administration Manufacturer and User Facility Device Experience Database. *Heart Rhythm* 1(4):399–405. DOI: 10.1016/j.hrthm.2004.05.006.

Hebert, M.A., B. Korabek, and R.E. Scott. 2006. Moving research into practice: A decision framework for integrating home telehealth into chronic illness care. *Int J Med Inform* 75(12):786–794. DOI: 10.1016/j.ijmedinf.2006.05.041.

Hekmat, K., B. Salemink, G. Lauterbach et al. 2004. Interference by cellular phones with permanent implanted pacemakers: an update. *Europace* 6(4):363–369. DOI: 10.1016/j.eupc.2004.03.010.

IARC [International Agency for Research on Cancer]. 2013. *IARC Monographs on the Evaluation of Carcinogenic Risks to Humans. Non-Ionizing Radiation, Part 2: Radiofrequency Electromagnetic Fields.* Volume 102. Lyon, France: IARC Press. http://monographs.iarc.fr/ENG/Monographs/vol102/mono102.pdf (accessed February 3, 2020).

ICNIRP [International Commission on Non-Ionizing Radiation Protection]. 1998. Guidelines for limiting exposure to time-varying electric, magnetic, and electromagnetic fields (up to 300 GHz). *Health Phys* 74(4):494–522.

ICNIRP [International Commission on Non-Ionizing Radiation Protection]. 2020. Guidelines for limiting exposure to electromagnetic fields (100 kHz to 300 GHz). *Health Phys* 118(5):483–524. DOI: 10.1097/HP.0000000000001210.

IEEE C95.1–1999. 1999. *IEEE Standard for Safety Levels with Respect to Human Exposure to Electric, Magnetic, and Electromagnetic Fields, 0 Hz to 300 GHz.* New York: IEEE [Institute of Electrical and Electronics Engineers].

IEEE C95.1–2019. 2019. *IEEE Standard for Safety Levels with Respect to Human Exposure to Electric, Magnetic, and Electromagnetic Fields, 0 Hz to 300 GHz.* New York: IEEE [Institute of Electrical and Electronics Engineers].

IEEE 802.11–2016. 2016. *IEEE Standard for Information technology–Telecommunications and Information Exchange between Systems Local and Metropolitan Area Networks--Specific requirements - Part 11: Wireless LAN Medium Access Control (MAC) and Physical Layer (PHY) Specifications*. New York: IEEE [Institute of Electrical and Electronics Engineers].

IEEE P802.11ax. 2017. *IEEE Draft Standard for Information Technology – Telecommunications and Information Exchange Between Systems Local and Metropolitan Area Networks – Specific Requirements Part 11: Wireless LAN Medium Access Control (MAC) and Physical Layer (PHY) Specifications Amendment Enhancements for High Efficiency WLAN*. New York: IEEE [Institute of Electrical and Electronics Engineers].

IEEE 802.15.1–2005. 2005. *IEEE Standard for Information technology – Local and metropolitan area networks– Specific requirements– Part 15.1a: Wireless Medium Access Control (MAC) and Physical Layer (PHY) specifications for Wireless Personal Area Networks (WPAN)*. New York: IEEE [Institute of Electrical and Electronics Engineers].

IEEE 802.15.4–2020. 2020. *IEEE Standard for Low-Rate Wireless Networks*. New York: IEEE [Institute of Electrical and Electronics Engineers].

IEEE 802.15.6–2012. 2012. *IEEE Standard for Local and metropolitan area networks - Part 15.6: Wireless Body Area Networks*. New York: IEEE [Institute of Electrical and Electronics Engineers].

ISO/IEC/IEEE 802–15–6:2017. 2017. *ISO/IEC/IEEE International Standard - Information technology – Telecommunications and Information Exchange between Systems – Local and Metropolitan Area Networks – Specific Requirements – Part 15–6: Wireless Body Area Network*. New York: IEEE [Institute of Electrical and Electronics Engineers].

Jalilian, M., M. Eeftens, M. Ziaei, and M. Röösli. 2019. Public exposure to radiofrequency electromagnetic fields in everyday microenvironments: An updated systematic review for Europe. *Environ Res* 176, Article Number: 108517. DOI: 10.1016/j.envres.2019.05.048.

Kainz, W., J.P. Casamento, P.S. Ruggera, D.D. Chan, and D.M. Witters. 2005. Implantable cardiac pacemaker electromagnetic compatibility testing in a novel security system simulator. *IEEE Tran Biomed Eng* 52(3):520–530. DOI: 10.1109/TBME.2004.843293.

Kim, J. H., J-K. Lee, H-G. Kim, K-B. Kim, and H. R. Kim. 2019. Effects of radiofrequency electromagnetic field exposure on central nerve system. *Biomol Ther (Seoul)* 27(3): 265–275. DOI: 10.4062/biomolther.2018.152.

Kouyoumjian, R. G. and P.H. Pathak. 1974. A uniform theory of diffraction for an edge in a perfectly conducting surface. *IEEE Proc* 62(4):1448–1462.

Leach, V., S. Weller, and M. Redmayne. 2018. A novel database of bio-effects from non-ionizing radiation. *Rev Environ Health* 33(3):273–280. DOI: 10.1515/reveh-2018-0017.

Lee, S., K. Fu, T. Kohno, B. Ransford, and W.H. Maisel. 2009. Clinically significant magnetic interference of implanted cardiac devices by portable headphones. *Heart Rhythm* 6(10):1432–1436. DOI: 10.1016/j.hrthm.2009.07.003.

Levitt, H. 2001. The nature of electromagnetic interference. *J Am Acad Audiol* 12(6):322–326.

Li, Y., X. Cheng, and N. Zhang. 2018. Deterministic and stochastic simulators for non-isotropic V2V-MIMO wideband channels. *China Commun* 15(7):18–29. DOI: 10.1109/CC.2018.8424579.

Lopez-Iturri, P., S. De Miguel-Bilbao, E. Aguirre et al. 2015. Dosimetric assessment of RadioFrequency power leakage from microwave ovens in complex scenarios. *USNC-URSI Radio Science Meeting (Joint with AP-S Symposium), Vancouver, BC*, 2015.07.19–24, New York: IEEE, pp. 322–322. DOI: 10.1109/USNC-URSI.2015.7303606.

Marques, G., R. Pitarma, N. M. Garcia, and N. Pombo. 2019. Internet of things architectures, technologies, applications, challenges, and future directions for enhanced living environments and healthcare systems: A review. *Electronics* 8(10), Article Number: 1081. DOI: 10.3390/electronics8101081.

Mattei, E., E. Lucano, F. Censi, M. Triventi, and G. Calcagnini. 2016. Provocative testing for the assessment of the electromagnetic interference of RFID and NFC readers on implantable pacemaker. *IEEE Trans Electromagn Compat* 58(1):314–322. DOI: 10.1109/TEMC.2015.2504602.

Mattei, E., F. Censi, G. Calcagnini and R. Falsaperla. 2021. Workers with cardiac AIMD exposed to EMF: Methods and case studies for risk analysis in the framework of the European regulations. *Int J Environ Res Public Health* 18, 9709. DOI: 10.3390/ijerph18189709.

McIvor, M.E., and S. Sridhar. 1998. Interactions between cardiac pacemakers and anti-shoplifting security systems. *N Engl J Med* 339(19):1394–1395. DOI: 10.1056/NEJM199811053391911.

Morzyński L. 2021. Wireless sensor networks. In *Occupational Noise and Workplace Acoustics – Advances in Measurement and Assessment Techniques* (pp. 83–121), ed. D. Pleban. Boca Raton: CRC Press.

Movassaghi, S., M. Abolhasan, J. Lipman, D. Smith, and A. Jamalipour. 2014. Wireless body area networks: A survey. *IEEE Commun Surveys Tuts* 16(3):1658–1686. DOI: 10.1109/SURV.2013.121313.00064.

Napp, A., S. Joosten, D. Stunder et al. 2014. Electromagnetic interference with implant- able cardioverter-defibrillators at power frequency. An in vivo study. *Circulation* 129(4):441–450. DOI: 10.1161/CIRCULATIONAHA.113.003081.

NFPA. 1982. *[National Fire Protection Association]. 2018. Standard on Personal Alert Safety Systems (PASS).* Quincy: NFPA.

Reiner, J., and M. Sullivan. 2005. RFID in healthcare: a panacea for the regulations and issues affecting the industry? UPS Supply Chain Solutions White Paper. United Parcel Service of America, Atlanta, Georgia, United States.

Salous, S. 2013. *Radio Propagation Measurement and Channel Modelling.* First Edition. United Kingdom: John Wiley & Sons.

Sánchez-Hernández, D. A. 2009. *High Frequency Electromagnetic Dosimetry.* Norwood: Artech House, Inc.

SCENIHR [Scientific Committee on Emerging and Newly Identified Health Risks]. 2015. *Opinion on Potential Health Effects of Exposure to Electromagnetic Fields (EMF).* Luxembourg: European Commission. http://ec.europa.eu/health/sites/health/files/scientific_committees/emerging/docs/scenihr_o_041.pdf (accessed February 3, 2020).

Tagnola, G., M. Parazzini, F. Sibella, A. Paglialonga, and P. Ravazzani. 2007. Electromagnetic interference and cochlear implants. *Ann Ist Super Sanita* 43(3):241–247.

Tandogan, I., A. Temizhan, E. Yetkin et al. 2005. The effects of mobile phones on pacemaker function. *Int J Cardiol* 103(1):51–58. DOI: 10.1016/j.ijcard.2004.08.031.

Tiikkaja, M., A.L. Aro, T. Alanko et al. 2013. Electromagnetic interference with cardiac pacemakers and implantable cardioverter-defibrillators from low frequency electromagnetic fields in vivo. *Europace* 15(3):388–394. DOI: 10.1093/europace/eus345.

Toivonen, T., T. Toivo, L. Puranen, and K. Jokela. 2009. Specific absorption rate and electric field measurements in the near field of six mobile phone base station antennas. *Bioelectromagnetics* 30(4):307–312. DOI: 10.1002/bem.20478.

United Nations, Department of Economic and Social Affairs. 2018. https://www.un.org/development/desa/en/news/population/2018-revision-of-world-urbanization-prospects.html (accessed 3 February 2020).

Walfisch, J., and H.L. Bertoni. 1988. A theoretical model of UHF propagation in urban environments. *IEEE Trans Antennas Propag* 36(12):1788–1796. DOI: 10.1109/8.14401.

Wi-Fi. 2020. https://www.wi-fi.org (accessed 3 February 2020).

Willimas, C. 2019. Zigbee green power. White paper. https://zigbeealliance.org/wp-content/uploads/2019/11/Green-Power-White-Paper.pdf (accessed February 3, 2020).

WHO [World Health Organization]. 1993. *Environmental Health Criteria 137: Electromagnetic Fields (300 Hz – 300 GHz)*. Geneva: WHO. http://www.inchem.org/documents/ehc/ehc/ehc137.htm (Accessed February 3, 2020).

WHO [World Health Organization]. 2006. *Electromagnetic Fields and Public Health. Base Stations and Wireless Technologies*. Geneva: WHO. https://www.who.int/peh-emf/publications/facts/fs304/en/ (accessed February 3, 2020).

Wust, P., B. Kortüm, U. Strauss et al. 2020. Non-thermal effects of radiofrequency electromagnetic fields. *Sci Rep* 10, Article number:13488. DOI: 10.1038/s41598-020-69561-3.

Yin, X., Y. He, C. Ling, L. Tian, and X. Cheng. 2015. Empirical stochastic modeling of multipath polarizations in indoor propagation scenarios. *IEEE Trans Antennas Propag* 63(12):5799–5811. DOI: 10.1109/TAP.2015.2486798.

Yun, Z., and M.F. Iskander. 2015. Ray tracing for radio propagation modeling: Principles and applications. *IEEE Access* 3: 1089–1100 DOI: 10.1109/ACCESS.2015.2453991.

Zeiler, W., R. Houten, G. Boxem, D. Vissers, and R. Maaijen. 2011. Indoor air quality and thermal comfort strategies: The human-in-the-loop approach. *11th International Conference for Enhanced Building Operations (ICEBO 2011)*, 2011.10.18–20, New York, United States.

Zhang, C., and J. Yu. 2013. Compressive sensing wireless channel modeling with digital map. *IEEE Antennas Wirel Propag Lett* 12:349–352 DOI: 10.1109/LAWP.2013.224701.

Zhang, Y., P.L. Jones, and R. Jetley. 2010. A hazard analysis for a generic insulin infusion pump. *J Diabetes Sci Technol* 4(2):263–283. DOI: 10.1177/193229681000400207.

Zheng, J., D. Simplot-Ryl, C. Bisdikian, and H. Mouftah. 2011. The internet of things. *IEEE Commun Mag* 49(11):30–31.

ZigBee. 2020. https://www.zigbee.org (accessed February 3, 2020).

Zradziński, P. 2015a. Difficulties in applying numerical simulations to an evaluation of occupational hazards caused by electromagnetic fields. *Int J Occup Saf Ergon* 21(2):213–220, DOI: 10.1080/10803548.2015.1028233.

Zradziński, P. 2015b. The examination of virtual phantoms with respect to their involvement in a compliance assessment against the limitations of electromagnetic hazards provided by European Directive 2013/35/EU. *Int J Occup Med Environ Health* 28(5):781–792. DOI: 10.13075/ijomeh.1896.00342.

Zradziński, P., J. Karpowicz, K. Gryz, and W. Leszko. 2018a. Evaluation of the safety of users of active implantable medical devices (AIMD) in the working environment in terms of exposure to electromagnetic fields – Practical approach to the requirements of European Directive 2013/35/EU. *Int J Occup Med Environ Health* 31(6):795–808. DOI: 10.13075/ijomeh.1896.00783.

Zradziński, P. 2018b. Evaluation of the inter-person variability of hazards to the users of BAHA hearing implants caused by exposure to a low frequency magnetic field. *Int J Radiat Biol* 94(10):918–925. DOI: 10.1080/09553002.2018.1454619.

Zradziński, P., J. Karpowicz, and K. Gryz. 2019. Electromagnetic energy absorption in a head approaching a radiofrequency identification (RFID) reader operating at 13.56 MHz in users of hearing implants versus non-users. *Sensors* 19(17):e3724. DOI: 10.3390/s19173724.

10 The Significance of a Posture-Related Evaluation of the Electromagnetic Field's Influence from Hand-Operated Devices

Patryk Zradziński and Tomasz Tokarski
Central Institute for Labour Protection—
National Research Institute (CIOP-PIB)

Kjell Hansson Mild
Umeå University

CONTENTS

DOI: 10.1201/9781003020486-10

10.1 INTRODUCTION

The many different factors that have an impact on a worker's body while performing work tasks can contribute to various adverse health effects. Excessive exposure to electromagnetic fields (EMF) can cause a number of biophysical effects that, depending on the frequency of the EMF the body is exposed to, can include nerve or muscle (e.g. cardiac excitation), vertigo and nausea, impaired blood flow, and a localised or whole-body rise in temperature, which may negatively influence the work ability and worker's safety or even cause health or life threats, including increased cancer risk (ICNIRP, 1998, 2010, 2020; Reilly 1998, 2002; Saunders and Jefferys, 2002, 2007; Kheifets et al., 2007, 2009; McNamee et al., 2009; IARC, 2002, 2013; SCENIHR, 2015; WHO, 1993, 2006, 2007, Wilén et al., 2004). Another factor affecting the worker's body by biomechanical influence is musculoskeletal system load (MSL), which may lead to such medical disorders as arthritis, tendinitis, neuritis, muscle pain or the degeneration of joints (NRCIM, 2001, Roman-Liu, 2010, Graveling, 2018). Hazards resulting from the simultaneous impact of electromagnetic and biomechanical factors often occur while manually operating industrial sources of EMF.

10.1.1 Biophysical Effects of EMF Exposure

The basic physical laws of the EMF are described by the Maxwell equations:

$$\text{–Faraday's law} \quad rot\ \boldsymbol{E} = -\frac{\partial \boldsymbol{B}}{\partial t} \tag{10.1}$$

$$\text{–Ampère's law} \quad rot\ \boldsymbol{H} = \boldsymbol{j} + \frac{\partial \boldsymbol{D}}{\partial t} \tag{10.2}$$

$$\text{–Gauss' law for electricity} \quad div\boldsymbol{D} = \rho \tag{10.3}$$

$$\text{–Gauss' law for magnetism} \quad div\boldsymbol{B} = 0 \tag{10.4}$$

where: H, magnetic field strength in A/m; B, magnetic flux density in T; E, electric field strength in V/m; D, electric displacement in C/m^2; j, current density in A/m^2; σ, electrical conductivity in S/m and ρ, charge density in C/m^3.

The metrics adopted for the assessment of biophysical non-thermal effects considered in evaluation of exposure to EMF at a frequency not exceeding 10 MHz are electric field strength (E_{in}, in V/m) and current density (j, in A/m^2) induced in the exposed body (ICNIRP, 1998, 2010; 2020; Directive 2013/35/EU, 2013; IEEE C95.1–2019, 2019; IEEE C95.6–2002, 2002; IEEE C95.3.1–2010, 2010). According to Faraday's law (10.1), exposure to time-varying magnetic fields causes an induced electric field E_{in} inside the organism, which causes a flow in the tissues with the conductivity σ of the eddy currents of density j, expressed by the relationship:

$$j = \sigma \boldsymbol{E}_{\mathbf{in}} \tag{10.5}$$

The commonly accepted metric of biophysical thermal effects, considered in evaluation of exposure to EMF, at frequency exceeding 100 kHz, is the specific energy absorption rate (SAR, in W/kg), and, in case of exposure to EMF at frequency exceeding 6 GHz, also the absorbed power density (S_{ab}, in (W/m^2) (Directive 2013/35/EU, 2013; ICNIRP 1998, 2020; IEEE C95.1–2019, 2019; Varmeeren and Martens, 2005; Varmeeren et al., 2007; Anzaldi et al., 2007; Findlay and Dimbylow, 2005; Wong et al., 2005; Nagaoka et al., 2004).

The SAR is a measure describing the EMF energy absorption in the organism and expressed as the time derivative of the incremental energy (dW) absorbed (dissipated) in an incremental mass (dm) contained in a volume element with a volume (dV) of given mass density (ρ) (ICNIRP 1998, 2020, IEEE C95.1–2019, 2019):

$$\text{SAR} = \frac{d}{dt}\left(\frac{dW}{dm}\right) = \frac{d}{dt}\left(\frac{dW}{\rho dV}\right) \tag{10.6}$$

The SAR value can also be determined from the j, E_{in} or rise in temperature T:

$$\text{SAR} = \frac{j^2}{\sigma\rho}; \quad \text{SAR} = \frac{\sigma E_{in}^2}{\rho}; \quad \text{SAR} = c_i \frac{dT}{dt}\Big|_{t=0} \tag{10.7}$$

where: c_i - specific heat capacity in J/(kg°C); $\frac{dT}{dt}\Big|_{t=0}$ - value of the derivative of temperature versus time in the tissue under consideration at instant $t = 0$, in °C/s.

All the mentioned metrics of biophysical EMF exposure effects (determined for the whole body or particular body sections) are usually evaluated by numerical simulations using digital model of the human body. The most commonly and traditionally used human body models in such simulations represent a standing human, upright with arms placed along the body, because they were developed using data collected through magnetic resonance imaging (MRI) and computed tomography (CT). The models may be homogeneous or heterogeneous, composed of up to over 300 tissues/anatomical structures (such as skin, fat, bones, muscles) with a spatial resolution down to 0.1 mm. There are models representing males, females (also pregnant) and children with a wide range of ergonomic (biomechanical) parameters such as height, body mass index, length and circumferences of particular parts of body (Christ et al., 2010; Conil et al., 2008; Dimbylow, 2005; El Habachi et al., 2010; Gandhi and Chen, 1992; Gosellin et al., 2014; Kramer et al., 2003, 2004; Lee et al., 2006; Nagaoka et al., 2004; Sandrini et al., 2004; Xu et al., 2000; Zankl et al., 2002; Zradziński, 2013, 2015a). In the recent years, flexible human models (allowing changes in the body posture) have been used more and more often, for example, with raised upper limbs, in a sitting posture or in other postures typical for public exposure (Zradziński et al., 2020, Goselin et al., 2014).

The results of research by Findlay and Dimbylow (2005) showed a relationship between SAR values averaged over the whole body of the body model and its posture, for example, the differences in SAR values reach 35% during exposure to plane waves at 10–300 MHz in sitting and standing postures. Similar research by Wong et al. (2005) showed differences of 50%, and Uusitupa et al. (2010) even 200% differences in local SAR values in the head and torso, when calculated for models in standing and sitting postures, or for models in a standing posture with raised hands and sitting on the ground, during exposure from dipoles at 100 MHz, and to plane waves at 300, 450, 900, 2100, 3500 and 5000 MHz, respectively. Differences were also shown in local SAR values in the extremities, reaching 400% between models in sitting and standing postures (Zradziński, 2015a). Due to the influence of the worker's body posture on the distribution and the level of E_{in}, j or SAR, it is important to use worker models with a realistic body posture, characterising the work performed during evaluated EMF exposure. Such an approach has been advised in international standards and recommendations, for example, EN 50505:2008, EN 50413:2019, which requires, along the assessment of direct effects of EMF exposure, the use of numerical models of the worker's body that correspond, as far as possible, to the assessed workplace exposure scenario in the real working environment.

Workers may be present in the vicinity of localised sources emitting relatively strong EMF, and in some cases the worker's torso or limbs may even be in contact with their cover; it is therefore likely that such exposure can cause significant biophysical effects in the body (Karpowicz and Gryz, 2007; Nadeem et al., 2004). According to Directive 2013/35/EU, in the case of 'a very localised source at a distance of several centimetres from the body, compliance with exposure limit values must be determined dosimetrically (e.g. by numerical simulations), case by case' (Directive 2013/35/EU, 2013). Investigations carried out by Jokela et al., respecting ICNIRP guidelines, show that such an approach should be taken into account for EMF sources closer than 20 cm to the body (ICNIRP, 2010, Jokela, 2007).

10.1.2 Biomechanical Load

Among the biomechanical factors that have the greatest impact on MSL, the most important are body posture, external force (type, direction of action and value of force) and time factor (Chaffin, 2009). These basic biomechanical factors, which characterise the load and fatigue caused by performing work activities (tasks), are considered together, and the development of musculoskeletal disorders (MSDs) is closely related to the combined impact of these factors. The proper selection of biomechanical parameters of these three factors (i.e. body posture, value direction, and type of external force and time of its impact) minimises the MSL and the possibility of developing MSDs. Therefore, assessing the MSL arising as a result of performing work activities plays an important role (NRCIM, 2001, Roman-Liu, 2010, Graveling, 2018).

Body posture while working depends on the ergonomic properties of the working environment, mainly on the spatial structure of the workplace, the way in which the work tasks are performed and the biomechanical parameters of the worker. The optimal body posture, with the lowest MSL during various tasks (except for a lying down posture) is a natural (neutral) posture, i.e. standing with the spine straightened and the upper limbs lowered close to the body. The more the posture of the body differs from the natural posture, the greater the MSL, as shown in Figure 10.1, on the basis of graphically presented data published by Nachemson (1981).

Work performed in uncomfortable body postures, such as while turning or bending, causes high values of compressive and cutting mechanical forces, as well as torque force in the spine and joints of the limbs. Such loads, if they are too high or occur too often, are a direct cause of injuries and MSDs.

10.1.3 EMF Exposure under MSL (Musculoskeletal System Load)

In order to minimise MSL, work activities should be performed while operating the device as close to the body as possible. However, this should be considered when available measures to reduce influence of EMF are analysed. The EMF increases rapidly when approaching the source, for example, along a line perpendicular to the

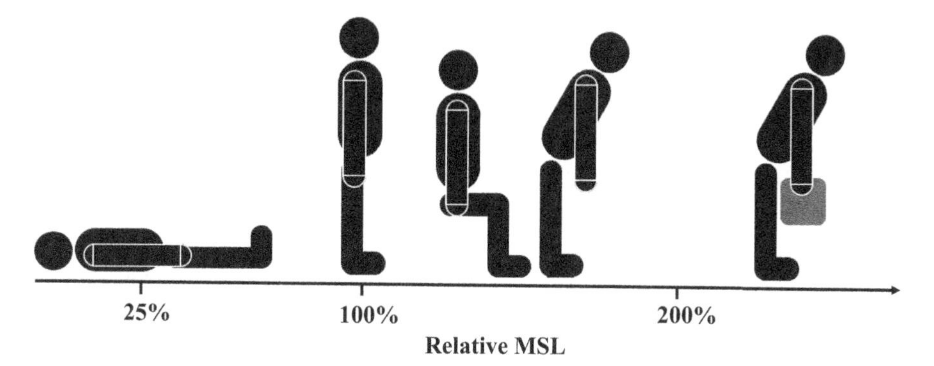

FIGURE 10.1 Musculoskeletal load (MSL) for different body postures (reference value: MSL for natural posture). (Authors' collection)

centre of the plane of a square-shape conductor with an edge of 40 cm; the magnetic field at distances: 20; 40; 60; 80; 100 cm drops up to 54%; 15%; 6%; 2.6% and 1.4% of the value at a distance of 10 cm away from the conductor, respectively (Zradziński et al., 2019), as shown in Figure 10.4c.

10.2 INDUSTRIAL SOURCES OF EMF AND MSL WHILE BEING OPERATED

EMF is a factor in the environment related to the use of electricity or the transmission of radio waves in all areas of human activity. The magnetic field occurs around charges that move (i.e. create an electric current) or due to the magnetisation of certain materials, and is proportional to the current causing them. The electric field occurs with both moving and stationary charges, and is related to the difference in the electric potential of the objects (i.e. it is proportional to the voltage). Emission or exposure to EMF depends on the intensity of electric current, voltage or output power in the EMF source, as well as the dimensions and physical structure of it (including the efficiency of electromagnetic shielding from the metal/metallised cover of the device).

In general, populations with high exposure to EMF include industrial workers operating EMF sources at a short distance, for example, induction heaters, plastic sealers and welders, welding arc or resistance devices, devices working in the Internet of Things (IoT) systems, such as radiofrequency identification (RFID) guns (Zradziński et al., 2020, Hansson Mild et al., 2009). Workers operating mentioned devices may be exposed to strong EMF, but only some of them may experience excessive MSL during EMF exposure.

10.2.1 Induction Heaters for Use in Metal Industry

Induction heaters are used to heat metal elements with induced eddy currents. The source of the EMF is the inductor, most often in the shape of a multi-turn coil, into which heated metal elements are inserted or approached. Currents flowing in the inductor may have an amperage of several hundred up to thousand amperes (A). Depending on the size of the heated load and the material it is made of, desired depth of penetration of area to be heated, frequencies from 50 Hz to several kHz are used (occasionally up to several MHz). Usually, while heating, the elements to be heated are moved along the inductor, or the inductor is moved along a stationary heated element. Smaller induction heaters (usually portable), which usually are used for local heating of parts of a larger metal structure, are mainly used in artistic metalwork, car repair services or the local hardening of tools. Currents flowing through the small inductor are much lower than currents in typical large industrial heaters. The inductor and the supplying cables give rise to a strong magnetic field. Typically, inserting the load into the inductor does not require the worker to be next to the field source (various feeders are often used). Loads can be heavy, and loading can cause excessive, high MSL. The worker usually performs the work in a standing or sitting posture. Figure 10.2a shows the possible posture of a worker operating an induction heater.

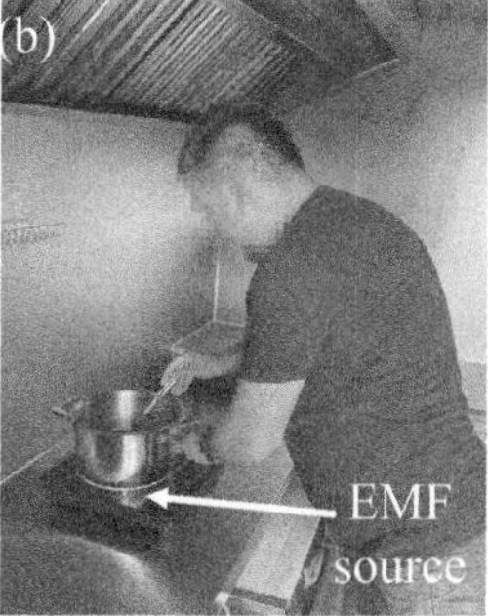

FIGURE 10.2 Various ways of operating industrial devices emitting EMF: (a) worker operating induction heater; (b) worker operating induction hob in a food truck; (c) worker operating RFID gun. ((a), Olly2/Bigstockphoto; (b) and (c), The authors' collection)

10.2.2 Induction Cooking Hobs for Use in Gastronomy

Induction cooking hobs are used to heat food with eddy currents induced in multi-layer ferromagnetic bottoms of pans or pots. The heat generated in the base of the vessel flows into the food inside the vessel due to the convection process. The source of the EMF is an inductor, in the shape of a multi-turn coil located below the vessel (Gryz at al., 2020). Induction cookers typically contain several heating zones of various dimensions, with the maximum heating power of approximately 3.2 and 3.7 kW, with and without booster, respectively. Frequencies from 20 kHz up to 100 kHz are used. According to the advice provided in the user manuals of the induction cooking hobs, vessels should cover the entire labelled heating zone, if they are not able to adjust the heating zone to the size of the vessels. The device is equipped with a sensor that switches off the supply of the heating coil in the absence of a vessel, but the use of vessels smaller than the heating zone or moved from its centre may not break the emission of EMF from the hob. The EMF level in the vicinity of an induction cooking hob while using vessels with dimensions smaller than the heating zone, or not cantered vessels, may be increased up to three times in comparison to the use of vessels covering the entire zone. A worker performs activities in a standing posture (at various distances from the hob housing, depending on the organisation of the operating space, even in contact with the device cover), as shown in Figure 10.2b. While at the hob, it may be exposed to strong EMF (at distances closer than 20 cm). Working with induction cooking hobs may cause excessive, medium MSL in the upper limbs, during hours of using the device with a limb position significantly differs than flexed at the elbow, at an angle of 90° (e.g. extended in elbow) (Gryz et al., 2020).

10.2.3 Radiofrequency Identification (RFID) Guns and IoT Systems

Radiofrequency identification (RFID) is the most common identification and tracking wireless technology. RFID systems are composed of readers and tags attached to the objects (Finkenzeller, 2010; Zradziński, 2019, 2020). RFID devices are used wherever identification, managing, controlling or tracking is desired, for example, in offices, shops, libraries, hospitals, etc., but also marking hazardous substances, bikes, animals, prisoners or in contactless cards and controlling time at sporting events in a public environment. Depending on the RFID system, various frequencies are used: about 125 kHz in low-frequency (LF) systems, moving up through 13.56 MHz in high frequency (HF), 433 MHz and 860–965 MHz in ultra-high frequency (UHF) to reach 2.45 and 5.8 GHz in super-high-frequency (SHF) systems. The sources of the EMF are the reader antennas of various dimensions, from several centimetres up to over one metre. RFID readers may be stationary, for example, in gates or fixed to walls, desks, or mobile (handheld guns). Such devices may be used as a part of the IoT system. HF and UHF RFID readers may be sources of strong EMF depending on the type of RFID tags used and the required reading range. Workers operate stationary readers (e.g. fixed to a desk) in a sitting or standing posture, while operating gun readers in various postures as necessary (Zradziński, 2020). Performing activities related to the operation of stationary RFID readers do not cause excessive MSL, while operating RFID guns may be associated with fatigue in the limb holding the gun, which may reduce the work comfort and cause excessive, medium MSL (Figure 10.2c).

10.2.4 Arc Welding Devices

Arc welding devices are used to connect metal elements. Depending on the welding method and type of welded elements, an alternating (AC) or rectified current (with direct, DC, component) is used, with a basic frequency in the range of 50–300 Hz, or several to several dozen kHz and an amperage of up to several hundred amperes. The source of the EMF is the electric circuit created by the welding electrode, welded elements and the cables connecting them to the welding generator. Depending on the needs, the welder adopts very varied body postures, for example, kneeling, leaning, sitting, standing with arms lowered or raised, for example, in posture shown in Figure 10.3a. When welding small parts, welding may be carried out on the welding table. A worker operating an arc welding device may be exposed to a very localised strong EMF near the welding electrode and the supplying cable. The welding electrode holder is a relatively light device that does not cause excessive MSL when the welder posture is close to the natural one. Hours of using the arc welding devices, in postures significantly different than the natural one, may cause excessive, medium MSL.

10.2.5 Resistance Welding Devices

Resistance welding devices (welders) are used to connect metal elements. A short-circuit current of up to several tens of kA (alternating or rectified with a DC component) is used to weld the elements. These devices produce harmonic EMF at a frequency of 50 Hz, or distorted by higher harmonics and DC component, and may produce EMF at higher frequencies, especially from modern devices using DC generators. There are two types of resistance welders: stationary and suspended.

A worker operating a stationary resistance welder inserts the welded elements between the electrodes (The elements vary in size from small to large.) and then starts the welding process. These activities are usually performed in a standing or sitting

FIGURE 10.3 Various ways of operating industrial devices emitting EMF: (a) worker operating arc welding device; (b) worker operating welding gun; c) worker operating dielectric welder. (Authors' collection)

posture. The worker usually has to be near the stationary resistance welder during the weld, when special tools that allow the welded elements to be fixed are not available. When staying near the welder, worker may be exposed to strong EMF. During EMF exposure, the work tasks performing typically do not cause excessive, high MSL, except for cases when welding large and heavy elements.

In the case of suspended resistance welders (welding guns), the worker fits the electrodes in the place of welding and then starts the welding process. The worker performs work in a standing posture, at a location determined by the dimensions of the welding gun, the location of the welding point, the range of upper limbs, etc., as shown in Figure 10.3b. While welding, workers cannot be away from the welding gun (They hold it in their hands over the welding run.). Workers may be exposed to strong EMF. The operation of such gun during EMF exposure is associated with the operation of a large and heavy tool (weighing up to several dozen kg), which can cause excessive, high MSL.

10.2.6 Dielectric Sealers and Welders

Dielectric sealers and welders are used to connect or shape thermoplastic materials. The source of the EMF is an electrode with a potential of up to several kV. The typical operating frequency of the device is 24–28 MHz (However, less frequently 13, 43 or 81 MHz may be used.) from the radiofrequency range. Dielectric welders generate strong radiofrequency electric and magnetic fields. As seen in Figure 10.3c, a worker operating a dielectric welder has to insert pieces of thermoplastic materials between the electrodes, presses the electrode clamping lever and then starts the welding process. The worker performs the task in a sitting or standing posture. If standing while welding, the worker does not have to stay near the electrodes in a strong EMF and is better able to step back for the duration of the welding. Performing activities related to the operation of a dielectric welder usually does not cause excessive MSL. (The welded elements are light.)

10.2.7 Summary of EMF Exposure and MSL Caused by Industrial EMF Sources

Table 10.1 discusses the typical conditions in which workers operate particular devices as various postures while operating the device, potential exposure to strong EMF and excessive MSL. A very good example of the work practice that is necessary in order to apply a posture-related evaluation of EMF exposure is the operation of resistance welders, especially suspended ones (welding guns). While using these devices, the operator is usually simultaneously exposed to strong EMF and an excessive, high MSL.

Many electric devices, such as electric handheld tools (e.g. drills, impact hammers, saws, angle grinders, etc.), machine tools, cutting machines, milling machines, lifts, soldering irons, etc. typically do not produce EMF at levels that are high enough to require consideration in the OHS system. Some devices consuming high amounts of electricity (exceeding 10 kW) may emit EMF at levels close to the exposure limits provided by the international guidelines and labour law, such as tiger saws or heavy handheld drills.

10.3 A Posture-Related Evaluation of Biophysical Effects Caused by EMF Exposure

10.3.1 Suspended Resistance Welders (Guns)

Suspended or handheld resistance welders (guns) are often used in automotive factories to weld metal components of car body. As seen in Figure 10.4, while working with a suspended resistance welder, operators very often hold the welder arms, where

TABLE 10.1
Summary of EMF Exposure and MSL Caused by the Use of Industrial EMF Sources

Device	EMF Source	EMF Exposure	Posture	MSL
Induction heaters	Large: fixed location and shape	Medium to **strong** (depending on current)	Sitting, standing	Medium to **high** (depending on elements weight)
	Small: movable, fixed shape or flexible wire	Medium to **strong** (depending on current)	various	Low
Induction cooking	Fixed location and shape	Medium to **strong** (depending on heating power)	Standing	Low to medium (depending of posture and time of use)
Arc welding devices	Movable, flexible shape	Medium	Various	Low to medium (depending of posture and time of use)
Resistance welding devices	Stationary, fixed location and shape	**Strong**	Sitting, standing	Low to **high** (depending on elements weight)
	Suspended (guns): movable, fixed shape	Strong	various	Medium to **high** (depending on the suspension system and gun's weight)
Dielectric sealers and welders	Fixed location and shape	Medium to **strong** (depending on electrode potential)	Sitting, standing	Low
RFID guns	Movable, fixed shape	Medium to **strong** (depending on reading range)	Various	Low to medium (depending of posture and time of use)
Tiger saws	Movable, fixed shape	Low to medium (depending on power of electric motor)	Various	Low to **high** (depending on saw's weight and posture)
Handheld drills	Movable, fixed shape	Low to medium (depending on power of electric motor)	Various	Low to **high** (depending on drill's weight and posture)

Standing posture, worker operating EMF source is standing with the spine straightened; sitting posture, worker operating EMF source is sitting on, for example, stool; various postures, worker operating EMF source is adopting postures different than standing and sitting, for example, kneeling, leaning, lying down.

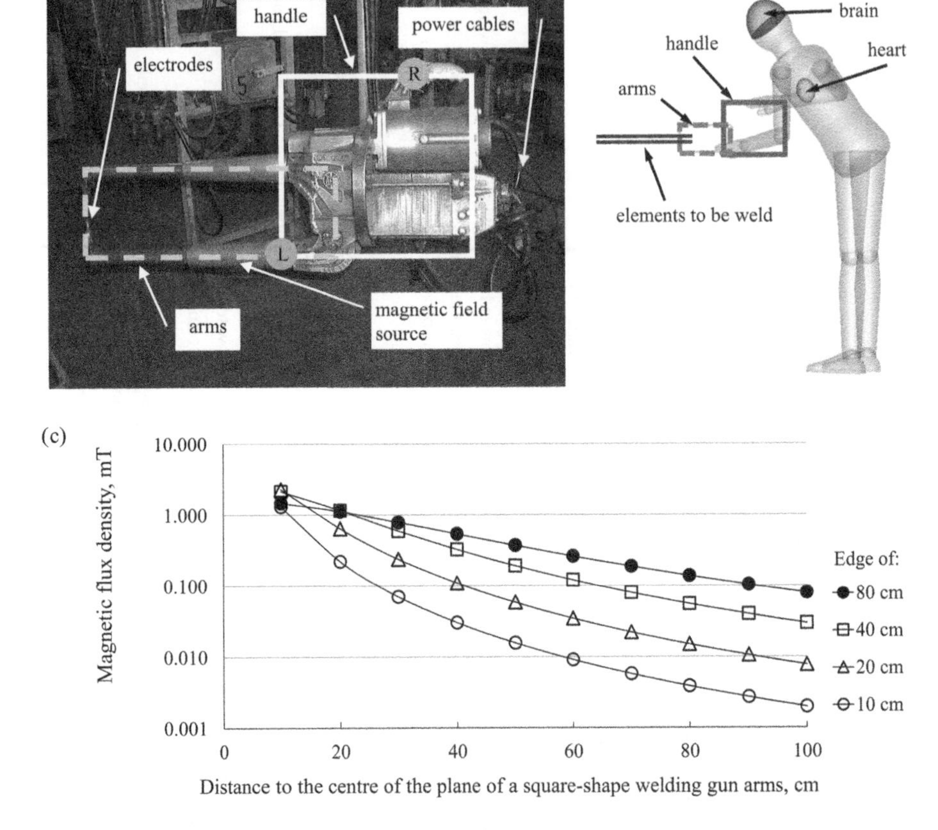

FIGURE 10.4 Suspended resistance welder (gun): (a) construction (dashed line, magnetic field source; light solid line, virtual handle; L and R dots, assumed locations of grip points for the left and right hand at the resistance gun handle); (b) the scenario of gun operating (numerical model of operator's body, CIOP-MAN, and the small-size gun for analysing biophysical effects from the EMF exposure) and (c) magnetic field distribution along a line perpendicular to the centre of the plane of a square-shape conductor [arms of welding gun of various dimensions (edges' length: 10–80 cm) and a welding current of 1 kA]. (Authors' collection)

the typical distance between the operator's head and the gun electrodes is approximately 50–120 cm, and the typical distance between the operator's waist and the gun electrodes is approximately 40–100 cm, though distances of a few centimetres are also possible. The mentioned distances depend on the size of the gun (in particular the dimensions of the gun arms), the location of the gun, the operator's posture while making the weld, and also on the height and upper limb range of the operator.

Depending on the application (e.g. thickness and dimensions of welded metal elements), resistance-suspended welders (guns) are used with a wide range of welding currents, power and dimensions. The length of the heads (taking into account the length of the arms and housing) of typical suspended resistance welders (guns) is in the range of approximately 40 cm to approximately 170 cm. Typical arm spacing is from about 10 to 40 cm, and arm length is from about 20 to 120 cm or more. The gun mass ranges from tens of kilograms up to about 100 kg. Each welding device model can be equipped with a number of electrodes with various parameters such as shape, dimensions, diameter, maximum welding current, etc.

EMF emitted by the welding guns is keyed in accordance with the control system settings and the manual release of subsequent welds by the operator. Resistance welders are supplied with one-, two- or three-phase voltage 230–400 V. Depending on the application and type of resistance welding, the current flowing through the electrodes at the time of welding may exceed 20 kA.

10.3.2 Numerical Modelling of the Electric Field Induced in the Operator of Welding Gun

10.3.2.1 Numerical Modelling of Suspended Resistance Welder (Gun)

As mentioned above, assessment of EMF exposure effects inside human body need evaluation by numerical modelling following metrics: E_{in} (alternatively: j, as per older international requirements) for EMF frequencies up to 10 MHz and SAR for frequencies exceeding 100 kHz. It follows that in the case of EMF sources with a frequency in the 100 kHz to 10 MHz, both E_{in} and SAR should be evaluated. The parameters influencing the value of these metrics are among others related to parameters of the EMF source such as dimensions and frequency of emitted EMF (more precisely the waveform of emitted EMF in time, which may be characterised by its amplitude–frequency spectrum) and EMF source location relative to the operator body (mostly with respect to the distance from the body and polarisation of EMF against particular body segments), as well as parameters of the body such as its electrical grounding, posture and dimensions.

The numerical model of an EMF source should correspond to the realistic EMF source. Such a model takes into account the shape and dimensions of the EMF source and the frequency of the emitted EMF. As an example, a suspended gun for resistance welding is typically modelled as a rectangular conductor with dimensions equal to the length of the gun's arms and arms gap, with a relevant welding current and frequency (Nadeem et al., 2004; EN 50505:2008, 2008). E_{in} and j values are linearly proportional, while SAR values are proportional to squared values of EMF intensity (E or H), which are linearly proportional to welding current. To make the analysis of the results of modelling easier, the welding current is usually considered to be 1 kA or 10 kA, which helps when scaling the obtained values of E_{in}, j or SAR to various welding currents used in various applications.

Simulations with the high-resolution model and low-frequency EMF require a long computational time often expressed in days. In order to reduce the calculation time, for any low-frequency magnetic field source the frequency scaling method is used. According to this method, simulations can be carried out for higher frequencies (not exceeding 5 MHz) with dielectric properties of tissues for frequency of interest (obtained E_{in} or j results should be divided by the scaling factor expressed as the ratio of the frequency at which the calculations were run and the frequency of interest).

For example, approximately 350 times reduction of a duration of calculations for simulations carried out with the use of the same workstation, numerical model and its resolution at 500 kHz as compared with 50 Hz was reported (Zradziński, 2016b).

10.3.2.2 Numerical Modelling of the Body of Operator

A key element of numerical modelling of exposure to EMF is the human body models being used. Operator's body model is characterised by its spatial resolution, dielectric parameters of tissues distinguish in the model and its contact with the ground (particularly important in the case of exposure to EMF with a dominant electric component), and above all the posture of the body. It is recommended (for example by the requirements from the EN 50505:2008 standard) to use body models that meet the following criteria: a height of 1.76 m ±8%, representing the human shape, internal organs and their dielectric properties with an appropriate model resolution. This advised height of numerical model was based on ICRP 110 Adult Reference Computational Phantoms, which for male models have a height of 176 cm (ICRP, 2002). Additionally, international recommendations and standards require the use in numerical modelling of EMF exposure of models of the human body that emulate the real human body as closely as possible, so they should represent the largest percentage of the population.

As seen in Table 10.2, there is significant variability in the biomechanical, anatomical and numerical parameters of models of human body developed and used by leading research centres around the world. The biomechanical parameters of adult models vary, for example, from 160 cm up to 199 cm in body height, from 47 kg up to 120 kg in body mass, and form 17.7 up to 36.1 in body mass index (BMI).

Figure 10.5a shows that the variability of biomechanical parameters of models of the human body dedicated to working with specified EMF software do not widely cover the biomechanical parameters of the largest percentage of the population (Zradziński, 2016a). The percentile of biomechanical parameters of the human body

TABLE 10.2
Variability of the Most Important Parameters of Human Body Models Used Worldwide in Numerical Modelling of EMF Exposure (Christ et al., 2010; Conil et al., 2008; Dimbylow, 2005; El Habachi et al., 2010; Gandhi and Chen, 1992; Gosellin et al., 2014; Kramer et al., 2003; Lee et al., 2006; Nagaoka et al., 2004; Sandrini et al., 2004; Xu et al., 2000; Zankl et al., 2002; Zradziński, 2013, 2015a)

Sex	Body Height (cm)	Body Mass (kg)	BMI	Number of Tissues/Organs	Spatial Resolution (mm)
Male	170–199	63–120	20.3–36.1	20–305	0.1–10
Female	160–186	47–81	17.7–28.0	34–305	0.1–10

BMI, body mass index

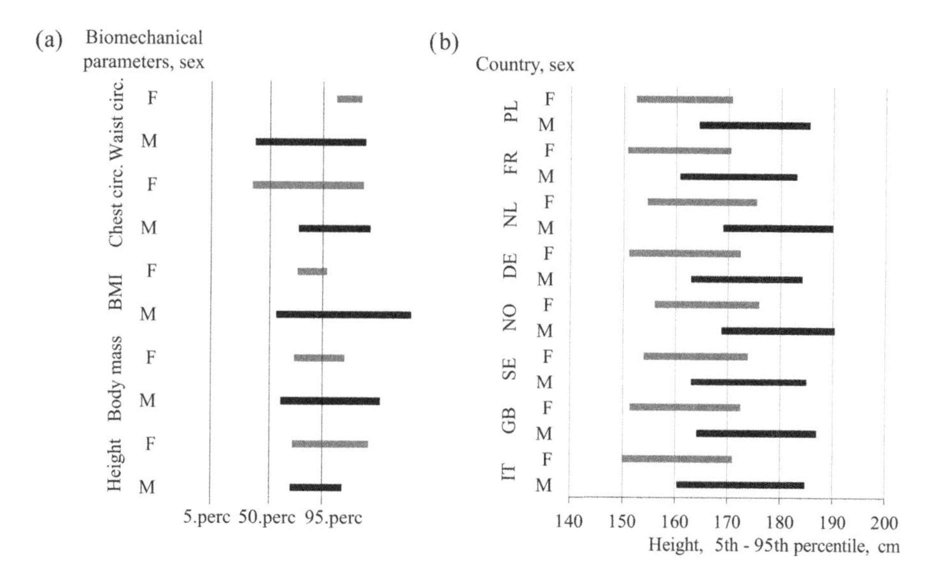

FIGURE 10.5 Variability of human body biomechanical parameters: (a) selected numerical body models (Bio Models, CST, Germany) in relation to dimensions of population in Poland (5th, 50th and 95th percentile); (b) the (5th to 95th) percentile ranges of height of various European populations based on data from ErgoDesign database (2000) (M, male; F, female; BMI, body mass index; PL, Polish; FR, French; NL, Netherlanden; DE, German; NO, Norwegian; SE, Swedish; GB, Great British; IT, Italian).

indicate what percentage of the particular population is characterised by smaller parameters values. For example, the 95th percentile indicates that 95% of population is characterised with lower parameter values, while the 5th percentile indicates that only 5% of population has lower values.

As seen in Figure 10.5b, there is a significant variability between the 5th and the 95th percentile ranges of biomechanical data among various European populations (ErgoDesign, 2000). It also needs to be pointed out that the presented systematic data were collected two decades ago, whereas the percentage of males and females with a height exceeding 200 cm has increased in populations all over the world in the recent years.

An example of models widely covering the population parameters is the family of flexible, semi-homogenous CIOP-MAN models, developed with the use of data on the 5th, 50th and 95th percentile of Polish males relating, among other things, to height (164–185 cm) and lengths of particular body parts (head, trunk, upper limbs determining the range of the upper limbs, and legs) (Gedliczka, 2001). The CIOP-MAN models included flexibility in the main joints of the human body, i.e. the shoulder, elbow, knee, wrist and spine, with full range of motion, allowing the body posture to be modified. Another good example of the latest high-resolution anatomical human body models that allow the body posture to be changed at the knee, elbow, hip, shoulders, wrists, ankles, fingers and so on, are the models developed by the IT'IS Foundation (The Foundation for Research on Information Technologies in Society (IT'IS), Switzerland) (Gosellin et al., 2014).

The variability in values of measures of the direct effects of EMF exposure calculated using numerical models of various biomechanical parameters were:

- Up to 20% of E_{in} in the brains of models 163 and 176 cm tall, under exposure to uniform 50 Hz EMF, as reported by Dimbylow (2005)
- Up to 30% between SAR values in adult Japanese models of various BMI, exposed to a plane wave with a vertical polarisation at a resonance frequency of used human body models, as reported by Hirata et al. (2010)
- Up to two times between SAR values in six different adult models exposed to a plane wave with a vertical polarisation at a frequency from 20 MHz to 2.4 GHz, as reported by Conil et al. (2008)
- Up to two times between SAR values in seven different models (6 adults and 1 child) exposed to plane waves for two orthogonal polarisations at a frequency from 300 MHz to 5 GHz, as reported by Uusitupa et al. (2010).

Another key issue when evaluating EMF exposure using numerical modelling is the tissue's dielectric parameters. Relative permittivity and electrical conductivity significantly change as a function of the frequency of EMF (Gabriel et al., 1996). Studies conducted by Dimbylow or by Hirata et al. on exposure of different models to a uniform 50 Hz EMF showed the possibility of differences of up to 30% and 25%, respectively, in the calculated values of E_{in}, along a twofold change in the electrical conductivity of tissues (Dimbylow, 2005, Hirata et al., 2011). In turn, Keshvari et al. (2006) showed 20% differences in local SAR values calculated for conductivity, and permittivity of all tissues increased from 5% to 20% set in child and adult head models exposed to EMF emitted from a half-wave dipole antenna at the frequencies of 900, 1800 and 2450 MHz.

10.3.2.3 Exposure Scenarios (Postures of the Operator)

One of the most important issues with numerical modelling of EMF exposure is the characterisation of the body posture of the workers operating the EMF source and the source locations against the workers' body. An example of exposure scenarios for the use of hand-operated radiofrequency-emitting devices is the analysis of EMF exposure during the use of radiofrequency identification (RFID) guns typically working as sensors in an IoT system. The use of RFID guns may be associated with fatigue in the limb holding the gun and reducing work comfort, as well as EMF exposure caused by the radiofrequency emission from its antenna (Zradziński et al., 2020). This study showed up to 4-times and 11-times variability in localised SAR in the head and torso of a person in various postures, who operates an RFID gun emitting EMF at 865 MHz. Another study related to EMF exposure from dielectric welders reported up to 36-times higher localised SAR values in models in a sitting posture in comparison to a standing one (Zradziński, 2015a).

It seems reasonable to use a simplified description of the body posture used in ergonomics for this purpose. It also allows the MSL to be analysed, and to assess hazards related to MSDs. The following description used in ergonomics for the description of a worker's body posture may be also used in numerical simulations of EMF exposure based on the 13 angles corresponding to the whole body motion range

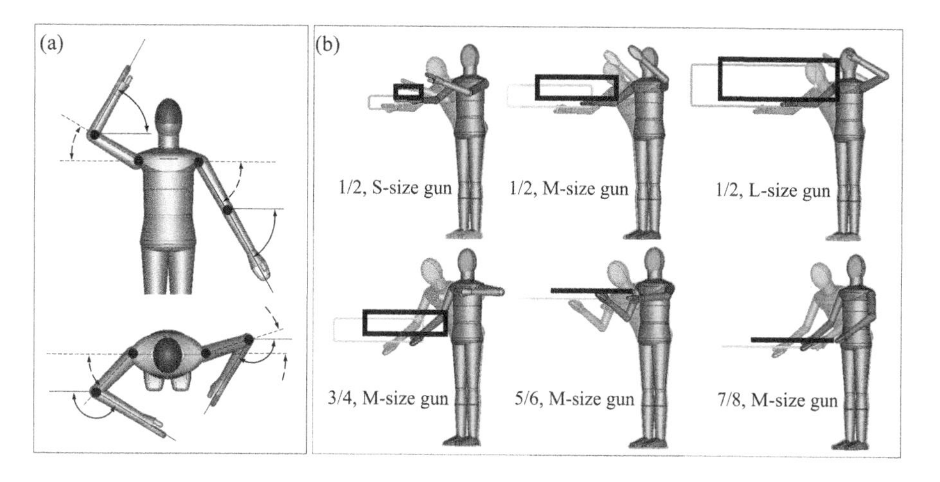

FIGURE 10.6 Resistance welding gun operator: (a) vertical and horizontal angles defining the ergonomic forearms and arms location; (b) examples of realistic exposure scenarios (S-size gun: gun arms 14 × 25 cm; M-size gun: gun arms 20 × 80 cm; L-size gun: gun arms 34 × 115 cm).

(Zradziński and Roman-Liu, 2009; Zradziński, 2010). These include the torso bending angle, vertical angles at the hips (thigh location) and knees (shank location), and vertical and horizontal angles of the elbows (forearm location) and shoulders (arm location), as shown in Figure 10.6.

In order to analyse the influence of realistically modelled worker posture when assessing the EMF exposure, it is also important to pay attention to the possible simultaneous exposure to high EMF and high MSL. An example of the work where both the exposures may reach relatively high levels can be found in operating a suspended gun for resistance welding. The ergonomic description of welder posture is of interest for the systematic analysis of such work activities. As seen in Figure 10.6, there is a high variability in the operator's posture while using a resistance welding gun, identified on the basis of observations at an automotive factory where welding guns were widely used to join the metallic elements of vehicles. The workers' posture differs between each exposure scenario, as shown in Table 10.3. A more detailed description of the analysed exposure scenarios was referred to in Zradziński (2016b).

10.3.2.4 Numerical Modelling of Electric Field Induced in Operator

The basic requirement for the numerical modelling of measures of the biophysical effects of EMF exposure is that the resolution set to the human body model should be better than 1/10 of the electromagnetic wavelength in tissues in the low-frequency range (regarding EMF sources such as induction heaters, arc welding equipment, resistance welders, etc.) and in the case of high-frequency field (regarding EMF sources such as wireless communication devices, for example, IoT devices, mobile phones, Wi-Fi routers, RFID readers, etc.)—better than 1/15 (IEC 62232-2022). This condition is met when, for example, the resolution is at least 19 mm and 3 mm for a frequency of 100 and 900 MHz, respectively. For frequencies exceeding 2 GHz, this

TABLE 10.3
Parameters Describing Analysed Examples of Realistic Workers Body Postures: Welding Gun Arms Plane Orientation and Forearm and Arm Vertical Angles

Posture	The Orientation to the Ground of the Plane of Welding Gun Arms (EMF Source)	Forearm Vertical Angle, Degree	Arm Vertical Angle, Degree
1 and 2	Vertical	0	−30
3 and 4	Vertical	−30	−60
5 and 6	Horizontal	30	−60
7 and 8	Horizontal	−30	−60

Odd numbers of postures, erect postures; even numbers of posture, postures with a torso bending angle of 40°

condition may be difficult to meet in the heterogeneous body models (e.g. about: 1.3 mm for 2100 MHz; 0.8 mm for 3600 MHz and 0.5 mm for 5000 MHz), due to limitations on computer workstation resources and insufficient resolution of MRI/CT scans used in the development of numerical body models.

As has been shown, it is easy to meet the above-mentioned resolution requirements for low-frequency EMF. However, according to ICNIRP guidelines, the E_{in} values taken for the compliance analysis should be the 99th percentile (1% of the highest values have to be omitted.) (ICNIRP 2010) or peak spatial (ICNIRP 2020) of values averaged over $2 \times 2 \times 2$ mm^3 of contiguous tissue in anatomical body models, while IEEE requirements state that they should be the maximum values over a 5 mm linear distance, so the resolution should be at least 2 mm (ICNIRP, 2010, 2020; IEEE C95.1–2019, 2019). In addition, Dimbylow (2005) has demonstrated that 99th percentile E_{in} values calculated under exposure to uniform 50 Hz EMF for a resolution of $2 \times 2 \times 2$ mm^3 are comparable to values calculated for finer resolutions.

Material elements in the vicinity of the workplace affecting the conditions of the worker's EMF exposure or the use of boundary conditions adequate to the examined exposure scenario should be also considered. For example, the use of inadequate boundary conditions resulted in differences of up to 100% between the results of limb-induced current in the bodies of workers exposed to the near-field EMF of a rod antenna from a mobile radio transmitting device (radiotelephone) (Zradziński et al., 2015b).

According to international recommendations and standards, calculations should be validated. One method of validation is to compare the EMF distributions measured near the real EMF source and those numerically modelled, or comparing the values of limb-induced current measured in the limbs of an exposed worker at EMF frequencies from 10 MHz up to 110 MHz and those numerically calculated (Zradziński, 2015b; Zradziński et al., 2020; Karpowicz et al., 2017). For such purpose, to validate numerical results by measurement results, the analytical formula to test the identity of the results of two independent studies derived from the assumption that the two results obtained with a particular uncertainties are equal may be used (Karpowicz et al., 2017).

Another validation method involves comparing the results of numerical modelling with the results of analytical calculations (EMF distribution or measures of the biophysical effects of exposure in simplified, homogenous human body models, for example, according to the requirements and methodology of EN 50413:2019 and EN 62226-2-1:2005). A recommended validation method is also to compare the numerical modelling results with the results of numerical modelling obtained for the reference model, though this is not usually used when evaluating workers' EMF exposure due to the lack of relevant models.

10.3.3 Posture-Related Evaluation of Electric Field (E_{IN}) Induced in Operator

An example of posture-related evaluation of E_{in} induced in worker body concerned operating of suspended resistance welders (welding guns). Numerical simulations were carried out for 50 Hz fundamental frequency of EMF.

To concentrate on the posture-related variability of EMF-exposure hazards, analyses of obtained results of E_{in} in the brain and the heart were based on relative values. The reference exposure scenario was related to a tall worker with biomechanical parameters corresponding to the 95th percentile dimensions of the male population in Poland, case 1, and an L-size (large) suspended resistance welding gun in which obtained values of E_{in} in the brain and the heart were identical.

The example results of numerical modelling showed a high variability in the values of E_{in} in both the brain and the heart in particular scenarios, as shown in Figure 10.7a. The values of E_{in} in the brain varies up to 140 times, while it is up to 105 times in the heart between the considered eight postures of using welding guns of three dimensions.

An analysis of the obtained results, which were divided into groups according to the size of the worker model and the welding gun, showed posture-related variability of approximately nine times and five times of E_{in} in the brain and the heart, respectively. The highest values of E_{in} in the brain were found for bended postures (up to three times higher than for erected postures), while they were the opposite in the case of E_{in} in the heart (up to twice as low as for erected postures).

In the exposure scenarios with vertical source polarisation and a higher left upper limb position (scenarios Nos 1 and 2), the values of E_{in} in the brain were up to 2.2, 2.0 and 1.7 times higher for S-, M-, and L-size guns, respectively, while values of E_{in} in the heart were up to 0.2, 0.4 and 0.7 times lower than the values calculated for scenarios with a lower left upper limb position (scenarios Nos 3 and 4). In addition, in the scenarios with horizontal source polarisation and higher left forearm position postures (scenarios Nos 5 and 6), the values of E_{in} in the brain were up to 4, 5 and 6 times higher, and the values of E_{in} in the heart were up to 6, 5 and 4 times higher for S-, M-, and L-size guns, respectively, than the values calculated for scenarios with lower left forearm position postures (scenarios Nos 7 and 8).

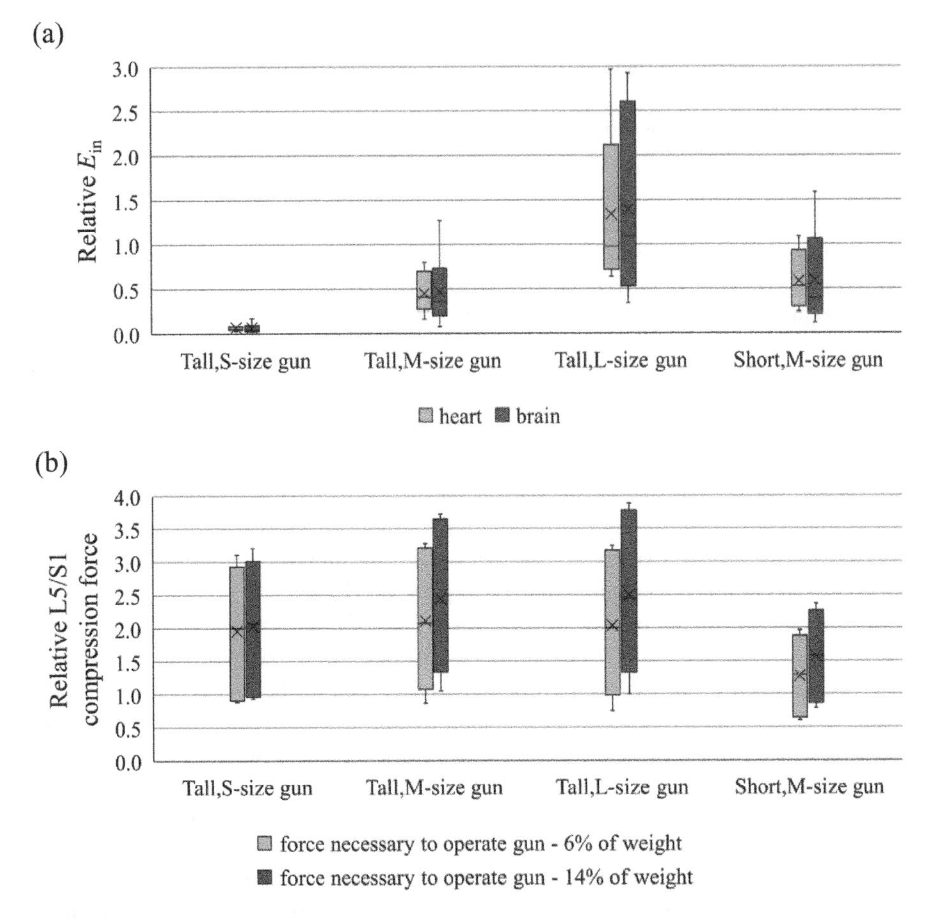

FIGURE 10.7 EMF exposure effects and MSL in welding gun operator calculated for cases of various worker postures and various sizes of resistance welding guns (as shown in Figure 10.6): (a) induced electric field strength, E_{in} in the brain and heart; (b) MSL characterised by L5/S1 compression force; reference value of E_{in} in brain or MSL in Tall worker, posture 1, and an L-size gun and force necessary to operate the welding gun equal to 14% of its weight. (Tall and Short: Numerical model of worker of dimensions corresponding to 95th and 5th percentile of Polish males; S-size gun, gun arms 14 × 25 cm; M-size gun, gun arms 20 × 80 cm; L-size gun, gun arms 34 × 115 cm; whiskers, minimum–maximum range; box, interquartile range; x, arithmetic average).

Note: The range of values is important for the worker: The highest E_{in} values in the brain may be associated with exceeding limits; depending on welding current, the highest values of L5/S1 may be assumed as high hazardous and may cause MSDs.

The E_{in} values calculated in the worker's body model with biomechanical dimensions corresponding to dimensions of the 5th percentile of Polish males [Short (5th)] were up to 50% higher than the values calculated in models corresponding to the 95th percentile dimensions [Tall (95th)]. For example, obtained results for the exposure scenario No 2, M-size gun and welding current of 15 kA showed that the value of E_{in} in the brain of Short (5th) model may exceed the ICNIRP basic restriction limit of 100 mV/m (110% of limit), while in the brain of Tall (95th) model E_{in} value was below the limit (70% of limit). The variability in E_{in} values calculated for workers corresponding to the 5th and the 95th percentile ergonomic (biomechanical) parameters for other populations may be different due to the mentioned differences in their dimensions.

While using a typical welding current (below 20 kA), the ICNIRP basic restriction limit related to E_{in} values in the brain for occupational exposure (100 mV/m) may be exceeded while working in these postures.

10.3.4 Evaluating the Influence of the Composition of Harmonics in EMF on the Electric Field Induced in the Operator

Welding guns are usually supplied by power frequency installations at 50 Hz in Europe (60 Hz in the US or Asia). Because of that an intuitive evaluation of an operator's exposure to the magnetic field emitted during the weld by the current flow in the gun's arms (electrodes) refers to the exposure limits set at that power frequency. Such an approach is subject to a very high uncertainty with regard to the results of the exposure evaluation. There are two general reasons for this: (1) the power frequency of supply is not the same thing as the power frequency variability of the output current, and (2) even when the same variability of output current is characterised by the power frequency fundamental component, it may take the form of a non-sinusoidal wave, which may be characterised by the frequency–amplitude spectrum including the component of the fundamental frequency (of the highest amplitude) along with at least several other components of frequencies multiplying the fundamental one (recognised as being higher harmonics) and with amplitudes exceeding 5% of the amplitude of the fundamental component.

In high-powered industrial devices, including welding guns (with a power of around 10 kW), such a situation is very common and relates to being supplied from an AC current from a single-, two- or three-phase installation (including a transformer or thyristor system increasing the current, and, in many cases, rectifying it to create DC current). In in the case of industrial installations, it usually means time-varying current with a relatively strong DC component and an AC component, with amplitude of the fundamental AC harmonic at the level not exceeding of tens of percent of the DC level, including also higher AC harmonics. Routine exposure assessment is typically based on the results of broadband measurements of the distribution of undisturbed EMF in the vicinity of the source. The results of the measurements carried out in this way do not provide information about the harmonic content. To consider harmonics in exposure evaluation, EMF waveform should be recorded to allow analysing of its amplitude–frequency spectrum. At low frequencies below 10 MHz, the EMFs are mostly distorted by harmonic components distributed over a large frequency band, as is the case with resistance welders, for example. Figure 10.8 shows an example of an EMF waveform and an amplitude–frequency spectrum recorded during the welding process.

The mentioned complex structure of frequency composition of the welding currents needs to be considered with respect to the humans' exposure evaluation rules.

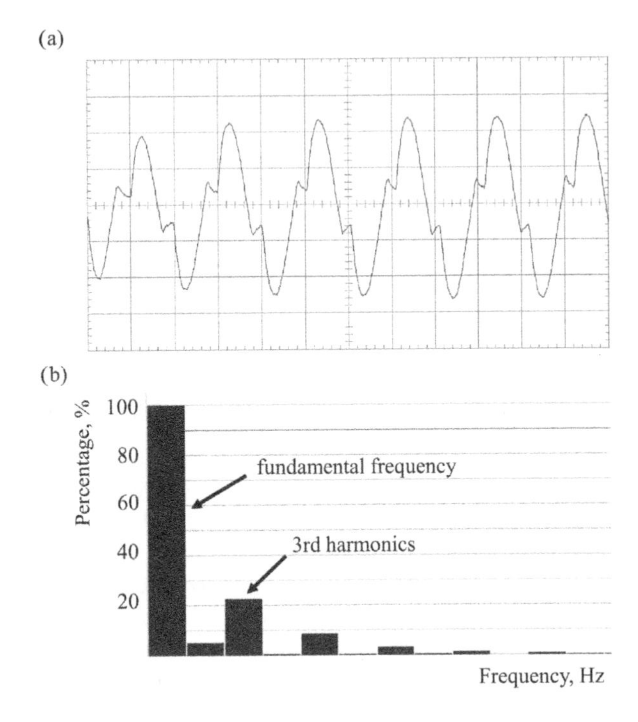

FIGURE 10.8 Example of magnetic field recorded during welding: (a) waveform; (b) an amplitude–frequency spectrum. (Authors' collection)

As mentioned, the strength of the electric field induced in the body is proportional to the frequency of the magnetic field affecting it. The higher the frequency, the lower the limit of exposure (i.e. according to Directive 2013/35/EU (2013) the high exposure limit at 100 Hz is half that of the limit at 50 Hz, whereas at 250 Hz it is just 20% of the limit at 50 Hz, increasing the exposure evaluation up to 200% and 500% in comparison to the 50 Hz one, respectively). International labour law, recommendations and standards (Directive 2013/35/EU; ICNIRP, 2010; IEEE C95.1–2019, 2019) require it to be determined whether, in situations involving the simultaneous exposure to fields of different frequencies (such as a magnetic field near a welding gun), these exposures are additive in their effects. In such situations, the following formula should be applied:

$$\sum_{j=1Hz}^{UR} \frac{A_j}{A_{R,j}} \leq 1 \qquad (10.8)$$

where A_j, a value at frequency j of the quantity (magnetic field strength, electric field strength, or induced electric field strength) characterising EMF exposure; $A_{R,j}$, a limit value at frequency j set for the quantity characterising EMF exposure (magnetic field strength, electric field strength or induced electric field strength); UR, upper range for the summation of exposures from the exposure components: UR = 5 MHz according to IEEE C95.1–2019; UR = 10 MHz according to ICNIRP.

In the evaluation of E_{in} or j, the higher the frequency, the lower the limit, and therefore the frequency summation of harmonics may mean the E_{in} or j move above the limits when their values for the fundamental frequency (evaluated based on the measured RMS value of the affected magnetic field) are close to, but not reaching, the exposure limits, as well as in the case of very high (exceeding 20%) amplitudes of higher harmonics. In the case of the frequency composition of welding currents (as shown in Figure 10.8), the situation is expected mainly in relation to DC currents used in the welding process. However, a much stronger influence on the exposure evaluation results may come from the mentioned misinterpretation with respect to the fundamental frequency in the welding current. In many cases, instead of the expected 50 Hz, it may be 100 Hz (the case of a rectified single-phase supply), or 150 Hz or even 300 Hz (the case of a three-phase supply, with a significant 600 Hz component in the case of rectification).

International recommendations and standards do not specify how many harmonics and what level of their contribution in relation to fundamental frequency should be considered in an exposure evaluation. For example, Kos et al. (2011) investigated the fundamental and the first odd harmonic with a contribution over 10% of the value of the fundamental frequency.

Typically, numerical modelling of the influence of EMF at low frequency on the human body is carried out using a sinusoidal (harmonic) EMF model with the frequency of interest (usually the fundamental frequency in the waveform observed in the EMF emitted from the modelled EMF source). In the case of exposure from a welding gun, the numerical modelling is usually performed at the expected power frequency (50/60 Hz). Harmonics and amplitude modulations (for pulsed exposure) are usually considered through the relevant scaling and summation of exposure results caused by components of exposure of various amplitudes and frequencies (as shown in equation 10.8).

10.3.5 Posture-Related Evaluation of MSL

MSL is assessed using observational, integrated or numerical methods. One of the commonly used measures of MSL is the value of compression force at L5/S1 intervertebral disc (spine load), typically calculated using the model developed by Chaffin and Anderson (1991).

The lowest MSL posture of the body (except for a lying posture), i.e. the standing posture with the spine straightened and the upper limbs lowered along the body (the natural posture), is characterised by compression force at L5/S1 intervertebral disc of approximately 320–440 N (Chaffin and Anderson, 1991; Bridger, 2018). L5/S1 compression force value depends significantly on the torso-bending angle (e.g. standing posture, bent at 35° – approximately 1450 N), load held in hands (e.g. standing posture with a 20 kg load in hands at a distance of 40 cm – 2100 N) and posture (e.g. sitting postures may reach approximately 650 N) (Chaffin and Anderson, 1991; Bridger, 2018).

As mentioned in Section 10.3.1., the portable resistance welders used in the industry are devices of large dimensions and, above all, weight, which is why they are suspended using special constructions. The most commonly used suspension systems are a guide rail system with trolleys, a wall or pillar crane, or a rigid suspension. The suspension system, individually developed for a given posture, should ensure that the worker performs operations with the welding gun using the least possible force. The highest force is required for rigid suspension. In the case of suspension with the use of a crane, the value of this force decreases with the distance from the axis of rotation of the crane (a longer crane beam). Typical minimum values of the force necessary to operate the suspended welding gun during a typical operation are about 2.5–6% of the weight of the gun. In the case of more dynamic work, or the use of rigid suspension, these values are much higher and may be at a level of approximately 12–14% of the weight of the gun, i.e. it may exceed 10 kgf (kilogram-force) (98 N).

In Figure 10.7b, the obtained results of L5/S1 compression force are presented as relative values to concentrate on the posture-related variability in MSL. The reference value was L5/S1 compression force (1000 N) obtained in the same posture [tall worker with biomechanical parameters corresponding to the 95th percentile dimensions of Polish males, case 1 and an L-size (large) suspended resistance welding gun] as in the case of E_{in} analysis, for force necessary to operate the welding gun equal to 14% of its weight.

The results of example calculations showed a high variability in the values of the L5/S1 compression force—five times the differences between values for both forces necessary to operate the gun equal to 6% and 14% of its weight, as shown in Figure 10.7b.

An analysis of the obtained results, divided into groups according to the size of the worker's model and welding gun, showed approximately (3.1–4.3) times and (2.8–3.9) times posture-related variability of L5/S1 compression force for force necessary to operate the welding gun equal to 6% and 14% of its weight, respectively. Higher variability was found for heavier (larger) guns. The highest MSL was found for bended postures—up to four times and three times higher than for erected postures for force necessary to operate the welding gun equal to 6% and 14% of its weight, respectively.

In the exposure scenarios with vertical source polarisation and a higher left upper limb position (scenarios Nos 1 and 2), the MSLs were up to 30% lower than the values calculated for scenarios with a lower left upper limb position (scenarios Nos 3 and 4)—opposite to E_{in} values in the brain. In addition, differences in MSL in the scenarios with horizontal source polarisation and higher left forearm position postures (scenarios Nos 5 and 6) and lower left forearm position postures (scenarios Nos 7 and 8) were below 10%.

The MSL calculated for a worker's body model with biomechanical dimensions corresponding to the dimensions of the 5th percentile of Polish males [Short (5th)] were up to 40% lower than the values calculated for a model corresponding to the 95th percentile dimensions [Tall (95th)], and it was opposite to E_{in} values. The variability in MSLs calculated for workers corresponding to the 5th and 95th percentile biomechanical parameters for other populations may be different due to the mentioned differences in the body dimensions.

The values calculated for force necessary to operate the welding gun equal to 14% of its weight were up to 1.4 times higher than the values obtained when the force necessary to operate the welding gun equals to 6%.

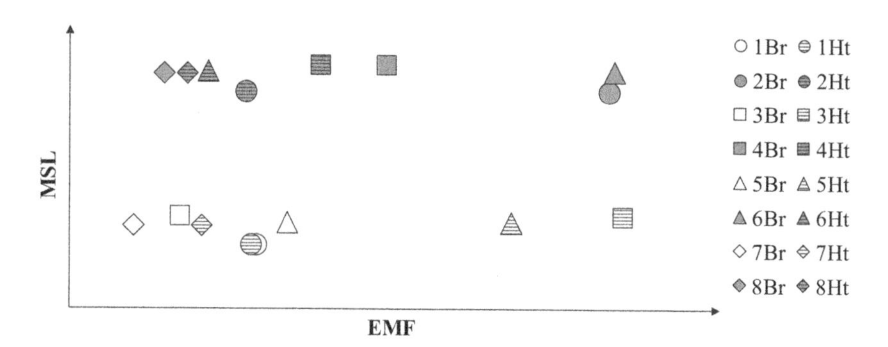

FIGURE 10.9 Posture-related combined evaluation of EMF exposure and MSL in Tall (95th) worker, an L-size (large) gun and force necessary to operate the welding gun equal to 14% of its weight (Br and Ht, referenced to E_{in} values in brain and heart, 1–8, postures considered).

10.3.6 Posture-Related Combined Evaluation of Biophysical Effects Caused by EMF Exposure and MSL

Figure 10.9 discusses the simultaneous posture-related evaluation of EMF exposure and MSL. The highest combined hazard was found for postures with workers bending and a higher upper limb position (postures Nos 2 and 6). Working in these postures is associated with high E_{in} values in the brain and excessive high MSL. On the contrary, the highest E_{in} values in the heart are associated with erected postures and a lower upper limb position (postures Nos 3 and 5), which are characterised by low MSL.

While using a typical welding current (below 20 kA), the ICNIRP basic restriction limit related to E_{in} values in the brain for occupational exposure (100 mV/m) may be exceeded while working in these postures. Additionally, MSL values associated to operating an M- or L-size gun and the force necessary to operate the welding gun equal to 14% of its weight in bended postures may exceed 3400 N—the level of L5/S1 compression force are assumed as excessive, high and may cause MSDs (NIOSH, 1981). The excessive, medium level (assumed as L5/S1 compression force from 2890 N to 3400 N) was found while working with bended postures and an S-, M- and L-size gun with the force necessary to operate the welding gun equal to 6% of its weight (NIOSH, 1981; EN 1005-2:2003 + A1:2008).

10.4 CONCLUSIONS

The discussed principles of evaluating the biophysical effects of EMF exposure also with respect to MSL and examples of its evaluation related to the manual operating of industrial sources of EMF (exemplified in details by resistance welding guns) showed that the key issues for a proper analysis of these aspects of the EMF exposure assessment are: the posture of worker while operating the EMF source (up to 9-times variability in E_{in} and up to 5-times in MSL); the composition of the EMF frequency (up to several times variability in E_{in} with respect to exposure evaluation at an assumed pure 50 Hz exposure); and the parameters related to the workers' anthropometric properties (up to two-times variability in E_{in} and in MSL) and tissue properties (up to 30% variability in E_{in}).

Since the limits of EMF exposure should take all frequencies encountered into consideration, it means that the differences in the fundamental frequency at 50 Hz and the harmonics content may be the exposure properties that may push the exposure evaluation above the limits, especially in the case of a fundamental frequency exceeding 50 Hz. This needs to be carefully considered.

In any case, in order to decrease the exposure and the levels of the biophysical effects of the influence of EMF on the human body (proportional linearly to the exposure level), it is advisable to increase the distance between the body of the worker and the EMF source. This action is more beneficial for the exposed operator than a detailed evaluation counting the frequency composition of EMF exposure. However, it must be emphasised that increasing the distance of the operator from the welding gun usually increases the MSL, which must then be compensated by ensuring relevant ergonomic support.

ACKNOWLEDGEMENTS

This chapter has been based on the results of the research tasks that has been carried out in Poland within the scope of the National Programme 'Improvement of safety and working conditions' (CIOP-PIB is the Programme's main co-ordinator), partly supported by the National Centre for Research and Development (within the scope of research and development), and by the ministry for labour issues (within the scope of state services) (2.G.07, II.N.18, II.N.19, II.PB.15, 2.R.11), as well as work carried out by the National Institute for Working Life, Sweden.

REFERENCES

Anzaldi, G., F. Silva, M. Fernandez, M. Quilez, and P. J. Riu. 2007. Initial analysis of SAR from a cell phone inside a vehicle by numerical computation. *IEEE Trans Biomed Eng* 54(5):921–930. DOI: 10.1109/TBME.2006.889776.

Bridger, R. S. 2018. *Introduction to Human Factors and Ergonomics*. Boca Raton: CRC Press, Taylor & Francis Group.

Chaffin, D. B., and G. B. J. Anderson. 1991. *Occupational Biomechanics*. New York: Wiley-Interscience.

Chaffin, D. B. 2009. The evolving role of biomechanics in prevention of overexertion injuries. *Ergonomics* 52(1):3–14. DOI: 10.1080/00140130802479812.

Christ, A., W. Kainz, E. G. Hahn et al. 2010 The virtual family – development of anatomical CAD models of two adults and two children for dosimetric simulations. *Phys Med Biol* 55(2):N23-N38. DOI: 10.1088/0031-9155/55/2/N01.

Conil, E., A. Hadjem, F. Lacroux, M. F. Wong, and J. Wiart. 2008. Variability analysis of SAR from 20 MHz to 2.4 GHz for different adult and child models using finite-difference time-domain. *Phys Med Biol* 53(6):1511–1525. DOI: 10.1088/0031-9155/53/6/001.

Dimbylow, P. J. 2005. Development of the female voxel phantom, NAOMI, and its application to calculations of induced current densities and electric fields from applied low frequency magnetic and electric fields. *Phys Med Biol* 50(6):1047–1070. DOI: 10.1088/0031-9155/50/6/002.

Directive 2013/35/EU. 2013. Directive of the European Parliament and of the Council of 26 June 2013 on the Minimum Health And Safety Requirements Regarding The Exposure Of Workers To The Risks Arising From Physical Agents (Electromagnetic Fields) (20th Individual Directive within the Meaning of Article 16(1) of Directive 89/391/EEC). *Official Journal of the European Union* O.J. No. L-179 of 29 June 2013, 1–21, Brussels, Belgium.

El Habachi, A., E. Conil, A. Hadjem et al. 2010. Statistical analysis of whole-body absorption depending on anatomical human characteristics at a frequency of 2.1 GHz. *Phys Med Biol* 55(7):1875–1887. DOI: 10.1088/0031-9155/55/7/006.

EN 50505:2008. 2008. *Basic Standard for the Evaluation of Human Exposure to Electromagnetic Fields from Equipment for Resistance Welding and Allied Processes*. Brussels: CENELEC [European Committee for Electrotechnical Standardization].

EN 50413:2019. 2019. *Basic Standard on Measurement and Calculation Procedures for Human Exposure to Electric, Magnetic and Electromagnetic Fields (0 Hz – 300 GHz)*. Brussels: CENELEC [European Committee for Electrotechnical Standardization].

EN 62226-2-1:2005. 2005. *Exposure to Electric or Magnetic Fields in the Low and Intermediate Frequency Range – Methods for Calculating the Current Density and Internal Electric Field Induced in the Human Body – Part 2-1: Exposure to Magnetic Fields 2D Models*. Brussels: CENELEC [European Committee for Electrotechnical Standardization].

EN 1005-2:2003. 2003. Safety of machinery. Human physical performance. Manual handling of machinery and component parts of machinery. Brussels: CENELEC [European Committee for Electrotechnical Standardization].

ErgoDesign. 2000. Electronic database of anthropometric and biomechanics data. Warszawa: Institute of Industrial Design.

Findlay, R. P., and P. J. Dimbylow. 2005. Effects of posture on FDTD calculations of specific absorption rate in a voxel model of the human body. *Phys Med Biol* 50(16):3825–3835. DOI: 10.1088/0031-9155/50/16/011.

Finkenzeller, K. 2010. *RFID handbook. Fundamentals and Applications in Contactless Smart Cards, Radio Frequency Identification and Near-Field Communication*. Chichester: John Wiley & Sons, Ltd.

Gabriel, S., R. W. Lau, and C. Gabriel. 1996. The dielectric properties of biological tissues: II. Measurements in the frequency range 10 Hz to 20 GHz. *Phys Med Biol* 41(11):2251–2269. DOI: 10.1088/0031-9155/41/11/002.

Gandhi, O. P., and J. Y. Chen. 1992. Numerical dosimetry at the power-line frequencies using anatomically based models. *Bioelectromagnetics* 13(S1):43–60. DOI: 10.1002/bem.2250130706.

Gedliczka, A. 2001. *Atlas of Human Measures. Data for Design and Ergonomic Evaluation*. Warszawa: Central Institute for Labour Protection.

Gosselin, M., E. Neufeld, H. Moser et al. 2014. Development of a new generation of high-resolution anatomical models for medical device evaluation: the Virtual Population 3.0. *Phys Med Biol* 59(18):5287–5303. DOI: 10.1088/0031-9155/59/18/5287.

Graveling, R. 2018. *Ergonomics and Musculoskeletal Disorders (MSDs) in the Workplace: A Forensic and Epidemiological Analysis*. Boca Raton: CRC Press, Taylor & Francis Group.

Gryz, K., J. Karpowicz, and P. Zradziński. 2020. Evaluation of the influence of magnetic field on female users of an induction hob in ergonomically sound exposure situations. *Bioelectromagnetics* 41(7):500–510. DOI: 10.1002/bem.22283.

Hansson Mild, K., T. Alanko, G. Decat et al. 2009. Exposure of workers to electromagnetic fields. A review of open questions on exposure assessment techniques. *Int J Occup Saf Ergon* 15(1):3–33. DOI: 10.1080/10803548.2009.11076785.

Hirata, A., O. Fujiwara, T. Nagaoka, and S. Watanabe. 2010. Estimation of whole-body average SAR in human models due to plane-wave exposure at resonance frequency. *IEEE Trans Electromagn Compat* 52(1):41–48. DOI: 10.1109/TEMC.2009.2035613.

Hirata, A., Y. Takano, O. Fujiwara, T. Dovan, and R. Kavet. 2011. An electric field induced in the retina and brain at threshold magnetic flux density causing magnetophosphenes. *Phys Med Biol* 56(13):4091–4101. DOI: 10.1088/0031-9155/56/13/022.

IARC [International Agency for Research on Cancer]. 2002. *IARC Monographs on the Evaluation of Carcinogenic Risks to Humans. Volume 80. Non-Ionizing Radiation, Part 1: Static and Extremely Low-Frequency (ELF) Electric and Magnetic Fields*. Lyon: IARC Press. https://publications.iarc.fr/Book-And-Report-Series/Iarc-Monographs-On-The-Identification-Of-Carcinogenic-Hazards-To-Humans/Non-ionizing-Radiation-Part-1-Static-And-Extremely-Low-frequency-ELF-Electric-And-Magnetic-Fields-2002.

IARC [International Agency for Research on Cancer]. 2013. *IARC monographs on the Evaluation of Carcinogenic Risks to Humans. Non-Ionizing Radiation, Part 2: Radiofrequency Electromagnetic Fields. Volume 102*. Lyon, France: IARC Press. http://monographs.iarc.fr/ENG/Monographs/vol102/mono102.pdf.

ICNIRP [International Commission on Non-Ionizing Radiation Protection]. 1998. Guidelines for limiting exposure to time-varying electric, magnetic, and electromagnetic fields (up to 300 GHz). *Health Phys* 74(4):494–522.

ICNIRP [International Commission on Non-Ionizing Radiation Protection]. 2010. Guidelines for limiting exposure to time-varying electric and magnetic fields (1 Hz – 100 kHz). *Health Phys* 99(6):818–836. DOI: 10.1097/HP.0b013e3181f06c86.

ICNIRP [International Commission on Non-Ionizing Radiation Protection]. 2020. Guidelines for limiting exposure to electromagnetic fields (100 kHz to 300 GHz). *Health Phys* 118(5):483–524. DOI: 10.1097/HP.0000000000001210.

ICRP [International Commission on Radiological Protection]. 2002. Basic anatomical and physiological data for the use in radiological protection: Reference values. ICRP publication 89. *Ann ICRP* 32(3–4):1–277. DOI: 10.1016/S0146-6453(03)00002-2.

IEC 62232-2022. 2022. *Determination of RF Field Strength, Power Density and SAR in the Vicinity of Radiocommunication Base Stations for the Purpose of Evaluating Human Exposure*. Geneva: IEC [International Electrotechnical Commission].

IEEE C95.1–2019. 2019. *IEEE Standard for Safety Levels with Respect to Human Exposure to Electric, Magnetic, and Electromagnetic Fields, 0 Hz to 300 GHz*. New York: IEEE [Institute of Electrical and Electronics Engineers].

IEEE C95.3.1–2010. 2010. *IEEE Recommended Practice for Measurements and Computations of Electric, Magnetic and Electromagnetic Fields with Respect to Human Exposure to Such Fileds, 0 Hz to 100 kHz*. New York: IEEE [Institute of Electrical and Electronics Engineers].

IEEE C95.6–2002. 2002. *Standard for Safety Levels with Respect to Human Exposure to Frequency Electromagnetic Fields, 0 Hz to 3 kHz*. New York: IEEE [Institute of Electrical and Electronics Engineers].

Jokela, K. 2007. Assessment of complex EMF exposure situations including inhomogeneous field distribution. *Health Phys* 92(6):531–540. DOI: 10.1097/01.HP.0000250620.32459.4c.

Karpowicz, J., and K. Gryz. 2007. Practical aspects of occupational EMF exposure assessment. *Environmentalist* 27:525–531. DOI: 10.1007/s10669-007-9067-y.

Karpowicz, J., P. Zradziński, J. Kieliszek, K. Gryz, J. Sobiech, and W. Leszko. 2017. An in situ and in silico evaluation of biophysical effects of 27 MHz electromagnetic whole body humans exposure expressed by the limb current. *BioMed Res Int* Article Number 5785482. DOI: 10.1155/2017/5785482.

Kashvari, J., R. Kashvari, and S. Lang. 2006. The effect of increase in dielectric values on specific absorption rate (SAR) in eye and head tissues following 900, 1800 and 2450 MHz radio frequency (RF) exposure. *Phys Med Biol* 51(6):1463–1477. DOI: 10.1088/0031-9155/51/6/007.

Kheifets, L., A. Ahlbom, C. Johansen, M. Feychting, J. Sahl, and D. Savitz. 2007. Extremely low-frequency magnetic fields and heart disease. *Scand J Work Environ Health* 33(1):5–12. DOI: 10.5271/sjweh.1059.

Kheifets, L., J. D. Bowman, H. Checkoway et al. 2009. Future needs of occupational epidemiology of extremely low frequency electric and magnetic fields: Review and recommendations. *Occup Environ Med* 66(2):72–80. DOI: 10.1136/oem.2007.037994.

Kos, B., Valic, B., Miklavcic, D., Kotnik, T., and P. Gajsek. 2011. Pre- and post-natal exposure of children to EMF generated by domestic induction cookers. *Phys Med Biol* 56(19):6149–6160. DOI: 10.1088/0031-9155/56/19/001.

Kramer, R., J. W. Vieira, H. J. Khoury, F. R. Lima, and D. Fuelle. 2003. All about MAX: A male adult voxel phantom for Monte Carlo calculations in radiation protection dosimetry. *Phys Med Biol* 48(10):1239–1262. DOI: 10.1088/0031-9155/48/10/301.

Kramer, R., H. J. Khoury, J. W. Vieira et al. 2004. All about FAX: A female adult voXel phantom for Monte Carlo calculation in radiation protection dosimetry. *Phys Med Biol* 49(23):5203–5216. DOI: 10.1088/0031-9155/49/23/001.

Lee, C., C. Lee, S. H. Park, and J. K. Lee. 2006. Development of the two Korean adult tomographic computational phantoms for organ dosimetry. *Med Phys* 33(2):380–390. DOI: 10.1118/1.2161405.

McNamee, D. A., A. G. Legros, D. R. Krewski, G. Wisenberg, F. S. Prato, and A. W. Thomas. 2009. A literature review: The cardiovascular effects of exposure to extremely low frequency electromagnetic fields. *Int Arch Occup Environ Health* 82(8):919–933. DOI: 10.1007/s00420-009-0404-y.

Nachemson, A. L. 1981. Disc pressure measurements. *Spine (Phila Pa 1976)* 6(1):93–97. DOI: 10.1097/00007632-198101000-00020.

Nadeem, M., Y. Hamnerius, K. Hansson Mild, and M. Persson. 2004. Magnetic field from spot welding equipment – Is the basic restriction exceeded? *Bioelectromagnetics* 25(4):278–284. DOI: 10.1002/bem.10197.

Nagaoka, T., S. Watanabe, K. Sakurai et al. 2004. Development of realistic high-resolution whole-body voxel models of Japanese adult males and females of average height and weight, and application of models to radio-frequency electromagnetic-field dosimetry. *Phys Med Biol* 49(1):1–15. DOI: 10.1088/0031-9155/49/1/001.

NIOSH [National Institute for Occupational Safety and Health]. 1981. *Work Practices Guide for Manual Lifting*. Publication No. 81–122. Cincinnati: Department of Health and Human Services (DHHS), NIOSH.

NRCIM [National Research Council and Institute of Medicine]. 2001. *Musculoskeletal Disorders and the Workplace: Low Back and Upper Extremities*. Washington: The National Academies Press.

Reilly, P. J. 1998. *Applied bioelectricity. From Electrical Stimulation to Electropathology*. New York: Springer-Verlag.

Reilly, P. J. 2002. Neuroelectric mechanisms applied to low frequency electric and magnetic field exposure guidelines. Part I: sinusoidal waveforms. *Health Phys* 83(3):341–355. DOI: 10.1097/00004032-200209000-00004.

Roman-Liu, D. 2010. Work-related activities: Rules and methods for assessment. In: *Handbook of Occupational Safety and Health*. ed. D. Koradecka, 483–498. Boca Raton: CRC Press.

Sandrini, L., A. Vaccari, C. Malacarne, L. Cristoforetti, and R. Pontalti. 2004. RF dosimetry: A comparison between power absorption of female and male numerical models from 0.1 to 4 GHz. *Phys Med Biol* 49(22):5185–5201. DOI: 10.1088/0031-9155/49/22/012.

Saunders, R. D., and J. G. Jefferys. 2002. Weak electric field interactions in the central nervous system. *Health Phys* 83(3):366–375. DOI: 10.1097/00004032-200209000-00006.

Saunders, R. D., and J. G. Jefferys. 2007. A neurobiological basis for ELF guidelines. *Health Phys* 92(6):596–603. DOI: 10.1097/01.HP.0000257856.83294.3e.

SCENIHR [Scientific Committee on Emerging and Newly Identified Health Risks]. 2015. *Opinion on Potential Health Effects of Exposure to Electromagnetic Fields (EMF)*. Luxembourg: European Commission. http://ec.europa.eu/health/sites/health/files/scientific_committees/emerging/docs/scenihr_o_041.pdf.

Uusitupa, T., I. Laakso, S. Ilvonen, and K. Nikoskinen. 2010. SAR variation study from 300 to 5000 MHz for 15 voxel models including different postures. *Phys Med Biol* 55(4): 1157–1176. DOI: 10.1088/0031-9155/55/4/017.

Vermeeren, G., J. Wout, L. Martens et al. 2007. Of a PEC ground on the whole-body averaged SAR. Materiały EBEA 2007. *The 8th Congress of The European Bioelectromagnetics Associacion*, Bordeaux, France, 2007.04.10–13, 52.

Vermeeren, G., and L. Martens. 2005. Assessment of the SAR for a walkie-talkie setup. *A Joint Meeting of The Bioelectromagnetics Society and The European BioElectromagnetics Association (BIOEM) 2005*, Dublin, Ireland, 2005.06.19–24, Abstract collection, 487–488.

WHO [World Health Organization]. 1993. *Environmental Health Criteria 137: Electromagnetic Fields (300 Hz – 300 GHz)*. Geneva: WHO. http://www.inchem.org/documents/ehc/ehc/ehc137.htm.

WHO [World Health Organization]. 2006. *Environmental Health Criteria Criteria 232: Static Fields*. Geneva: WHO. https://www.who.int/peh-emf/publications/EHC_232_Static_Fields_full_document.pdf?ua=1.

WHO [World Health Organization]. 2007. Environmental Health Criteria criteria 238: Extremely Low Frequency (ELF) Fields. Geneva: WHO. https://www.who.int/peh-emf/publications/Complet_DEC_2007.pdf?ua=1.

Wilén, J., R. Hörnsten, M. Sandström et al. 2004. Electromagnetic field exposure and health among RF plastic sealer operators. *Bioelectromagnetics* 25(1):5–15. DOI: 10.1002/bem.10154.

Wong, M. F., V. Dronne, E. Nicolas, F. Jacquin, and J. Wiatr. 2005. Influence of human body shape on EMF exposure at 100 MHz. *A Joint Meeting of The Bioelectromagnetics Society and The European BioElectromagnetics Association (BIOEM) 2005*, Dublin, Ireland, 2005.06.19–24, Abstract collection: 492–493.

Xu, X. G., T. C. Chao, and A. Bozkurt. 2000. VIP-man: An image-based whole-body adult male model constructed from color photographs of the visible human project for multi-particle Monte Carlo calculations. *Health Phys* 78(5):476–486. DOI: 10.1097/00004032-200005000-00003.

Zankl, M., U. Fill, N. Petoussi-Henss, and D. Regulla. 2002. Organ dose conversion coefficients for external photon irradiation of male and female voxel models. *Phys Med Biol* 47(14):2367–2385. DOI: 10.1088/0031-9155/47/14/301.

Zradziński, P., and D. Roman-Liu. 2009. Metodyka oceny jednoczesnego oddziaływania czynników elektromagnetycznych i biomechanicznych na pracowników obsługujących podwieszane zgrzewarki rezystancyjne. [Methodology for combined assessment of electromagnetic and biomechanics factors affecting workers operating suspended gun for resistance welding]. *Acta Bio-Optica et Informatica Medica* 15(4):399–403.

Zradziński, P. 2010. *Ergonomically Realisctic Assessment of Hazards Related to electromagnetic Fields Exposure while the Use of Welding Devices, EMC Europe 2010*, Wrocław, Poland, 2010.09.13–17.

Zradziński, P. 2013. The properties of human body phantoms used in calculations of electromagnetic fields exposure by wireless communication handsets or hand-operated industrial devices. *Electromag Biol Med* 32(2):226–235. DOI: 10.3109/15368378.2013.776434.

Zradziński, P. 2015a. Difficulties in applying numerical simulations to an evaluation of occupational hazards caused by electromagnetic fields. *Int J Occup Saf Ergon* 21(2):213–220. DOI: 10.1080/10803548.2015.1028233.

Zradziński, P., J. Karpowicz, J. Kieliszek, and K. Gryz. 2015b. Walidacja modeli numerycznych w procedurze wykorzystania symulacji numerycznych do oceny narażenia pracownika w strefie bliskiej na pola elektromagnetyczne częstotliwości radiowych. In: *Ochrona przed promieniowaniem jonizującym i niejonizującym. Nowe uregulowania prawne, źródła, problemy pomiarowe*, eds. M. Zmyślony, and E. Nowosielska, 213–226. Warszawa: Wojskowa Akademia Techniczna (WAT).

Zradziński, P. 2016a. Uwarunkowania wykorzystania numerycznych modeli pracowników do oceny zagrożeń bezpośrednich wynikających z narażenia na pole elektromagnetyczne. [Conditions of using numerical workers' models while assessing direct hazards related to exposure to electromagnetic field]. *Podstawy i Metody Oceny Środowiska Pracy* 90(4):75-89. DOI: 10.5604/1231868X.1222127.

Zradziński, P. 2016b. A comparison of ICNIRP and IEEE guidelines to evaluate low frequency magnetic field localised exposure. *Proceedings of the 2016 17th International Conference on Computational Problems of Electrical Engineering (CPEE), Sandomierz, Poland*, 2016.09.14–17. New York: IEEE. DOI: 10.1109/CPEE.2016.7738764.

Zradziński, P., J. Karpowicz, and K. Gryz. 2019. Electromagnetic energy absorption in a head approaching a radiofrequency identification (RFID) reader operating at 13.56 MHz in users of hearing implants versus non-users. *Sensors* 19(17):e3724. DOI: 10.3390/s19173724.

Zradziński, P., J. Karpowicz, K. Gryz, and V. Ramos. 2020. An evaluation of electromagnetic exposure while using ultra-high frequency radiofrequency identification (UHF RFID) guns. *Sensors* 20(1):e202. DOI: 10.3390/s20010202.

11 Managing Electromagnetic Hazards by Applying Non-Binding Safety Measures

Sachiko Yamaguchi-Sekino
National Institute of Occupational Safety and Health Japan (JNIOSH)
National Institute of Information and Communications Technology (NICT)

CONTENTS

11.1 INTRODUCTION

Electromagnetic hazards sometimes occur in the workplace, since industrial machines and medical equipment are driven by high-energy sources. In contrast to legally binding protection measures against acute occupational hazards (such as electric shocks), protection measures against non-lethal biophysical symptoms, which may be experienced by workers due to substantial exposure to electromagnetic field (EMF), may not be mandatory in various countries. Nowadays, however, the management of electromagnetic hazards present nearly everywhere has become necessary in order to create safer and healthier workplaces. For example, the United States Department of Labor, Occupational Safety and Health Administration (OSHA) recommends health and safety programmes for the workplace based on seven actions (OSHA, 2016), with the key three areas defined as being: (1) hazard

DOI: 10.1201/9781003020486-11

TABLE 11.1
The Core Elements of the Health and Safety Programmes for the Workplace Recommended by OSHA (2016)

Core Elements	Actions Included	Category in this Chapter
1. Management leadership		
2. Worker participation		
3. Hazards identification and assessment	Hazards identification Risk assessment	Inspection of work environment
4. Hazards prevention and control	Control selection Control implementation	Management of work practice
5. Education and training	Education Training	Education and training
6. Programme evaluation and improvement		
7. Communication and coordination for host employers, contractors, and staffing agencies		

identification and assessment, (2) hazard prevention and control, and (3) education and training (Table 11.1).

In this chapter, the 'Hazard identification and assessment' named— **'Inspection of the Work Environment'**—is a procedure for estimating hazards to health or safety from exposure to various ambient factors in the workplace. Understanding how much exposure to a particular factor poses a health or safety hazard to workers is important in order to appropriately eliminate, control and reduce those hazards and related risk. After the workplace hazards have been identified, work practices to prevent them should be established. In this chapter, the 'Hazard prevention and control' named— **'Management of Work Practices'**—will contribute to the development of prevention measures (NIOSH). **'Education and training'** are important tools for informing managers and workers about workplace hazards and relevant interventions, so the work can be safer and more productive.

This chapter explains the general rules regarding the application of these concepts to the management of electromagnetic hazards using non-binding safety measures. The definition of the term 'electromagnetic hazards' in this chapter is: 'non-lethal biophysical annoying (or irritating) symptoms that may be experienced by workers and which disturb their activities or safe and productive work ability but are not prohibited by law.'

11.2 MANAGING ELECTROMAGNETIC HAZARDS BY APPLYING NON-BINDING SAFETY MEASURES

The concept of managing electromagnetic hazards by applying non-binding safety measures is based on a common strategic approach to protect workers from occupational hazards, as proposed by various organisations. Although names of the actions used differ among the proposers, the principles are mostly common throughout the world. This section introduces the management of electromagnetic hazards using non-binding safety measures based on categories proposed by OSHA (2016) described in Table 11.1. The first part introduces processes for identifying hazards and assessing risk in terms of protecting workers against electromagnetic hazards (Section 11.2.1). In the second part, the details of selecting and implementing intervention measures are explained (Section 11.2.2). Lastly, trials for education and training will be introduced (Section 11.2.3).

11.2.1 Inspection of the Work Environment

Inspection of the Work Environment is the primary measure to prevent occupational diseases or disorders associated with hazardous materials or environmental factors.

Identifying hazards is the first stage of the assessment of related risk. This step identifies hazards associated with the job and the workplace. With regard to EMF exposure, health and safety hazards are sufficiently documented, briefly, sensational effects (caused by induced electro stimulation) and heat caused by absorbed electromagnetic energy are health hazards related to direct EMF exposure (ICNIRP, 1998, 2009, 2010, 2014, 2020). In particular, protection against electric shocks is legally binding, because of the severe damage that it can cause, and, therefore, it is excluded from hazards covered by the term 'electromagnetic hazards'. However, indirect EMF effects, coming from exposure effects in humans and nearby physical objects, for example, contact currents, also need to be avoided (ICNIRP, 2010, 2020). Other hazards relevant for indirect EMF effects include malfunctions in electronic devices, including medical implants or projectile hazards when ferromagnetic objects are attracted by magnets.

Risk assessment is the second step, with this procedure evaluating the likelihood and consequences of an injury or illness occurring in the workplace. Exposure assessment is an essential process when estimating the risk caused by the hazards identified. A basic knowledge of the physical features of EMF is required in order to carry out the evaluation. The factors listed below need to be taken into consideration when making an assessment:

- **Frequency of EMF:** The frequency of EMF component used in the workplace needs to be checked, because the biological effects caused by EMF depend on the operating frequency.
- **Inhomogeneity:** Highly inhomogeneous energy absorption occurs in the body even during exposure to a uniform EMF, but this inhomogeneity of effects increases significantly when the affecting EMF is not uniform.
- **Wave Properties of EMF Propagation:** High-frequency EMF is recognised as being electromagnetic waves with various wave properties, such as the property of hitting an object and then changing direction (reflection), the property of wrapping around an object (diffraction), and the superposition of radio waves (interference).
- **Distance Attenuation:** Electromagnetic wave intensity (power density or the strength of electric and magnetic fields) has the property of distance attenuation; for example, the power density decreases by as much as four times along doubled distance from the emitting antenna.

Furthermore, appropriate and calibrated equipment is required to take measurements of the parameters of EMF exposure relevant for an evaluation of electromagnetic hazards or the efficiency of the applied protection measures. For example, an isotropic probe is usually required to take measurements, since the direction from the exposed worker to the electromagnetic sources may differ significantly.

Figure 11.1 shows the example of an on-site measurement of EMF emitted by a high-frequency furnace, arc furnace and magnetic particle tester (Yamaguchi-Sekino and Okuno, 2014). In this case, these industrial machines were evaluated as possibly harmful for workers. On-site measurements were performed for the risk evaluation using a 100 cm^3 isotropic probe with a recorder and a non-metallic tripod. Since no specific measurement standard exists for EMFs emitted from the equipment used, measurement points were set at the height above the ground of the head, chest and limb for an average person with an estimated height of 180 cm. Then the measured exposure levels were evaluated by the relative value against the limits of workers' exposure (i.e. occupational reference levels provided by ICNIRP (2010), in Figure 11.1, see % of each figure). According to the measured data, the magnetic particle tester showed the highest relative levels of exposure (23–99% of the exposure limit). Although the exposure levels reached nearly 100% of reference level, the risks associated with the work process was evaluated as 'middle to low', taking into account the work postures and actual distance from the exposure source. As a result

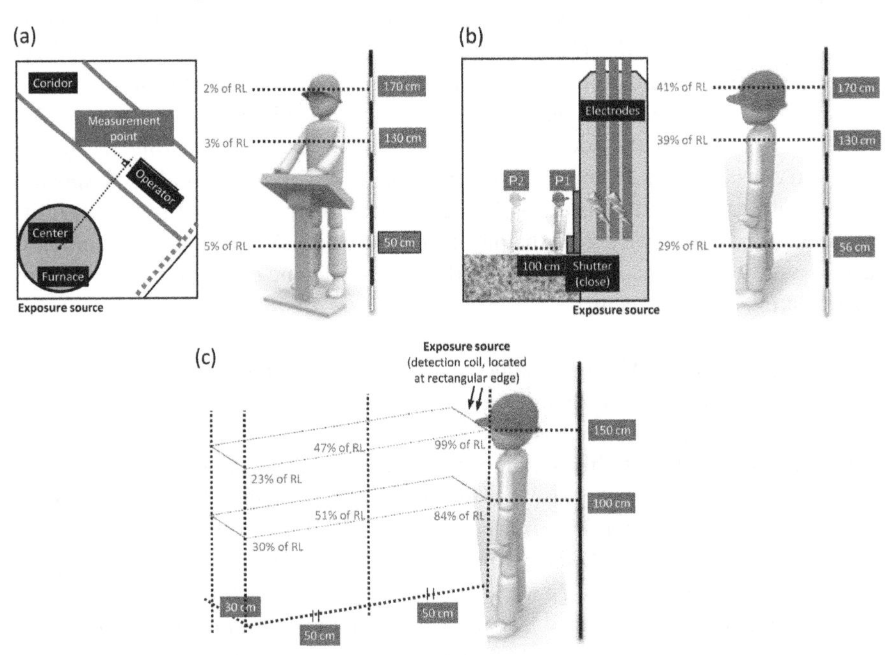

FIGURE 11.1 An example of an on-site measurement of EMF emitted by: (a) a high-frequency furnace at the operator position, (b) a high-frequency furnace during the processing (ventilation and blower) and (c) magnetic particle tester; the body height was estimated as 180 cm; % of RL—exposure level (measured magnetic field plus SD) versus relevant limit (occupational reference level), (ICNIRP, 2010; Yamaguchi-Sekino and Okuno, 2014).

of the risk assessment, a modification of the work area beside the tester was suggested to the manager for establishment of safer work environments.

A number of studies have independently reported risk assessments of EMF in the workplace; extremely-low-frequency EMF (ELF-EMF) exposure from switching and transforming stations (Korpinen et al., 2011), an uninterruptible industrial power supply (Tesneli and Tesneli, 2014), arc-welding equipment (Zoppetti et al., 2015); intermediate frequency EMF exposure from induction cooktops (Christ et al., 2012); electronic article surveillance (EAS) system (Roivainen et al., 2014); and radio frequency EMF (RF-EMF) exposure from air traffic controls (Joseph et al., 2012a,b), broadcasting stations (TV or radio) (Valic et al., 2012; Osei et al., 2016; Politanski et al., 2018), shortwave and microwave diathermy (Shah and Faeeow, 2013; Andrikopoulos et al., 2017) and military uses (Halgamuge, 2015; Sobiech et al., 2017). The results of compliance with the exposure limits (e.g. ICNIRP, 2010) are dependent on exposure sources and the location of the measurements. SCENIHR report 2015 (SCENIHR, 2015) is available for more detailed measurement result. The exposure evaluation is an essential step for risk assessment regarding EMF exposure, though the various factors affecting the results (frequency, inhomogeneity, wave properties, and distance attenuation) need to be taken into consideration when evaluating the levels of exposure.

Regarding the policies for managing RF-EMF hazards, Dhungel et al. (2015) performed a worldwide survey on risk management policies and practices, and revealed that 76.5% of countries set specified exposure limits for occupational settings, although the implementation levels differ among counties (Dhungel et al., 2015).

11.2.2 Management of Work Practices

Once the hazards identification and risk assessment have been carried out, the appropriate selection and implementation of management tools need to be discussed. The next step will be to typically establish a 'hierarchy of interventions for reducing occupational hazards' (Figure 11.2), which is based on the concept of 'hierarchy of

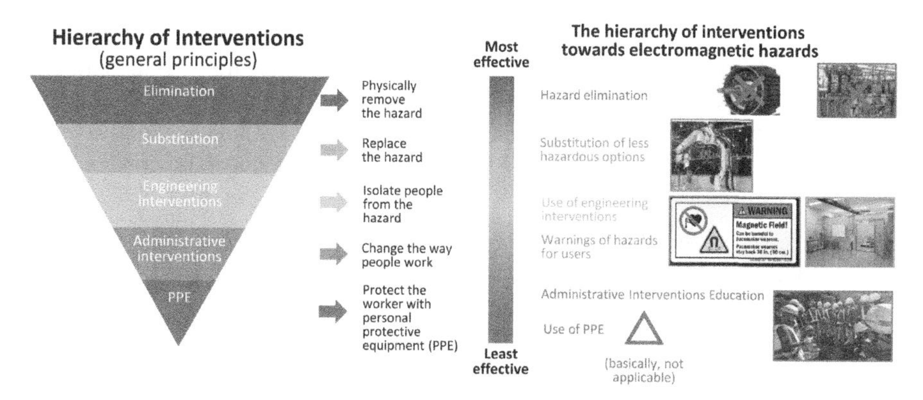

FIGURE 11.2 Hierarchy of interventions towards hazards in the work environment: general principles by NIOSH (NIOSH) (left side) and application towards electromagnetic hazards (right side).

controls' (NIOSH), where the methods of interventions at the top of the graph are potentially more effective and protective than those at the bottom. The establishment of this hierarchy normally leads to the implementation of inherently safer systems, where the risk of illness or injury has been substantially reduced (NIOSH).

However, when considering protection from electromagnetic hazards, some of the solutions raised may not be suitable to be applied directly in the workplace. As shown in Figure 11.2, taking measures of 'elimination' and 'substitution' may be very expensive, as they may require drastic changes in the production processes; however, measures related to 'engineering interventions' and 'administrative interventions' are easier to introduce in actual working conditions. Personal protection equipment (PPE) is basically not applicable to electromagnetic hazards. The relevant protective suits are available in some cases only, for example, the protection against RF-EMF exposure such as for the work near radars.

11.3 EDUCATION AND TRAINING

Education and training programmes provide employers, managers, supervisors and workers with:

- Knowledge and skills needed to make the work safe, and to avoid creating hazards that could place themselves or others at risk.
- Awareness and understanding of workplace hazards, and how to identify, report and manage them.
- Specialised training, when the work involves unique hazards.

Developing education programmes are active in certain societies of workers, for example, construction workers and medical personnel. For example, managing EMF hazards in the use of a magnetic resonance imaging (MRI) system requires a safety educational programme to be drawn up in advance, because the system uses multiple sources of EMF and cryogen, which might lead to severe injury to patients or users (See Section 11.4 for more details.). Therefore, a number of supplier-released guidance tools (posters, text and DVDs) were developed by MRI system operators and provided for educational purposes for their customers. With regard to a standardised educational tool for MRI system operators, Crisp and Dawdy built an education tool for a safety programme of MRI together with educators and technical experts (Crisp and Dawdy, 2017). Their tools took 10–20 minutes in length, depending on the level of lessons involved.

11.4 MANAGING ELECTROMAGNETIC HAZARDS BY APPLYING NON-BINDING SAFETY MEASURES USING THE EXAMPLE OF AN MRI SITE

MRI systems use multiple EMF sources, such as the static magnetic field (SMF), a time-varying EMF and radio frequency EMF. Therefore, possible adverse health effects were a major concern among MRI system operators (e.g. radiographers or service engineers), nurses, doctors and other company personnel. Protection from

SMFs is the most considerable issue among MRI system operators. With regard to 'Inspection of the Work Environment', several studies have reported the actual or estimated parameters of SMF affecting workers or induced electric field values during routine MRI examinations (McRobbie, 2012; Karpowicz and Gryz, 2013a; Bonutti et al., 2015; Gourzoulidis et al., 2015; Yamaguchi-Sekino et al., 2014; Zilberti et al., 2016; Berlana and Ubeda, 2017; Delmas et al., 2017; Fatahi et al., 2017; Walker et al., 2020). However, it is difficult to apply normal general measures for the 'Management of Work Practices' to the MRI environment due to two reasons:

1. Interventions covering 'hazard elimination' and the 'substitution of less hazardous options' are not applicable, because SMF emitted by the magnet of the MRI scanner is the principle factor necessary for the intentional use of the scanner in the medical diagnostics and is always present when using permanent or superconducting magnets,
2. 'Use of engineering interventions', such as building shielding of SMF very close to MRI systems is impossible, because the centre of the system needs to be easily accessible by the patients and medical personnel, and also the presence of metallic objects near the patient's position may significantly disturb the quality of diagnostic information collected over the patient's examination.

To protect the quality of medical data collected during patient's examination inside MRI scanner (against RF-EMF signals from outside systems, such as radio and TV broadcasting) the radiofrequency shielding is installed around all MRI scanner rooms (several metres away from MRI magnets). So, workers are not exposed to time-varying EMF emitted by scanners during their duty outside the MRI room. Outside the MRI room also SMF is already comparable to the geomagnetic natural level, because it decreases over the distance and active shielding of MRI magnets, reducing the SMF level outside the intentional location of patients. The applicable 'engineering interventions' are limited only to setting up the area with restricted access or the use of a detachable patient bed in order to prepare diagnostic coil settings in the pre-clinical area to reduce SMF exposure of MRI personnel. The 'administrative interventions' are useful to reduce temporal sensations that may be experienced by workers in the vicinity of the MRI scanner. It has been identified scientifically that displacement in the gradient SMFs induces temporal sensations in humans (ICNIRP, 2009, 2014). To avoid these temporal effects, self-motivated motion control (management) around MRI systems was suggested in general (ICNIRP, 2009, 2014). Therefore, these limited 'engineering interventions' and 'administrative interventions' were used in general (Yamaguchi-Sekino et al., 2015; Gourzoulidis et al., 2015; Karpowicz and Gryz, 2013b). This approach differs from exposure protection from other industrial equipment, because it involves primarily individual behavioural changes rather than organizational measures, though the company organization should support personnel in this direction, for example, by providing sufficient time for particular duties performed near the magnets and by reducing the time pressure on workers' movements.

Yamaguchi-Sekino et al. has also proposed supporting technical measures—'setting a 30 cm access restriction area from MRI systems', if the situation permits

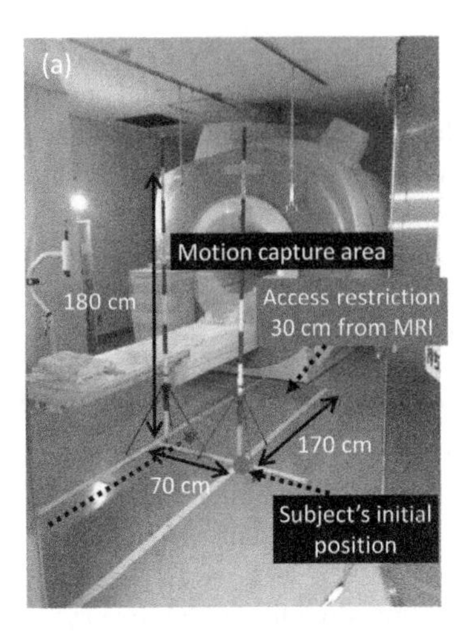

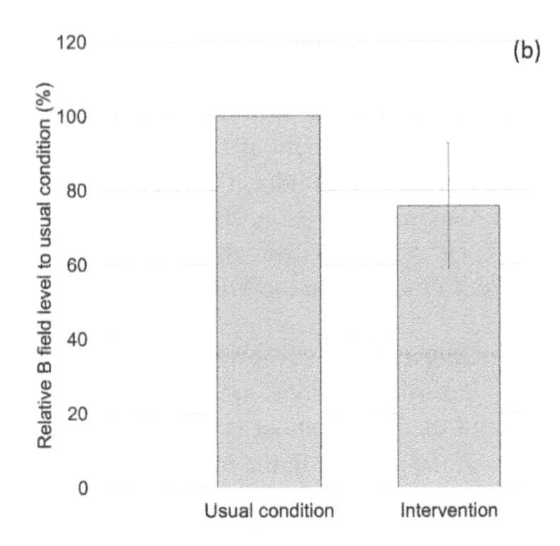

FIGURE 11.3 Experimental setup: (a) a motion recording system used in a 3 T MRI system room; the position of the reflection marker for motion capture and the Hall sensor for SMF measuring; and (b) the recorded SMF levels (peak B) for each subject; the results were expressed as relative value to usual condition (without intervention). $N = 6$; the error bar represents the standard division of the result.

(Yamaguchi-Sekino et al., 2015). Their study also reported that these measures did not affect subjects' motions, while the observed level of exposure to SMF was reduced by 25% compared with usual conditions (Yamaguchi-Sekino et al., 2015) (Figure 11.3).

Although RF and ELF-EMF exposure from MRI scanners is not present as long as operators do not remain in the MRI room during data acquisition, Gourzoulidis et al. (2015) measured such EMF components during the data acquisition next to the patient's bed in the position where exposure reaches the maximum value. The authors of this study reported that the measured values complied with the EU Directive (Directive 2013/35/EU, 2013), although hot spots in the RF ranges were detected behind the bore. Considering the location of the hot spots, the authors concluded that they are not concerned, because the personnel had limited opportunities to enter those locations.

Another EMF hazard around the MRI environment comes from the projectile effect caused by the mechanical force interacting between ferromagnetic objects and the MRI magnet, as explained, for example, by Kangarlu (Kangarlu and Robitaille, 2020). Karpowicz and Gryz performed an experimental and on-site evaluation of the projectile effect in an imaging diagnostic centre (Karpowicz and Gryz, 2013b). The authors of this study showed that in the laboratory conditions, metallic objects started to move towards the magnet under lower field (2.2–15 mT) when they are placed on a smooth surface compared with the relevant levels of SMF moving freely suspended objects. From the results of the on-site evaluation, they also confirmed that an SMF of 3 mT is reasonable for the evaluation where prevention measures related to projectile effects should be applied.

11.5 CONCLUSION

This chapter explains the management of electromagnetic hazards using non-binding safety measures from an occupational health and safety perspective. The author hopes that this chapter will help to reduce EMF hazards in the workplace where the use of strong EMF sources is required.

ACKNOWLEDGEMENTS

The author thanks Dr. Jolanta Karpowicz for her suggestions.

REFERENCES

Andrikopoulos, A., A. Adamopoulos, I. Seimenis, and C. Koutsojannis. 2017. Microwave diathermy in physiotherapy units: a survey on spatial and time heterogeneity of the electromagnetic field. *J Radiol Prot* 37(2):N27-N41. DOI: 10.1088/1361-6498/aa6e63.

Berlana, T., and A. Úbeda. 2017. Occupational exposure of NMR spectrometrists to static and radiofrequency fields. *Radiat Prot Dosimetry* 177(4):397–406. DOI: 10.1093/rpd/ncx058.

Bonutti, F., M. Tecchio, M. Maieron, D. Trevisan, C. Negro, and F. Calligaris. 2016. Measurement of the weighted peak level for occupational exposure to gradient magnetic fields for 1.5 and 3 Tesla MRI body scanners. *Radiat Prot Dosimetry* 168(3):358–364. DOI: 10.1093/rpd/ncv308.

Christ, A., R. Guldimann, B. Bühlmann, M. Zefferer, J.F. Bakker, G.C. van Rhoon, and N. Kuster. 2012. Exposure of the human body to professional and domestic induction cooktops compared to the basic restrictions. *Bioelectromagnetics* 33(8):695–705. DOI: 10.1002/bem.21739.

Crisp, S., and K. Dawdy. 2018. Building a magnetic resonance imaging safety culture from the ground up. *J Med Imaging Radiat Sci* 49(1):18–22. DOI: 10.1016/j.jmir.2017.10.005.

Delmas, A., N. Weber, J. Piffre, C. Pasquier, J. Felblinger, and P-A. Vuissoz. 2017. MRI 'exposimetry': how to analyze, compare and represent worker exposure to static magnetic field? *Radiat Prot Dosimetry* 177(4):415–423. DOI: 10.1093/rpd/ncx060.

Dhungel, A., D. Zmirou-Navier, and E. van Deventer. 2015. Risk management policies and practices regarding radio frequency electromagnetic fields: results from a WHO survey. *Radiat Prot Dosimetry* 164(1–2):22–27. DOI: 10.1093/rpd/ncu324.

Directive 2013/35/EU. 2013. Directive of the European Parliament and of the Council of 26 June 2013 on the Minimum Health And Safety Requirements Regarding The Exposure Of Workers To The Risks Arising From Physical Agents (Electromagnetic Fields) (20th Individual Directive within the Meaning of Article 16(1) of Directive 89/391/EEC). *Official Journal of the European Union* O.J. No. L-179 of 29 June 2013, 1–21, Brussels, Belgium.

Fatahi, M., J. Karpowicz, and K. Gryz. 2017. Amirmohammad Fattahi, Georg Rose, Oliver Speck. Evaluation of exposure to (ultra) high static magnetic fields during activities around human MRI scanners. *MAGMA* 30(3):255–264. DOI: 10.1007/s10334-016-0602-z.

Gourzoulidis, G., E. Karabetsos, N. Skamnakis et al. 2015. Occupational electromagnetic fields exposure in magnetic resonance imaging systems - Preliminary results for the RF harmonic content. *Phys Med* 31(7):757–762. DOI: 10.1016/j.ejmp.2015.03.006.

Halgamuge, M.N. 2015. Radio hazard safety assessment for marine ship transmitters: measurements using a new data collection method and comparison with ICNIRP and ARPANSA limits. *Int J Environ Res Public Health* 12(5):5338–5354. DOI: 10.3390/ijerph120505338.

ICNIRP [International Commission on Non-Ionizing Radiation Protection]. 1998. Guidelines for limiting exposure to time-varying electric, magnetic, and electromagnetic fields (up to 300 GHz). *Health Phys* 74(4):494–522.

ICNIRP [International Commission on Non-Ionizing Radiation Protection]. 2009. Guidelines on limits of exposure to static magnetic fields. *Health Phys* 96(4):504–514. DOI: 10.1097/01.HP.0000343164.27920.4a.

ICNIRP [International Commission on Non-Ionizing Radiation Protection]. 2010. Guidelines for limiting exposure to time-varying electric and magnetic fields (1 Hz – 100 kHz). *Health Phys* 99(6):818–836. DOI: 10.1097/HP.0b013e3181f06c86.

ICNIRP [International Commission on Non-Ionizing Radiation Protection]. 2014. Guidelines for limiting exposure to electric fields induced by movement of the human body in a static magnetic field and by time-varying magnetic fields below 1 Hz. *Health Phys* 106(3):418–425. DOI: 10.1097/HP.0b013e31829e5580.

ICNIRP [International Commission on Non-Ionizing Radiation Protection]. 2020. Guidelines for limiting exposure to electromagnetic fields (100 kHz to 300 GHz). *Health Phys* 118(5):483–524. DOI: 10.1097/HP.0000000000001210.

Joseph, W., F. Goeminne, G. Vermeeren, L. Verloock, and L. Martens. 2012a. In situ exposure to non-directional beacons for air traffic control. *Bioelectromagnetics* 33(3):274–277. DOI: 10.1002/bem.21706.

Joseph, W., F. Goeminne, G. Vermeeren, L. Verloock, and L. Martens. 2012b. Occupational and public field exposure from communication, navigation, and radar systems used for air traffic control. *Health Phys* 103(6):750–62. DOI: 10.1097/HP.0b013e31825f78d5.

Kangarlu, A., and P.M.L. Robitaille. 2000. Biological effects and health implications in magnetic resonance imaging. *Concepts in Magnetic Resonance* 12(5):321–359. DOI: 10.1002/1099-0534(2000)12:5<321::AID-CMR4>3.0.CO;2-J

Karpowicz, J., and K. Gryz. 2013a. The pattern of exposure to static magnetic field of nurses involved in activities related to contrast administration into patients diagnosed in 1.5 T MRI scanners. *Electromagn Biol Med* 32(2):182–191. DOI: 10.3109/15368378.2013.776428.

Karpowicz, J., and K. Gryz. 2013b. Experimental evaluation of ballistic hazards in imaging diagnostic center. *Pol J Radiol* 78(2):31–37. DOI: 10.12659/PJR.883943.

Korpinen, L., H. Kuisti, R. Pääkkönen, P. Vanhala and J. Elovaara. 2011. Occupational exposure to electric and magnetic fields while working at switching and transforming stations of 110 kV. *Ann Occup Hyg* 55(5):526–536. DOI:10.1093/annhyg/mer013.

McRobbie D. 2012. Occupational exposure in MRI. *Br J Radiol* 85(1012):293–312. DOI: 10.1259/bjr/30146162.

NIOSH [National Institute for Occupational Safety and Health], 2023. NIOSH- hierarchy of controls. https://www.cdc.gov/niosh/topics/hierarchy/default.html (accessed April 3, 2023).

Osei, S., J.K. Amoako, and J.J. Fletcher. 2016. Assessment of levels of occupational exposure to workers in radiofrequency fields of two television stations in Accra, Ghana. *Radiat Prot Dosimetry* 168(3):419–426. DOI: 10.1093/rpd/ncv326.

OSHA [Occupational Safety and Health Administration]. 2016. *Recommended Practices for Safety and Health Programs*. Washington: OSHA. https://www.osha.gov/sites/default/files/publications/OSHA3885.pdf (accessed on June 20, 2022).

Politański, P., H. Aniołczyk, E. Gadzicka, A. Bortkiewicz, and M. Zmyślony. 2018. Electromagnetic fields exposure assessment among workers at broadcast centers in Poland. *Med Pr* 69(5):477–482. DOI: 10.13075/mp.5893.00685.

Roivainen, P., T. Eskelinen, K. Jokela, and J. Juutilainen. 2014. Occupational exposure to intermediate frequency and extremely low frequency magnetic fields among personnel working near electronic article surveillance systems. *Bioelectromagnetics* 35(4):245–250. DOI: 10.1002/bem.21850.

SCENIHR [Scientific Committee on Emerging and Newly Identified Health Risks]. 2015. *Opinion on Potential Health Effects of Exposure to Electromagnetic Fields (EMF)*. Luxembourg: European Commission. http://ec.europa.eu/health/sites/health/files/scientific_committees/emerging/docs/scenihr_o_041.pdf (accessed June 20, 2022).

Shah, S.G., and A. Farrow. 2013. Assessment of physiotherapists' occupational exposure to radiofrequency electromagnetic fields from shortwave and microwave diathermy devices: a literature review. *J Occup Environ Hyg* 10(6):312–327. DOI: 10.1080/15459624.2013.782203.

Sobiech, J., J. Kieliszek, R. Puta, D. Bartczak, and W. Stankiewicz. 2017. Occupational exposure to electromagnetic fields in the Polish Armed Forces. *Int J Occup Med Environ Health* 30(4):565–577. DOI: 10.13075/ijomeh.1896.00696.

Teşneli, N.B., and A.Y. Teşneli. 2014. Occupational exposure to electromagnetic fields of uninterruptible power supply industry workers. *Radiat Prot Dosimetry* 162(3):289–298. DOI: 10.1093/rpd/nct340.

Valič, B., B. Kos, and P. Gajšek. 2012. Occupational exposure assessment on an FM mast: electric field and SAR values. *Int J Occup Saf Ergon* 18(2):149–159. DOI: 10.1080/10803548.2012.11076924.

Walker, M., A. Fultz, C. Davies, and D. Brockopp. 2020. Symptoms experienced by MR technologists exposed to static magnetic fields. *Radiol Technol* 91(4): 316–323.

Yamaguchi-Sekino, S. and T. Okuno. 2014. Example of measurement of magnetic fields generated by industrial machines. JNIOSH special research report (SRR). SRR-No.44-2-1. (in Japanese).

Yamaguchi-Sekino, S., T. Nakai, S. Imai, S. Izawa, and T. Okuno. 2014. Occupational exposure levels of static magnetic field during routine MRI examination in 3T MR system. *Bioelectromagnetics* 35(1):70–75. DOI: 10.1002/bem.21817.

Yamaguchi-Sekino, S., M. Sekino, and T. Nakai. 2015. Effectiveness of safe working procedure on SMF exposure levels and work performances in 3 T MRI system operations. *IEEE Trans Magn* 51(11):5000904. DOI: 10.1109/INTMAG.2015.7157570.

Zilberti, L., O. Bottauscio, and M. Chiampi. 2016. Assessment of exposure to MRI motion-induced fields based on the International Commission on Non-Ionizing Radiation Protection (ICNIRP) guidelines. *Magn Reson Med* 76(4):1291–1300. DOI: 10.1002/mrm.26031.

Zoppetti, N., A. Bogi, I. Pinto, and D. Andreuccetti. 2015. Evaluation of human exposure to complex waveform magnetic fields generated by arc-welding equipment according to European safety standards. *Radiat Prot Dosimetry* 163(3):292–305. DOI:10.1093/rpd/ncu188.

12 Occupational Exposure to the Electromagnetic Field and Precautionary Approaches to Health Issues

Kjell Hansson Mild
Umeå University

CONTENTS

12.1 INTRODUCTION

Many occupations may entail quite high exposure to electromagnetic field (EMF), especially those that involve work near electrical equipment that uses a large amount of electric power, for example, welding equipment, induction heaters, radiofrequency

DOI: 10.1201/9781003020486-12

heaters and sealers, glue dryers or magnetic resonance imaging machines (Hansson Mild et al., 2009). International guidelines and legislation (ICNIRP, 1998, 2010, 2020; EU directive, 2013) for EMF are set in order to ensure that the field humans experience is not harmful to health. At present, they are based on the current scientific knowledge on the prevention of acute effects. Exposure to intense low-frequency electric and magnetic fields may cause nerve excitation due to the induced current in tissue (recognised as acute effects at low-frequency EMF exposure). The uncontrolled excitation of the central and peripheral nervous system is of special concern. Nerve excitation by using an intense magnetic field is used for therapeutic purposes in electromedicine; but it is not something one would want to occur uncontrolled in the working environment. In addition, exposure to intense microwaves may lead to heating the body, or parts thereof, in a way that would be hazardous to health (recognised as acute effects at high-frequency EMF exposure). The heating effect of microwaves is also used in electromedicine in the form of shortwave and microwave diathermy; but, in order to prevent unwanted heating in the working environment, the guidelines limit the exposure levels so that heating does not occur.

The guideline limits incorporate a large safety margin with respect to the thresholds of these acute effects and therefore do not represent a precise delineation between safety and hazardous. Normal exposure levels are in most cases much lower than the guideline limits. However, concerns have been expressed about health and safety from occupational exposure to EMFs present below guidelines, and a precautionary step might be advisable. This chapter offers some examples of such measures and their justification.

12.1.1 What is known about the Health Effects of EMFs?

The World Health Organisation (WHO) and national agencies are continuing to evaluate the health risks of exposure to EMF. Scientific studies have reported various biological effects from exposure to EMF at intensities lower than those permitted with regard to preventing acute effects, for example, limits issued by the International Commission on Non-ionizing Radiation Protection (ICNIRP) guidelines and the European Union (EU) directive. However, these effects are measurable reactions to exposure and are not necessarily harmful to health in every case of exposure. Some studies suggest that the effects are associated with intensity and frequency 'windows'. See further for a recent update of the report from the Scientific Committee on Emerging and Newly Identified Health Risks (SCENIHR, 2015).

Epidemiological studies, particularly regarding EMF in the low-frequency range, have been reviewed by several different health agencies. Many studies report small increases in leukaemia or brain cancer in groups of people living or working in magnetic field of extremely low frequency (ELF) with an intensity above about 0.4 μT. Several studies also associated workplace EMFs with breast cancer, and some have suggested a possible link between occupational EMF exposure and Alzheimer's disease. Recent clinical studies have reported that EMF can cause heart rate variability and sleep disturbance, see further SCENIHR (2015).

The United States (US) National Institute for Environmental Health Sciences (NIEHS, 1999) concluded about the risk of children developing leukaemia, '*ELF*

EMF exposure cannot be recognized as entirely safe because of weak scientific evidence that exposure may pose a leukemia hazard'. The WHO cancer expert agency IARC (International Agency for Research on Cancer) evaluated magnetic field and cancer (IARC, 2002), and made the classification as IIB, which means that ELF magnetic field is considered to be a possible carcinogen to humans.

In the Netherlands, the Committee on Electromagnetic Fields of the Health Council has recently analysed the scientific data on a possible relationship between exposure to low-frequency magnetic fields and the occurrence of various types of cancer in adults. They found an association between occupational exposure and the risk of developing male breast cancer, brain cancer and pancreatic cancer. The committee considers the associations found in the workplace to be suggestive of a causal relationship between occupational exposure and these types of cancer. As a precaution, it, therefore, recommends restricting occupational exposure to magnetic fields to as low a level as is reasonably possible (Health Council, 2022a).

This Committee also analysed the scientific data on a possible relationship between exposure to magnetic fields and the occurrence of neurodegenerative diseases. For occupational exposure, the committee found indications suggesting an increased risk of ALS and Alzheimer's disease. As a precaution, it therefore recommends restricting occupational exposure to magnetic fields to as low a level as is reasonably possible (Health Council, 2022b).

In addition, epidemiological reports on radiofrequency (RF) field have suggested associations between exposure at levels lower than the limits and some adverse health effects. The question of health hazards related to the use of mobile phone has been debated since the mid-1990s. At first, the problems were subjective symptoms associated with the use of a mobile phone, for instance, headache, dizziness, fatigue, heating behind the ear, burning face, etc., see further Oftedal et al. (2000) and Sandström et al. (2001). Wilén et al. (2004) were able to show that some of the symptoms were correlated with phones with high-energy deposition measured as the Specific Absorption Rate in Watt/kg (SAR) in combination with a longer calling time per day.

A problem still being hotly discussed is the possible connection between the use of mobile phones and brain tumours. We published our first study on this in 1999 (Hardell et al., 1999), and since then several other studies have been published. In 2011, IARC evaluated the studies on cancer and mobile phone use and, based on our own study Hardell et al. (2013a,b,c), Hardell and Carlberg (2015) and the international study Interphone (Cardis et al., 2011) along with some studies related to occupational RF exposure, decided to classify 'Radiofrequency Electromagnetic Fields' (RF-EMF) as possibly carcinogenic to humans (Group IIB) (IARC, 2013). The epidemiological studies on cell phone use reported a slightly increased risk for glioma (a malignant form of brain cancer) and acoustic neuroma (a non-cancerous type) among heavy users. Although the key information came from mobile telephone use, IARC considered that the three types of exposure entail basically the same type of radiation, and the classification holds for all types of radiation within the RF part of the electromagnetic spectrum, including the radiation emitted by base-station antennas, radio/TV towers, radar, Wi-Fi, smart metres.

Since then, two large animal studies on occurrence of tumours and RF exposure to rats and mice have been published. In the US, the National Toxicology Program

(NTP, 2018) announced that male rats exposed to EMF (at level comparable to the ICNIRP general public exposure limit), such as cell phone radiation, developed higher rates of cancer. The same RF/microwave radiation that led male rats to develop brain tumours also caused DNA breaks in their brains. In Italy, Falcioni et al. (2018) studied brain and heart tumours in Sprague-Dawley rats that had been exposed from their prenatal life until their natural death to EMF with characteristic like a mobile phone RF field. They found an increased incidence of tumours in the brain and heart in RF-EMF-exposed rats.

In our studies of the risk of malignant brain tumours in children in association with their mobile phone use, Hardell et al. (2004) reported that, for the age group 20-29 years, this risk with a >5 year latency for analogue phones was OR = 8.17, 95% CI = 0.94 – 71, and for cordless phones OR = 4.30, 95% CI = 1.22-15. The large CI was due to a low number of cases and controls. This was later followed up by Hardell et al. (2011), and with a larger number of cases and controls. It was found that the risk of astrocytoma was highest in the group with the first use of a wireless phone before the age of 20; mobile phone use OR = 4.9, 95% CI = 2.2-11, cordless phone use OR = 3.9, 95% CI = 1.7-8.7. In conclusion, an increased risk was found for glioma and the use of a mobile or cordless phone. The risk increased with latency time and cumulative use in hours, and was the highest in subjects with first use before the age of 20.

These findings indicate that it is of special importance to apply a precautionary approach when it comes to children's use of mobile phones. Markov and Grigoriev (2015) noted that and pointed out that children and teenagers tend to 'need' to communicate 24 hours a day. There is clearly a need to read the manual and not hold the phone directly to the head, and use a headset. In the manual it is said that the testing of the phone is done at a distance between 5 and 25 mm from the head in order to satisfy the SAR values allowed for mobile phones, see further Gandhi (2019).

These new developments have led to an advisory committee recommending that the IARC reassesses the cancer risks associated with RF radiation. This should be a 'high priority', according to the panel's report (Advisory group, 2019). See also Lin (2018).

The problem of setting exposure limits for EMF based on low-level effect is that the interaction mechanisms are not well understood, especially concerning weak field and non-thermal effects. Since concepts like *exposure* and *dose* (the measure of cumulative or long-term EMF influence) are not clearly defined, and we do not know the priorities on what to avoid, is it the time derivative for the magnetic field intensity or the rms value (root mean square), peak SAR or mean value? So which factor is of most importance to consider? Most epidemiological studies of health effects have measured the dose using various forms of mean values of exposure, such as the time average of the magnetic field during a working day or over 24 hours. Others have used the highest value found in a day as a measure. Only a few studies have attempted to create a dose in the form of an integration of exposure over time, such as in the form of microtesla-hours. We do not know, however, what the correct dimension is, that is, is an exposure to 20 μT for 0.5 h equivalent to 0.5 μT for 20 h? Is the EMF health effect linearly dependent on the 'dose', or is it, as in many biological contexts, a non-linear relationship? Should various frequencies—basic tones and harmonics—be included when assessing the weighted average of a dose? Before these fundamental questions about what constitutes a 'dose' in these contexts is better understood, our risk assessment will be more or less arbitrary when it comes to long-term health effects from EMF influence. See further Hansson Mild and Mattsson (2017).

Taking this into account, the only way is to avoid unnecessary exposure to EMF in all its forms by applying a low-cost precautionary approach to the exposure situation at hand.

12.2 THE PRECAUTIONARY PRINCIPLE

Research is continuing in many countries into possible health effects from EMF exposure, and it should be reflected in the exposure guidelines when new results are at hand. However, science cannot, in principle, prove absolute safety, so any risk assessment is, by definition, associated with some degree of uncertainty. While science provides the starting point for assessing risks, a decision on what constitutes an acceptable risk is essentially a value judgement. It has been suggested that 'better safe than sorry' approaches (which means taking precautionary measures in order to cope with the remaining uncertainties) might be useful as a substitute for absolute assurance, given existing weak evidence of a health risk. The type of precautionary approach chosen critically depends on the strength of evidence for a health risk, and the scale and nature of the potential consequences.

What should people who are concerned about EMF potential health effects from long-term exposure do while scientists seek to improve information? A cautious, 'better safe than sorry', approach is intuitively obvious, and both socially and politically attractive. What are examples of such approaches? How do they apply to concerns about EMF?

The Precautionary Principle (PP) is a term used to characterise a 'better safe than sorry' attitude towards potentially hazardous technologies that has already appeared in many international environmental treaties. For the countries of the EU, the PP was explicitly enshrined in the Treaty of Maastricht treaty. In Title XVI, it states that 'Community policy on the environment shall contribute to....protecting human health...' and '...shall be based on the precautionary principle...' (Article 191 point 2, replaced by Article 174 point 2 of the Lisbon Treaty) As part of the declaration signed at the 1999 Third Ministerial Conference on Environment and Health, the WHO was encouraged to take into account 'the need to rigorously apply the PP in assessing risks and to adopt a more preventive, proactive approach to hazards'. The PP itself remains undefined. It has been interpreted to require prudent action to be taken when there is sufficient scientific evidence (but not necessarily absolute proof) that inaction could lead to harm and where action can be justified on reasonable judgements of cost effectiveness. An interpretation of the Treaty requirements in any particular case evolves as it is applied. Sometimes this evolution takes place in the courts of law. For further details, see Science for Environment Policy EC (2017).

In the case of EMFs, applying the PP is particularly problematic. It is not clear which aspect of exposure, that is, duration or field intensity, should be limited. Furthermore, the matter of whether there is 'sufficient scientific evidence' that exposure to EMF could lead to harm remains subject to debate. In the absence of established risk factors, cost effectiveness is impossible to demonstrate. However, making assumptions about existing risks, a risk–benefit analysis can and has been performed.

12.3 PRUDENT AVOIDANCE

The concept of 'Prudent Avoidance' was initially developed in the US by Nair et al. (1989), specifically in the context of concerns about EMF and as a precautionary approach distinct from ALARA (As Low as Reasonably Achievable). It has since gained wider recognition, for instance, early on in Sweden and later elsewhere in the world. Although it is widely agreed that the potential health risk from low-level EMF exposure is small, it is difficult to quantify. Therefore, many people feel that, until additional research has been completed to provide better information about possible health consequences, people should lower their exposure to EMF. Simply put, Prudent Avoidance means taking simple, easily achievable, low-cost measures to reduce EMF exposure, even in the absence of a demonstrable risk. The terms 'simple', 'easily achievable' and 'low cost' are not defined.

Prudent Avoidance was initially proposed for the actions of individuals, whereas the PP could be interpreted as a regulatory measure. See also Dolan et al. (1998) and Sahl and Dolan (1996).

12.4 HOW HAVE POLICIES PROMOTING CAUTION BEEN APPLIED?

One way is to try to put the recommended actions into perspective by establishing priorities. For example, the Swedish Radiation Protection Agency stated in their policy about EMF that countermeasures with regard to EMF exposure are considered to have lower priority than steps taken in radiation protection areas, such as radon, natural UV radiation, leakage from nuclear power plants and radiation from medical use of radioactive sources. Countermeasures to magnetic fields are considered to have the same priority as countermeasures in areas like dental and veterinary radiography, and industrial use of radioactive sources. Thus, provided the cost is reasonable, protective measures should be considered in order to protect people from high magnetic field exposures of long duration. They recommend working towards the design or location of new power lines and electrical installations so as to limit exposure to magnetic field, avoid locating new housing, schools and pre-schools in close proximity to electrical installations generating elevated magnetic field.

A high magnetic field is considered to exist if the values are ten or more times what can be considered as 'normal' for that particular type of environment.

See further at: http://www.ssm.se. For mobile phones, they state that reducing unnecessary exposure is justified. This can be done, for example, by using hands-free equipment or the speakerphone setting.

12.5 EXAMPLES OF PRECAUTIONARY APPROACHES IN OCCUPATIONAL EXPOSURE

Just as individuals can exercise Prudent Avoidance, government regulators, electric power companies and other companies where EMF exposure may occur, can also exercise prudence. Some examples are given here, divided into two different categories according to EMF frequencies; first we will deal with the ELF range and then with RF field (or microwaves).

12.5.1 ELF

Certain occupations are associated with high-field exposures. The Swedish Trade Union Confederation (LO) had a demand that all workplaces should be surveyed for ELF magnetic field and practical measures should be taken to reduce high exposures so that no worker will be exposed to more than 0.2 μT as an average over the workday. This can be achieved by, for instance, marking out zones, reducing magnetic field, relocating workplaces and having an altered organisation of work. They, along with the National Institute of Environmental Health Sciences in the US, also encourage manufacturers of electric appliances to consider alternatives that reduce magnetic field at a minimal cost. In the European standard (EN 12198-1), the emission of EMF from machines was taken. The manufacturer of machines should label them according the levels of emissions:

- Level 0: No restrictions
- Level 1: Only for use by professionals
- Level 2: Where special working instructions are needed to avoid overexposure

The Swedish National Board of Occupational Health and Safety (AV, 1995), now the Swedish Work Environment Authority), together with four other Swedish authorities, issued a text for applying the PP to ELF magnetic field exposure. They jointly recommend the following:

> If measures generally reducing exposure can be taken at reasonable expense and with reasonable consequences in all other respects, an effort should be made to reduce field radically deviating from what could be deemed normal in the environment concerned. Where new electrical installations and buildings are concerned, efforts should be made already at the planning stage to design and position them in such a way that exposure is limited.

For an individual who is concerned about possible health effects, the first step is to try to get as much information as possible about the workplace and the possible exposure to EMF that exists. The most efficient way of reducing exposure is to increase the distance to the EMF sources. Since the magnetic field often drops off dramatically about 1 m from the source, workers can stand back from electrical equipment, and work stations can be moved out of the 1 m range of stronger EMF sources. One should also use a low EMF design wherever possible. One should also look for the possibility of reducing the EMF exposure times.

Anti-theft devices can emit localised field in excess of the given reference values (guidelines) and, therefore, a precautionary approach could be used to keep a distance from these apparatuses. This should also be considered when planning new workplaces. For further information, see the report by Bernhardt et al. (2002).

12.5.2 RF Exposure

Most guidelines for occupational exposures state that exposure should be kept low and must not exceed the limit values. However, in many situations there may be a very fine distinction between being within the limits or above them. Therefore, with respect to this kind of work, it is perhaps of even more importance to apply a PP in order to stay within the limits.

This is especially true for work near RF dielectric heaters, and sealers and glue dryers, where RF exposure is strong and very heterogeneous. Here, it is very important to strictly adhere to a good work practice, including maintenance and operating procedures. Improper maintenance may lead to excess EMF leakage from the machine, and small changes in the near environment may also lead to higher exposure levels. In an International Labour Office (ILO, 1998) several practical examples are given for the application of shielding devices and effects on ground planes and reflectors on operator exposure. Eriksson and Hansson Mild (1985) and Wilén et al. (2004) have done extensive measurements of EMF near RF sealers, and Adair et al. (1999) also gives useful information about the exposure near sealers.

For most people, the most common source of RF exposure is connected with the mobile phone use. Concerned individuals can take a few simple steps to minimise potential risks. Time is a key factor in how much exposure a person receives. People who must conduct extended conversations every day could switch to a type of mobile phone that places more distance between their bodies and the source of the RF, since the field strengths drop off dramatically with distance. For example, they could switch to a headset (hands-free device) and carry the mobile phone at the waist or in the hand, or use conventional phones.

The mobile phone industry needs to start designing mobile phones in such a way that it minimises the user's exposure to any RF fields that are not necessary for the device's function.

It is known that the differences between various makes and models with respect to the SAR values can be twentyfold or more. A precautionary approach would be to buy a phone with a low value, rather than the one that only just meets the recommended standard. Choosing a mobile with a low SAR value is also beneficial from the point of view of communication: the low-SAR phone does not need to upregulate the power as much as a high-SAR device, and hence longer battery life and longer reach is achieved.

Gandhi (2019) recently published a paper discussing how the mobile phones exceed the SAR limits when held close to the body. When held against the body, most mobile phones will exceed the safety guidelines by factors of 1.6–3.7 times for the European/ICNIRP guidelines (local SAR averaged over 10 g of tissue) or by factors as high as 11 if SAR values were to be measured and averaged over 1 g of tissues, as required by the US FCC (Federal Communication Commission). This is also reflected in the manual for the phones, where you can read in the fine print that the phones have been tested at a distance of 0.5–2.5 cm from the body in order to meet the exposure standards! Gandhi points out that, in spite of the manufacturer's recommendations, he finds it hard to believe that one can carry out a conversation when the telephone is held up to 25 mm away from the ear canal.

12.6 APPROACHES TO REDUCING EMF EXPOSURE

12.6.1 Individuals

Individuals may want to reduce their exposure to EMF, because they fear that there are health consequence if they do not. In this case, it is an individual's responsibility to take whatever measures they feel are appropriate to their situation and circumstances.

12.6.1.1 Electric Power

Most people spend a significant part of their time at their workstation. Examples of Prudent Avoidance may then include repositioning electrical equipment in the work space, such as a computer or UPS, or moving to an area with a lower magnetic field within the same room. Similar actions may be taken at other places where individuals spend extended periods.

The US National Institute for Environmental Health Sciences (NIEHS, 2002) says in their educational booklet:

> Although scientists are still debating whether EMF is a hazard to health, the NIEHS recommends continued education on ways of reducing exposures. This booklet has identified some EMF sources and some simple steps you can take to limit your exposure.

Then they continue and give some advice on how to reduce exposure:

> Magnetic fields from appliances decrease dramatically about an arm's length away from the source. In many cases, rearranging a bed, a chair, or a work area to increase your distance from an electrical panel or some other EMF source can reduce your EMF exposure. ... Sometimes electrical wiring in a house or a building can be the source of strong magnetic field exposure. Incorrect wiring is a common source of higher-than-usual magnetic fields.

However, they also indicate that other more costly actions such as burying power lines, moving out of a building or restricting the use of office might not be warranted.

12.6.1.2 Welding

In welding, there are some simple things that can be done to reduce the exposure. When the workplace is designed, make sure to maximise the distance between the welder, the power source and the welding equipment. Place the equipment on the right/left side of the welder, as he is right or left handed; this is in order not to have the cable wrapped or draped around the body. In an electric arc, route the electrode/torch and current return cable together. The photo presents an example of weld-fume reduction equipment fixed with the welding electrode supplying cable (Figure 12.1). This way of using them caused a significant reduction in their distance from the welder's body and increase in exposure to the magnetic field. That unnecessary magnetic field exposure could be easily avoided by having both the items of equipment (electric supplying of the electrode and fume ventilation) properly mechanically supported separately.

12.6.2 National Authorities

In 1999, New Zealand issued a standard for electromagnetic field in the RF range that complies with the guidelines recommended by the ICNIRP. The Ministry of Health and the Ministry of the Environment make it clear that it is essential to ensure the credibility of the standard and agree that 'there are no established adverse effects from exposures to RF field that comply with the ICNIRP guidelines and the New Zealand standards'. However, in view of the **residual scientific uncertainty,** they advocate the application of low- or no-cost interventions to minimise unnecessary RF exposure. This should not be done in an arbitrary way. However, if alternative

FIGURE 12.1 An example of weld-fume reduction equipment fixed with the welding electrode supplying cable, causing increased unnecessary magnetic field exposure of the welder.

options are available, for example when designing or locating a radio transmitter, the one resulting in the lowest incidental exposures should be chosen, all other things being equal. Furthermore, the telecommunications industry is encouraged to voluntarily minimise EMF emissions by mobile phones and their base stations, as a means of demonstrating to the public that it is in their own business interest to reduce exposure.

12.6.3 Company Actions

12.6.3.1 Electric Power

If companies want to practice a policy of Prudent Avoidance, there are many strategies that can be pursued. Power companies, for example, when designing or routing new transmission lines, can use the following (Figure 12.2):

- Design conductor configuration to minimise EMF.
- Reverse-phase conductors in double-circuit lines to minimise magnetic field by cancellation.
- Locating lines to limit exposure in areas of concentrated population, including schools, day care centres and hospitals, and widening right-of-way corridors.
- Electrical substations inside buildings can cause substantial exposure to magnetic field and should be sited in a way to minimise long-term exposure.

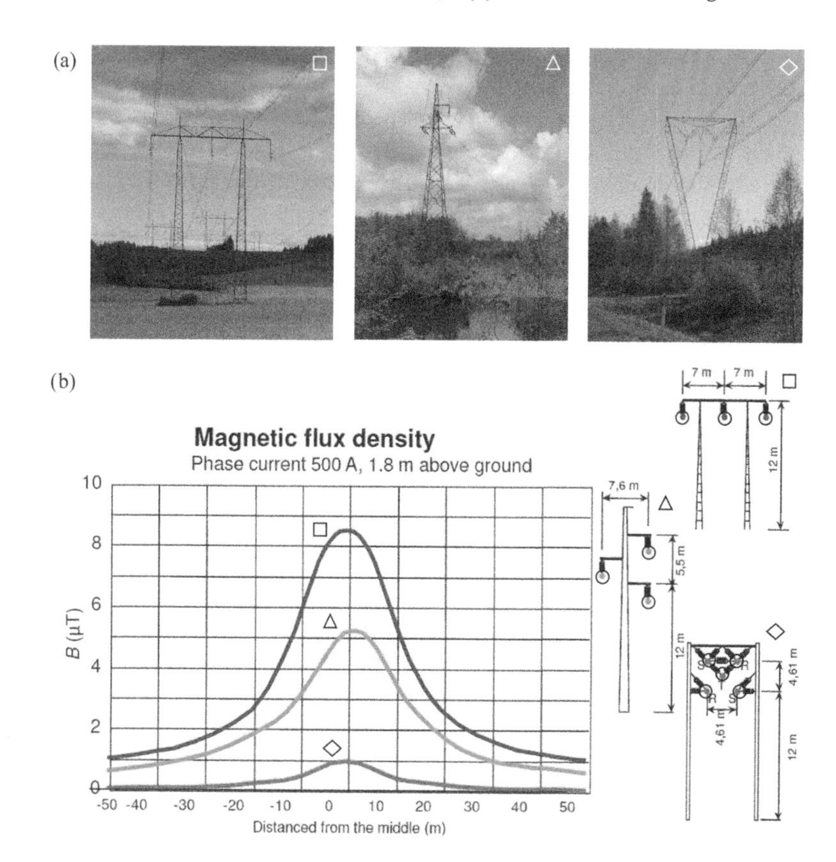

FIGURE 12.2 Variability of magnetic field near the high-voltage power lines with different configuration of conductors for high-voltage power lines: (a) examples of different configuration of high-voltage phase conductors; (b) calculations of the magnetic field under a power line for three different line configurations. Note that, with the triangular configuration, almost a tenfold reduction is obtained as compared to the normal with all three phases on the same height; this is beneficial both for the people living nearby or workers that have to spend time under the line. See further Greenebaum and Hansson Mild (2018).

12.6.3.2 Mobile Telecommunications

Radiofrequency levels near base stations encountered by the general public are low and amount to a small fraction of international guideline limits. RF from distant TV and radio transmitters are higher than those from nearby mobile phone masts. Therefore, base stations in general do not require a precautionary approach with respect to public exposure. However, because of local sensitivity to the issue, authorities may consider recommending that new mobile telephone base stations or masts be sited away from schools and day care centres.

12.6.3.3 Dielectric Heaters

Working near dielectric heater, such as a plastic welding machine or a glue dryer, it is important to consider that the working frequency is around 27 MHz. This is close to the resonance frequency for a standing man in contact with high-frequency ground. Thus, if the operator is standing on a reinforced concrete floor, they will be absorbing substantially more RF energy than if they were free standing (insulated from ground). It is often only necessary to separate the distance from the floor by a few centimetres, so a wooden platform would make a large difference in RF influence. This is a simple measure to apply in order to reduce the exposure. However, it is important not to make the separation distance from the ground too large, because then the ergonomics will be a problem.

12.7 INFORMATION NEEDS

To be able to act prudently, individuals need a better understanding of the sources of EMF, in order to identify the options available to limit their exposure. Education material on EMF provides this kind of information, and gives people and organisations the opportunity to make such informed choices.

The public exposure to RF is increasingly dominated by mobile phone use. However, in occupational settings, high exposures sometimes occur, and here information about the sources and various factors that may influence the exposure levels is needed, in order for the employers and workers to be able to act prudently. This information should be included in the instructions and the maintenance practice at each workplace.

During the last couple of decades, several new technologies have been introduced into our everyday life, for instance, mobile phones and wireless technology, though often without proper information about the technology and its possible consequences. This lack of information has raised concerns among people who feel that the new technologies were imposed on them. Those who suffer from ill health of unknown cause often blame EMF. In the future, we will see many more new developments and applications that will lead to some increases in our everyday exposure to EMF. Therefore, it is of considerable importance to devote sufficient resources to informing the people about EMF and its possible effects on human health.

REFERENCES

Adair, E., J. Bergeron, C. K. Chou et al. 1999. Human exposure to electric and magnetic fields from RF sealers and dielectric heaters: A COMAR technical information statement. *IEEE Eng Med Biol Mag* 18(1):88–90.

Advisory group recommendations on prioritites for the IARC monographs. 2019. *Lancet Oncol* 20(6):763–764. DOI: 10.1016/S1470–2045(19)30246–3.

Bernhardt, J., A. F. McKinlay, and R. Matthes (eds.). 2002. *Possible Health Risk to the General Public from the Use of Security and Similar Devices*. Oberschleissheim: ICNIRP.

Cardis, E., B.K. Armstrong, J.D. Bowman et al. 2011. Risk of brain tumours in relation to estimated RF dose from mobile phones: results from five Interphone countries. *Occup Environ Med* 68(9):631–640. DOI: 10.1136/oemed-2011-100155.

Directive 2013/35/EU. 2013. Directive of the European Parliament and of the Council of 26 June 2013 on the Minimum Health And Safety Requirements Regarding The Exposure Of Workers To The Risks Arising From Physical Agents (Electromagnetic Fields) (20th

Individual Directive within the Meaning of Article 16(1) of Directive 89/391/EEC). *Official Journal of the European Union* O.J. No. L-179 of 29 June 2013, 1–21, Brussels, Belgium.

Dolan, M., K. Nuttall, P. Flanagan, and G. Melik. 1998. The application of prudent avoidance in EMF risk management. In *EMF, Risk Perception and Communication: Proceedings Int. Seminar, Ottawa, Ontario, Canada, 31 Au. – 1 Sept. l998,* eds. M. H. Repacholi, and A. M. Muc, 281–308. Geneva: WHO [World Health Organization].

EN 12198-1:2000. 2000. *Safety of Machinery: Assement and Reduction of Risks Arising from Radiation Emitted by Machinery, Part 1: General Principles.* Brussels: CENELEC [European Committee for Electrotechnical Standardization].

Eriksson, A., and K. Hansson Mild. 1985. Radiofrequency electromagnetic leakage fields from plastic welding machines. Measurements and reducing measures. *J Microwave Power* 20(2):95–107. DOI: 10.1080/16070658.1985.11720296.

Falcioni, L., L. Bua, E. Tibaldi et al. 2018. Report of final results regarding brain and heart tumors in Sprague-Dawley rats exposed from prenatal life until natural death to mobile phone radiofrequency field representative of a 1.8 GHz GSM base station environmental emission. *Environ Res* 165:496–503. DOI: 10.1016/j.envres.2018.01.037.

Gandhi, O. 2019. Microwave emissions from cell phones exceed safety limits in Europe and the US when touching the body. *IEEE Access* 7:47050–47052. DOI: 10.1109/ACCESS.2019.2906017.

Greenebaum, B., and K. Hansson Mild. 2018. Environmental and occupational DC and low frequency electromagnetic fields. In: *Bioengineering and Biophysical Aspects of Electromagnetic Fields*, eds. B. Greenebaum and F. Barnes, 29–53. Boca Raton: CRC Press.

Hansson Mild, K., and M. O. Mattsson. 2017. Dose and exposure in bioelectromagnetics. In: *Dosimetry in Bioelectromagnetics*, ed. M. Markov, 101–118. Boca Raton, FL: CRC Press.

Hansson Mild, K., T. Alanko, G. Decat et al. 2009. Exposure of workers to electromagnetic fields: a review of open questions on exposure assessment techniques. *Int J Occup Saf Ergon* 15(1):3–33. DOI: 10.1080/10803548.2009.11076785.

Hardell, L., A. Näsman, A. Påhlsson, A. Hallquist, and K. Hansson Mild. 1999. Use of cellular telephones and the risk for brain tumours: a case-control study. *Int J Oncol* 15(1):113–116.

Hardell, L., K. Hansson Mild, M. Carlberg, and A. Hallquist. 2004. Cellular and cordless telephones and the association with brain tumours in different age group. *Arch Environ Health* 59(3):132–137. DOI: 10.3200/AEOH.59.3.132-137.

Hardell, L., M. Carlberg, and K. Hansson Mild. 2011. Pooled analysis of case-control studies on malignant brain tumours and the use of mobile and cordless phones including living and deceased subjects. *Int J Oncol* 38(5):1465–1474. DOI: 10.3892/ijo.2011.947.

Hardell, L., M. Carlberg, and K. Hansson Mild. 2013a. Use of mobile phones and cordless phones is associated with increased risk for glioma and acoustic neuroma. *Pathophysiology* 20(2):85–110. DOI: 10.1016/j.pathophys.2012.11.001.

Hardell, L., M. Carlberg, F. Söderqvist, and K. Hansson Mild. 2013b. Case-control study of the association between malignant brain tumours diagnosed between 2007 and 2009 and mobile and cordless phone use. *Int J Oncol* 43(6):1833–1845. DOI: 10.3892/ijo.2013.2111.

Hardell, L., M. Carlberg, F. Söderqvist, and K. Hansson Mild. 2013c. Pooled analysis of case-controls studies an acoustic neuroma diagnosed 1997-2003 and 2007-2009 and use of mobile and cordless phones. *Int J Oncol* 43(4): 1036–1044. DOI: 10.3892/ijo.2013.2025.

Hardell, L., and M. Carlberg. 2015. Mobile phone and cordless phone use and the risk for glioma: Analysis of pooled case-control studies in Sweden, 1997-2003 and 2007-2009. *Pathophysiology* 22(1):1–13. DOI: 10.1016/j.pathophys.2014.10.001.

Health Council. 2022a. https://www.healthcouncil.nl/documents/advisory-reports/2018/04/18/power-lines-and-health-part-i-childhood-cancer (accessed September 19, 2022).

Health Council. 2022b. https://www.healthcouncil.nl/documents/advisory-reports/2022/06/29/power-lines-and-health-neurodegenerative-diseases (accessed September 19, 2022).

IARC [International Agency for Research on Cancer]. 2002. *IARC Monographs on the Evaluation of Carcinogenic Risks to Humans. Volume 80. Non-Ionizing Radiation, Part 1: Static and Extremely Low-Frequency (ELF) Electric and Magnetic Fields.* Lyon: IARC Press. https://publications.iarc.fr/Book-And-Report-Series/Iarc-Monographs-On-The-Identification-Of-Carcinogenic-Hazards-To-Humans/Non-ionizing-Radiation-Part-1-Static-And-Extremely-Low-frequency-ELF-Electric-And-Magnetic-Fields-2002 (accessed January 20, 2020).

IARC [International Agency for Research on Cancer]. 2013. *IARC Monographs on the Evaluation of Carcinogenic Risks to Humans. Non-Ionizing Radiation, Part 2: Radiofrequency Electromagnetic Fields.* Volume 102. Lyon, France: IARC Press. http://monographs.iarc.fr/ENG/Monographs/vol102/mono102.pdf (accessed January 20, 2020).

ICNIRP [International Commission On Non-Ionizing Radiation Protection]. 1998. Guidelines for limiting exposure to time-varying electric, magnetic, and electromagnetic fields (up to 300 GHz). *Health Phys* 74(4):494–522.

ICNIRP [International Commission On Non-Ionizing Radiation Protection]. 2010. Guidelines for limiting exposure to time-varying electric and magnetic fields (1 Hz to 100 kHz). *Health Phys* 99(6):818–836. DOI: 10.1097/HP.0b013e3181f06c86.

ICNIRP [International Commission on Non-Ionizing Radiation Protection]. 2020. Guidelines for limiting exposure to electromagnetic fields (100 kHz to 300 GHz). *Health Phys* 118(5):483–524. DOI: 10.1097/HP.0000000000001210.

ILO [International Labour Office]. 1998. *Safety in the Use of Radiofrequency Dielectric Heaters and Sealers: A Practical Guide.* Geneva: ILO.

Lin, J. C. 2018. Clear evidence of cell-phone RF radiation cancer risk. *IEEE Microwave Magazine* 19(6):16–24. DOI: 10.1109/MMM.2018.2844058.

Markov, M., and Y. Grigoriev. 2015. Protect children from EMF. *Electromagn Biol Med* 34(3):251–256. DOI: 10.3109/15368378.2015.1077339.

Nair, I., M. G. Morgan, and H. K. Florig. 1989. *Biologic Effects of Power Frequency Electric and Magnetic Fields.* Washington, DC: Congress of the U.S., Office of Technology Assessment. https://www.princeton.edu/~ota/disk1/1989/8905/8905.PDF (accessed January 20, 2020).

NTP [National Toxicology Program]. 2018. Peer review of the draft NTP technical reports on cell phone radiofrequency radiation. https://ntp.niehs.nih.gov/ntp/about_ntp/trpanel/2018/march/peerreview20180328_508.pdf (accessed January 20, 2020).

NIEHS [National Institute of Environmental Health Sciences]. 1999. NIEHS report on health effects from exposure to power-line frequency electric and magnetic fields: Prepared in response to the 1992 Energy Policy Act (PL 102-486, Section 2118). https://www.niehs.nih.gov/health/assets/docs_p_z/report_powerline_electric_mg_predates_508.pdf (accessed January 20, 2020).

NIEHS [National Institute of Environmental Health Sciences]. 2002. NIEHS educational booklet. EMF: Electric and magnetic fields associated with the use of electric power. https://www.niehs.nih.gov/health/topics/agents/emf/index.cfm (accessed December 11, 2019).

Oftedal, G., J. Wilén, M. Sandström, and K. Hansson Mild. 2000. Symptoms experienced in connection with mobile phone use. *Occup Med* 50(4):237–245. DOI: 10.1093/occmed/50.4.237.

Sahl, J., and M. Dolan. 1996. An evaluation of precaution-based approaches as EMF policy tools in community environments. *Environ Health Perspectives* 104(9):908–911. DOI: 10.1289/ehp.96104908.

Sandström, M., J. Wilén, G. Oftedal, and K. Hansson Mild. 2001. Mobile phone use and subjective symptoms: comparison of symptoms experienced by users of analogue and digital phones. *Occup Med* 51(1):25–35. DOI: 10.1093/occmed/51.1.25.

SCENIHR [Scientific Committee on Emerging and Newly Identified Health Risks]. 2015. *Potential Health Effects of Exposure to Electromagnetic Fields (EMF)*. Luxembourg: European Commission. https://ec.europa.eu/health/scientific_committees/emerging/docs/scenihr_o_041.pdf (accessed January 20, 2020).

Science for Environment Policy. European Commission. 2017. *The Precautionary Principle: Decision-Making under Uncertainty*. Future Brief 18. Luxembourg: European Commission. https://ec.europa.eu/environment/integration/research/newsalert/pdf/precautionary_principle_decision_making_under_uncertainty_FB18_en.pdf (accessed January 14, 2020).

The Swedish National Board for Occupational Safety and Health. 1995. Low-frequency electrical and magnetic fields: The precautionary principle for national authorities: Guidance for decision-makers. https://www.osti.gov/etdeweb/servlets/purl/464381 (accessed January 20, 2020).

Wilén, J., R. Hörnsten, M. Sandström et al. 2004. Electromagnetic field exposure and health among RF plastic sealer operators. *Bioelectromagnetics* 25(1):5–15. DOI: 10.1002/bem.10154.

Appendix

LIST OF ABBREVIATIONS

1G	First generation (mobile radiocommunication networks)
2G	Second generation (mobile radiocommunication networks)
3G	Third generation (mobile radiocommunication networks)
4G	Fourth generation (mobile radiocommunication networks)
5G	Fifth generation (mobile radiocommunication networks)
AFH	Adaptive frequency hopping
AIMD(s)	Active implantable medical device(s)
AL(s)	Action level(s)
AR	Augmented reality
ARP	Antenna rotation period
BDR	Basic data rate
BEM	Boundary element method
BLE	Bluetooth low energy
CML	Current Measured at Limb
CW	Continuous wave
EAS	Electronic article surveillance
EC	European Commission
ECG	Electrocardiogram
EDR	Enhanced data rate
EEC	European Economic Community
EEG	Electroencephalograms
EF	Electric field
ELF	Extremely low frequency
ELF-EMF	Extremely-low-frequency electromagnetic field
ELV(s)	Exposure limit value(s)
EM	Electromagnetic
EMBB	Enhanced mobile broadband
EMC	Electromagnetic compatibility
EM-ergonomics	Electromagnetic ergonomics
EMF(s)	Electromagnetic field(s)
EMG	Electromyogram
EMR	Electromagnetic radiation
ERP	Effective radiated power
ESU	Electrosurgical Unit
EU	European Union
FDTD	Finite difference time domain
FIT	Finite integration technique
HetNet	Heterogeneous Networks

HF	High frequency
HPMP	High-power microwave pulses
HSE	Health and Safety Executive (U.K.)
IARC	International Agency for Research on Cancer
ICD(s)	Implantable cardioverter-defibrillator(s)
ICNIRP	International Commission on Non-Ionizing Radiation Protection
ICOH	International Commission on Occupational Health
ICRP	International Commission on Radiological Protection
IEC	International Electrotechnical Commission
IEEE	Institute of Electrical and Electronics Engineers
IEI-EMF	Idiopathic environmental intolerance attributed to electromagnetic fields
ILO	International Labour Organisation
IM	Impedance method
IMT-A	International Mobile Telecommunications-Advanced
IoT	Internet of things
IP	Internet protocol
ISM	Industrial scientific and medical (with respect to EMF frequency)
ITS	Intelligent transportation systems
IUD(s)	Intrauterine contraceptive device(s)
JEM	Job exposure matrix
LF	Low frequency
LR	Long-range
Massive MTC	Massive machine-type communications
MF	Magnetic field
MIG	Metal inert gas (welding)
MoM	Method of moments
MR	Mixed reality
MRI	Magnetic resonance imaging
MSL	Musculoskeletal load
MW	Microwave
NIOSH	National Institute on Occupational Safety and Health (U.S.)
NRCIM	National Research Council and Institute of Medicine
OHS	Occupational health surveillance
P2P	Point to point
PASS	Personal alert safety system
PDA(s)	Personal digital assistant(s)
PE-DE	Penetration depth
PM	Pulse modulation
PPE	Personal protection equipment
PRP	Pulse repetition period
QSF	Quasi-static electromagnetic field
RF	Radiofrequency
RF-EMF	Radio frequency electromagnetic field
RF EMR	Radiofrequency electromagnetic radiation
RFID	Radio frequency identification

RMS	Root-mean-square
RL	Ray launching
SAD(s)	Social alarm device(s)
SCENIHR	Scientific Committee on Emerging and Newly Identified Health Risks (European Commission)
SEF	Static electric field
SHF	Super-high frequency
SMF	Static magnetic field
SR	Short range
SRD(s)	Short-range device(s)
UHF	Ultra-high frequency
ULF	Ultra-low frequency
URLLC	Ultra-reliable low latency communications
UTD	Uniform theory of diffraction
UWB	Ultra-wide band
VR	Virtual reality
WBANs	Wireless body area networks
WHO	World Health Organisation
Wi-Fi	Wireless fidelity
WLAN(s)	Wireless local area network(s)
WMAN(s)	Wireless metropolitan area network(s)
WPAN(s)	Wireless personal area network(s)
WSN(s)	Wireless sensor network(s)
WWAN(s)	Wireless wide area network(s)

SUBMULTIPLE AND MULTIPLE UNITS

Prefix to Unit	Symbol	Submultiple or Multiple Meaning	
nano	n	$\times 10^{-9}$	(× 0,000 000 001)
micro	μ	$\times 10^{-6}$	(× 0,000 001)
milli	m	$\times 10^{-3}$	(× 0,001)
–	–	$\times 10^{0}$	(× 1)
kilo	k	$\times 10^{3}$	(× 1000)
mega	M	$\times 10^{6}$	(× 1000 000)
giga	G	$\times 10^{9}$	(× 1000 000 000)
tera	T	$\times 10^{12}$	(× 1000 000 000 000)
peta	P	$\times 10^{15}$	(× 1000 000 000 000 000)
eksa	E	$\times 10^{18}$	(× 1000 000 000 000 000 000)
zetta	Z	$\times 10^{21}$	(× 1000 000 000 000 000 000 000)

QUANTITIES AND CORRESPONDING SI UNITS

Symbol	Quantity	Unit
$\boldsymbol{H}$	Magnetic field strength	Ampere per metre (A/m)
$\boldsymbol{H}_{inc}$	Incident magnetic field strength	Ampere per metre (A/m)
$\boldsymbol{B}$	Magnetic flux density	Tesla (T)
$\boldsymbol{E}$	Electric field strength	Volt per metre (V/m)
E_{ave}	Electric field strength average	Volt per metre (V/m)
E_{in}	Strength of electric field induced in human body	Volt per metre (V/m)
$\boldsymbol{E}_{ind}$	Induced electric field strength	Volt per metre (V/m)
$\boldsymbol{E}_{inc}$	Incident electric field strength	Volt per metre (V/m)
$\boldsymbol{D}$	Electric flux	Coulomb per square metre (C/m^2)
$\boldsymbol{S}$	Power density	Watt per square metre (W/m_2)
S_{ab}	Absorbed power density	Watt per square metre (W/m_2)
S_{ave}	Power density value average	Watt per square metre (W/m_2)
$S_{ave/ARP/6\ min}$	Power density value averaged over the antenna rotation period (ARP) or 6 minutes	Watt per square metre (W/m_2)
$S_{ave/PRP}$	Power density value averaged over the pulse repetition period (PRP)	Watt per square metre (W/m_2)
S_{inc}	Incident power density	Watt per square metre (W/m_2)
S_{eq}	Plane-wave equivalent incident power density	Watt per square metre (W/m_2)
S_{peak}	Peak power density value	Watt per square metre (W/m_2)
T	Temperature	Degree Celsius (° C)
T	Pulse repetition period	Second (s)
$\boldsymbol{U}$	Voltage	Volt (V)
$\boldsymbol{I}$	Current	Ampere (A)
J	Current density	Ampere per square metre (A/m^2)
τ	Pulse width	Second (s)
σ	Conductivity	Siemens per metre (S/m)
ρ	Volume density of electric charge	Coulomb per cubic metre (C/m^3)
λ	Wavelength	Metre (m)
μ	Magnetic permeability	Henry per metre (H/m)
μ_o	Magnetic permeability of vacuum	$4\pi \times 10^{-7}$ H/m
μ_r	Relative magnetic permeability of medium (equal to one, 1, in case of air or vacuum)	–
ε	Permittivity	Farad per metre (F/m)
Z_0	Wave impedance of a free space	$120\pi\ \Omega \approx 377\ \Omega$
f	Frequency	Hertz (Hz)
v	Velocity	Metre per second (m/s)
t	Time	Second (s)
SA	Specific (energy) absorption	Joule per kilogram (J/kg)
SAR	Specific (energy) absorption rate	Watt per kilogram (W/kg)
U_{ab}	Absorbed energy density	Joule per square metre (J/m^2)
U_{inc}	Incident energy density	Joule per square metre (J/m^2)
U_{eq}	Plane-wave equivalent incident energy density	Joule per square metre (J/m^2)

ELECTROMAGNETIC EQUATIONS

EMF's behaviour and interaction with the material objects (including the human's body and the medium in which EMF propagation occur) are defined by Maxwell's equations:

$$\text{Faraday's equation: } rot\,\boldsymbol{E} = -\frac{\partial \boldsymbol{B}}{\partial t} \tag{A.1}$$

$$\text{Amper's equation: } rot\,\boldsymbol{H} = \boldsymbol{J} + \frac{\partial \boldsymbol{D}}{\partial t} \tag{A.2}$$

$$\text{sourceness of electric field: } div\boldsymbol{D} = \rho \tag{A.3}$$

$$\text{sourcelessness of magnetic field: } div\boldsymbol{B} = 0 \tag{A.4}$$

$$\text{conservation of electric charge: } div\boldsymbol{J} = -\frac{\partial \rho}{\partial t} \tag{A.5}$$

$$\text{electric field property: } \boldsymbol{D} = \varepsilon \boldsymbol{E} \tag{A.6}$$

$$\text{magnetic field property: } \boldsymbol{B} = \mu \boldsymbol{H} \tag{A.7}$$

$$\text{Ohm's equation: } \boldsymbol{J} = \sigma(\boldsymbol{E} + v \times \boldsymbol{B}) \tag{A.8}$$

Wavelength and frequency are in close relationship in the air:

$$f = c/\lambda \tag{A.9}$$

where c - light's velocity.

The wavelength of EMF in the vacuum or the air can be quickly estimated from the following formula:

$$\lambda_{\mathrm{m}} = 300/f_{\mathrm{M}} \tag{A.10}$$

where λ_{m} is expressed in metres, f_{M} is expressed in MHz.

A magnetic field can be specified equivalently as magnetic field strength, ***H***, and also as magnetic flux density, ***B***, related to the following formula:

$$\boldsymbol{B} = \mu \boldsymbol{H} \tag{A.11}$$

Magnetic permeability in a vacuum and in air, as well as in non-magnetic (including biological) materials has the value $\mu = 4\pi \times 10^{-7}$ H/m. For practical use, corresponding values of magnetic flux density and magnetic field strength, which are applicable to a vacuum and in air, as well as in non-magnetic (including biological) materials, are as follow (based on eq. A.11):

---------		***H*, A/m**	***B*, μT**	***B*, mGs**
Magnetic field strength	***H***, A/m	1	1.25	12.5
Magnetic flux density	***B***, μT	0.8	1	10
	B, mGs	0.08	0.1	1

Index

For Product Safety Concerns and Information please contact our EU representative GPSR@taylorandfrancis.com Taylor & Francis Verlag GmbH, Kaufingerstraße 24, 80331 München, Germany

Printed and bound by CPI Group (UK) Ltd, Croydon, CR0 4YY
08/05/2025
01864412-0008